African Urban Life

African Urban Life

THE TRANSFORMATION OF OUAGADOUGOU

by Elliott P. Skinner

Princeton University Press

Princeton, New Jersey

Copyright ℗ 1974 by Princeton University Press
ALL RIGHTS RESERVED
L.C. Card: 72-14032
ISBN: 0-691-03095-2

Library of Congress Cataloging in Publication
data will be found on the last printed page of this book.

Printed in the United States of America by Princeton
University Press, Princeton, New Jersey

Publication of this book has been aided
by The Program for Research on Black and
Urban Studies, Columbia University.

To my father and to the memory of my mother.

This book appears at a time when the ethics of individual anthropologists are being severely questioned, and when the relevance of our discipline to the modern world is seriously challenged. Some anthropologists have even implied that given the history of anthropology, it cannot be successfully practiced by its "objects," the peoples of the Third World, unless they become completely westernized. The suggestion is that phoenix-like anthropology must die if it wishes to take on new life. The problems of ethics insofar as it deals with the neutrality of our discipline, is of course related to the fiction that man can be objective about man. The human condition precludes this, and will always do so. Man's views of himself or of others have always been conditioned by values or shaped by definite goals. If anthropology is being challenged by Third World peoples, it is because they can now insist that anthropologists view them in all their humanity and deal with all their problems rather than highlight only some aspects of their societies and cultures. Moreover, these people reject the notion that it took the West to make them conscious of themselves. To the contrary, they are now reasserting their humanity after being considered objects by the West. Of course there are some anthropologists who cannot accept the facts of contemporary life. Many of them are retreating into the realm of folklore, or are concentrating on the analysis of the symbolic structures of religious beliefs no longer meaningful to the people involved. These anthropologists may even achieve some temporary prominence in the discipline. But it is they and not anthropology who are doomed; for other anthropologists, including those from Third World groups, will tackle issues in the contemporary world. The science of man will not disappear as long as man, a sentient being, remains interested in humanity. I hope that this study contributes to an understanding of urbanization, one of the major forces in the Third World.

I have been able to undertake the basic research for this book through the generous assistance of a number of persons and institutions. I owe a special debt to Dr. Paul Bohannan of the African Urban Studies Project of Northwestern University

for the fellowship which permitted me to conduct field work in
Ouagadougou from June 1964 to February 1965. Yet, this
work could not have been accomplished had I not received
permission from, and the full support of Dr. J. Issoufou
Conombo, presently Ministre des Affaires Étrangères de la
République de Haute-Volta, and then Mayor of the town of
Ouagadougou. During most of my field work, I had the
friendship of Mme. Conombo, now deceased, and the kind assistance of M. Salifou Ouédraogo, now Director de Cabinet
du Ministre des Affaires Étrangères, but then Surveillant
General, at the Lycée Philippe Zinda Kaboré in Ouagadougou.
To the judges of the Customary and Municipal courts of
Ouagadougou, I owe a special debt for permitting me to audit
their cases. I am also grateful to Mesdames Georgette Com-
bary and Justine Ouedraogo, to Monsieur Jean Hochet, and
the numerous Aides-Sociales of the Direction des Affaires
Sociales du Ministère de la Santé Publique et de la Population for their help in procuring data in their clinics, offices,
and juvenile shelters. My wife and family dutifully shared my
experiences in the field. Thanks to their comfort and support
during the initial fieldwork; during three subsequent years
spent in Ouagadougou as United States Ambassador to Upper
Volta; and during this period of writing, I was able to finish
this task.

 I received the encouragement of my former teachers and
colleagues at the Department of Anthropology, Columbia
University, during this long period of research and writing.
Professors George Bond and Joan Vincent were kind enough
to read this manuscript and to provide valuable advice based
on their extensive field research in Africa. Mrs. Vera Chimene
gave unsparingly of her advice, energy, and time in preparing
the major part of this manuscript, and Miss Nora Stevenson
worked long and hard to complete it for publication. The
Urban Center of Columbia University under the directorship
of Ambassador Franklin H. Williams and Lloyd A. Johnson
graciously supported the study of the field data. Finally, I
wish to thank the Program for Research on Black and Urban
Studies of Columbia University for its contribution toward
the publication of this book.

ELLIOTT P. SKINNER

Columbia University
In the City of New York
January 1973

CONTENTS

TEXT ILLUSTRATIONS

PLATES   *(following p. 114)*

Panorama of the city
Woman resisting kinsmen's demand that she return to her husband
Children, with birth certificates in hand, waiting to register for school
Republican Guard repelling attack by Mogho Naba's army on
   Territorial Assembly
Changing house types in Ouagadougou
Mogho Naba and officials at Moslem ceremony marking the end of
   Ramadan
Catholic baptismal ceremony
Traditional religious sacrifice at modern, urban crossroad
Health care in urban clinic
Roadside vendors
Central market
Commercial zone
Mother and children preparing cakes for sale
View of residential section

xii

African Urban Life

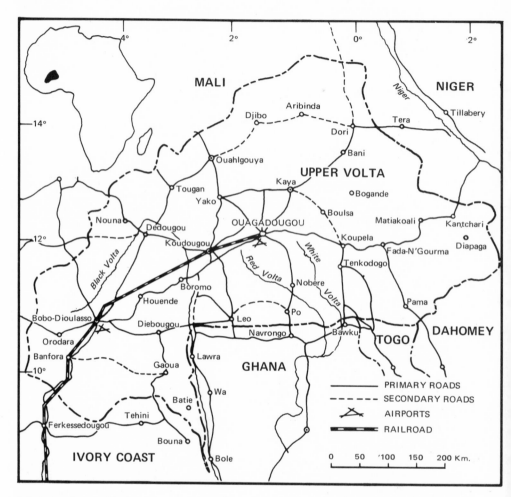

Map I. Upper Volta

Urbanization is producing drastic and perhaps revolutionary changes in contemporary Africa. All over the continent people are moving from their rural villages into the burgeoning towns intent on achieving a better life and, by implication, a modern life. Yet, most of the African cities do not have either the facilities or the resources to accommodate their mushrooming populations. Many city planners, politicians, and social scientists lament the plight of the migrants in the cities and consider them to be "'displaced persons,' the DPs of the development process as it now typically occurs in most of the world; a human flotsam and jetsam that has been displaced from traditional life."[1] A few social scientists believe that neither urbanization nor modernization is desirable or even feasible in all African countries. Others suggest that, if, in fact, these processes are inevitable, they could take place more effectively and at a lower human cost if postponed until the societies are economically further developed.[2] However, the facts are that whether the cities are ready for them or not, the migrants keep flocking into town intent upon entering the modern world economically, politically, and socially.

The present growth of cities in Africa is quite distinct in the history and evolution of urban centers. The early and medieval cities in Egypt, Nubia, the North African and East African littorals, and the western Sudan shared many of the basic characteristics of the so-called preindustrial cities of the Middle East and Europe.[3] They had relatively large populations; were centers of trade, politics, and religion; were ethnically heterogeneous and socially stratified; and above all were crucibles of intellectual and cultural life. The later refugee towns and royal cities (or seats) in the complex Guinea Coast

---

[1]Daniel Lerner, "Comparative Analysis of Processes of Modernisation," in Horace Miner (ed.), *The City in Modern Africa* (London: Pall Mall Press, 1967), p. 22.

[2]*Ibid.*

[3]Gideon Sjoberg, "The Preindustrial City," *The American Journal of Sociology, LX,* No. 5 (March 1955), 438–45; John Sirjamaki, *The Sociology of Cities* (New York: Random House, 1964), pp. 39–62.

societies had dense populations but were ethnically more homogeneous and functionally less specialized.[4] Nevertheless, all of these agglomerations represented a stage in the urbanization process in Africa which everywhere was characterized by relatively dense human agglomerations and greater functional specialization than in the rest of the societies of which they were a part.

Urbanization in contemporary Africa is taking place against a different background of world economic, political, and social history.[5] The preindustrial cities of Europe became industrialized, and then imperial expanding Europe carried both specific urban forms and much of its industrial basis into countries that it conquered, settled, and colonized.[6] Europeans also conquered and colonized Africa, but because of historical and economic factors they did not transfer the whole urban-industrial complex to that continent. Instead, they used Africa as a major source of human and primary commodities. They transformed the indigenous towns to suit their purposes; established trading posts; opened mines; created plantations and built ports and roads; but they established few industrial complexes. The only towns they created were either administrative or commercial centers. The result is that Africa is the least industrialized and least urbanized of all the continents.[7]

Africa still has the fewest population centers in the world

---

[4]William Bascom, "Urbanization among the Yoruba," *The American Journal of Sociology,* LX, No. 5 (March 1955), 446–54; Aidan Southall (ed.), *Social Change in Modern Africa* (London: Oxford University Press, 1961), pp. 1–13; Hilda Kuper (ed.), *Urbanization and Migration in West Africa* (Berkeley and Los Angeles: University of California Press, 1965), pp. 1–21.

[5]Gerald Breese, *Urbanization in Newly Developing Countries* (Englewood Cliffs, N.J.: Prentice-Hall, 1966), pp. 26–30; Peter C. W. Gutkind, "The African Urban Milieu: A Force in Rapid Change," *Civilisations, XII,* No. 2 (1962), 167–91.

[6]Louis L. Snyder (ed.), "The Conquest and Exploitation of Africa," in *The Imperialism Reader* (New York: D. Van Nostrand Co. Inc., 1962), pp. 177–256; W. Alphaeus Hunton, *Decision in Africa* (New York: The International Publishers, 1957); Raymond Kennedy, "The Colonial Crisis and the Future," in Ralph Linton (ed.), *The Science of Man in the World Crisis* (New York: Columbia University Press, 1945), p. 310.

[7]Aidan Southall, "The Impact of Imperialism upon Urban Development in Africa," in Victor Turner (ed.), *Colonialism in Africa* (Cambridge, England: The University Press, 1971), pp. 216–55; William A. Hance, "The Economic Location and Functions of Tropical African Cities," *Human Organization, XIX* (1960), 135–36.

containing one million persons or more, and only about 10 per cent of its people live in urban centers. This situation is now changing rapidly as a result of the nationalist movements and the attainment of political independence in most parts of Africa. People have started to move into the proto-cities in large numbers, and today Africa is experiencing the highest rate of urban growth (a 69 per cent increase in urban populations between 1950 and 1960) in the world. Whereas, in 1963 Lagos (Nigeria) had a population of 500,000 persons, its present population is over 1,200,000, and, with a population growth of 12 per cent per year, its projected population in 1985 will be over 4 million. Kinshasa, the capital of Zaire (formerly the Congo) now has a population of 1.3 million and is growing at a rate of 14 per cent per year. Similar population growth is expected in Accra (Ghana), Abidjan (Ivory Coast), Johannesburg (Republic of South Africa), Nairobi (Kenya), and Addis Ababa (Ethiopia). It is estimated that by the end of this century some 300 million Africans will live in cities of more than 20,000 inhabitants, as compared to 36 million in 1960.[8] This major migratory trend toward the city is bound to cause fundamental changes in the lives of the people of Africa.

The absence of major economic development and industrialization in Africa is having an effect on the nature of African urbanization. True, and as Mabogunje has pointed out, urbanization does not necessarily imply industrialization.[9] But as Kahl states: "Although economic development, industrialization and urbanization can be conceived of as separate variables, in most real instances the three unfold as an over-all complex."[10] Until quite recently *modern* urbanization was largely dependent upon economic development and industrialization. It was also possible to talk about an urban-industrial complex. Today, in some highly industrial nation-states, urbanization in specific areas can take place without industrialization; and likewise, industrialization can occur without

[8]Breese, pp. 26–30; Bowen Northrup, "The Lure of Lagos: City Is Beset By Woes, but People Flock There," New York: *The Wall Street Journal*, January 25, 1972, p. 1.

[9]Akin L. Mabogunje, *Urbanization in Nigeria* (London: The University of London Press, 1968), p. 22.

[10]Joseph A. Kahl, "Some Social Concomitants of Industrialization and Urbanization," *Human Organization, XVIII* (1959), 53.

5

large-scale urbanization.[11] Nonetheless, the two or three processes normally support each other.

In Africa, urbanization has now reached the stage where it needs to be supported by important economic and industrial development. At a comparable stage in European and American urbanization, the migrants who flocked to the industrial towns could find work in the factories.[12] In contrast, the new African towns cannot provide sufficient employment for their growing populations.[13]

While most urban people during the period of rapid growth of European and American cities were industrial workers, most of the people in the emerging African cities are engaged in public works, in government, or in the secondary or so-called consumer industries. And while European and American cities were self-sufficient economically or used resources from economically rich and productive hinterlands, the African cities are largely parasitic entities living off the surplus of relatively poor rural subsistence farmers.[14] The economic problems of the African towns and African countries are exacerbated by their dependence for revenues on the sales of primary products which are subject to the vagaries of an insecure and unstable world commodity market.[15] The result is that any downward economic spiral in commodity prices or commercial stagnation can generate both rural discontent and urban disorders.

Another quality of the urban centers of contemporary Africa is the great influence which they have on the political life of all citizens within their nation-states. This influence is greater than that of European and American towns at a comparable stage in development and is a new development in the history of Africa. Historically, most centralized indigenous

[11]Herbert J. Gans, "Urbanism and Suburbanism as Ways of Life: A Reevaluation of Definitions," in Sylvia F. Fava (ed.), *Urbanism in World Perspective* (New York: Thomas Y. Crowell, Co., 1968), pp. 63–80.

[12]Sirjamaki, pp. 90ff.

[13]William A. Hance, *Population, Migration, and Urbanization in Africa* (New York and London: Columbia University press, 1970), pp. 276–81, 393; P. C. Lloyd, *Africa in Social Change* (Baltimore: Penguin Books, 1967), pp. 119ff.

[14]Mabogunje, pp. 315-19.

[15]Andrew M. Kamarck, *The Economics of African Development* (New York: Frederick Praeger, 1967), pp. 63–65; Kwame N'Krumah, *Neo-Colonialism: The Last Stage of Imperialism* (London: Nelson Co., 1965).

African states had several loci of government.[16] After European conquest, the colonial powers largely administered their African territories through traditional rulers and white officials from many regional or provincial centers.[17] The officials at these levels tended to act as proconsuls or *vrais chefs de l'empire* who felt that they had to protect their charges from the central bureaucrats in the colonial and metropolitan capitals.[18] Those officials in the capitals, not needing either the vote or approval of the rural Africans, paid little attention to them as long as law and order were maintained, taxes paid, and labor provided.

In contrast, most African urban centers, especially the capital cities, function as a "primate or great city."[19] As such they control not only the resources of the rural people but also their political lives. Most of the African states are now governed either through a centralized party or a civilian or military bureaucracy located in the capital city. The officials here not only make the decisions that affect both the resident urban population and rural people, but, more than the European officials, they hold their representatives in the rural areas responsible for mediating the policies of the state on that level.[20] The result is that both the local officials and the rural people are encouraged to look to the cities for guidance in most areas of life. This inevitably leads many people to migrate to town, the center of modern life and political power.

The nationalist and independence movements that stimu-

[16]Ronald Cohen and John Middleton (eds.), *From Tribe to Nation in Africa* (Scranton, Penna.: Chandler Publishing Co., 1970); Lucy Mair, *Primitive Government* (Baltimore: Pelican Books, 1962), pp. 125–247; Jacques Maquet, *Power and Society in Africa* (London: Weidenfeld and Nicolson, 1971), pp. 85–123.

[17]Lloyd A. Fallers, *Bantu Bureaucracy* (London and Chicago: The University of Chicago Press, 1965); Margery Perham, *Colonial Sequence: 1930–1949; 1949–1969* (London: Methuen and Co., Ltd., 1967, 1970); Raymond L. Buell, *The Native Problem in Africa,* 12 vols. (New York: Macmillan, 1928); Frederick D. Lugard, *The Dual Mandate in British Tropical Africa* (London: W. Blackwood, 1929).

[18]Robert Delavignette, *Les Vrais Chefs de L'Empire* (Paris: Larose, 1934).

[19]Mabogunje, pp. 319–25; cf. the concept of "centrality" as discussed by W. W. Deshler in "Urbanization in Africa: Some Spatial and Functional Aspects," *Items* (Social Science Research Council), *XXV,* No. 3 (September 1971), 28.

[20]Aristede Zolberg, *Creating Political Order* (Chicago: Rand McNally & Co., 1966); Maxwell Owusu, *Uses and Abuses of Political Power: A Case*

lated the rapid growth of African towns have also influenced the nature of African urbanization, especially the inhabitants' view of their relationship to the town. During the late colonial period and in countries still under white-minority rule, the political authorities made and are making efforts to limit the movement of Africans to town. The reasons they gave were demographic, economic, hygienic, social, and political.[21] These efforts never successfully halted the influx of migrants to town and are still ineffectual in the white-ruled countries. The rural citizens of the new, independent African states now feel no inhibition about moving to the cities. They go there to redeem the pledges made to them by politicians—that independence would bring the good life, and almost by implication the good life meant urban life.

For both the rural and urban elite, the end of colonialism has been viewed as providing the opportunity for them to participate in all aspects of urban life and to be free psychologically as well as politically from European rule. European colonialism as it appeared in the towns of Africa was more than a system of economic exploitation. It was a system of domination and exclusivity practiced by a white minority which considered itself culturally and racially superior to the Africans.[22] This means that consciously or subconsciously,

Study of Continuity and Change in the Politics of Ghana (Chicago and London: The University of Chicago Press, 1970), pp. 241–324; Claude E. Welch, Jr. (ed.), *Soldier and State in Africa* (Evanston: Northwestern University Press, 1970), pp. 270–301; Martin Kilson, "African Political Change and the Modernization Process," *Journal of Modern African Studies, I,* No. 4 (1963), 426.

[21]Valdo Pons, *Stanleyville: an African Urban Community under Belgian Administration* (London: Oxford University Press, 1969); J. Van Velsen, "Labour Migration as a Positive Factor in the Continuity of Tonga Tribal Society," in Aidan Southall (ed.), *Social Change in Modern Africa* (London: Oxford University Press, 1961), p. 239. Southall also notes (in Turner, p. 243) "the tendency of colonial authorities to treat Africans as if they did not belong in urban areas. In West Africa, where there was already an African urban tradition, this factor did not apply either to the old towns or to the new towns that grew up within the same countries. It was most characteristic of the mine-based towns of southern Africa, where Africans from the rural areas were expected to stay in town only as long as they were employed"; cf. J. Clyde Mitchell, "Structural Plurality, Urbanization and Labour Circulation in Southern Rhodesia," in J. A. Jackson, (ed.) *Migration* (Cambridge, England: Cambridge University Press, 1969), p. 161.

[22]Georges Balandier, *Ambiguous Africa* (New York: Random House, (1966), p. 269, *et passim;* Georges Balandier, "The Colonial Situation,"

Africans engaged in the process of socio-cultural change, which is urbanization, attempt to eliminate the legacy of the colonial situation. They try to achieve a form of psychological autonomy unknown during the colonial period. Yet they are often constrained to use modern European mechanisms in order to urbanize and modernize.[23]

Urbanization in contemporary Africa is a legacy of European conquest and colonial rule.[24] Nevertheless, Mabogunje is quite correct in rejecting the claim that urbanization is a peculiarly European and American phenomenon and the corollary assumption "that modern industrial development is the only basis for urban agglomeration."[25] On the other hand, the present rate of urbanization on that continent cannot be understood without taking the previous European impact and its continuing influence into consideration. The Africans who are moving into towns are not only moving into denser population agglomerations, but they are attracted by the amenities of modern city life: new types of jobs, modern education, effective health services, and opportunities to lead different types of lives.

Contemporary African urbanization, then, is a process by which large numbers of persons are moving into towns and are acquiring new material and nonmaterial cultural elements—including new occupations, new patterns of behavior and forms of organization, new ideas and new values. Many of these cultural elements have come from Western European cities and are specific to urban life. Yet, many of the social

---

in Pierre L. Van den Berghe (ed.), *Africa: Social Problems of Change and Conflict* (San Francisco, Calif.: Chandler Publishing Co., 1965), pp. 36–57.

[23]Frantz Fanon, *The Damned* (Paris: Présence Africaine, 1963), pp. 121–63.

[24]I believe that Southall is fundamentally correct when he states (in Turner, pp. 252–53): "Western imperialism had a negative and destructive impact upon many of those lines of development in African society which could have led towards the foundation of urban living properly rooted in African culture." Nevertheless, he insists that "For better or worse the imperial intervention created the new African nations, with their capital cities and their small towns, their ports, mines, industries, commerce, and communications centers." He concludes: "Whatever regret there may be that this was done by Europeans, whose obtrusive difference of race, culture and technological power made antagonism inevitable and rapid integration impossible, the facts of history have to be recognized."

[25]Mabogunje, p. 33.

and cultural institutions found in these towns are quite new. They represent the product of the interaction of heterogeneous African and non-African groups with different socio-cultural backgrounds within towns. Urbanization in Africa is further complicated by the fact that the *raison d'être* of towns in which it is taking place is changing even though the towns continue to serve as the purveyors of cultural influences from the outside world.

The aim of this study is to view Ouagadougou, the capital of Upper Volta, as a framework in which to analyze the human activities characteristic of African urbanism. The city is seen as a node where a whole complex network of economic, social, and political relations meet. As such, and as Arensberg has pointed out, Ouagadougou, like many towns and cities, provides "a demographic field for human interaction, a cultural environment for human behavior and a form or forms of social organization, as well as an arena for economic and political activity."[26] It is an ideal setting for delineating and studying the processes by which people become urbanized.

The major thesis of this study is that the attempt of people in Ouagadougou to modernize and adapt to the urban milieu is characterized by a conscious manipulation of all institutions within the town and components of urban life. People utilize any skill they may have and any institution that may facilitate adaptation to life in town. Thus, we shall see that the civil servants, the dominant group in town, have no commitments to their jobs, but continually take examinations in order to receive better pay and more perquisites. Rural farmers attempt to earn a living in town, but retire to the peri-urban areas to cultivate farms so that they can live in the towns. People who had lived in Ouagadougou for years without formal association, formed and used almost all types of associations for political purposes when this was neces-

[26]Conrad M. Arensberg, "The Urban in Crosscultural Perspective," in Elizabeth M. Eddy (ed.), *Urban Anthropology: Research Perspectives and Strategies,* Southern Anthropological Society Proceedings, No. 2 (Athens: University of Georgia Press, 1968), p. 4; Conrad M. Arensberg, "The Community Study Method," *American Journal of Sociology, LX* (1954), 106–24; Joan E. Vincent, "The Dar es Salaam Townsman: Social and Political Aspects of City Life," *Tanzania Notes and Records,* No. 71 (May 1970), pp. 149–56.

sary, and promptly abandoned the associations when their usefulness was over. People join and abandon political parties as a function of the opportunities they present. They also join religious organizations for the same purposes, and non-Christians often give their babies Christian names so that later they will be admitted to the parochial schools.

The manipulation of regional and kin ties by the Ouagadougou people is quite common, but there is no behavior that can be identified as "tribalism" in the sense it is used by many anthropologists.[27] It is possible that the kin and regional loyalties found among Ouagadougou's urban population are of a special type and "not confined to Africans."[28] Gluckman did suggest, perhaps facetiously, that "tribalism acts, though not as strongly, in British towns: for in these Scots and Welsh and Irish, French, Jews, Lebanese, Africans, have their own associations, and their domestic life is ruled by their own national customs."[29] The fact is that European scholars do not normally refer to this type of behavior as "tribalism," therefore, the concept does not have cross-cultural validity and should now be discarded. Instead of attributing the tendency of people in towns to surround themselves with relatives and home-town folk to "tribalism," or, worse yet, "retribalism,"[30] it might be better to view this behavior as the manipulation of

---

[27]Clifford Geertz, "The Integrative Revolution, Primordial Sentiments and Civil Politics in the New States," in *Old Societies and New States* New York: The Free Press, 1963), pp. 109ff.

[28]Max Gluckman, "Anthropological Problems arising from Industrial Revolution," in Southall, *Social Change,* p. 76.

[29]*Ibid.*

[30]Abner Cohen defines "retribalization" as a case where "an ethnic group adjusts to the new realities by reorganizing its own traditional customs, or by developing new customs under traditional symbols, often using traditional norms and ideologies to enhance its distinctiveness within the contemporary situation." *Custom and Politics in Urban Africa* (Berkeley and Los Angeles: University of California Press, 1969), pp. 1, 3, 191. Note, he does not state why he uses the term "ethnic group" and not "tribe" in a definition of "retribalization." Immanuel Wallerstein is a bit more logical in his distinction between "tribalism" and "ethnicity." He uses the latter concept to mean a "persistence of loyalties and values, which stem from a particular form of social organization." The social organization he has in mind is the "tribe," but uses the concept "tribe" for the group in the rural areas, and "ethnic group" for the one in the town. "Ethnicity and National Integration in West Africa," in *Cahiers d'Etudes Africaines, I,* No. 3 (1960), 129–39.

sentiment for political and economic self-protection. The principle of the *Mafia* or *Landtsmanschaft* works as well in Ouagadougou as in the United States of America.

It must be pointed out that the ability of urban Africans to be "manipulative" is not unlimited. Differences in education, which in turn influence income and style of life, are becoming increasingly important. Definite ranking with associated values is emerging among the sociological categories found in Ouagadougou, and this limits or conditions the way in which people interact with each other. If this study does not identify clear-cut classes in Ouagadougou, it is because the social categories found are not yet sharply delineated.[31] Cross-cutting ties of kinship, common rural origin, traditional social statuses, and relatively open educational, occupational, and economic opportunities have so far prevented sharp lines from developing.[32] Moreover, the lack of economic development in Ouagadougou, expatriate retention of control of the economy, and the rise of a civil service elite have all contributed to the existing social situation. What remains to be seen is what type of social stratification will develop in such an environment, especially since many of the leaders espouse, if not believe in, an ideology of social consciousness (or socialism) grounded in the African reality.

The methodology used in studying Ouagadougou was influenced by my belief that African urban life cannot be understood unless all the institutions and aspects of a town are studied. Familiarity with the traditional society and culture of the Mossi people who comprised the overwhelming majority of the town's population facilitated an ethnographic approach. Moreover, the compact nature of the town and its modest population made it possible for me to cover most of the town myself. I was also fortunate in having personal acquaintance with a large cross section of the Mossi in town (and this included many persons previously known in the rural districts of Manga and Nobéré) which afforded an unusual access to many areas of life and almost unlimited opportunities for participant observation. I was able to observe and to analyze

---

[31]Michael Banton, "Social Alignment and Identity in a West African Town," in Kuper, pp. 144–46.

[32]Cf. W. B. Schwab, "Social Stratification in Gwelo," in Southall, *Social Change,* pp. 139–41; Leonard Plotnicov, *Strangers to the City: Urban Man in Jos. Nigeria* (Pittsburgh: University of Pittsburgh Press, 1967), pp. 45–46.

the "social networks" of a key number of individuals from all social strata. This necessitated several trips to the peri-urban villages of Ouagadougou and even to rural areas to observe the interaction between rural and urban people. The existence of a demographic survey of the town obviated the difficult and acutely politically sensitive task of an individual census. Use was made of questionnaires when possible, and when deemed necessary or indeed valuable. The municipal courts of Ouagadougou proved to be a mine of information. One could observe there many areas of conflict in traditional Mossi culture and society but, more importantly, note the difficulties that emerged from living in town and the nature of the numerous adaptations to urban environment. Municipal and government documents completed the sources of data gathered and used for this study.

The basic data for this study were collected during 1964 and 1965, but the book could not be published until I had completed a tour of duty as United States Ambassador to the Republic of Upper Volta, 1966–1969. This assignment, the first of its kind ever given to an anthropologist, permitted me to observe the town of Ouagadougou from another vantage point. True, I could no longer jump on a velo-moter and rush about to every ceremony, nor could I slip unobtrusively into the markets and other public places. Nevertheless, I was able to keep abreast of the changes that were taking place in Ouagadougou and could leisurely compare my earlier knowledge with data that came from perusing the changing urban scene. Developments were noted although not written down, but items of interest that appeared in the local news or other media were systematically saved. By the end of 1969, I believed that I had a good knowledge of urbanization in Ouagadougou as well as an understanding of Upper Volta. Having first studied among the Mossi on the village and district level, I had followed migrants to the town and had lived there like many of my rural friends. Later, I served on the level of the Upper Volta nation-state as did many members of the African elite I first met as proto-politicians in the rural areas. This book, then, is the summation of more that fifteen years' experience with the Upper Volta and its peoples, and represents more than two years of systematic field work. Its subject matter, urbanization, is the most important social factor in contemporary Upper Volta.

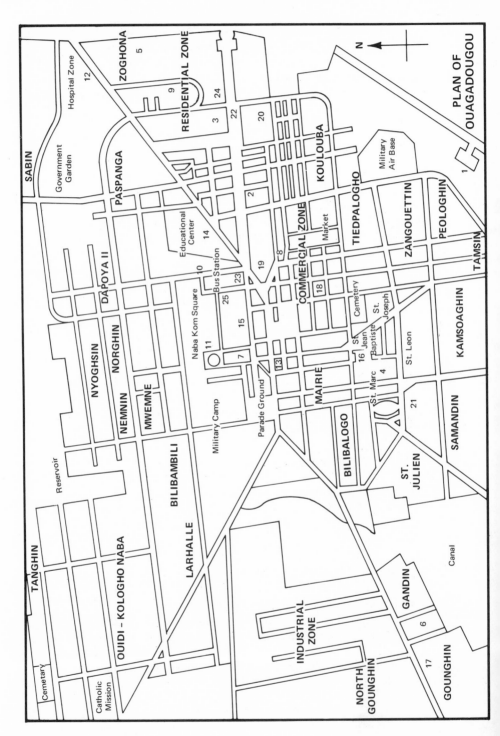

Map II.

CHAPTER I

The Development of Ouagadougou

Geography, trade, and poltics have played key roles in the development of Ouagadougou. The town, located about 12.14° north latitude and 3.29° west longitude, is strategically placed between the Saharan bend of the Niger River and the forest zone of West Africa.[1] Since this region is fairly flat and relatively well watered, it was apparently ideal for early human settlement. Ouagadougou is situated on part of that vast lateritic plateau characteristic of much of the western Sudan. It is traversed by two main ravines and several smaller ones which, during the rainy season, drain water into the White Volta, one of a complex of three Volta rivers (the Black, Red, and White) from which the territory of Upper Volta derives its name. The climate of Ouagadougou is also typical of the Sudan. There is a dry season which begins about mid-October and lasts until mid-May or early June. The first months of this season are characterized by moderate temperatures rarely exceeding 76°F. and the blowing of the rather dusty and dry harmattan. Beginning in March the temperature often reaches as high as 106°F.; this lasts until broken by the rains which start at the end of May, reducing the heat to between 74°F. and 86°F. The annual rainfall in and around Ouagadougou seldom exceeds 33 inches and the relative humidity for the year ranges between 12 and 16 per cent. The main vegetation in the Ouagadougou area is a mixture of grass and orchard bush, now modified by the activities of man. At one time the fauna included lions, elephants, hippopotami, buffalo, monkeys, various types of antelope, and a vast variety of bird and insect life.

Trade was probably a significant factor in the development of Ouagadougou.[2] The town lies within the northern quadrant

[1]Paul Barlet, "La Haute Volta (Essai de présentation géographique)," *Etudes Voltaiques* (N.s. 1962), Mémoire No. 3, Ouagadougou, pp. 11–77.

[2]A. Adu Boahen, "The Caravan Trade in the Nineteenth Century," *Journal of African History, III*, No. 2 (1962), 356; cf. Ivor Wilks, "The Northern Factor in Ashanti History: Begho and Mande," *Journal of African History, XI*, No. 1 (1961), 25–34.

of the Voltaic area, a region extending from Salaga (Ghana) in the south to Ouahigouya (Upper Volta) in the north, inhabited by the Moré-Dagbane-speaking peoples, many of whom conducted extensive trade between the West African forest zone and the desert. It is highly probable, therefore, that such large-scale societies as Mossi, Dagomba, and Mamprussi found in this region owe their development to the activities of those caravaneers who either organized polities among the indigenous populations or stimulated their development. Barth and other early travelers reported the existence of more than five caravan trails crossing the area, and the Mossi and Dagbane peoples have traditions that their states were founded by mounted warriors who might well have been the escorts of caravans.[3]

According to Mossi traditions, their society developed as a result of the expansion of the Dagomba people of the Gold Coast (modern Ghana) into the Volta region and their subsequent conquest and partial assimilation of the autochthonous peoples such as the Ninisi, Foulsé, and Habé. The resulting population, the Mossi, developed four important kingdoms and lesser principalities under rulers called *naba* (pl. *nanamsé*). All of these rulers, and most of their subordinates in the provinces, districts, and villages, were members of the royal lineage and were linked by bonds of kinship, ritual, and military power. The important Mossi political units developed complex hierarchical administrative structures which extended the power of the Mogho Naba (king of the world) into the smallest villages and funneled goods and services back to them.

The precolonial Mossi village populations were divided into noble, commoner, serf, and slave, segmentary patrilineal groups who lived in polygynous, extended family households. The Mossi marriage system was based on the exchange of women between lineages linked by long-term reciprocal relations. However, since the older men were the ones who controlled most of their lineages' resources, they were the ones who obtained most of the wives. The young men either had to wait until their elders died to inherit wives or sought wives (*pughsiudsé*) from chiefs against the promise of provid-

[3]Henry Barth, *Travels and Discoveries in North and Central Africa* (New York: Harper and Brothers, 1859), pp. 643-49.

ing goods and services to their benefactors and giving them their first daughters to serve as future *pughsiudsé*. Lineage heads also supervised the economic activities of the people under their charge. These activities included the cultivation of several varieties of millet, sorghum, maize, rice, okra, sweet potatoes, cotton, and indigo, the herding of livestock, and trade, both local and to Timbuktu and the forest zones.

The traditional religion of the Mossi included belief in an otiose deity called Winnam, Winde, or Naba Zid'winde. Associated with Winnam was a female deity called Tenga whose local manifestations and propitiatory agencies were *tengkouga* (sing. *tengkougré*) which took the form of clumps of trees, mountains, rocks, or rivers and were served by spirits called *kinkirsé*. Earth priests or *tengsobadamba* (sing. *tengsoba*) appealed to the *tengkouga* on behalf of the local populations for help in sickness, for rain and good crops, and for children.

The Mossi founded Ouagadougou during an expansionist drive that ultimately took them into the Niger River bend where they sacked and burned Timbuktu (c. 1328), and attacked both Walata and Banku. The actual founding of the royal capital is the subject of several oral histories recounted by the autochthonous Ninisi or Nyonyonse of this region. According to a historical account furnished by the contemporary Ouagadougou Naba (an earth priest with ritual control over the land), the Ninisi of this region were commanded by his ancestor, Zabra Soba Koumbemba (head war chief), a *tengsoba* (*tenga* is Moré for village).[4] Zabra Soba was so honored (*wogé* in Moré) and respected by other earth priests and the people in the area that they referred to his village as Wogé Zabra Soba Koumbemb' tenga. When the Mossi under Naba Oubri arrived in the Ouagadougou area (c. A.D. twelfth century), many Ninisi and several *tengsobadamba* fled—some going as far as Tougan where they became known as Samogho; others, such as Zabra Soba and his people, remained. Zabra Soba then agreed to help Oubri conquer the region. According to the agreement, Oubri was to take all the conquered lands on the left, that is west of Ouagadougou which for the Mossi is toward the "front," and Zabra Soba was to keep all the lands on the right-hand side, that is east and therefore

[4]Yamba Tiendrébéogo, *Histoire et coutumes royales des Mossi de Ouagadougou* (Ouagadougou, 1964a), pp. 8ff.

17

the "back." Zabra Soba and his descendants were to be left in control of his village Wogé Zabra Soba Koumbemb' tenga. In time the name of the village was allegedly transformed by Malinke traders who substituted *Ouaga* for *Wogé* and *dougou,* their word for village, for the Mossi *tenga.*

The various traditions about the establishment of the court at Ouagadougou all concur that the royal successors of Oubri (the Mogho Nanamsé) did not return to the Ouagadougou area until the time of Mogho Naba Niandfo (c. 1441–1511), the ninth successor of Oubri.[5] The reasons for this ruler's breaking the pact with the descendants of Zabra Soba Koumbemba are unclear. Traditions only state that since the Ouagadougou Tengsoba, in his role as earth priest, consecrated the Mogho Naba's "bonnet" (crown), the king preferred to live close to the earth priest. If so, the Ouagadougou Naba suffered as a result of this decision because he subsequently lost all effective control of the area. He became a religious official for the Mogho Naba and remained under this ruler's political control. The Ouagadougou Naba did retain proprietory rights over errant animals, and the privilege of granting immunity to all fugitives. If a condemned criminal saw the Ouagadougou Naba and cried out to the priest, "I ask pardon of the Ouagadougou Naba and also of the protective spirits of the earth," his life could be spared.

Ouagadougou apparently reached its zenith as the capital of the Oubri dynasty during the reign of Mogho Naba Ouaraga (c. 1666–81).[6] It was Ouaraga who organized the royal court and laid the foundation for much of Ouagadougou's present physical structure. Ouaraga surrounded his palace-complex, Na'Tenga (village of the chief), with a number of hamlets housing his retainers. Two of these hamlets, Bilbalgo and Bilibambili, housed his superannuated pages (*soghondamba*). In another hamlet, Dapoya (*da poré,* behind the house), behind the palace wall, dwelt a group of retainers. A number of lesser officials at court such as the Kamsaogho Naba (chief eunuch), the Samand' Naba (chief of palace serfs), the Pwe Naba (head diviner), Nemdo Naba (chief of livestock),

[5]Ibid., p. 22.

[6]Elliott P. Skinner, *The Mossi of Upper Volta* (Stanford, Calif.: Stanford University Press, 1964b), pp. 31–59; see A. A. (Dim) Delobson, "Le Mogho Naba et Sa Cour," *Bull. du Comité d'Etudes Hist. et Sc. de L'A.O.F.,* XI, 3 (July–September 1928), 386–421.

Bend'Naba (chief of musicians), Kamboinsi Naba (chief of royal guards), and others lived in hamlets in the vicinity of Na'Tenga.[7] Some of these hamlets were later to become wards such as Kamsaoghin, Samandin, and Pwese.

The important senior officials of the Mogho Naba, the provincial governors, such as the Ouidi Naba, the Larhalle Naba, and the Goungha Naba, lived in large hamlets about 2 kilometers away from Na'Tenga. Their households had the same organizational plan as that of the Mogho Naba. Thus, in the hamlet named Ouidi, inhabited by the Ouidi Naba of the Mogho Naba, there were subsections named Bilbalse and Ouidi for this minister's own Baloum Naba and Ouidi Naba. The villages and hamlets of the autochthonous Ninisi and their earth priests, about 3 kilometers from Na'Tenga, formed part of the capital, as did the hamlets inhabited by Moslem merchants[8] and by groups of semi-nomadic and sedentary Fulani pastoralists. Most of these hamlets remained fixed, although many of their inhabitants, including éven the great officials, occasionally moved their houses for ritual or religious reasons. The entire palace-complex, Na'Tenga, and the market (from which the king derived substantial income) moved after the death of an encumbent Mogho Naba or when a reigning monarch was advised to do so by his religious counselors. When the palace-complex moved, those retainers who served the monarch moved their hamlets also. These moves did not entail too much labor, however, since the houses were built of sun-dried bricks with straw roofs or beaten earthen roofs. Today there are numerous areas around Ouagadougou known to have been the sites of former palace-complexes and of the tombs of former Mogho Nanamsé.

Early travelers reported that precolonial Ouagadougou was a whole complex of villages scattered over 12 square kilometers and linked by footpaths to Na'Tenga and to the market place. That the entire complex inhabited by some 5,000 persons was never walled has been attributed to the strength of the Mogho Naba's kingdom. Each homestead within the villages and hamlets, whether the king's palace, or the houses of nobles, commoners, serfs, or slaves, was surrounded by its own

[7]Tiendrebéogo, 1964a, pp. 83ff.

[8]A. A. (Dim) Delobson, *The Empire of the Mogho-Naba,* trans. Kathryn A. Looney (Human Relations Area Files, New Haven, Conn., 1959), p. 105.

19

gardens or "village" farm. The regular or "bush" farms of
the Ouagadougou people were located at the capital's perim-
eter or in neighboring areas.[9] Crozat, a Frenchman and one of
the first Europeans to visit Ouagadougou described it as:

A large denuded plateau that one perceives from a vast
distance, four to five kilometers as one comes from the
north; a wide expanse of land with immense lougans; a line
of ponds; small portions of waste land where one suspects
ferruginous rocks underlie the rank weeds; some clusters of
large trees; and here and there groups of Bambara-type
huts half hidden by millet stalks—such is Ouagadougou.
The capital, like the smallest Mossi hamlet, is only an agricultural village, and, were it not for the deforestation of the
area, nothing would reveal to the traveller that here is the
great center and the residence of a sovereign. But the inhabited area here is truly considerable; and the groups of
houses, if not denser, are incomparably more numerous. As
far as the eye can see, other comparable groups of agricultural hamlets—really dispersed small farms—are in view,
or are suspected to be all over the plateau and are like
suburbs of this rustic town *ville campagnarde.* Also, one
should say right away that each one of these groups of small
huts has a particular name, even that of the group of royal
huts which is called Kounkounbissi (summit). The name
Ouagadougou, which my predecessors in Mossi country
gave to the complex of hamlets neighboring the royal habitation is that which, for convenience sake, I will continue
to use in my turn, although it is in reality, the name of the
province [sic].[10]

Crozat described the palace of the Mogho Naba (Na'Yiri,
house of the chief) in Na'Tenga as a walled complex of buildings. The central ones were built out of sun-dried bricks in
the Sudanese style, whereas the scores of other buildings were
typical Mossi round mud-brick and straw huts with conical
roofs. There were sections within the palace compound for
receptions and affairs of state, others which served as living

[9]Louis Binger, *Du Niger au golfe de Guinée par le pays de Kong et le Mossi, 1887–1889* (Paris: Hachette, 1892), I, 459–60.

[10]Dr. Crozat, "Rapport sur une mission au Mossi, 1890," *J. O. de la Rép. franc*; 5–9 October 1891, p. 4,835.

quarters for the ruler's wives and relatives, and stables for animals. The Mossi judged this complex of buildings to be quite luxurious, but the first Europeans to visit Na'Yiri said that it differed only in scale from the quarters of the common people. Crozat gives the following description of the Mogho Naba's reception area:

> Before the group of royal huts, which are surrounded by a small *tata* (adobe wall), extends a large, semi-circular court-yard with its soil well beaten and carefully maintained. In front of the door the earth has been mounded in the form of a small terrace some thirty centimeters high and equally semi-circular. The door, being the door of the palace, is, by its oddness, worthy of description. It shows that sump-tousness of decor preoccupies the Mossi kings less than their exaggerated concern for security. It is the extremity of a small, very narrow corridor, parallel to the facade, de-limited by two walls which, at the same time, form a part of the enclosure, a sort of passage contrived in the thickness of *tata* whose dimensions appear exaggerated. Thus, the open-ing of the door is perpendicular to the direction of the fa-cade; it is not even eighty centimeters large.
>
> It is on this terrace that the chief holds his audiences; it is there that he stays every morning when his favorites come to offer him their homage and where every Friday he receives all the notables of Ouagadougou, the marabouts, and the merchant strangers, coming to take part in the great weekly ceremony. It is there where I, myself, will be received.[11]

The royal capital of Ouagadougou gained a certain renown in the western Sudan not only because the Mossi people con-trolled a large territory, but also because it had become an im-portant trade and market center.[12] Sultan Mohammed Bello of Sokoto, whose Hausa merchants had had extensive trade with the Mossi before the arrival of the Europeans, knew much about Ouagadougou.[13] However, it was Henry Barth, the renowned German traveler in the western Sudan, who really revealed the importance of Ouagadougou as a trade and

[11]*Ibid.*

[12]Joseph Dupuis, *Journal of a Residence in Ashantee* (London, 1824), Part II, p. CVII.

[13]Hugh Clapperton, *Second Voyage dans L'intérieur de l'Afrique,* trans. M. M. Eyries and de la Renaudière (Paris, 1829), II, 323.

market center. He listed it as a major point in the itinerary of about five caravans moving between Timbuktu and Salaga in northern Ghana, and between the territory which is now the Republic of Niger and Kong in the northern Ivory Coast.[14] In view of the administrative and commercial activities which took place in Ouagadougou, that town was both esteemed and feared, not only by the Mossi subjects of the Mogho Naba but also by caravaneers and surrounding peoples. Crozat tells of the trouble he encountered in even trying to get a guide to Ouagadougou:

> I did not hide from myself the difficulties that awaited me in that town. I arrived there menaced by a defiance which had only grown stronger since I left Yako [a town northwest of Ouagadougou]. I have said that my guide from Kougi, Moussa Keita [no doubt a trader] had abandoned me specifically because he feared to displease [the Mossi chiefs]. As for Abdoulaye, a Mossi whom I had brought from Bobo-Dioulasou, he was no longer recognizable since he arrived in his own country. I needed my most earnest entreaties to persuade him to follow me to Ouagadougou.[15]

The ordinary Mossi seldom went to Ouagadougou unless summoned there. Or they visited the town for judicial purposes, to accompany chiefs or notables, or to attend the market. The main reason for this was the ordinary Moagha's fear of approaching a chief who might recruit him for some unwelcome task or exact some kind of tribute.

The non-Mossi populations in traditional Ouagadougou consisted primarily of Hausa merchants, Moslems, and the Fulani herdsmen. They all lived in special quarters of the town commanded by their own headmen, but under the overall control of the Baloum Naba, the head steward of the palace and, by extension, "mayor" of the administrative capital of Ouagadougou.[16] The Mogho Naba and his officials encouraged these non-Mossi to remain in Ouagadougou because of their value to the community. Nevertheless, it was always made quite clear to them that they remained in the capital at the sufferance

[14]Barth, pp. 643–49; cf. Dr. Krause, "Krause's Reise," *Peterman's Mittheilungen* (Berlin, 1887–88), pp. 42ff.

[15]Binger, I, 465–67.

[16]Tiendrébéogo, 1964a, p. 104.

of the Mossi officials and should not interfere in the domestic affairs of their hosts.[17]

Although the Mossi always welcomed strangers, they remained suspicious of them. They were quite suspicious of the first Europeans, especially of Crozat, who appeared in Ouagadougou stating, "Our merchants will bring you the money and the goods you lack, and you will give us in return those things which you have in excess ... and this exchange will make us both greater, richer, and stronger."[18] Mogho Naba Sanum diplomatically agreed to permit traders to visit the town telling Crozat that he would "be pleased to see other Frenchmen come here, provided that they are not too numerous. As for your black traders and French merchants, they could come and trade with the Mossi in all security; we will not maltreat them."[19] Unfortunately for the Mogho Naba, the French were as interested in territory and glory as in trade, and when a later Mogho Naba, Wobogo, refused to surrender his country, the French resorted to force. Wobogo's army was no match for the French and their auxiliaries, and, after a brief show of resistance, Mogho Naba Wobogo fled, never to return to his capital. The French capture of Ouagadougou on September 5, 1896, inaugurated a new era in the history of the town.[20]

It took the people of Ouagadougou some time to reconcile themselves to the defeat of their Mogho Naba. When, one day after the battle, Lieutenant Voulet left the capital to pursue the fleeing monarch, the inhabitants of Ouagadougou rose in support of their king. So infuriated was Voulet by this act that, upon his return, he put Ouagadougou to the torch and destroyed much of Na'Tenga and the surrounding hamlets. Later, when Voulet left the capital to return to his base at Bandiagara for provisions, the people of Ouagadougou rejoiced, repaired the palace-complex, and awaited the return of their king. But this was not to be. Voulet returned in January 1897, and the Ouidi Naba and other officials surrendered to him. The French deposed Wobogo and elected Sighiri, his brother, Mogho Naba. The people of the capital accepted

[17]Elliott P. Skinner, "Processes of Political Incorporation in Mossi Society," in Cohen and Middleton, *From Tribe to Nation in Africa*, p. 195.
[18]Crozat, p. 4,849.
[19]*Ibid.*
[20]Skinner, 1964b, pp. 148–53.

23

French rule, and the conquerors began to transform Ouaga-dougou.[21]

A number of forces combined to transform Ouagadougou. Immediately after the conquest, the French used Ouaga-dougou as a military camp from which to subdue the remaining Volta region. By 1899 the base was designated head-quarters of the Second (Volta) Military Territory and its resident officers charged with establishing peace and order. These early resident officers, such as Scal, Amman, Pinchon, and Dubreuil, quickly recruited Mossi to build a large military camp (Camp Militaire) with its attending parade ground (Place d'Armes) on the site of the palace-complex of Mogho Naba Wobogo. They also permitted their African soldiers to bring their wives and relatives to Ouagadougou[22] and lodge them either in the military camp or in nearby Bilibambili, then inhabited mainly by ex-pages of the Mogho Naba and a few semi-sendentary Fulani. A number of foreign Senegalese and Soudanese soldiers even received wives from the Mogho Naba.

The administrative and material aid which the French military command required from the Mogho Naba and his chiefs led to other physical and demographic changes in Ouaga-dougou. The early military commanders called upon the Mogho Naba to help feed the garrison and to facilitate its housekeeping. The ruler used his administrative hierarchy to requisition goods, materials, and labor for the capital. Many rural Mossi were sent to the capital, and many of these men, attracted by the jobs and money in Ouagadougou, remained in the growing town. They were joined by large numbers of laborers who were recruited by the provincial ministers, placed at the disposal of the military government, and lodged in the vicinity of their households. Many of the men and their spouses who later joined them became inhabitants of burgeoning settlements in the hamlets of the Goungha, Larhalle, and Ouidi Nanamsé. Tradition has it that the quarter called Kologho Naba (approach the chief) was founded when the Ouidi Naba, at the request of the Mogho Naba, invited his kinsmen to join him in Ouagadougou. They came, "approached the chief," and established a ward of their own.

[21]*Ibid.*

[22]*L'Afrique Française: Bulletin du Comité de l'Afrique Française et du Comité du Maroc,* X (Paris, 1900), 147–48.

The economic activities of the early French administrators in the Upper Volta did much to change the traditional economic life of Ouagadougou.[23] An early commander moved the Ouagadougou market from its ancient site in front of the Mogho Naba's palace to the southeast about 1 kilometer. European commercial houses sent African representatives to establish trading centers in its vicinity. This additional economic activity induced many more members of such traditional African merchant groups as the Dioula and Hausa to come to Ouagadougou and to settle there. These merchants undertook a lively trade with residents now needing, in addition to goods, specie with which to pay taxes. Many rural Mossi organized caravans to Ouagadougou where they sold their goods to get the necessary specie from the administration and merchants with which to pay taxes.[24] Inevitably some of the caravaneers stayed on and augmented the town's population.

The Catholic missionaries were another important factor in the growth of modern Ouagadougou. On June 25, 1901, Father Guillame Templier and three other White Fathers established a mission in Ouagadougou south of the military zone and near the Mogho Naba's new palace. The four Europeans in Ouagadougou at that time, especially the Commander, Captain Ruef, referred to as an "Israelite," were reportedly glad to have the missionaries, whose arrival increased the number of white men in the capital by 100 per cent. Captain Ruef sent a number of African children to the missionaries to be cared for and educated.[25] He thereby increased the Ouagadougou population and laid the basis for the development of the "Saint" wards in which missionized Africans settled.

In 1904, the French created the colony, Haut-Sénégal et Niger, with Ouagadougou as the *chef-lieu* (chief town) of a *cercle* (a French administrative unit) also called Ouagadougou. The town's population had now grown to more than 8,000, of

[23]Unpublished document in the archives of the *Centre Voltaique de la Recherche Scientifique* (formerly I.F.A.N.), Ouagadougou.

[24]Eugène Mangin, *Les Mossi: Essai sur les us et coutumes du peuple Mossi du Soudan occidental* (reprinted from *Anthropos,* 1916), Paris, 1921. Trans. Ariane Brunel and Elliott Skinner and reissued by Human Relations Area Files, New Haven, Conn., 1959, pp. 61-62.

[25]Paul Baudu, *Vieil Empire, Jeune Eglise* (Paris; Editions La Savane, 1956), p. 17.

25

whom 12 were Europeans. The new *commandant de cercle* and his aides, whom the Mossi called *kadanga neba* (people of the *cercle*), immediately created a new complex of buildings near the Place d'Armes and Bilbalgo (the settlement of the Baloum Naba). The various commandants, Lambert, Carrier, Vidal, and d'Arboussier, continued the tasks of the former military commanders. They laid out streets, planted trees, and provided a more permanent water supply by building dams across the swamps—in fine, they continued building Ouagadougou. This work was expensive, and the people of the town and of the *cercle* were severely taxed.[26] The immediate effect of this taxation was to force even more people from the rural areas to migrate to Ouagadougou than had come during the first years after the conquest. Ironic as this may seem, some people believed that they could escape excessive taxation in the town, which was far removed from rural district chiefs who often penalized their subjects by extracting additional revenue from them. Others migrated to the plantations, mines, and towns in the Gold Coast (Ghana) and Ivory Coast in order to raise money for the taxes.

The creation of the Haut-Sénégal et Niger colony, which included Mossi country, increased European and African commercial activity in Ouagadougou. The Compagnie Francaise de la Côte d'Ivoire built a store in Ouagadougou and staffed it with Africans from the Soudan. The store asked for and received land upon which to build houses for their clerks. In 1907–1908 many more Hausa, who traded kola nuts and salt between Salaga and Timbuktu, joined their countrymen and settled in the Hausa quarter called Zanguettin. They were soon joined by Yoruba traders from Salaga who decided to move to Ouagadougou because their traditional trade in cloth and kola nuts to Timbuktu-bound Dioula and Hausa merchants was curtailed by the French. Many of these Yoruba later sent for their wives, and these women started petty trading in the town's markets.

By the time Commandant d'Arboussier replaced Vidal in 1911 as head of the *Cercle* of Ouagadougou, the town had changed appreciably. The western part of Ouagadougou, demarcated by the ravine called Kardiogo, was being laid

[26]Louis Tauxier, *Le Noir du Soudan: Pays Mossi et Gourounsi* (Paris: Larose, 1912), p. 538; Baudu, p. 43.

out, and both bicycles and motorcycles were already circu-
lating on the new streets.[27] The roads leading from Ouagadougou to the Ivory Coast in the south and to the Niger
River in the north were now completed, and the first automobile arrived from Bobo-Dioulasso in March 1913. However, d'Arboussier's plans for developing the town came to a
halt because of the impending war and later by World War I
itself. Nevertheless, the town's population continued to increase, and, while there was no census of the town's African
population in 1913, it was noted that there were about fifteen
European men living there.[28]

Ouagadougou grew spectacularly in 1914 (See Table I)
because the town was used as a collecting point and garrison
for African soldiers recruited for World War I. Orders for
general mobilization arrived on August 2, 1914, and by
August 8, 1914, the local officials had started to procure the
recruits. Among the first to volunteer were some of the 2,500
Voltaic ex-servicemen who had previously been drafted to
fight in Morocco and who had subsequently settled in town.
Several hundred Mossi "cavaliers" (horsemen) were also

TABLE I. **Population Growth of Ouagadougou
from 1914–62**

Year	Africans	Europeans	Total
1914	19,332	12	19,344
1919	19,000	75	19,075
1926	12,015	223	12,238
1931	10,500	268	10,768
1936	14,050	150	14,200
1945	17,639	161	17,800
1946	17,000	120	17,120
1948	19,360	340	19,700
1951	37,300	378	37,678
1956–60	50,000	1,500	51,500
1961–62	57,779	1,347	59,126

SOURCE: "Recensement Démographique de la Ville de
Ouagadougou" [Resultats Provisoires], Rép. de Haute-
Volta, Ministère de l'Économie Nationale, Direction de la
Statistique et des Études Économiques, Ouagadougou,
Haute-Volta (June 1962), p. 9.

[27]*Ibid.*, p. 57.
[28]*Ibid.*, p. 61.

summoned to Ouagadougou and 500 were chosen.[29]   Commanded by d'Arboussier, these troops left Ouagadougou and conquered northern Togoland from the Germans on August 27, 1914.   The Mossi horsemen were returned and demobilized "happy to have mounted and fought like in days of yore,"[30] but the foot soldiers were retained.   In February 1915, the French easily recruited an additional 500 infantrymen from among the several hundred who had been summoned to Ouagadougou.   But when, in October 1915, additional thousands of Mossi were summoned to Ouagadougou so that 6,700 infantrymen could be recruited, there was opposition.   A missionary source reported that: "Theoretically, we knew that this call should have been for volunteers, but this time the number [of volunteers] was again very insufficient, thus it was necessary to 'draft' men so that the number required could be obtained."[31]   Later on, M. Blaise Diagne, the African deputy from Senegal to the French parliament, and one Lieutenant Mademba visited Ouagadougou and succeeded in recruiting 10,000 men from among those who had been summoned to the town.

   Many soldiers settled in Ouagadougou after the war ended. There were several reasons for this.   First, all veterans received a pension, albeit a small one, but because this was an important source of money, many men remained in Ouagadougou "where the money was" rather than returned to their villages, where they risked being forgotten by the administration.   Second, many veterans remained around Ouagadougou to seek jobs as policemen or as *gardes de cercles,* for which they had priority.   Third, many of the ex-soldiers, having been to Europe, could no longer tolerate the conservative traditional political regime in the rural areas. They preferred to live in Ouagadougou near the French administrators, most of whom were veterans themselves and understood the plight of ex-soldiers.   The administration for its part took an active interest in the veterans and, among other things, procured house lots for them in the Bilbalgo ward.   Many veterans settled here and, using their new prestige, obtained farm land for cultivation in the peri-urban areas.

[29]*Ibid.*, p. 65.
[30]*Ibid.*, p. 66.
[31]*Ibid.*, p. 70.

The final impetus to the growth of Ouagadougou took place in 1919 when the French created the Upper Volta as a separate colony in French West Africa and designated the town of Ouagadougou as its capital.[32] Ouagadougou was centrally located in this new 105,900-square-mile territory bounded on the south by the Ivory Coast, the Gold Coast (later Ghana), Togo, and Dahomey; on the east by Niger; and on the north and west by the French Soudan (later Mali). Therefore its choice as capital made sense from a geographic as well as from a commercial point of view. But when Lieutenant-Governor M. Edouard Hesling arrived on November 9, 1919, to take command of the colony, Ouagadougou did not impress him as a town worthy of being the capital of a new colony. He mobilized the people and started to build a new governmental complex.[33]

Hesling's new buildings were located east of the "ancient" complex of buildings in Ouagadougou across Kardiogo ravine and on a slight plateau known as Tang'Zugu (hilltop). The name of the area was soon changed to Koulouba, imitating a similar complex of government buildings at Bamako, Soudan. Thus did Hesling start the eastward growth of the town, a direction taken because it was feared that the giant ravine on the north would prevent northward development. The only inconvenience was that the colony's administrative center and government quarters east of the ravine were now separated from the *cercle* headquarters, the military camp, and the commercial center. Hesling ordered that the two areas be joined by a bridge, and he extended a street called Avenue Binger into the new area where it became Avenue du Gouvernment. The Governor thereafter constructed buildings on both sides of the town. These included school buildings, a new hospital, and a football stadium called Stade Mangin. He ordered the parceling out of lots for commercial and residential use in the old part of the town as well as the new. He traced many streets and avenues in the town, had them bordered with shade trees, and finally had a road build around Ouagadougou.[34] Ouaga-

[32]"Ouagadougou: Chef-Lieu de la Haute Volta," *Renseignements Coloniaux et Documents,* Suppelèment à l'*Afrique Française* de Janvier 1921, XXXI, p. 5.
[33]*Ibid.*
[34]See "Plan de la Ville de Ouagadougou," *Annuaire de l'Afrique Occidentale Française,* 1921, Plan IX.

dougou now took on the characteristics of a planned town with imposing buildings. However, since these majestic buildings were constructed out of sun-dried bricks (*banco*), the town was jocularly referred to throughout French West Africa as Bancoville.

Governor Hesling's public works program caused the most radical displacement of the African population of Ouagadougou since the conquest. These retainers of the Mogho Naba, such as the Dapoya Naba and ex-slaves, who had not accompanied the monarch to his new Na'Tenga, were evacuated from the area east of the Place d'Armes. They settled in a locality called Nindaogo Kango, a former execution ground bordering the swamps about 2 kilometers to the northeast. The newcomers called this area Dapoya II. The Hausa and other immigrant merchant groups who lived east of the Place d'Armes (ancient Zanguettin or Zangana) were also moved to make way for a hospital. But instead of going with the Dapoya (who were non-Moslem), they elected to move about 2 kilometers southwest in the direction of an old village called Pallentenga to a new area, Tiedpalogho (new place). Their new quarter retained the name Zanguettin but is sometimes called Zanguettin II.

The Governor's decision to reserve an area behind the military camp for a station on the projected Abidjan-Niger railway also resulted in the displacement of a number of traditional quarters. A quarter called Mwene inhabited by Moslems was moved about 50 meters north into Bilibambili, but as late as 1967 their abandoned mosque still stood because people feared to destroy it. Two other quarters, Noaghin and Nyoghsin, were moved about 1½ kilometers northward toward the swamp, parallel to Dapoya II. However, because these people were moved as groups their removal caused little social disorganization. The new areas were not parceled out and people still built their houses close to each other. Later, when plots were demarcated, the existing socio-cultural relationships were subordinated to geometry, with the result that there was a confusion between sociological relationships and geometric ones. Of course, people grumbled, but judging from conversations with some of those who remember this reorganization of Ouagadougou, there was surprisingly little overt opposition to this project because they all feared and respected the power of the Europeans.

Governor Hesling planned to develop Ouagadougou economically as well as transforming it physically. We are told that:

Because of its location Ouagadougou is slated to become the great market place of Upper Volta. Already an important market before our occupation, it is becoming more and more the center of native commerce where merchants coming from the south with their cargoes of shoddy European goods and kolas meet those coming from the north with salt and beasts. A network of roads, actually passable for automobiles only during two-thirds of the year, has put the new capital in communication with Bamako and the Ivory Coast on one side, and with Togoland and Dahomey on the other. Other roads, just as passable, connect Ouagadougou with all the other towns of the *cercles* of the colony, as well as the subdivisions of Mossi country. There are some bridges to repair, but light trucks, or semi-heavy ones, would be able to travel to Bouake, the provisional terminus of the Ivory Coast railway, or to Atakpame, the terminus of the Togoland railroad, in five days. Ouagadougou is the capital of the country, but its economic importance, independent of its political situation, is what makes it ideally suited to be the final stop of the future Mossi railway. Something worthy of note is that in all French West Africa it is the only capital of a colony which is truly central and is no further than two days' journey by automobile from any part of the *cercle* of which it is the main town.[35]

Under the aegis of Albert Sarraut, the colonial minister who had elaborate plans to develop the French colonies, Governor Hesling tried to commercialize cotton production in the Upper Volta and made Ouagadougou the collecting point for this produce. Many thousands of peasants were sent to the town carrying bales of cotton which they had cultivated "in a common field under the authority of the village chief, and for a salary which was theoretically to be distributed among them afterwards."[36] Of course, many peasants were not paid, but all had the opportunity to see urban life for the first time, and some remained in Ouagadougou.

[35]"Ouagadougou: Chef-Lieu."
[36]*L'Afrique Française,* XLII (1932), 520.

The 1920's witnessed more commercial enterprises establishing warehouses in Ouagadougou and mission-inspired efforts to start and expand small-scale industries there. In 1912 the White Sisters had established a workshop (*ouvroir*) for making carpets and now expanded its operations, recruiting hundreds of young girls and women from the rural areas to work.[37] Later there would be complaints that these girls were exploited by the nuns. But the girls and their husbands did become the founders of new urban and Christian families.

Governor Hesling worked hard to develop both the town of Ouagadougou and the colony of Upper Volta, but he worked the Mossi and other Voltaic populations even harder. Some of his African subalterns, now retired and still living in Ouagadougou, claim that they had no choice but to put the local people to work. The truth here is difficult to ascertain, but during the Hesling regime thousands of Mossi and other Voltaics fled Ouagadougou and the labor recruiters in the countryside and migrated to the Gold Coast. The wartime African population of 19,332 declined to 12,015, in 1926. In contrast, the European population, primarily engaged in administration and commerce, rose from 12 to 223 during that same period.

It was also during Governor Hesling's regime that the municipal structure of Ouagadougou was put in place. Ouagadougou was transformed into a *commune-mixte* according to the decree of December 4, 1926 (activated on January 1, 1927) and was now officially recognized as a town, but one which did not require a complex administrative organization. The Governor appointed a French official as Administrateur-Maire (Administrator-Mayor), who, although performing some of the duties of French mayors, was both an officer in the civil service and an officer in the judiciary police. His task was to work closely with the *cercle* commander, the Governor, and the traditional officials who supervised the various quarters in the emerging town.

The physical, municipal, and demographic growth of Ouagadougou stopped and declined during the Great Depression. The economy of the country was based on cotton, and, when the world cotton market collapsed, the economy of Upper Volta soon became bankrupt. The colony stagnated. Even the carpet factory felt the economic disaster, and the mission

[37]Baudu, p. 158.

"resigned itself to having to discharge a number of its girls. With the crisis continuing throughout the world, orders ... [for carpets] no longer arrived."[38] The African population in the town declined further, to 10,500 in 1931 (the smallest number of people in the town since the conquest) representing almost a 50 per cent loss of population since World War I. Finally, because of financial insolvency and the desire of the Ivory Coast planters to have unbridled access to Mossi manpower, Upper Volta was discontinued as a colony on September 5, 1932, and Ouagadougou lost its status and role as a colonial capital. The administrative services moved to the Ivory Coast, many European merchants left the town, and the African population continued its decline.[39]

The *Journal of the Post* of Ouagadougou for 1931–36 reveals that there was little activity in the town. Exceptions were the steady flow through the town of forced laborers to and from the Ivory Coast and the arrivals and departures of the representatives of commercial houses notifying the Resident of the prices offered for agricultural products. Ouagadougou even lost its position as the largest urban agglomeration in the former colony, dropping to third behind Bobo-Dioulasso and Koudougou, two towns located in the agriculturally richer western part of the territory. The population figures for the three towns from 1914 to 1945 show this quite clearly. (See Table II) The population increases in Bobo-Dioulasso and

TABLE II. Comparative Urbanization in Upper Volta

Year	Ouagadougou	Bobo-Dioulasso	Koudougou
1914	19,344	5,000	2,000
1926	12,238	6,749	11,525
1931	10,768	11,060	9,379
1936	14,200	10,250	15,920
1945	17,800	28,785	19,027
1953	32,077	43,400	8,700
1962	59,126	45,000	8,000

SOURCE: "Recensement Démographique de la Ville de Ouagadougou" [Resultats Provisoires], Rép. de Haute-Volta, Ministère de l'Économie Nationale, Direction de la Statistique et des Études Économiques, Ouagadougou, Haute-Volta (June 1962), p. 9.

[38]*Ibid.*

[39]Virginia Thompson and Richard Adloff, *French West Africa* (Stanford, Calif.: Stanford University Press, 1958), p. 153.

Koudougou were partially due to the presence of forced laborers there, but, after 1932, many people voluntarily migrated there from Ouagadougou in an effort to obtain work in order to pay taxes.

Ouagadougou's population did not start to increase again until after 1936. In 1938 Mogho Naba Kom went to Abidjan and after a passionate plea secured from Minister Marius Moritet the nomination of a chief administrator for the Upper Volta to reside at Ouagadougou.[40] French officials admitted that there was a need to deal with the particular interests of the Mossi, since their interests did not "always coincide with those of their neighbors."[41] Mossi country was reorganized under the Haute-Côte d'Ivoire (Upper Ivory Coast) in 1938. With the arrival of M. Louveau as Resident at Ouagadougou, the town began to recover and the African population increased to 14,200. It was still rising slowly when World War II broke out in 1939.

Ouagadougou After World War II

With the mobilization of men for World War II, Ouagadougou once again became an armed camp, and people started to flock to the town.[42] France fell so quickly, however, that few of the soldiers recruited in Ouagadougou could be shipped to Europe. The result was that the town's population increased by only 4,000 persons during the war, reaching 17,800 in 1945. The decline in 1946, slight as it was, reflected the exodus of those men who had been brought to the capital after the capitulation of pro-Vichy French West Africa. This was to be the last decline in Ouagadougou's population; since that period, the growth has been spectacular.

The population of the town almost doubled between 1946 and 1951. This rapid increase was again due to political, geographic, social, and economic factors, but they were of a slightly different order from those of the early colonial period. The most important political factor was the decision of the French Government on September 4, 1947, to recreate the Upper Volta colony and to redesignate Ouagadougou as its capital. This decision was based on the desire of the French

[40]Tiendrébéogo, p. 75.
[41]Thompson and Adloff, p. 174.
[42]Baudu, p. 208.

to clip the wings of M. Félix Houphouet-Boigny whose radical Rassemblement Démocratique Africain was viewed as endangering their colonial rule; on the desire of the Mossi chiefs to escape the tutelage of Abidjan and to recreate the Upper Volta; and on the administration's need for Mossi labor to extend the Abidjan-Niger railroad to Ouagadougou. A political deal was made in which the Upper Volta was recreated, and the Mossi chiefs promised the French to provide labor and material for building the railroad.[43]

As soon as Ouagadougou was renamed capital, French and African civil servants arrived to staff the new administrative services. Other persons drifted into town eager to seek low-level employment with the government or with private enterprises. By the late 1940's there were about 5,000 foreign-born Africans in Ouagadougou, comprising one-third of the 17,800 inhabitants of the town. Ouagadougou became truly cosmopolitan in population and culture.

Much of the recent heavy migration of Upper Volta people into Ouagadougou has been for economic reasons and only secondarily for other reasons. Many illiterate cultivators migrated to town in the hope of finding nonagricultural employment. Educated Voltaics have also migrated into town for economic reasons, because there were few jobs in the rural areas for educated persons except in the government administration. Some persons did migrate to Ouagadougou for social reasons, but it is difficult to determine whether they fled to town to get away from relatives, or were pulled into town by urban relatives. Few people, especially Mossi, admit voluntarily that they left home because of bad relations with spouses or kinsmen. It is only when people give contradictory answers or give testimony at the numerous court trials that one finds out about runaway wives or deserting husbands. Similarly, it is only when juvenile delinquents are interrogated either in Ouagadougou or at their rural homes that one discovers that they were runaways. On the other hand, people have always been invited to Ouagadougou by kinsmen or sent to join relatives in the town. The oldest male inhabitant of the Bilbalgo ward was invited to Ouagadougou by his father's sister's son whose mother had been sent there as a wife of the Baloum Naba. Chiefs and fathers still send *pughsiudsé* to husbands in the town, and, as we shall see, residents of Ouagadougou ask their

[43]Skinner, 1964b, pp. 181ff.

35

rural kinsmen to send children to help about the house. Reciprocally, rural dwellers often ask their urban relatives to host children attending school or to take illiterate children and "teach them how to live in the town."

Ouagadougou attracts persons interested in all types of education. Very young boys often startle the police by claiming that the reason they ran away was to get an education unobtainable in the rural areas. Moslem boys often add that they left home for Ouagadougou because they preferred a secular education to a Koranic one. More formally, graduates of primary schools in the eastern part of the Upper Volta come to Ouagadougou for further training. Moslems, too, send their children to Ouagadougou to be educated by Imams, and a number of Imams actively recruit Moslem boys from rural areas to train them.

Ouagadougou is still not a town that attracts people primarily interested in pleasure or adventure. Perhaps this is because it is a Mossi town and the Mossi normally do not migrate anywhere, not even to Ghana and the Ivory Coast, for any but economic reasons.[44] Interviews with unemployed or idle youths, persons whom one could expect to have come to Ouagadougou for pleasure, indicate that they had resided in town a rather long time before they even started going to the movies, their chief source of entertainment. What emerges from such interviews is the conviction these youths have that it is easier to make a living in Ouagadougou than elsewhere in the Upper Volta. They believe that all one has to do is to go to one of the markets, help some passing African or European woman with her shopping bags, and one will get enough money to buy food and clothing.

Postwar Ouagadougou also has attracted a large number of Mossi who fled to the Gold Coast and even to the Ivory Coast to avoid forced labor and returned home (when they heard that the postwar reforms had "cooled the country") only to discover that they could no longer live in their rural villages.[45] They were later to be joined by many thousands of

[44]Albert S. Balima, "Note sur la situation sociale et les problèmes de travail en Haute-Volta," *Revue Internationale du Travail, LXXXII*, No. 4 (October 1960), 404–408.

[45]Elliott P. Skinner, "Labour Migration and its Relationship to Socio-Cultural Change in Mossi Society," *Africa, XXX,* No. 4 (October 1960b), 385.

rural persons who had migrated to the coastal cities after 1950 and also wished to live in an Upper Volta town. The significance of external migration for the demographic growth of contemporary Ouagadougou cannot be stressed too highly. This phenomenon was noted in the rural areas in 1955-57 but never became the subject of specific inquiry. Women questioned in the urban health centers about why they came to Ouagadougou reported that their husbands refused to live in the *weogho* (bush or rural area) on returning from the coasts. More specific data were: among the 164 young male nonresidents of Ouagadougou who applied to the Labor Office in Ouagadougou during the week of October 19 to October 24, 1964, some 96 had worked outside the Upper Volta. What was even more indicative of the relationship between external migration and internal urbanization was the tenor of the 147 letters requesting jobs dating from January 1963 to November 1964, which the Labor Office in Ouagadougou had received from Voltaics living in foreign areas. These letters (See Appendix I) indicated that most of the applicants, whether "boys cuisinier" (cook-stewards), craftsmen, tradesmen, or clerks of various types, were not only interested in returning home but also specified, as a matter of course, work *in* the town of Ouagadougou and often for a government bureau *in* the town of Ouagadougou.

Rural youngsters who plan to migrate to Ouagadougou have even developed a pattern of migrating first to the Ivory Coast in order to be better prepared for urban life in this town. Young men reported that they encountered less parental resistance if they initially sought permission to go to the Ivory Coast rather than to Ouagadougou. The parents believed that the "foreignness" of the Ivory Coast would stimulate the migrants to work, whereas they would become wastrels in the familiarity of Ouagadougou. However, once such a migrant returns home with evidence of his maturity and good character, he encounters almost no resistance when he departs for Ouagadougou. Youths also report that migrating to the Ivory Coast instead of to Ghana is now good linguistic preparation for the subsequent move to Ouagadougou. The diversity of languages in the Ivory Coast forces the migrant to pick up French as a *lingua franca,* whereas in Ghana he learns English. The youths believe that those who know some French have greater opportunities for jobs in Ouagadougou than the

37

TABLE III.   Ethnic Composition of
Ouagadougou (1962)

Group	Number	Percentages
Mossi	44,201	74.8
Fulani (Peulh)	2,254	3.8
Boussansé	1,947	3.3
Gourounsi	1,819	3.1
Europeans	1,347	2.3
Bobo Sam	1,267	2.1
Samogho	724	1.2
Gourmantche	489	.8
Others (including non-Voltaic Africans)	5,078	8.6
TOTAL	59,126	100.0

SOURCE: "Recensement Démographique de la Ville de Ouagadougou" [Resultats Provisoires], Rép. de Haute-Volta, Ministère de l'Économie Nationale, Direction de la Statistique et des Études Économiques, Ouagadougou, Haute-Volta (June 1962), p. 13.

youths who know only Moré or English.   Thus in this competition for scarce jobs, external migrants have a better chance than those persons who migrate directly to Ouagadougou.

The profile of Ouagadougou's population, based on the last complete census (1962), shows quite clearly the two main factors which have led to the growth of the town: the heavy influx of Mossi into the town and the extreme youth of the population.   The census gives the ethnic concentration of Ouagadougou as follows (See Table III).

The Mossi characteristics of the town have increased because of the departure in 1960 of many non-Voltaic civil servants who, until that time, were the cultural elite of Ouagadougou and dominated many of its institutions.   The percentage of Mossi was much higher in 1968 than it was in 1962 since the population of the town had increased to an estimated total of 110,000 in 1968.   Ouagadougou's position in the middle of Mossi country where the population density is over 60 persons per square mile, in contrast to the rest of the Upper Volta where the density is only 40 persons per square mile, has undoubtedly influenced the ethnic characteristics of the town.   In fact, the 1962 census shows that more than half the town's population claimed to have been born in the Ouagadougou region. (See Table IV)

The other dominant feature of Ouagadougou's demographic

TABLE IV.   Birthplaces of Ouagadougou Residents (1962)

Place of Birth	Number	Place of Birth	Number
Ouagadougou	33,877	Fada N'Gourma	395
Koudougou	1,688	Dori	376
Kombissiri	1,557	Boulsa	335
Bobo-Dioulasso	1,307	Dédougou	309
Zinaré	1,218		
Ouahigouya	1,216	*Foreign African Areas*	
Manga	1,112	Mali	1,134
Tenkodogo	1,105	Ivory Coast	573
Kaya	1,051	Niger	569
Zorgho	825	Nigeria	451
Saponé	820	Senegal	321
Boussé	651	Dahomey	318
Koupéla	624	Ghana	254
Léo	589	Mauritania	91
Tougan	557	Guinea	68
Yako	496	Congo	24

SOURCE: "Recensement Démographique de la Ville de Ouagadougou" [Resultats Provisoires], Rép. de Haute-Volta, Ministère de l'Économie Nationale, Direction de la Statistique et des Études Économiques,
Ouagadougou, Haute-Volta (June 1962), p. 13.

profile is the extreme youth of its population (See Table V)
This is a common feature of African towns in the process of
dynamic development. Some 28,591 persons, or 49.5 per cent
of the total population are listed as less than twenty years old;
91.5 per cent of the population under fifty; and only 5 per cent
of the population is over fifty five years old. Thus, the majority are relatively young persons still capable of a rather active
life. The male to female ratio among the youth is almost equal
with no substantial imbalance in the sex ratio among any of
the age groups. The .1 per cent majority of male children over
female under five is about standard for any population in the
world. The larger, but still rather small preponderance of .5
per cent males over females in the five to fifteen age group
indicates the tendency of more boys than girls to migrate
or run away to the town for education, to find work, or
loaf. The slight increase of females (40.7 per cent) to males
(39 per cent) in the groups over fifteen years of age reflects the
norm for the entire country where at the age of marriage females outnumber males by .1 per cent.[46]

The demographic equality of the sexes in Ouagadougou is

[46]"Recensement Démographique de la Ville de Ouagadougou," pp. 11–12.

TABLE V.   Bar Graph of the Population of Ouagadougou (By Age and Sex;
Based on the 1962 Census)

	Male (Age Unknown: 269)	Female (Age Unknown: 155)
60+ yrs	876	1,040
60 yrs	586	446
55 yrs	696	576
50 yrs	927	748
45 yrs	1,433	1,142
40 yrs	1,806	1,516
35 yrs	2,495	2,071
30 yrs	2,965	2,866
25 yrs	3,227	3,348
20 yrs	2,955	3,325
15 yrs	2,635	2,254
10 yrs	3,157	3,029
5 yrs	4,165	3,454
1 yr	1,627	1,490

Number (scale: 4,000 3,000 2,000 1,000 0 4,000 3,000 2,000 1,000)

SOURCE: "Recensement Démographique de la Ville de Ouagadougou" [Re-
sultats Provisoires], Rép. de Haute-Volta, Ministère de l'Econömie Nationale, Direction de la Statistique et des Études Économiques, Ouagadougou, Haute-Volta (June
1962), pp. 11–12.

due to the tendency of males migrating to town to bring multiple wives with them or send for them. This is probably the
reason why there is a disparity of 1.1 per cent of females over
males in the fifteen to twenty age group; 1.2 per cent females
over males in the twenty to twenty five age group; and .4 per
cent of females over males in the twenty five to thirty age
group. The preponderance of 1.0 per cent males over females
in the thirty to thirty five age group and the .7 per cent males
over females in the thirty to fifty age group probably indicates
either that an earlier group of male immigrants did not wish to
bring wives with them or that older women prefer to remain at
home. Females do not again outnumber males in the population until sixty years of age and over. In Ouagadougou, as in
some Western countries, they outnumber males by some .8
per cent. The implication of these demographic features in
Ouagadougou is that even if immigration were to cease, an
unlikely occurrence, the town's population could still be expected to increase at quite a rapid rate.
    The physical development of Ouagadougou, like its demo-

40

graphic growth, went forward at a swift pace with the restoration of Upper Volta after World War II. However, this time France paid for refurbishing and reequipping the capital and its services. The new Upper Volta Government lost no time transforming the former "Bancoville" into a worthy capital.[47] New roads and avenues were laid out, trees were planted, the ravines at the northern part of the town were converted into reservoirs, and new quarters were taken in hand, parceled into lots, and distributed among the people. A whole complex of buildings was constructed in 1953 for the Governor and for the administration, and a new palace was even built for Mogho Naba Sagha II. A system of reservoirs capable of holding about 4 million cubic meters of water was constructed, and a station capable of storing, purifying, and distributing 1,000 cubic meters of potable water was put into operation. In addition, a network for the production and distribution of electrical power was finished. By December 1954, when the Mossi railroad reached Ouagadougou, the construction of the railroad station was completed. About the same time, the Buffet Hotel was completed to take care of travelers; a motor park and an industrial zone were laid out; the main streets and avenues of the town were paved; the runways of the airport were lengthened and nightlanding facilities installed; and a modern college and apprenticeship center in the Zone Scolaire was completed.

As is readily apparent on the plan of Ouagadougou (see Table VI) the commercial zone lies closest to the center of the town and includes part of Avenue Binger. Establishments represented here range from the great colonial enterprises to large African enterprises, modern markets, banks, and governmental offices. The commercial zone is bordered on the south by the Catholic mission and its satellite areas. As one would expect, the administrative and residential zones are quite modern and well laid out. Lying to the east of the center of Ouagadougou and quite near to the peripheries, these two areas enclose the presidential palace, ministerial buildings, and embassies, as well as the residences of ambassadors and other high-status Africans and Europeans. Koulouba, a quarter to the south of the administrative and residential zones, has been developed as the residential area for civil servants and is

[47]French Union Assembly Debates, June 24, 1949, p. 768.

TABLE VI. Major Quarters and Wards of Ouagadougou

Bilbalgo Originally a hamlet created by Mogho Naba Ouaraga to house his pages. Much land here was allocated to war veterans and officials of the administration, but area is now becoming delapidated. Presently a center of urban development.

Bilibambili Originally created by Mogho Naba to house pages. Traditionally contained both Mossi and Fulani populations, but now houses Moslems as well. Presently a center of urban development incorporating subquarters of Mwemne and Norghn.

Dapoya II The second site of residence of the Dapoya Naba and ex-slaves. (The original name was Nindaogo Kango.) Contains the largest African population. Civil servants are entering and displacing cultivators.

Gounghin North and South Largest quarter in the town, but one of the least developed. Houses Protestant mission of Assemblies of God. A new military camp is being built here. Its subquarters are Baoghin, Bendogo, Bourgretenga, Gandin, S. O. M., Zone Industrielle and the original Ouagadougou.

Koulouba Originally "Tang'Zugu" or "hilltop." Contains a complex of government buildings built by Hesling. Though originally a residential area for African civil servants, the area is rapidly being transformed.

Kamsaoghin Originally a hamlet occupied by officials of the Mogho Naba. Urban development is taking place here.

Larhalle A small and still underdeveloped area. It was the original residence of the Larhalle Naba and his retainers. Hamdalaye, its subquarter, is inhabited mostly by Moslems of the Tidjaniyya sect.

Mairie Originally part of Bilbalgo. The area includes the present Town Hall and former prison complex.

Nemne An area in the process of rapid change. Round traditional houses are disappearing.

Nyoghsin Inhabited by smiths who manufacture figurines, art works.

Ouidi Original residence of the Ouidi Naba. Quarters such as Kologho Naba were founded by relatives who came to join the Mogho Naba. The area houses many immigrant Moslems.

Paspanga An ancient quarter of ritual significance to the Mogho Naba during installation ceremonies. Contains the barracks of the military, and military personnel and police are acquiring land here. The area is undergoing rapid change.

Peologhin Inhabited by Hausa, Yoruba, and Mossi populations.

Samandin Originally a hamlet occupied by officials of the Mogho Naba. Now a center of urban development, though not heavily populated.

St. Joseph, St. Julien, St. Léon, St. Jean-Baptiste, St. Marc Satellite areas of the Catholic mission. The areas house many early Christians and their descendants.

Tanghin An unallotted quarter; round houses predominate.

TABLE VI. (Continued)

Tiedpalogo Presently a center of urban development. A new area and very heterogeneous.

Zoghona Relatively underdeveloped. La Rotunde area of this quarter may expand at the expense of Zoghona and aid in its transformation.

Zangouettin Often called Zangouetin II. Second site of residence of Hausas and other important merchant groups. Mainly Hausa, Yoruba, and Mossi populations.

rapidly being transformed. It is becoming quite modern and may, in fact, soon be absorbed into the residential and administrative zones. Modern institutions such as hospitals and the Centre Voltaique des Recherches Scientifique lie in Zone Scolaire, located to the north of the residential zone.

For the most part, the African wards of Ouagadougou[48] ring the central area of the town, with the administrative, residential, and industrial zones lying outside the circle. Dapoya II is the most populous of the African quarters in the town. All these quarters, especially Dapoya II, are in the process of rapid change. In Dapoya II, the civil servants are crowding out the cultivators who formerly lived there and who are now moving further out of town. Moderate concrete structures are therefore replacing the older houses which were built of *banco* in Sudanese style.

A complex of many traditional African quarters lies to the south and southwest of the commercial zone. Areas such as Kamsaoghin and its adjoiners and Samandin were traditionally occupied by the Mossi retainers of the Mogho Naba, and most of the houses are of mud-brick plastered with cement.

[48]Cf. F. Bellot, "Étude sur la toponymie des quartiers de Ouagadougou," *Notes Africaines,* XLII (April 1949), 61–64. There is no agreement as to the correct number of quarters in Ouagadougou. For example, on August 29, 1968, the Town Hall listed the following quarters: "Sambin, Tanghin, Larhalle, Tampoui, Ouidi, Gounghin, Samambili, Bourgretinga, Baoghin, Bendogo, S.O.M., Gandin, Zone Industrielle, Kamboisin, St. Joseph, Kamsaonghin, Tamsin, Radio, P.T.T., Tiedpalogo, Zangoetin I et II, Samandin, Chateau d'eau (route de PO), Peolonghin, St. Léon, Palemtinga, Bedogo, Paspanga II, Depot de Gardes, Gendarmerie, Koulouba, Zone des Ambassades, Dag-Noe, Zog-Na, Zone Commerciale, Bilbalogo, Poedogo, St. Julien, St. Jean-Baptiste, Cite des Fonctionnaires, Camp Militaire, Bilibambili, Transafricaine, Norghin, Moemin, Nemnin, Nogsin, Dapoya II, Gare Routière, Paspanga."

Bilbalgo was formerly the hamlet of the Baloum Naba; and Gounghin, the largest quarter in the town, was traditionally inhabited by the Gougha Naba, a provincial governor. Traditionally, Moslem and Fulani populations occupied Bilibambili. These areas shade off into Ipelesse, an unallotted area occupied by migrant squatters living almost exclusively in traditional-type huts.

Completing the ring of African quarters surrounding the central area of the town are Ouidi and Tampouy. Ouidi, the residence of the Ouidi Naba (Prime Minister of the Mogho Naba), was first inhabited by relatives of this official and is now emerging as an important Catholic religious and educational center. North and across the reservoir from Ouidi is Tampouy. Like the other quarters in this northern area, it is still relatively indigenous in house types and living arrangements. However, it is also a potential area of expansion for persons who have been displaced from the core of the town. Already people from the other quarters of Ouagadougou are eagerly seeking house lots there.

Most of the quarters of Ouagadougou appear fated to change their physical and sociological characteristics. New quarters such as Kologho Naba and the different "zones" have emerged and many of the preexisting quarters have been or are in the process of being absorbed by them. Not many residents of contemporary Ouagadougou now recognize the ancient boundaries of Mwemne, or care about the distinctions between Nemne, Nyoghsin, and Bilibambili. Similarly, the small quarters of the retainers of the Mogho Naba near Na'Tenga are almost indistinguishable from each other and are in the process of being absorbed either by the Mission or Kamsaoghin. By far the greatest casualties among the traditional quarters are the small subquarters within the housing complexes of the important provincial ministers. Today, except for the older people actually living in these areas, no one remembers that each traditional chief had a Bilbalgo, Samandin, Dapoya, and other quarters within his own "village." The Dapoya *of* Ouidi and others like it have ceased to be physical, political, or sociological entities.

There are a number of modern public areas of Ouagadougou located near the present limits of its town. The airport extends from the southeast to the southwest along the outskirts of the town, south of Koulouba. The municipal stadium of Ouagadougou is located due west of Na'Tenga. The municipal abbatoir and its cattle pen are on the northeastern edge of the town. Also in this area is a still undeveloped section called the Bois de Boulogne. Some attempts have been made to transform this area into a park for the town's inhabitants, but so far financial problems have delayed this project.

The municipality has many plans for Ouagadougou. It would like to pave most of the streets of the town, provide water and light for all the inhabitants, take over and develop the peripheral quarters, and build sanitary canals in place of the marshy and unsightly ditches which still drain the town. The problem is that the town has no money to realize these projects. Nevertheless, the urban inhabitants are demanding that these things be done, and migrants to Ouagadougou expect the municipal authorities and national government to find the means which will allow them to participate in the activities of the modern world.

Residential quarter in transition

CHAPTER II

Occupations and Economic Activities

Civil Servants and Clerks

Public administration has always been the most prestigious, if not the most economically rewarding, occupation of the Ouagadougou elite. The Mogho Naba and his officials derived their incomes from the work of the larger group of resident farmers, from the control of trade, and from their official duties as rulers and administrators. When the French conquered the town, their administrators replaced the traditional authorities both in the prestige gradient and in actual incomes. They set the occupational standards for the still largely farmer population of the emerging town. To become a civil servant (*fonctionnaire*) or a general clerk (*commis*) became the occupational goal of Africans who desired affluence, prestige, and power. Africans became more attracted to administration when they discovered that civil service status gave some Africans (the Senegalese citizens of France) theoretical equality in salary, privileges, and security with Frenchmen holding the same rank. The civil service was also seen as the most valuable occupation because, in contrast to private employment where indeterminate factors were important for promotion, it promised advancement on the basis of intelligence, educational qualifications, and success on examinations. Finally, both the civil service and clerical work drew people because there were no large-scale extractive and manufacturing industries that could have absorbed the emerging group of literate Africans in the town.

Most censuses of Ouagadougou indicate that civil servants and clerks comprise the largest percentage of the persons employed in the town (cultivators excluded). The census of 1962 (see Table VII) which grouped civil servants and clerks under one category showed that these workers represented some 43.9 per cent of the nonagricultural workers. More precise data from a still-unpublished employment census of 1967 (see Table VIII) showed that the civil servants alone numbered about 50 per cent of the nonagricultural workers in Ouagadougou.

TABLE VII. Occupational Groups in Ouagadougou
(Based on the 1962 Census)

Occupations	Number	Occupations	Number
Cultivators	4,655	*Dolotières* (Millet	
Civil servants		beer makers and sellers)	124
and clerks	2,154	Butchers	110
Domestic servants	845	Jewelers	76
Laborers	816	Ironsmiths and solderers	69
Merchants	751	Electricians	53
Soldiers	709	Barbers	52
Chauffeurs	671	Painters	51
Masons	407	Bakers	50
Tailors	312	Shoemakers	44
Carpenters	305	Weavers	26
Mechanics	290	Kola sellers	24
Missionaries and		Plumbers	18
Moslem teachers	149	Watch repairers	13
		TOTAL	12,774

SOURCE: "Recensement Démographique de la Ville de Ouagadougou" [Resultats Provisoires], Rép. de Haute-Volta, Ministère de l'Économie Nationale, Direction de la Statistique et des Études Économiques, Ouagadougou, Haute-Volta (June 1962), p. 14.

If the clerical and managerial staffs of both public and private sectors are added to the civil service-clerk category, this group accounts for about 65 per cent of the town's nonagricultural workers. These percentages are not only significant for the occupational structure of the town, but have always influenced the lives of its inhabitants.

The salaries and perquisites of the *fonctionnaires* in Ouagadougou are based on the ranking of their jobs, their length of service, and their number of dependents[1] (see Table IX). Since one's rank determines one's earning capacity, civil servants in Ouagadougou have always sought to increase their earnings by taking examinations for better paying jobs. The result is an absence of professionalism or commitment to specific types of jobs, or to technical competence within the service. Instead, there is a constant attempt to manipulate the service in the

[1]The government used to pay its employees approximately $10.00 per month per child, up to 6 children, until age seventeen, but by 1967 it had reduced this family allowance to about $3.00 per child. In addition to this allowance, civil servants receive annual leaves, sick leaves (women receive 14 weeks' maternity leave), and substantial pensions upon retirement.

TABLE VIII. Employment Statistics

	Laborers and Apprentices	Journeymen	Employees (Clerks and Retainers)	Management and Staff	Total
Public Sector (Status)					
Civil servants	0	0	2,031	1,211	3,242
Non-civil servants (including police and military)	1,789	901	1,001	573	4,264
TOTAL OF PUBLIC SECTOR	1,789	901	3,032	1,784	7,506
Private Sector (Occupations)					
Agriculture, forestry, and herding	6	7	25	5	43
Extractive industries	0	0	0	0	0
Manufacturing industries, and workshops	610	305	40	46	1,001
Construction and public works	710	1,010	104	70	1,894
Commerce, banking, liberal professions, missionaries	905	301	750	299	2,255
Transport	101	382	265	82	830
Domestic service	435	0	848*	0	1,283
TOTAL OF PRIVATE SECTOR	2,767	2,005	2,032	502	7,306
GRAND TOTAL	4,556	2,906	5,064	2,286	14,812

SOURCE: "Direction du Travail, de la Main-d'Oeuvre et de la Formation Professionnelle," Ministère du Travail et de la Fonction Publique, Rép. de Haute-Volta, 1967, pp. 2ff.

*Not counted along with "white-collar" employees.

interest of better paying jobs and important fringe benefits. For example, young people leaving school with the appropriate academic diplomas or certificates focus upon the best paying civil service jobs available. They take examinations for various jobs and choose the one that ensures the highest salary. Thereafter, they continue to take tougher examinations for still better jobs, and as we shall see later on, seize any opportunity for additional study abroad so that they can improve their chances for still higher paying jobs. This

TABLE IX. Salary Scales for Educational Levels

Category	Employment Grade	Educational Standard	Level	Qualifications for Recruitment	Career	Index	Gross Annual Salary (C.F.A.)*	Gross Monthly Salary (C.F.A.)	Retention of 6% for Pension (C.F.A.)	Net Monthly Salary (C.F.A.)	Residence Allowance 10% (C.F.A.)	Net Monthly Pay (C.F.A.)
A	Management and Direction	Superior	1	Doctorate Graduate Diploma Professional Schools	Top Salary	1,000	1,940,000	161,667	9,700	151,967	16,166	168,133
					Starting Salary	375	727,500	60,625	3,637	56,988	6,062	63,050
			2	Master's Degree + Competitive Exam	Top Salary	750	1,155,000	121,250	7,275	113,975	12,125	126,100
					Starting Salary	350	582,000	48,500	2,910	45,590	4,850	50,440
B	Supervisor	Secondary	1	Baccalauréate and Competitive Exam + Specialization	Top Salary	520	1,008,800	84,067	5,044	79,023	8,406	87,429
					Starting Salary	250	485,000	40,417	2,425	37,992	4,041	42,033
			2	Baccalauréate and Competitive Exam	Top Salary	460	892,400	74,367	4,462	69,905	7,436	77,341
					Starting Salary	220	426,800	35,567	2,134	33,433	3,556	36,989
C	Specialized Work	First Cycle	1	B.E.P.C. and Competitive Exam + Specialization	Top Salary	300	582,000	48,500	2,910	45,590	4,850	50,440
					Starting Salary	165	320,100	26,675	1,600	25,075	2,667	27,742
			2	B.E.P.C. and Competitive Exam	Top Salary	265	514,100	42,842	2,570	40,272	4,284	44,556
					Starting Salary	150	291,000	24,250	1,455	22,795	2,425	25,220
D	Specialized Work	Elementary Certificate		C.E.P.E. and Competitive Exam	Top Salary	210	407,400	33,950	2,037	31,913	3,395	35,308
					Starting Salary	100	194,000	16,167	970	15,197	1,616	16,813

SOURCE: "Projet de Classement Indiciaire et Echelle des Traitements" (Tableau No. 1), Ministère du Travail et de la Fonction Publique, Rép. de Haute-Volta. 1967.
*The salaries are in C.F.A. which until 1968 were 250 = $1.00.

**TABLE X.   Monthly Salaries (in C.F.A.) of
Clerks Employed in the Private Sector**

Grade	Bank Salary	Machine Shops and Electric Company Salary
1	5,030	5,030
2	8,050	7,685
3	9,900	9,410
4	12,100	11,760
5	15,100	13,915
6	18,050	16,390
7	25,450	23,100

SOURCE: "Projet de Classement Indiciaire et Echelle des Traitements" (Tableau No. 4), Ministère du Travail et de la Fonction Publique, Rép. de Haute-Volta, 1967. (In general, wage scales were fixed by various conventions; the wages of clerks not so fixed are comparable to those paid by the machine shops and the Electric Company.)

constant mobility creates problems for heads of departments who are often helpless in preventing skillful cadres from moving elsewhere. They sometimes try to frustrate this but seldom succeed since this is against the ethos of the service.

Most clerks in the private sector of Ouagadougou are civil servants *manqué*. They are persons who cannot become *bona fide* civil servants either because they lack the educational or moral qualifications, or the necessary civil status. Their occupational and economic status is normally inferior to that of civil servants, but like them, they have comparable salary scales and perquisites based on occupational category, length of service, and most important, the nature of their firm's business (see Table X). Like the civil servants, the *commis* are also highly mobile, but this mobility is usually toward the higher paying and prestigious civil service. Clerks, too, constantly take examinations, and those whose civic status permits them to become *fonctionnaires* ultimately do so.

The *fonctionnaires* and *commis* remain quite conscious of their economic advantages over the rest of the Ouagadougou population, but consider their status as a function of individual effort and of their contribution to the service. Their economic model was always the Europeans in similar positions, and during the colonial and decolonization periods, their major effort was to gain parity with them. European employers, both government and private, did provide important perquisites for their white employees. These included more generous vacations than the Africans, indemnities for the rigors of climate, and allowances for the education of children. The civil servants and clerks felt discriminated against in comparison with the Europeans and lobbied against these differentials until equality was achieved.

Given their preoccupation with governmental and clerical jobs as sources of incomes, not too many *fonctionnaires* and *commis* sought other means to augment their incomes. Almost none entered business, but with the rapid growth of Ouagadougou after 1953, many acquired house lots on which to construct houses either for themselves or for rent. A small but influential group of *fonctionnaires* in Ouagadougou has become "gentlemen farmers" or "civil servant farmers." They include ministers and their staffs, deputies, municipal councilors, politicians, and ordinary clerks. As members of the elite group in Ouagadougou, these men have had little difficulty obtaining land—even valuable rice land—from peri-urban and rural chiefs.[2] They either bring rural relatives to settle on these farms as cultivators or hire youths in Ouagadougou to go and work there. The gentlemen farmers visit their nearby farms on weekends during the planting season to supervise what is being done. When, for example, there is a shortage of weeders, they are the ones who hire the additional help in Ouagadougou and dispatch them to the farms. Or when, as in the summer of 1964, there is insufficient water for growing wet rice, these men provide water in large tanks for irrigation.

Gentlemen farmers view their peri-urban or rural farms as a source of basic staples for their families and only secondarily as a source of income from the sale of produce. The result is that the economics of these farms are difficult to unravel. Not only is there a lack of bookkeeping, but kinship factors play an important role in the production and distribution of food. For example, relatives or friends settled on these farms are not given a fixed salary. Instead, they are given sums of money periodically, provided with money for taxes, and given such

[2] At Boulbi, 20 kilometers from Ouagadougou, more than 50 per cent of the plots of land developed for irrigated rice fields by Taiwanese agricultural experts are owned by civil servants.

51

gifts as bicycles and clothing. These relatives may also consume as much of the food produced as they need and cultivate their own crops, which presumably they do sell for cash. In essence, the relationship between the gentlemen farmers and their dependents on these farms does not differ fundamentally from that which exists between elders and dependents in the rural areas. The main difference here is that the dependents in the urban areas expect and receive sums of money and are assured of some income during the year.

There are other reasons why members of the *fonctionnaire* group keep peri-urban and rural farms. These men view their farms both as security against the vagaries of administrative and political life and as a source of income after retirement. They plant grafted mangoes and oranges among the cereal so that these fruits will bring them enough income to live on if they should be fired by the government. Finally, there is a sentimental reason why many *fonctionnaires* invest surplus money in farms. Many, if not the majority, of the older elite were born in the rural areas and have certain traditional attitudes about land and farming. They enjoy, or profess to enjoy, the rustic peace and "natural" life of the farms in contrast to the bustle of Ouagadougou. Through the possession of the peri-urban or rural farms the gentlemen farmers of Ouagadougou combine present economic gain and future economic security, while maintaining ties with kinsmen and the soil.

Domestic Servants

Domestic servants, a service group, are the next largest group of nonagricultural workers in Ouagadougou. These are the rural persons who migrated to town in order to improve their lives, and, in the absence of many opportunities for employment, became domestic servants. Initially most of the domestic servants worked for Europeans, especially bachelors, who did not bring their wives and families to Ouagadougou. As Africans also entered the civil service, they too started to employ domestics. Today, almost all civil servants and clerical workers (both African and European) in Ouagadougou have domestic servants. The larger European households usually have a cook-steward, a launderer, a gardener, and, when there are children, a male (and only infrequently a female) nursemaid. The households of ordinary African civil servants and second-grade European technicians have at least a cook-steward who cooks, cleans the house, and launders clothes. Even young unmarried male civil servants and clerks have their "boys" to take care of the housework, laundry, and cooking.

It is really difficult to ascertain the number and character of domestic servants in Ouagadougou. The Ministry of Labor listed some 1,283 domestics in 1963, but these figures must be used cautiously since many domestic servants are linked to their "employers" by kinship or friendship ties. To complicate matters, often these persons are not really considered as domestic servants, but as kinsmen who help about the household. The status "domestic servant" is therefore not only ambiguous, it is imprecise and difficult to define. For example, many "domestic servants" are not given the wages established by the government or recognized by the Ministry of Labor.

Table XI lists the minimum salaries of domestics (*gens de*

TABLE XI. Salaries and Job Descriptions of Domestics

Grade	Definition of Job	Monthly Salary (C.F.A.)
1	Beginning steward or one with up to eight months of experience, assistant steward, assistant cook	5,030
2	Steward with more than eight months of experience, children's nurse, housekeeper doing ordinary work	5,330
3	Night watchman, day watchman charged with upkeep of house, ordinary house-worker doing routine work as well as washing and ironing	5,790
4	Cook-Steward working for a bachelor living alone or in a household where no child-supplement payment is being received for children or additional persons	6,800
5	Family cook	7,470
6	General cook for more than five persons not belonging to the same family	8,660
7	Chief steward	11,960

SOURCE: "Direction du Travail, de la Main-d'Oeuvre et de la Formation Professionnelle," *Statistiques*, 1966, p. 4.

maison) in Ouagadougou, as stipulated by the government in 1964.

None of these salaries includes food and lodging. If the servant is fed at work, his employer may withhold 2,175 C.F.A. per month, and if he sleeps there, 435 C.F.A. may be withheld for his room. And it is precisely because of these two provisions that many persons in Ouagadougou do not normally pay their "domestics" even the minimum salaries.

Most of the domestics in Ouagadougou are men or boys. The older and experienced men usually work for Europeans and high-ranking African civil servants, and the young boys work for less prestigious persons. There are only a few African female domestics and they are usually employed as nursemaids by Europeans and top-grade African civil servants. This shift away from employing men as nursemaids is the result of changes in the status of the women of Ouagadougou. Undoubtedly, as many more enter the modern occupational system, they will replace men in a number of domestic-type occupations.

Cultivators

The large number of cultivators living in Ouagadougou (see Table VII) are persons who are qualified neither for the highly skilled and prestigious civil service and clerical jobs, nor for the relatively unskilled domestic service occupations. Except for the older people indigenous to the town, the primary reason urban men earn their living as cultivators is because they can find no other type of employment and cannot live off incidental earnings. Many cultivators do not consider farming to be an "occupation," and a man thus engaged is likely to tell the census taker that he is "unemployed." Only further questioning elicits the information that he is actively farming; then his comment is likely to be "mam ko bala," which means, "I am only cultivating."[3] Farming as an occupation in Ouagadougou must therefore be regarded as a substitute for other work and, as far as the majority of cultivators are concerned, a very poor one. With the possible exception of a small group

[3]Peter B. Hammond, "Economic Change and Mossi Acculturation," in William R. Bascom and Melville J. Herskovits (eds.), *Continuity and Change in African Cultures* (Chicago: The University of Chicago Press, 1959), pp. 244–45.

54

of commercial vegetable gardeners, people do not migrate to Ouagadougou to remain cultivators. They go to Ouagadougou to seek work and when, during the planting season, they can find nothing to do or calculate that the money they are earning will be insufficient to purchase their basic food needs for the coming year, they seek land to cultivate. The exception are those men who had been encouraged by kinsmen in the civil service to come and live in town and cultivate peri-urban farms for them.

Census data show that a large percentage of cultivators now living in Ouagadougou are immigrants from the rural areas of Mossi country. A personal survey of 111 resident cultivators showed that 86, or 77.5 per cent, were migrants and only 25, or 22.5 per cent, were born in Ouagadougou. Of these, 103 (92.8 per cent) were Mossi, 3 Yarsé, 2 Gourounsi, 1 Lobi, 1 Boussanga, and 1 Bobo. Some of these men had household plots in the peripheral urban quarters, but all had their fields in a belt of land extending between 5 to 25 kilometers beyond the town's boundaries in such places as Cissin, Saba, Bassoko, Nabagalé, Lanoagha-yiri, Pabre, Boulbi, and in Larhalle Naba Weogho (land belonging to the Larhalle Naba).[4]

Ouagadougou resident cultivators obtain farm land in a variety of ways. Among the 111 surveyed, 19 of the 25 who were born in the town obtained farm land from relatives who previously had obtained land from provincial governors or from chiefs in the peri-urban areas. The remaining 6 cultivators had personally obtained land from chiefs. Among the 86 migrant cultivators, 11 worked for relatives who had obtained land from various sources; 27 worked for themselves on land similarly obtained by relatives; and 48 had personnally received land from chiefs on the recommendations of friends or relatives. As in the traditional system, none of the latter paid the chiefs for using the land. It was sufficient that they needed land for their subsistence and there was unoccupied or unused land in the district. Of course, they gave the chiefs such traditional gifts as kola nuts, helped in his fields, and gave a present of grain after the harvest. The change here was that they could

---

[4]It should be pointed out that by World War I there was a shortage of cultivable land for families wishing to remain in the town. "Cultivable lands being lacking in the vicinity of Ouagadougou, some married Christians of the capital have had the idea to go and, in effect, install themselves (at Pabré)," Baudu, p. 63.

not plant fruit trees upon the land and had to promise to vacate the field at the end of the planting season if so requested
by the chiefs. Since they were not villagers, they had to allay
the chiefs' fear that they would seek to retain the land by planting trees and seeking long-term tenure.[5]

The Ouagadougou cultivators raise cereals such as sorghum
and millet on their farms and rice when they are lucky enough
to obtain swampy land. Few are able to grow maize due to the
infertility of the soil on "bush" farms and the high cost of
fertilizer. Instead, they grow such other crops as peanuts,
sweet potatoes, beans, manioc, and herbs whose leaves they
use as condiments for sauces.

The farming practices of Ouagadougou cultivators are similar to those of their rural brothers, except that their fields
are far from town. Those whose farms are from 4 to 7 kilometers away from the capital go there daily. Men with bicycles
transport their wives to the fields. They can work later than
those men without transportation and normally send their
wives home earlier with wood for the family's fuel or to be
sold for pocket money. A number of men, breaking sharply
with the male's traditional role, have started to transport
bundles of wood either for fuel or for sale. Cultivators working more than 10 kilometers away from Ouagadougou sometimes move to their farms during the planting season, returning to Ouagadougou only for specific purposes. Some
polygamous men leave one wife (or a wife with a young baby)
in Ouagadougou to take care of them when in town or to help
relatives working in town. Other wives and children never
leave the farms during the planting season, and their lives there
are even more "traditional" than in town. For one thing, there
are no daily markets which the women can visit; nor are there
mills where they can mill their cereal. These farm homesteads
have the traditional *néré* upon which the women grind their
cereals.

The usual labor unit among the Ouagadougou cultivators is
the nuclear family: a man, his wife or wives, and minor children. Some individuals are assisted by relatives who visit the
farms during vacations or on weekends. In general, the nuclear family does most of the work according to the traditional
division of labor: men clear the brush and break the soil while

[5]Skinner, 1964b, p. 122.

all the family sows, cultivates, and harvests the crops. Older cultivators do not expect or receive aid from their grown sons regardless of whether they are employed in other occupations or on their own farms. Nucleation of farming has gone so far among some Ouagadougou cultivators that husbands and wives even cultivate their peri-urban farms separately or with the help of young boys hired for 100 C.F.A. per day. Yet there are some exceptions to this. Three Moslem teachers in Tiedpalogho regularly have their youthful charges work on the farms during the planting season, and a Moslem Imam of Ouidi similarly used his married students and their wives. However, these are unusual cases, for the students are under the care and tutelage of their teachers. When the average farmer needs help, he employs laborers from town or uses the sossosé, a "work bee" in which friends and neighbors help in return for food and drink. The sossosé is most frequently used by farmers after the harvest to transport grain from their peri-urban farms into town, and by quarter chiefs, both to transport the grain and to thresh it.

An increasing number of cultivators are taking advantage of cultural and demographic changes in Ouagadougou to become commercial vegetable gardeners. They are producing recently introduced crops (tomatoes, sweet potatoes, carrots, beets, lettuce, cabbages, and cucumbers) for resident Europeans and a growing body of Africans with "modern" tastes. The origin of this type of gardening in Ouagadougou is closely linked with the arrival of Europeans. The early Catholic missionaries established vegetable gardens, Jardins des Pères, near a ravine west of Bilbalgo. Later, the administration, with the help of the missionaries, established its own truck garden near the reservoir north of Paspanga quarter. Many of the Africans employed as laborers became skilled gardeners, but did not develop their own gardens due to the lack of clients. With the growth of Ouagadougou and the influx of Europeans, and the spread of European food habits to the local population, many men abandoned ordinary cultivation and switched to vegetable gardening. This occupation paid much better, and by using irrigation, the gardeners could produce vegetables throughout the year.

The vegetable gardeners of Ouagadougou do have a problem procuring adequate land in or near the town and close to permanent sources of water. They now grow vegetables

57

wherever land and water are available, especially near ravines. Gardens are found along the railroad tracks leading into town; along the Ouahigouya and Bobo-Dioulasso roads; on the banks of the reservoir north of town; on vacant plots behind the Palais de Justice and in front of the Post Office, and on sidewalks near the Auto Gare. Some of these plots are worked by people who owned them before they were seized by the administration. They now continue to cultivate the unused portions of public domain. Those plots near the railroads and reservoirs are cultivated by gardeners who have no formal title to the land and know that the government or municipality may dispossess them at any time. Many such gardeners are among those seeking suitable plots outside the town where they can expand commercial gardening and increase their incomes. It is probably only a matter of time before consideration of health, taxes on urban plots, or esthetics induce the municipality to forbid all cultivation within Ouagadougou.

Precise information about the incomes of the Ouagadougou cultivators, including the gardeners, is hard to obtain. The Upper Volta Government found this task so formidable that no data on such incomes appeared in the 1962 census for Ouagadougou. A 1964 survey did obtain data on incomes and expenditures of cultivators, but these data are still unpublished and relatively incomplete (See Table XII). Not only do urban cultivator-gardeners dislike revealing income-expenditure information, they also have difficulty keeping track of their intermittent income and expenditures. Cultivators sell and buy grain as necessary; they also sell wood to buy what they need or desire. They save money to pay taxes and to buy such expensive items as bicycles and clothes, but readily sell their bicycles when and if there is a pressing need for cash.

The average monthly income of the cultivator-gardeners in Ouagadougou during 1964 was 1,094 C.F.A., or approximately $4.40 and their expenditures, 1,536 C.F.A., about $6.10 (See Table XII). Thus, the cultivator-gardeners appear to spend more than they earn. This contradiction is explained by the fact that these people do earn more than they normally account for—by selling bundles of wood and engaging in petty commerce. That commerce rather than agriculture provides the largest source of income for cultivators is not contradictory once it is recognized that much of the food produced is consumed and only that part sold is regarded as revenue-

TABLE XII. Monthly Per Capita Incomes and
Expenditures (in C.F.A.) of Cultivator-Gardeners in
Ouagadougou (Circa 1964)

	577 Individuals	76 Households
Sources of Income	Income	Income
Agriculture	39	296
Livestock	7	54
Hunting	0	0
Fishing	0	0
Handicrafts	34	260
Commerce	704	5,344
Salaries	48	366
Pensions	44	336
Miscellaneous	218	1,656
TOTAL	1,094	8,312
Nature of Expenditure	Expenditures	Expenditures
Foods, domestic	520	3,950
Foods, imported	21	163
Beverages	37	284
Tobacco and kola	40	301
Clothing, domestic	23	174
Clothing, imported	3	26
Secondhand materials	564	4,283
Light and heat	68	519
Housekeeping	9	70
Lodging	1	7
Miscellaneous	240	1,820
TOTAL	1,526	11,597

SOURCE: Data furnished the researcher by the Direction de
la Statistique et des Études Économiques, Ouagadougou,
Haute-Volta.

producing. Furthermore, many of the foodstuffs are sold having first been converted into cooked food. It is also not surprising that hunting and fishing are listed as providing no
income for the cultivator-gardeners and the rearing of livestock only a minimal amount. Indeed, the results of such
activities are consumed within families. That the members of
this group derive only a small income from their traditional
handicrafts is attributable to the growing preference of even
low-income people for foreign-manufactured household items,
especially those made of tin or plastic. A few cultivator-gardeners do gain income from pensions since Upper Volta has

59

what is perhaps the largest single group of French army veterans in the world outside the Metropole. In Table XII, the income shown as being derived from salaries represents money which the cultivator-gardener earned either through dry-season activities or by cultivating for others.

Laborers and Skilled Workmen

The activities of the laborers and skilled workmen in Ouagadougou are primarily supportive of the tasks of administrators and clerks. These persons make up the fourth largest occupational group, ranking after the cultivators, civil servant-clerks, and domestic servants. In 1963 the Ministry of Labor reported that there were 1,300 laborers and apprentices and 1,315 skilled workmen in Ouagadougou, totaling 2,635 persons. In 1967 there were 4,772 of these workers altogether. Most of these men are employed by large French civil engineering and construction firms such as the Société Française d'Entreprise de Dragages et de Travaux Publics (S.F.E.D.T.P.), the Société Lorraine de Travaux Publics Africains (S.L.T.P.A.), and the Société Auxiliaire d'Entreprise de Constructions en Afrique (S.A.D.E.C.) engaged in constructing government-sponsored projects to improve the physical appearance of Ouagadougou, offices for private firms in Ouagadougou, and villas for civil servants. Other skilled workmen and laborers are employed by the Municipality of Ouagadougou to construct schools and other public works, while only a minority work for local African enterprises such as the Société Coopérative pour les Oeuvres Meubles et Bâtiments (S.C.O.M.B.) or at private-home construction.

There is the belief that there are not sufficient skilled workmen in the town, and complaints are heard about the difficulty of obtaining modern electrical and plumbing services. This shortage is said to be due to the preference of the young for civil service or clerical jobs. Most of the oldest and skilled workmen were trained in Ouagadougou by the mission and by the colonial administration. But a goodly number of them served apprenticeships in Bobo-Dioulasso during the decade 1930 to 1940 when that town replaced Ouagadougou as the economic hub of the Upper Volta. A few others learned their trades in Ghana and the Ivory Coast, and skilled Voltaics in these countries are still writing letters of application for jobs

TABLE XIII. Minimum Hourly Wages (in C.F.A.) for Skilled Workers

| Building Trades and Public Works | | Electric Company | |
Category	Hourly Wages	Category	Hourly Wages
1. Grade A	29	1. Laborer	29
1. Grade B	30.15	2. Skilled Laborer	35
2. [Probationer]	35	3. Assistant Worker	43
3. Less than 1 yr	43	4. Worker	53
4. More than 1 yr	45	5. Worker first degree	68
4. First echelon	53	6. Worker second degree	80
5. First echelon	68	7. Worker third degree	129
6.	80		
Top Grade	129		

| Others | |
Category	Hourly Wages
1. [Probationer]	29
2. [Probationer]	35
3. Less than 1 yr	43
3. More than 1 yr	45
4. First echelon	53
4. Second echelon	59
5. First echelon	68
5. Second echelon	71
6.	80
Top Grade	118

SOURCE: Direction du Travail, de la Main-d'Oeuvre et de la Formation Professionnelle," *Statistiques*, 1966, p. 6.

to the Upper Volta Ministry of Labor. The technical schools in Ouagadougou are beginning to graduate a number of craftsmen each year, but owing to the rapid growth of the town and the increasing rate of technological change, it may be some time before there is a sufficient number of skilled workmen to meet the needs of the town. This pay scale does not reflect the true income for most workers since they usually earn more than the minimum wages. Also, because of the general shortage of skilled workers, many civil service craftsmen do extra work for the private sector. It is therefore difficult to discover the real income of these men. It is also difficult to obtain data on the incomes of such skilled craftsmen as shoemakers, jewelers, barbers, watch repairers, and weavers. Even those who are willing to talk declare that their incomes vary from day to day and claim not to keep records. The Senegalese jewelers,

61

TABLE XIV.   Monthly Salaries (in C.F.A.) for Skilled Craftsmen,
Engineers, and Managers

Category	Monthly Salary	Indemnity	Total
M-1	30,000	12,000	42,000
M-2	34,300	13,720	48,020
M-3	41,000	16,400	57,400
M-4	45,800	18,320	64,120
M-5	49,600	19,840	69,440

Classification	Basic Salary	Indemnity	Total
Position 1			
Beginning engineers, Class A	48,300	19,320	67,620
Beginning engineers, Class B	55,800	22,320	78,120
Position 2			
Experienced engineers, Class A	61,000	24,400	85,400
Experienced engineers, Class B	69,300	27,720	97,020
Position 3			
Management, First echelon	74,700	29,880	104,580
Management, Second echelon	112,100	44,840	156,940

SOURCE: "Direction du Travail, de la Main-d'Oeuvre et de la Formation Professionnelle," *Statistiques,* 1966, p. 7.

TABLE XV.   Number of Workers Employed by Ouagadougou Enterprises
in 1967

	1–10	11–25	26–100	100–300	300–1,000	1,000+	Total
Agriculture							
Animal Husbandry	1	2	—	—	1	—	4
Forestry	1	2	—	—	1	—	4
Industries	4	5	12	1	—	—	22
Construction &							
public works	8	5	4	2	—	—	19
Stores, banks, insur-							
ance companies	60	10	11	—	1	—	82
Liberal professions*	27	4	1	—	—	—	32
Transport & forward-							
ing agencies	6	1	4	1	—	—	12
Household help	1,002	—	—	—	—	—	1,002
Public & semi-private							
enterprises	1	3	1	—	1	—	6
Public service	—	—	—	—	—	—	0
TOTAL	1,109	30	33	4	3	1	1,180

SOURCE: Unpublished data furnished by the Ministère du Travail et de la
Fonction Publique, Rép. de Haute-Volta, 1967.
    *"Liberal professions" are bars, private schools, etc.

especially, are loath to discuss incomes. They are always afraid that any answers they give to inquirers would be used against them by a government anxious to know the source of their gold supply. Thus, one is forced to use the normally unsatisfactory data from the government, while recognizing that the ordinary practitioners of these trades, in contrast to their supervisors, have additional incomes.

While there is a growing number of skilled craftsmen in Ouagadougou, there are still few African supervisory or managerial personnel. One reason for this is that until quite recently there were no schools to train people for the high-echelon jobs in the various occupations, and no youngsters bright enough to study abroad opted for the manual crafts. Therefore, most highly placed technicians, engineers, and foremen are Europeans. Table XIV gives the minimum monthly salaries (in C.F.A.) earned by these people. African youngsters are now becoming aware of the nature of the salaries earned by both managerial personnel and engineers and can be expected to seek training for these positions.

Industry and Commerce

There are few industries in Ougadougou to meet the needs of the government and its workers. On the *Liste Commerciale et Industrielle* distributed by the Chamber of Commerce, Agriculture, and Industry of the Upper Volta, there is a blank space under the category "Industries in Ouagadougou." This is not entirely true since there are a few industries in the town, if only minor ones. The Ministère du Travail et de la Fonction Publique (1967)[6] lists 22 industries including: Bravolta (manufacturing and distributing beer, soda, and ice), the C.F.D.T. (seeding, baling, and exporting cotton), the S.F.E.D.T.P. (making bricks), Et Anguelis et Fils (manufacturing wooden furniture), Jacobs (manufacturing objects out of iron and steel), Centre de Tannage (curing hides and making leather articles), and S.I.C.O.V.O. (making clothing). As is readily observable, all these companies, except C.F.D.T., are primarily engaged in producing consumer goods. Moreover, all of them combined employ fewer than 500 persons (See Table XV).

[6]Ministère du Travail et de la Fonction Publique (Ouagadougou, 1967).

Ouagadougou has a growing body of consumers and commercial enterprises are growing in number and variety to meet their needs. Commerce, then, rather than industry provides employment for the people of Ouagadougou and can be said to be more important to the life of the town. There are 721 persons listed as *commerçants* in the 1962 census, and of these more than 500 were Africans. Of course, the actual number of people engaged in commerce is much higher since, as we shall see, almost all of the cultivators and their wives and even the wives of civil servants and clerks trade any surplus produce. If one adds to these the innumerable young people who hawk storebought goods along the streets, the number of *commerçants* in the town is over 5,000.

Despite the numerous African petty traders, commerce in contemporary Ouagadougou is still dominated by the giant French import and export companies and by smaller French and Lebano-Syrian traders. The early French trading company, the Société Commerciale du Soudan Français, which arrived in Ouagadougou around 1911, has become the Société Commerciale de l'Ouest Africain (S.C.O.A.). In addition, there are branches of such giant houses as Cie Française de l'Afrique Occidentale (C.F.A.O.), Cie Industrielle de la Côte d'Ivoire (C.I.C.I., now known as King), Cie Française de la Côte d'Ivoire (C.F.C.I.), Peyrissac, and others. These large companies furnish most of the materials and equipment for major construction in the town. Some of them, such as Peyrissac, have expanded their commercial activities to meet the growing urban population's need for consumer goods.

The major suppliers of consumer goods to the town's population are the sixteen or more rather large general stores. These include the Coopérative Centrale de Consommation de Haute Volta (government-owned) and the Société Monoprix, the local equivalent of a five-and-ten-cent store, which opened in 1962.[7] These stores, and the more specialized ones, make it possible for the inhabitants of Ouagadougou to obtain novelties, office supplies, bicycles, stoves, photographic equipment, shoes, liquors, and indeed almost all modern consumer goods. In addition, the 82 or more service establishments in the town provide such up-to-date services as airline tickets, automobile insurance, and the like. There is even one "repossesser" in

[7]This enterprise folded in 1967.

TABLE XVI. **Important Stores and Service Establishments in Ouagadougou**

Type of Service	Number
General and commercial retail	16
Yard goods and clothing	16
Furniture	9
Automobiles, tires, and accessories	8
Electrical appliances	8
Food stores	8
Hardware and building material	8
Variety (notions)	8
Motor scooters and bicycles	7
Shoestores	7
Bookstores and stationers	6
Gift shops	3
Pharmacies	3
Jewelers	2
Photographic and optical equipment	2
Construction and public works	20
Trucking companies and travel agencies	12
Insurance companies	9
Garages	7
Gasoline, oil, and Gas distributors	7
Furniture builders	5
Architects and surveyors	4
Hairdressers (Europeans)	3
Metal works	3
Painters	3
Photographers (Europeans)	3
Plumbing works	3
Attorneys	2
Bakeries	2
Banks	2
Bricklayers	2
Tilers	2
Automobile driving school	1
Cleaning, pressing, and dyeing	1
Repossessors	1

SOURCE: La Chambre de Commerce de Ouagadougou, André Aubaret, Président, 1964.

town to deprive financially embarrassed consumers of the goods he or she cannot afford (See Table XVI).

The major French commercial houses and three Ouagadougou Mossi traders export primary raw materials which pass through Ouagadougou enroute to the coastal ports. But the town has lost that air of a natural produce export mart it possessed during the 1920's. Then, long lines of peasants could be seen transporting baskets full of cotton, peanuts, shea-butter nuts, kapok, and other produce to collection centers set up in the markets or in the courtyards of the major commercial firms. One still sees the large trucks of the Transafricaine Company and of the Mossi exporters carrying produce to the town's railroad yards, but this only emphasizes Ouagadougou's status as an importing and consuming town rather than an exporting one.

European ownership and direction of trade and commerce in Ouagadougou is so overwhelming that there is little economic competition between the whites and the local people except for the three large Mossi traders. But even these three men have not been able to affect European control. There is more competition between an African-run building society (S.C.O.M.B.) and the European construction and furnishing enterprises, but although the local people may grumble, they have launched no campaign to obtain government building contracts for the African company. To the contrary, the leader of this firm declares that they have to struggle against the people's belief in the superiority of European builders. The result is that there has been little pressure for the Africanization of the managerial cadres, despite the absence of African directors and managers in any of the large firms. With few exceptions, the Voltaics in these commercial establishments hold only sales and other less important positions. The first reason for this is that those who would want such jobs prefer the civil service. A second is the subtle opposition of the Voltaics to foreign Africans obtaining these positions. A third reason is the persistence among Europeans of the racialistic notion that Africans are incompetent to run large enterprises. Lastly, French businessmen give jobs to wives, relatives, and even to relatives of men seconded by France to the Voltaic Government. The right of Europeans to employ other Europeans is so widely accepted that no official questioned the following advertisement which ran in the official *Bulletin Quotidien* for several days: 'Offre d'Emploi—Radio-Télé Service, Avenue ..., demande jeune vendeuse européene pour disques.''[8] The result of this attitude is that the most impor-

---

[8] *Bulletin Quotidien d'Information,* Distribué par le Service de l'Information de la République de Haute-Volta, Thursday, 19 November 1964.

tant aspects of commerce in Ouagadougou remain in European hands.

In contrast to many West African towns[9], Ouagadougou has never had a large Lebano-Syrian business community — presently, there are thirty small family-run shops and about five major businesses. Moreover, between 1966 and 1968 the relative commercial position of the Lebano-Syrians in the town appeared to have been declining, even though their numbers were not. As late as 1956 the Lebano-Syrians were important retailers of European goods. Some of them even hired Dioula, Hausa, and Yarsé to collect vegetable products, fish, and kola nuts which they transported and sold. Men like Jaja (a famous Lebanese trader who lived in Mopti, Mali) traded throughout British and French West Africa, shifting goods from one region to another and making profits from differential prices in the two areas.

Beginning in the early 1960's, several developments curbed the trade of the Lebano-Syrians: Europeans began to open small retail stores; the government started its cooperatives; the Monoprix opened its doors;[10] and many of these groups hired African clerks who spoke local languages as well as French. The Lebanese thus lost their monopoly in the retail trade and had to compete with groups which could sell goods at cheaper prices. Secondly, the Lebano-Syrians lost their linguistic advantage in that rural or even urban people could now find African clerks at competing stores who spoke their languages. Lastly, the independence of the Upper Volta and the neighboring African states also disrupted the commercial network of the Lebano-Syrians. Currency changes in Ghana and Mali, the periodic closings of frontiers between the now-independent states, and the opposition by these two governments to Lebano-Syrians also affected their trade.

The Hausa, Yarsé, and Dioula traders — groups whose names were synonymous with trade and commerce in precolonial Ouagadougou — lost their domination of traditional commerce after the conquest and never were able to compete against the Europeans and Lebano-Syrians. The Europeans disrupted trade between the forest and the desert zone, and

[9]Fuad I. Khuri, "Kinship, Emigration, and Trade Partnership among the Lebanese of West Africa," *Africa*, xxxv, No. 4 (October 1965), 385–95.

[10]When the Monoprix closed in 1967, the building it occupied was divided into smaller sections and rented to Lebano-Syrians.

large European trading companies took over all remaining trade and prevented the traditional traders from entering the new economy. African traders still trade kola nuts and locally manufactured products such as blankets, beads, baskets, and bracelets in the Ouagadougou markets, but the donkey caravans which formerly traversed Ouagadougou on their treks north and south are rapidly disappearing.

In contrast, the Yoruba and Mossi, the last two African groups to practice trade and commerce in Ouagadougou, are either maintaining their positions or are expanding. The Yoruba kola nut traders from Ilorin and Ibadan settled in Ouagadougou during the first decade after the conquest, and their wives retailed goods bought from European and Lebano-Syrian traders. They restricted their activities to the market places until recently when competition from female Mossi petty traders forced them to become itinerant traders. A few Yoruba women abandoned retail trade and became hairdressers or cooked-food vendors. The Yoruba men abandoned long-distance trade as soon as they settled in Ouagadougou. A number of them traded in the markets or became barbers, laundrymen, or photographers. A Yoruba is the only African in the town who owns a wholesale soft drink and beer outlet.

The Mossi were not active traders in precolonial Ouagadougou but are emerging as the most important African trader group in the town. True, they always controlled the local commerce in foodstuffs and implements, but they were indifferent long-distance traders. A few of the early missionaries encouraged a number of their converts to engage in commerce, but these joint enterprises failed.[11] Later on, individual Mossi became traders and they became quite successful. Two Mossi are among the largest exporters and importers in the town. Their commercial activities cover all of Mossi country, the non-Mossi areas of the Upper Volta, and foreign countries as well. These men have become models for those Africans in Ouagadougou interested in large-scale and even medium-scale commerce. They are said to be successful because they are less exploitative than European firms. The townspeople declare that they pay more for produce than do the Europeans, thereby helping the rural farmers to get better prices from the competing Europeans.

[11]Baudu, p. 78.

The Markets

The markets of Ouagadougou, rather than the European and Lebano-Syrian stores, are the largest centers of commerce. Most of the African population and a large percentage of the Europeans shop in the markets. The ordinary cultivator, laborer, or even junior civil servant or clerk in the town can meet most of his daily needs in the main market and never has to patronize the stores. Men and women in the peripheral quarters have been able to get what they need in their local markets and have not visited the central market or stores for years.

The markets of contemporary Ouagadougou are more numerous than they were in precolonial times and are now being modernized and sanitized. But they are much the same in structure and function as the early markets of the town.[12] As has been noted, Governor Hesling shifted the main market of Ouagadougou to the commercial zone in 1920 as part of his replanning program. About this time the market became a regular "daily market," thus departing from the traditional "three-day" market pattern. A *Zabre Daga* (evening or night market) also emerged in the town and was located south of the main market, where the Central Mosque now stands. It is possible that the *Zabre Daga* evolved independently of the daily market, and only later did daytime merchants start shifting there when the daily market closed. This market was finally transferred to its present site between Tiedpalogho, the commercial zone, and Koulouba when its original site was taken for building the Mosque.

As Ouagadougou's population grew, a number of smaller markets emerged in the various quarters to serve their needs. There is the *Nab'Raga* (chief's market) once located near the Mogho Naba's new palace, but moved to Samandin in 1967. It was once a daily market but is now also a night market. The *Sankre ra-le* (the small market of Sankre), a market between Bilibambili, Dapoya II, and Norghin is specialized and used for the sale of small animals. It is now mainly a large daily market, but is becoming a night market. Other small markets (*ra-le damba*) named after the wards they serve include: the Market of the mission; the *Rado Daga,* the wood market in Ouagadougou located between Bilibambili and

[12]Crozat, p. 4, 848; Binger, I, 113.

Ouidi; the *Larhalle ra-le;* the *Ouidi ra-le;* the *Kamsaoghin ra-le;* the *Gounghin ra-le;* the *Sabin ra-le;* the *Auto Gare ra-le;* a small market that specializes in secondhand clothing; and the *Zoghona ra-le.*

The local produce in the Ouagadougou markets is brought from the countryside and most imported goods are procured from European and Lebano-Syrian stores. Big African traders truck their produce from the country districts, going as far afield as Ouahigouya to the north, Poitenga to the east, Kou-dougou to the west and Manga-Nobéré to the south. Lesser merchants drain the three-day periodic markets at Kombissiri, Tanghin-Dassouri, Yako, and Saba, among others, for food-stuffs which they then bring into the town. People from the peri-urban villages also provide local commodities for the market. They either take goods directly to the markets or to the main roads for sale to ordinary passers-by enroute to town, or to middlemen going there. Merchants who sell European pro-ducts—from pins to bicycles—obtain their wares wholesale at the nearby stores. They either retail these goods, or distribute them to other merchants in the same market, or to traders in the smaller markets.

The merchants in the market of Ouagadougou are reluctant to give information about their incomes. They insist that they do not know their precise earnings, but there are indications that they fear an increase in the rent of their stalls if they divulged their true incomes. One Mossi vendor of bicycle parts estimated the value of his inventory to be some 40,000 C.F.A. and guessed that he earned about 5,000 C.F.A. profit each month from the constant turnover of his goods. Another man stated that his profit was quite small and gave the follow-ing example. He said that he bought a package of 20 cigarettes for 60 C.F.A. and sold 3 cigarettes for 10 C.F.A., having 2 cig-arettes per package to sell for profit. This low margin of profit raises the question of whether the individual could survive as a trader given a smaller margin on all of his goods.

The African merchants in the Ouagadougou markets, by cleverly manipulating cash and credit transactions, are able to compete with the larger commercial houses from which they buy merchandise. Merchants in the market can and do sell for 59,000 C.F.A. motor scooters which cost 63,000 C.F.A. at such stores as Camico. Some merchants even quote clients lower prices than the cost of articles in stores, obtain the article on credit from the larger stores, and resell them at what appears to be a loss. Investigation reveals that the merchant does not lose because his main interest in such a transaction is cash. Once he gets the cash he either loans out the money, at a profit, to other merchants or buys secondhand scooters or bicycles and resells them at a large profit. Merchants declare that this constant circulation of capital makes it difficult for them to gauge their overall profits. Obviously this was an evasion, since they must know what they are doing or they would go bankrupt.

Petty trading outside the market place provides an income for many people in Ouagadougou. Young male traders selling goods around town are highly visible, but most petty traders are women. The wives of urban cultivators engage in petty trading, and so do the wives of tradesmen, merchants, clerks, and even civil servants. So widespread and ubiquitous is this type of trade that one is tempted to look behind its relatively marginal economic utility to other socio-cultural factors making for its appearance and persistence. Whereas petty trading among Mossi women (and here one can talk about Mossi women since they are the dominant group in Ouagadougou and the women of the same socio-economic level in other groups tend to follow suit) in the rural[13] areas is limited to markets and to motor stops along the heavily traveled roads, it is practiced almost everywhere in Ouagadougou, wherever there is a possibility of commerce: in front of the hospital, in front of the cinemas, near workshops, near bridges—in fact, there is not a single street in Ouagadougou, not even in the residential quarter, where women are not found sitting quietly at the curb peddling some kind of produce. Many women even trade from unattended tables set in front of their houses while they go about their domestic duties, or delegate some young child to watch over the goods and to call out when a buyer appears.

Petty trading usually goes on all day, from early morning when the women try to catch those persons going off to work, to ten o'clock at night or even later, when the object is to cater to those persons simply strolling the streets. The merchandise

[13]Elliott P. Skinner, "Trade and Markets among the Mossi People," in Paul Bohannan and George Dalton (eds.), *Markets in Africa* (Evanston: Northwestern University Press, 1962), pp. 237–78.

sold by these traders includes matches, cigarettes, chewing tobacco, kerosene, kola nuts, peanuts, peanut balls for stew, cooked food, including vegetables in season, sugar, canned milk, fruit, candy, chewing gum, and so forth. There is also very little capital invested in goods, and profits are very small. Judging from what the women say and from surveys of their activities, many of these petty traders invest as little as 100 C.F.A. and make as little as 10 to 25 C.F.A. profit a day. But even the women with somewhat greater inventories make little profit because, unless they trade in front of their own houses, they must pay a daily market tax to the municipal tax collectors who circulate about the town.

The widespread incidence of petty trading with its very small profit is possibly the most effective occupational adaptation of unlettered wives to life in town. True, the wives of cultivators farm during the short rainy season, lasting only about four months, but they have little to do during the rest of the year. Unskilled wives of nonfarmers have even less to do since many of their traditional domestic duties are made easier because of the presence of wells in their own yards or standpipes nearby, and the availability of mills for grinding cereals. The result is that unless these women turn to petty trading, they have relatively little to do.

Petty trading permits the urban women to maintain the ideal that a woman should make a contribution to her family's income. Rural women are accustomed to having and using produce and money to supplement whatever meals their children receive from the head of the household. In contrast, not all the women in Ouagadougou have fields from which they can derive a small income. Even those who do have fields find that the town *di ligidi* (eats money) much faster than the rural areas and that they, like their nonfarming sisters, need to engage in commerce in order to "stretch" their incomes. By so doing, they can at least try to fulfill the economic norms of women, even within the new environment of the modernizing town.

Female Occupations

Making and Selling Beer (Dolo *or* Dam)

A number of women have been able to employ traditional techniques for making a living in Ouagadougou. One such technique, beer-making, provides the basis for the most lucrative of the legitimate traditional female occupations. The 1962 census listed 124 *fabricants de dolo* (brewers of millet beer) in the town. By 1964 there were about 400 beer brewers in town, and an additional 100 women who retailed beer acquired from the brewers. Most of these *dolotières* (makers and sellers of millet beer) are older women. Only one of the 25 *dolotières* interviewed was under thirty years of age, and, as we shall see later, this fact complicated her conjugal life. Of these 25 *dolotières,* only 9 were born in Ouagadougou; the others migrated to the town from rural areas.

Generally the *dolotières* are independent-minded women who use beer-making to become economically self-sufficient. Only 2 of the 25 women had "inherited" their occupation from a female relative; all the others drifted into this type of commerce. They got started by economizing "little by little," bought and resold beer from established *dolotières,* and eventually started their own business. One woman, who described herself as the wife of a "war veteran and cultivator," began selling beer while her husband was away in Algeria. She said that she did not want to remain idle—there being no one to prepare the fields for cultivation—and decided to sell beer to "increase" the money that her husband sent. Yet, even though her husband has now returned, she has retained her occupation.

The task of making and selling beer is a difficult, if profitable, one for the women of Ouagadougou. It costs about 600 C.F.A. to prepare a pot of beer, and the typical *dolotière* prepares fifteen pots every third day. The *dolotière* must advertise her brew by giving a taste (*lenga* in Moré) to prospective buyers. If she is too generous with her free gifts and does not thereby gain new customers, she loses money. If, however, business is good, and the *dolotière* earns 750 C.F.A. for each of her fifteen pots, she makes a profit of some 3,250 to 3,450 C.F.A. every third day on an average investment of 7,550 to 8,000 C.F.A. In a month's time a successful *dolotière* may make as much as 32,000 C.F.A., an income higher than that of many civil servants and greater than that of all laborers. Not all of this income is profit. The owner of a successful *ram zandé* (cabaret) has to pay 6,000 C.F.A a year for a license in addition to her other expenses.

Innumerable groups of three or four new beer sellers take turns selling *dolo* in small cabarets and collectively pay for the licenses. Poor women can thus get started in the business, gradually build up a clientele, and, if successful, open their own *ram zandé*. They may manufacture *dolo,* but normally they buy the beer from wholesale brewers or from *dolotières* who have overproduced. The latter often sell surplus beer at reduced rates in the afternoon or risk having it spoil. A few women in the outlying quarters such as Zogona and Tampouy sometimes brew small pots of beer for retail in front of their houses. This is against the law, and roving tax collectors either fine them 25 C.F.A. for roadside vending or threaten to take them to court. Few cases end in court because most tax collectors recognize that selling beer is traditional for some women and thus a legitimate way of earning a living.

Barmaids

The occupation of barmaid, in contrast to *dolotière,* is viewed with much apprehension by the local population. The first African women who began working in Ouagadougou bars during the period between 1955 and 1957 were neither indigenous to the town nor to the country. They included the wife of a Senegalese bar owner, the Afro-European wife and daughters of a civil servant from Guinea, and the Senegal-born, Afro-European wife and daughters of a Gourmantche school teacher. There was little adverse comment on the activities of these women qua barmaids. This may have been due either to foreign birth of these women, to their families' ownership of the bars, or to their membership in the civil servant group. However, as more bars opened and low-status foreign-born women began working in them, a certain onus attached itself to the occupation of barmaid. These women are now judged to be part-time prostitutes, must receive special police permits, and must submit to special medical examinations. The result is that few girls with relatives in town dare accept such employment, and thus, most of the barmaids in Ouagadougou are immigrants to the town.

Despite public opprobrium, a number of factors are encouraging more young women to become barmaids. First is the fact that literate but undereducated women have few avenues of employment and can profitably use their limited education as barmaids. Indeed, the wife of a policeman once worked as a barmaid in a "European" bar in the commercial zone without being considered a part-time prostitute. Second, a few former barmaids and young women once considered prostitutes are now gainfully employed as barmaids in local restaurants run by Catholic lay missionaries. Perhaps these precedents will make it possible for barmaids to work at their chosen occupation without arousing undue suspicion.

Prostitutes

Prostitution is an ancient profession in Ouagadougou. But here, as in other parts of Africa, is is functioning within a newer context. One of the first Europeans to arrive in Ouagadougou signaled the existence of well-dressed prostitutes there.[14] Prostitution increased in Ouagadougou after the French established an army base there and grew appreciably during World War I when thousands of Voltaic soldiers came to Ouagadougou. Oral tradition indicates that the Fulani women of Bilibambili became celebrated as the prostitutes of the army. Songs satirizing the amorous relations of these women with soldiers were heard as recently as 1964 during a local celebration at the Place d'Armes.

The influx of strangers into Ouagadougou after 1919, when the town became the capital of the Upper Volta, resulted in a change in the ethnic origin or the town's prostitutes. Foreign women, especially Songhay and Hausa from Niger,[15] so dominated this occupation that all prostitutes in Ouagadougou are still believed to be strangers. The town's Mossi believe that a certain, rather young, female habitué of the local bars is the "first Moaga prostitute" they have ever seen. Perhaps the emphasis here should be on "modern" prostitutes since the traditional Mossi prostitutes still frequent the markets especially the *Zabre Daga,* the *Nab'raga,* and, increasingly, the *Sankre ra-le.* They are probably less visible than in early days because they no longer appear better dressed than ordinary housewives. Their dress is rather plain in comparison with that of stranger prostitutes in the town.

Of the approximately 700 prostitutes scattered throughout the various quarters of Ouagadougou, about 200 of these are Voltaics. Many female petty traders augment their scanty incomes by part-time prostitution. This is especially true

[14]G. E. Lambert, "Le Pays Mossi et sa Population," *Étude historique économique et géographique suivie d'un essai d'ethnographie comparée.* Ouagadougou, 1967 [Archives de CVRS, Ouagadougou].

[15]Cohen, pp. 51–70.

of a number of Fulani women who sell kola nuts in Bilibambili. They and their Mossi counterparts in the markets normally visit the homes of their clients after work. These women
usually charge no fixed fee but accept presents of money,
clothing, or both.

The 100 or so "Sudanese" (Marka and Bambara) prostitutes
in town live primarily in Tiedpalogho and Bilibambili, but also
in Dapoya II. These women are circumspect in their behavior
and use procurers to solicit clients. They normally entertain
men for short periods, but may establish rather long-term
relationships with them, especially visiting merchants, until
the men leave or they quarrel. Under these circumstances, it
is difficult to determine the income of these women. They may
receive from 500 C.F.A. to 2,000 C.F.A. for an evening's entertainment, depending upon the affluence, or satisfaction, of
the client. Men who remain with prostitutes for long periods
may spend tens of thousands of francs buying them presents
and expensive clothing. In return, the prostitutes keep house
for these clients and act like temporary wives.

The most professional group of prostitutes in Ouagadougou
lives in Tiedpalogho. These women are mainly of Nigerien,
Nigerian, and Ghanaian origin. They run the gamut from
women who solicit clients in front of their brothels to flashy
young women who frequent the leading African and European
bars in Tiedpalogho and the commercial zone. The brothel
prostitute commands no more than 200 to 300 C.F.A. per visit
fom her predominantly African clients. She may average
1,500 to 2,000 C.F.A. a day at certain periods of the month.
Her more glamorous sister may earn as much as 5,000 C.F.A.
per day since she frequents air-conditioned bars and often dis-
criminates against Africans in favor of the more affluent Europeans. These women not only earn more, but they normally
spend large amounts of money on clothing. They frequently
support paramours, and, if some of them are to be believed,
only work to take care of children at home.

Most people in Ouagadougou are tolerant of the prostitutes.[16] Some long-term residents indicate surprise (perhaps
ritual ignorance) when the activities of these women are discussed. Yet, when Ghanaian women groups pass in review
during official parades, they are always greeted with knowing

[16]Bely Thiemko, *La Prostitution: Vue sur le drame social en Haute Volta.*
Ouagadougou, École Nationale d'Administration, 23 June 1961.

76

smiles and some laughter. In general, people are not very concerned with the activities of prostitutes. They say that most brothel prostitutes serve strangers and migrants and therefore pose no moral danger to the town's population. The "modern" prostitutes work in bars in the commercial area and in Tiedpalogho and are scarcely seen by the town's population. Thus their activities are ignored. Few women have been charged with prostitution in the Ouagadougou courts. Two prostitutes were in prison in 1964 for robbing and killing a French soldier, but the charge was murder. Those foreign prostitutes summoned to court in 1964 were charged with passport irregularities rather than prostitution. During a case which dealt with fighting in public, a Voltaic woman revealed to the judge that she was "in the business." Somewhat embarrassed, he ignored this revelation of illegal behavior and fined her for fighting while drunk.

Hairdressers

Hairdressing has been transformed from a traditional skill to a profession in the main market of Ouagadougou. The hairdressers are primarily non-Voltaic Ghanaian and Nigerian women who use chemicals to straighten, plait, and dye hair in the marketplace. The hair-straightening techniques of Afro-American women are known to a few members of the elite population, but no establishments practicing these techniques have been founded. There are beauty parlors operated by European females, but few African women patronize these. Most African women prefer to patronize the hairdressers in the marketplace or groom their own hair.

Dressmakers

In contrast to hairdressing, dressmaking is a new skill only now being acquired by town women. Traditionally, all tailoring in this culture area was done by men, but Catholic nuns taught a few women to make clothes for themselves, their children, and the public at large. There are now several small clothes and dressmaking establishments in Ouagadougou operated by dressmakers who were trained by "Sisters." One of them, *Au Chant du Rossignol,* was established and directed by a woman who had taken an advanced course in dressmaking in Paris. She and the other dressmakers are expanding their activities and training young women to make clothes. One

77

woman has even hired a male tailor to do the more laborious sewing. But many dressmakers complain that no girl with the intelligence and education to obtain a civil service position ever considers dressmaking as a career. There is the case of a young woman who was sent to France for a course in dressmaking, but when she returned, took a typist job in the Town Hall. She does claim that it was the lack of money to start her own establishment that prevented her from becoming a dressmaker. However, judging from the prestige of the civil sevice in Ouagadougou, among females as well as males, it is doubtful whether she will ever become a professional dressmaker.

Occupations of Youths and Children

Ouagadougou has turned out to be a Mecca for the youth of the country as well as for the adults. The numbers and ages of children, especially boys, who run off to town are unknown. However, a conservative guess is that there are some 2,000 migrant children, ranging from ten to fifteen years of age who are actually employed or seeking employment in the town.

Besides domestic service, most employed youngsters are petty traders. Those boys who agreed to be interviewed gave a variety of sources for the money or goods with which they started their trading. Quite a number of them simply asked relatives for some goods and hawked these along the streets. Others received small sums of money from relatives to start their activities and have been trying to meet their own personal needs as well as keep enough money to replace their stock. Still others raised money for petty trading by carrying packages for Europeans in the market. None of these boys have large inventories of goods, but what they have is quite varied. Often it includes pens and pencils, shoelaces, pins, a variety of mosquito repellents, pills of various sorts, and usually mirrors, brushes, and combs. The total cost of their merchandise seldom exceeds 1,000 C.F.A., and a boy may make a profit of from 50 to 100 C.F.A. on a successful day.

A group of about 200 boys works as charioteers, transporting goods, wood, or water around the market and other commercial areas. These boys rent small, four-wheeled wagons from older men (primarily Mossi and Yoruba) for about 200 C.F.A. a day and strive to make at least 300 C.F.A. a day so that they can pay the cost of hire and gain 100 francs profit.

Since these boys are seldom paid more than 25 C.F.A. per load, they have to hustle all day to make a living. They start early in the morning, taking the wares of their merchant patrons to the market place from the adjacent storage areas. After this, they tarry around the market, or seek jobs such as transporting water and fuel for beer-makers or taking pots of *dolo* from the brewers to retailers. Later in the afternoon, the youths return to the central market to transport merchandise to the *Zabre Daga*. Finally, late at night they return the merchandise to its storage areas.

There are too many young charioteers in Ouagadougou for the available work. Besides, these youths are gregarious and share jobs and incomes with their friends. This inevitably leads to a shortage of money with which to hire the wagons, and thus the inability to earn a living. Some youths resort to petty theft in order to get enough money to hire the wagons. They obviously feel that it is better to use illegal means in order to work than not to work. We shall see that the scarcity of work for charioteers led to the formation of gangs or "protective associations" to control the access to work in specific areas.[17]

There are about twenty shoeshine boys in Ouagadougou. These youths are more highly organized than the charioteers and have definite territories, mainly bars, which are "off limits" to interlopers. Sometimes these boys travel in pairs and by 1964 had adopted the blue jumper of the U.S. Navy, "ruptured duck" and all, as a uniform. (They bought these in the used clothing areas of the Auto Gare market.) Generally, these shoeshine boys are quite aggressive in their pursuit of work. They often surreptitiously clean the shoes, or even sandals, of a potential client "as a favor" and disclaim any interest in a fee. The coerced clients, whose shoes usually do need cleaning, seldom fail to give the youngsters 10 or 15 C.F.A. The only way one can avoid this is to make sure that boys do not start shining one's shoes.

The most ambiguous occupation of the young boys in Ouagadougou is that of common laborer. A number of employers in Ouagadougou regularly go to the Auto Gare where they pick up young migrants from the rural areas and promise

[17]Jean Houchet, *Inadaptation Sociale et Delinquance Juvenile en Haute Volta,* Recherches Voltaiques, No. 9, Paris-Ouagadougou, CNRS-CVRS, 1967–68, p. 70.

them work in return for a place to stay, food, and money. Many employers take a paternalistic attitude toward these boys, pay them nothing or a pittance, claiming that they are members of the family. This may continue until the youths discover that their peers are getting about 75 to 100 C.F.A. per day plus food and lodging. Their most common reaction to this knowledge is to abscond with their master's property. Such cases are so common in the towns that judges try to ascertain whether the youngster accused by his master of theft had been paid the agreed wage. Some employers appear genuinely shocked when told by the judge that behind the façade of generosity and benevolence they may be attempting to exploit and manipulate the youths.

There are, in fact, a number of employers who attempt to educate their young workers as well as provide employment for them. One Ghanaian restauranteur had great success with "seasonal" kitchen help until one youngster stole her money. Over the years she employed boys who came to Ouagadougou as seasonal workers. Some youngsters returned to her each season and "served their apprenticeship" until they finally settled in town. Three of this woman's employees gave evidence against the young thief, thus providing proof of her kindness. They would not have done so had they considered her unfair.

The occupational opportunities for young girls in Ouagadougou are much more limited. As mentioned earlier, only a very few of them obtain employment as nursemaids with African and European families. The rest of them must work as petty traders. They, too, are often given goods by their relatives to trade but, unlike the boys, many earn their own capital by making and selling fried cakes on the streets and in the markets of the town. The one hazard for the young girl petty traders is that they drift into part-time prostitution in order to augment their income. Perhaps this is inevitable since many of these young girls now wander all over Ouagadougou day and night hawking their wares near bars, dance halls, and cinemas, and witness all types of urban behavior.

Marginal Occupations

Fishing was a very marginal occupation among the Voltaic populations, but it is now emerging as a supplementary occupation in Ouagadougou. Formerly, only dried and smoked fish from the Niger River was sold in the town's market. Today, men fish in the town's reservoirs and either sell their catch in the central market or on the streets. None of the fishermen in Ouagadougou can gain an adequate income from fishing. Four out of the ten fishermen interviewed augment their incomes by farming.

Hunting has also become a marginal occupation for the people in Ouagadougou. Gone are the days when a Binger could report that the banks of the swamps at the northern end of the town were "full of game. My table is always well provided. Diawe even succeeded in providing meat for my men." All types of game in the area were reduced by the early military commanders who shot harmless animals for food and lions for safety. A game reserve was created in the Bois de Boulogne in the northern part of the town, but hunting was permitted in all other areas. Just after independence (about 1961) a hunting ban was imposed throughout the whole country and was not lifted until 1964. Today only African and European "sportsmen" hunt. The traditional hunters who still live in the town have turned to economic pursuits more consistent with urban life.

One major impediment facing the Ouagadougou people in their attempt to adapt to an urban economy is the scarcity of jobs. Yet, no one really knows the rate of unemployment in the town nor the extent of what has been called "underemployment." This situation is complicated by the presence in town of persons who consider themselves "unemployed," but who actually farm during the planting season. They therefore could be viewed as victims of seasonal unemployment. Underemployment, like seasonal employment, is also difficult to measure. Many of the "apprentices" who work in garages and workshops would take other employment if it were available. As it is, they work with craftsmen for small sums of money and also learn a trade. Similarly, those youths who work with the charioteers try to make the best adjustment to the scarcity of jobs.

The real unemployed in Ouagadougou are not the illiterate migrants who take any job they can find and often resort to farming, but the trained and educated persons who cannot find jobs. The Ministry of Public Offices and Labor states that unemployment in Upper Volta involves "exclusively the urban population and among these a growing number of persons holding *Certificat d'Etudes* [elementary school certificates] or the B.E.P.C. [comparable to high school diploma]." Many of these young people have never learned how to farm, having been reared in the urban area, and are ill-prepared or unwilling to seek occasional labor. Some who grew up in the rural areas are often so alienated from farming that they do not consider intermittent farming or vegetable gardening alternatives to unemployment. A number of young people, wise enough in urban ways, seek help at the employment office (Service de la Main-d'Oeuvre), but very few get jobs there. However, this agency does provide some information about unemployment in the town. The statistics in Tables XVII and XVIII were provided by the Employment Bureau in Ouagadougou.

These partial statistics confirm the rather critical employment situation in Ouagadougou. They also provide data about the type of persons seeking work and the availability of certain types of employment. It is not surprising that the highest number of persons sought work in domestic service, followed by those seeking employment in construction and public works (see Table XVII). Not only do these figures suggest that the job-seekers are relatively unskilled but also that they are quite aware that domestic service and construction provide the best opportunities for steady employment. These are also the two areas where persons, once employed, can learn modern skills and therefore have the best opportunity for future employment. It is also understandable why there were no applicants for the first three professional categories of jobs, nor for agricultural labor apprenticeships or government employment. Vacancies in most government bureaus are filled through competitive examinations or through the "combine," a word that connotes nepotism, friendship, or corruption. Top vacancies in the private sector are filled mainly by non-Voltaics on the basis of experience or the combine. No citizen of Upper Volta with good qualifications voluntarily chooses to work for the private sector. Young persons seeking agricultural labor or apprenticeships never go to the Employment Agency but use their own personal or kinship networks.

The small number of jobs actually offered through the Employment Agency reflects widespread ignorance of its function and the importance of personal contacts for procuring jobs.

82

TABLE XVII. Applications and Job Placements from June 1, 1964 to August 31, 1964

Type of Employment		Management	Technical Staff	Master Craftsmen	Clerks, Assistants	Journeymen	Laborers Messengers, Watchmen	Apprentices	Total
	Placed / Not Placed								
A. PRIVATE SECTOR									
Agriculture	P	—	—	—	—	—	—	—	0
	NP	—	—	—	—	—	—	—	—
Construction, public works	P	—	—	—	—	9	—	—	9
	NP	—	—	—	2	53	—	—	55
Commerce	P	—	—	—	—	—	—	—	0
	NP	—	—	—	31	—	9	—	40
Industries	P	—	—	—	—	1	—	—	1
	NP	—	—	—	—	23	—	—	23
Transportation	P	—	—	—	—	—	—	—	0
	NP	—	—	—	—	32	—	—	32
Domestic servants	P	—	—	—	4	—	—	—	4
	NP	—	—	—	58	—	8	—	66
TOTAL A	P	0	0	0	4	10	0	0	14
	NP	0	0	0	91	108	17	0	216
B. PUBLIC SECTOR									
General employment		—	—	—	—	—	—	—	0
Technical services		—	—	—	—	—	—	—	0
TOTAL B		—	—	—	—	—	—	—	0
TOTAL A & B	P	—	—	—	4	10	—	—	14
	NP	—	—	—	91	108	17	—	216

SOURCE: Data furnished by the Service de la Main-d'Oeuvre in Ouagadougou, 1964.

TABLE XVIII. Job Applications and Job Offers for September 1964

Type of Employment		Professional Category							
		Management	Technical Staff	Master Crafsmen	Clerks, Assistants	Journeymen	Laborers, Messengers, Watchmen	Apprentices	Total
A. PRIVATE SECTOR									
Agriculture	Applications (A)	—	—	—	—	—	—	—	—
	Offers (O)	—	—	—	—	—	—	—	—
Construction and public works	A	—	—	1	1	—	—	—	2
	O	—	—	—	—	1	—	—	1
Commerce	A	—	—	—	11	—	7	—	18
	O	—	—	—	1	—	—	—	1
Industries	A	—	—	—	—	32	—	—	32
	O	—	—	—	1	1	—	—	2
Transportation	A	—	—	—	—	7	—	—	7
	O	—	—	—	—	—	—	—	—
Domestic servants	A	—	—	—	15	—	4	—	19
	O	—	—	—	4	—	—	—	4
TOTAL A	A	—	—	1	27	39	11	—	78
	O	—	—	—	6	2	—	—	8
B. PUBLIC SECTOR									
General administration		—	—	—	—	—	—	—	—
Technical services		—	—	—	—	—	—	—	—
TOTAL B	A	—	—	—	—	—	—	—	—
	O	—	—	—	—	—	—	—	—
TOTAL A & B	A	—	—	1	27	39	11	—	78
	O	—	—	—	6	2	—	—	8

SOURCE: Data furnished by the Service de la Main-d'Oeuvre in Ouagadougou, 1964.

Most people get all types of jobs through friends and relatives, and it is only newly arrived persons or organizations without contacts who ask the help of the agency.

The outlook for jobs for salaried workers in Ouagadougou, as in all of Upper Volta, was bright until 1964, when the government listed some 32,788 employed. The situation worsened in 1965 when employment fell to 26,244. This led the largely civil servant labor unions (see Appendix II) to challenge the Yaméogo Government, and to bring about its downfall. Employment reached its nadir in 1966, with the figure of 22,576. It gradually increased to 23,999 in 1967 and to 28,607 in 1968. Nevertheless, the number of unplaced job-seekers rose from 3,314 in 1966 to some 5,345 in 1968 out of a total of 7,363 job requests. Unless some means can be found to ease the unemployment situation, especially in Ouagadougou, dissatisfied urban job-seekers will continue to exist, and with them, political problems both for the municipal and national governments.

The data of this chapter suggest that the attitude of Ouagadougou's population toward occupations and economic activities is highly manipulatory. Civil servants and clerks are not professional-minded and regard *position* as more important than *profession*. They take any examination that promises higher paying jobs and are convinced that they can perform the necessary tasks. Those persons who, because of educational deficiencies or unacceptable civil status, cannot become civil servants, become clerks—a kind of civil servant *manqué*. Both of these occupations are characterized by mobility based on individual merit rather than ascribed status. Nevertheless, family and ethnic links are manipulated for gaining employment and achieving high positions in these occupations, as in most others.

The absence of major industrial activities in Ouagadougou has limited the ability of migrants to find employment in the town. The most common alternative is employment as domestic servants in the households of civil servants and clerks. Often both employer and employee seek to manipulate family and regional ties so as to facilitate relations within novel and changing domestic patterns. The result is often a form of exploitation of kin relations unknown in the rural areas. Those migrants who, in the absence of—or despite—family ties to civil servants, cannot obtain employment in Ouagadougou cultivate crops in the peri-urban areas of the town so that they can continue to live in Ouagadougou. They do so because they hope eventually to get urban employment and abandon agriculture which is not an occupation in the modern sense. Moreover they seek to earn more money than they can derive from farming. Meanwhile, they attempt to derive as many material benefits either from these farms or from the high-status persons who have placed them on the farms. The latter, in turn, receive comestibles, and the satisfaction of providing employment for migrant relatives.

Migrants in Ouagadougou and the resident population tend to take advantage of every new occupational niche and are loathe to hold any occupation in contempt. When European conquest and economic control reduced long-distance trade and stimulated local retail trade, the Yoruba and other stranger merchants quickly adapted to the changes. As Mossi traders entered the market place, the Yoruba shifted to newer professions made possible by the changing culture of the town. Mossi merchants, plagued by a lack of capital, instituted subtle techniques whereby they manipulated credit from French, Lebanese, and Syrian stores in order to build up their own capital. Women, also, use their traditional skills and attributes to earn a living in town. Successful millet beer makers, the *dolotières,* are able to earn as much as middle-range civil servants and clerks, and in the process help less adventurous women to earn a living retailing beer. The prostitutes in Ouagadougou have been able to ply their trade by working with migrants and merchants. They have remained "invisible" to most of the resident population through a process of mutual toleration. But when, as in the case of barmaids, a profession normally held in disrepute became a source of employment for many literate local women, it soon lost its earlier opprobrium.

Despite the willingness of new migrants to Ouagadougou to use any economic device in order to remain in town, the absence of jobs does create problems. Women, especially local young girls, drift into part-time prostitution when unable to earn a living through legitimate petty trading. Young boys faced with the stiff competition and limited market for their services as charioteers organize gangs to protect certain territories. Unemployment, also, is related to the development of youthful robber gangs in Ouagadougou. But more detrimental to the political stability in the town is the presence of migrants unable to find jobs through work agencies and who, in the dry season, can find nothing to do. These people make up the crowds which are mobilized by civil servants (angry or frustrated over the lack of jobs or more often, inadequate incomes) to attack the government. The tendency of the Ouagadougou population to criticize the government has increased over the years. The impersonality which permits civil servants to achieve personal mobility also has its drawbacks. People do not feel responsible for the economy of either the town or the nation-state and more readily attack the government they hold to be responsible for their economic and personal problems.

Young men seeking employment

CHAPTER III

Kinship and Kin Relations

Urban life is having subtle and sometimes drastic effects on the traditional social organization of the population of Ouagadougou. This is understandable given the growing economic differentiations of the town's inhabitants; the increasing differences in opportunity among them; and the conscious or unconscious desire of many persons to become modern without the means to do so. Changes in kinship terminology only highlight changes in actual kin behavior. And changes in household composition have accompanied changes in the relations between relatives, the latter changing from general and reciprocal to specific, intermittent, and above all, manipulative. Commitment to urban life has even influenced the social behavior of cultivators in town; and this influence is readily apparent among the laborers, tradesmen, merchants, clerks, and civil servants.

The importance of kinship, whether in the use of traditional kinship terminology or in actual behavior, is becoming increasingly diverse among the several categories of people who live in the town. Most Mossi cultivators interviewed are familiar with their traditional kinship[1] nomenclature and use these terms when talking to or about relatives. The continued use of Moré, the language in which their kin terminology is imbedded, has undoubtedly contributed to the retention of these usages. Members of this group have remained more tradition oriented than the others and have retained many more social links with kinsmen (both within and out of Ouagadougou) than members of other social categories. More than any of the other groups, cultivators in town still depend upon kinsmen in the town and upon traditional chiefs for various types of aid such as, for example, peri-urban fields and land upon which to build houses.

Surprisingly, the elder civil servants (there are scarcely any elder clerks in the town) make as much of their kinship terminology as do the cultivators, and similarly, kinship played an

---

[1] The Mossi have a variant of the "Omaha" kinship system.

important part in their early lives. Though educated in town, they retained contact with their traditional villages, and when they returned home for holidays, they found their social systems relatively intact. Even after their appointments (which were usually to posts outside Upper Volta) they seldom spent vacations in Ouagadougou, preferring to return to their natal villages. In fact, many of the elder civil servants acquired property in Ouagadougou and settled there only after World War II. All these factors have induced the elder civil servants to retain their traditional kinship terminology. Even while speaking French, they often utilize traditional kinship terms when referring to relatives and unconsciously translate these kin terms into the nearest French equivalent rather than use European kinship terms. Thus, an elder Mossi civil servant would refer to his uncle as *le grand frère de mon père* (which in Moré is *mam ba kasanga*) rather than simply, *mon oncle,* the normal French usage.

What is striking in contemporary Ouagadougou is the young people's relative ignorance of their traditional kinship systems. This is especially true among the urban-born, school children, and the younger civil servants. The reasons for this lack of knowledge are complex. Urban-born children, both educated and uneducated, do not learn the tratitional kin terms because they have little contact with extended kin, especially rural ones. They are often embarrassed when confronted with these relatives and refer to them as "relatives of parents" or, if educated, use a French-like terminology to denote the nature of the affiliation. Thus, the female siblings of fathers and mothers are referred to as *tante paternelle* (paternal aunt) and *tante maternelle* (maternal aunt), and comparable terms are used for paternal male siblings. They use the terms, *cousin* and *cousine* for the children of all parental siblings, thereby eliminating the traditional distinctions between them. Yet, they have sharpened the referential distinction between grandparents. Young people address both paternal and maternal grandparents as *yarba,* but refer to them specifically as maternal or paternal grandmothers and grandfathers.

The persistence of traditional kin relations has acted as a brake on certain kinds of terminological innovations. As seen above, terms of address for ascending generations have remained traditional even among French-speaking individuals.

They address even their French-speaking mothers' brothers as *yesba* and fathers' brothers as *ba* rather than *oncle*. In some cases even generational or relative age indicators are used. The use of French terms of address for these individuals is considered a presumption and as an unwelcome affectation. Oldsters jokingly criticize young persons heard using French referential terms when speaking about relatives, thereby embarrassing the youthful innovators. Young people do use personal names when addressing relatives of their age, and use increasingly the Moré word *zoa* (friend) when referring to these persons.

Not only changing kin relations but status differences are modifying the use of traditional terminology. Urban youths are frequently embarrassed by having to use traditional kin terms for younger and rural kinsmen even of an ascending generation. This is especially true of kinsmen occupying an inferior position in the household of the speaker. I once caused a youth a great deal of embarrassment by trying to discover the traditional terms for his father's younger sister who did household chores in his home. He said that he referred to and addressed the girl by her *Christian* name. When asked for either a term of reference or address, the respondent gave the French terms; he first called her his *cousine* and later said she was his *tante paternelle*. When I pressed for the Moré term and the respondent suspected the real import of the question, he gave the Moré term, *ton* (sister). It was only when the true relationship could no longer be hidden that he gave the term, *pogodoba* (father's sister).

Kin relations are still important in the lives of the Ouagadougou people, but the number of kinsmen with whom they interact is restricted. For one thing, extended kinsmen in Ouagadougou seldom live in the same household or even in the same ward. An investigation of the relationship between kinship and household composition among cultivators, merchants and craftsmen, and civil servant-clerks in Ouagadougou provided the data given in Table XIX.

These data show that more than 63 per cent of the cultivators in Ouagadougou live in nuclear family groups, 17.6 per cent in fraternal joint families, and the remainder in families composed of various agnatic and affinal kin. Noteworthy is the absence of the patrilineal extended family so characteristic of the rural Voltaics. Nuclear family households among the

TABLE XIX.   Composition of Surveyed Households in Ouagadougou

Category of Kin Living with Respondent	Occupational Status of Respondent		
	Cultivators	Merchants and Craftsmen	Civil Servant-Clerks
Male Household Heads			
Alone with wives and children	54	18	33
Classificatory brothers and brothers' families	15	14	21
Koranic teachers and students of the teachers	4		
Mothers	3	3	4
Wives' sisters	2	1	4
Sister	1*		3
Father	1		1
Wives' mothers	1	1	
Mother and wife's mother	1		
Sons and their families	1	3	1
Brother's son and family		1	
Brother, son, and son's family		1	
Mother's brother		1	
Wife's mother and sister		1	
Sisters' sons		1	5
Mother and brother			1
Friend's sister			1
Female Household Heads			
Alone (aged and childless)	2		
Children			1
Foster son's Wife		1	
Total Number of Respondents	85	46	75

*Sister's husband was deceased.

merchants and craftsmen represented more than 39.1 per cent of the total, fewer than among the cultivators.   In contrast, the percentage of fraternal joint families in this group is 30.4 per cent, almost twice that of the cultivators. Generally, the make-up of the households of the merchants and craftsmen is more complex than the cultivators'. The incidence of nuclear families among clerks and civil servants is fairly high, 44 per cent, but while higher than among the merchants and craftsmen, it is not as high as among the cultivators. The 28 per cent of fraternal joint families in the group is also fairly high, and so is the incidence of multi-kin households.

A number of caveats must be recognized when using the foregoing data. First, the relatively high incidence of nuclear families reported for all groups may be related to the difficulty of getting house plots large enough to house extended kin groups. Second, Ouagadougou's recent phenomenal growth must be taken into account. Thus, the true pattern of Ouagadougou families may not emerge until the children of the families now found there come of age and marry. Despite these caveats, an attempt must be made to explain the high incidence of nuclear families in the town and the possible implication of this for the traditional kin relations.

The radical shift from the traditional extended family among the Ouagadougou population, especially among Mossi cultivators, is the result of several related factors. Many young nonagricultural workers leave the homes of cultivator fathers because of a desire to change their style of life. This invariably means constructing square houses with all their appurtenances. Some young men take over a portion of the parental compound, but most try to build elsewhere. The latter solution is preferred not only because it frees them from psychological tensions, but also because the parental compounds are usually too small to accommodate all the sons.[2] Once employed, these young men almost automatically seek their own house plots. When asked why they move away from their parents, the standard reply is: "Since I was growing big, I wanted to have my own *chez-moi* and leave room for my brothers and sisters with the old people." Indeed, the departure of young men is facilitated by the Mossi practice, both in the rural areas and in town, of placing boys in separate buildings as soon as they pass puberty. This is possibly the reason why no cases were found where parents resented the departure of their sons.

Young men who remain cultivators leave their parental compounds and establish nuclear households for some of the same reasons as those who have nonagricultural occupations. Not many urban cultivators, whether native or migrant, have enough cultivable land in the peri-urban zone to share with their sons. Therefore, many youths must seek land through the agency of influential extended kinsmen or from rural chiefs. This results in breaking up the traditional work group and facilitates the economic and social independence of the

[2]Elliott P. Skinner, "Intergenerational Conflict among the Mossi: Father and Son," *Journal of Conflict Resolution,* v, No. 1 (March 1961), 55–60.

sons. Even when young men are able to work with their fathers, they have a greater opportunity than rural youths to attain economic independence. Most earn some money in town from employment during the dry season and use it to meet the greater expenses of urban life. Urban life also forces young men to assume the status of adults more rapidly. For example, they pay their own taxes, often arrange their own marriages, and, given the limitation of household space in their fathers' growing families, obtain land upon which to build homes for their own wives and young families. Thus, even when youths remain cultivators the extended family gives way to a nuclear one.

Household heads who are merchants, craftsmen, clerks, and civil servants, but who retain traditional attitudes, foster the growth of nuclear families in Ouagadougou. These men still segregate their sons at puberty in out-buildings. They say that the boys are *tranquille* (at ease) by themselves, can study better in the relative solitude of their own rooms, and can entertain friends without disturbing their families. Several civil servants (including former President Yaméogo) placed youthful sons in houses or rooms which are some three to four blocks removed from the families' homestead. The young men sleep in the "bachelor quarters" and entertain their friends there but eat all meals at the homes of their parents. They eventually marry and move out of these quarters leaving them for their younger brothers.

The conservatism of many of the older men in nonagricultural professions has also played a role in the nucleation of Ouagadougou households. A number of these men were abroad between 1945 and 1960 and had acquired many of the traits the young people hope to acquire. Nevertheless, even the most progressive among them tended to value things of little interest to the young people. For example, many of the elder "gentleman farmers" of this group take a delight in spending weekends in the rural areas. In contrast, the young people have no interest in farms or farming and prefer to amuse themselves in town. The result is that even when they live together in the same household, parents and children of the educated group do not normally interact. For example, during this research, it was almost impossible to engage an educated father and son in any joint discussion. Either the father or the son found some excuse to leave a situation which placed one or the other at a disadvantage: the father because he showed an interest in some topic which his son felt was "primitive" or not important; the son because he disliked being erudite before his father even though the father would be proud of him. During an interview with a former important African colonial administrator, his son remained quiet except to remark that he never knew that his grandmother was a daughter of a Mossi king. The father responded that this indicated that the young man had never shown any interest in those things. The gap existed even though occupationally and intellectually these two men were more similar than most fathers and sons. It is therefore not surprising that the young people of even this group move away.

The presence of more fraternal-joint households among the noncultivators than among the cultivators is more likely a function of greater income than of greater regard for kinsmen. Relatively wealthy people in Ouagadougou are always the involuntary hosts of rural relatives. Moreover, given the value of hospitality, which even urbanites respect and use to validate their own superior statuses, it is not unusual to find rural relatives living with kinsmen in town. In fact, most of the "joint households" turn out, on closer examination, to be households in transition. A large percentage of the "brothers" (it was often impossible to determine the exact genealogical links between "brothers") are new arrivals looking for work. My suspicion is that in time many of these "brothers" will marry and find their own homes, or those who are already married will move out as their families grow larger. There is no indication that economic bonds encourage "brothers" to maintain joint households over any significant period of time.

The presence of "mothers" in the compounds of all occupational groups in Ouagadougou is not surprising given the universality of this living arrangement among most Voltaic populations. Mossi mothers usually live with their sons when widowed or abandoned by husbands in favor of younger wives. The surprising thing is that mothers are not present in *more* households. Perhaps one reason is that the Ouagadougou population is so young that mothers of immigrants are still childbearing wives in the rural areas. Another verified reason is that some rural widows prefer to remain where they have many strong social ties. One important official of the *Cercle* of Ouagadougou built a house for his mother in his native village some 15 miles away and hired local people to farm her land and to keep her granaries filled. His stated reason for so doing was to permit the "old lady" to remain in her own environment and not to bother her with the problems of urban living.

The presence of the mothers of wives or other affinal kin in Ouagadougou compounds is a distinct departure from the traditions of most Voltaic groups. Not only did a woman's own male children (agnatic or affinal kin) take care of her, but her role as a married daughter's confidant placed such a strain on her relations with her son-in-law that she seldom visited his household. Men both feared and respected their mothers-in-law, but had little to do with them. Significantly, some of the mothers-in-law came to town to help care for their working daughters' children; others simply preferred to live in Ouagadougou with their daughters rather than with sons in rural areas.

Relative wealth is the reason why more sisters' sons (ya-gensé)[3] live in the households of clerks and civil servants than in either those of cultivators or merchants and craftsmen. Most Voltaic groups have the classic close relationship between a man and his sister's son. Among the Mossi this includes, among other things, the right of a boy to live with his mother's brother, or seek asylum there. Three of the young men interviewed simply took advantage of their mothers' brothers' (yasenamba) presence in Ouagadougou to migrate and look for work. One of the two others was in school and did chores for his yesba's family during off hours.

The presence of Koranic students in the households of their teachers deserves comment. This pattern is fairly old in Ouagadougou and dates back to the time of Mogho Naba Komi (c. 1780) who permitted Moslems to settle in the town. Young Koranic students then came to study and lived with Imams. The living arrangement is usually transitory since, as each Koranic student finishes his studies, he takes his family and leaves. However, the stability of the household type is maintained since young students are constantly being re-

[3] Peter B. Hammond, "Mossi Joking," *Ethnology*, III, No. 3 (July 1964), 259–67; see also Elliott P. Skinner, "The Effect of Co-residence of Sisters' Sons on African Corporate Patrilineal Descent Groups," *Cahiers d'Etudes Africaines*, IV, No. 16 (1964a), 467–78.

cruited by the teacher. Some teachers utilized the Mossi *pughsiuré*[4] (a system whereby a man who received a wife returned his daughter to the benefactor) to provide spouses for their students and, by so doing, gathered satellite families around them. These students continue their studies while their wives help the women of the teacher's household. When these scholars graduate and depart, they aid their former teachers by sending daughters as *pughsiudsé* wives to future students.

There are a few female-headed households in Ouagadougou. This type is relatively rare in rural Upper Volta, being found among those women whose high political status engenders marital instability and among certain strong-willed female beer sellers. One Ouagadougou household canvassed is headed by an old millet beer seller. The second is a literate barmaid who lives with her three sons and an adopted boy and girl in a compound inhabited by Senegalese. She claims 'to have been married to a soldier who was killed in Indo-China. After his death she had a series of alliances, bore two more children, and now considers herself a "fallen woman" with no hope of remarrying. A third female household head is the widow of a civil servant-politician who died at an early age leaving behind eight children. This woman is only nominally the head of a household, since most decisions concerning her household are made by her husband's male relatives whose home she visits almost daily. Her three grown but unmarried sons live in bachelor quarters but eat with her daily.

There is a definite relationship between habitation and kin relations among the various occupational categories in Ouagadougou. Where cultivator household heads host younger unmarried brothers, the nature of their relationship is usually a function of occupation. Where the unmarried brothers are cultivators and work for their brothers, commensality is the rule. Where the young cultivators do not work with their elder brothers, they seldom share even the evening meal with their hosts. Nevertheless, in both cases, the young men contribute to the economy of their hosts' households. This may include bundles of faggots for fuel and gifts of produce and money earned during the dry seasons. The hosts and their

[4]Elliott P. Skinner, "The Mossi Pogsioure," *Man,* xxviii (February 1960a), 1–4.

wives do not view these gifts as payments for services received and continue to support the young men during periods of unemployment and financial embarrassment. Where a young married cultivator shares a compound with an elder cultivator brother, each family prepares its own meals. Although there is some sharing of food, there is little formal cooperation in this sphere. The brothers keep separate granaries (for the most part they cultivate their individual plots) and, for all intents and purposes, the arrangement is that of two families living together. They cooperate in their living arrangements but are quite distinct social entities.

Many young merchants or apprentices who lodge with their elder cultivator brothers usually eat only the evening meal at home. They give their elder brothers money to cover the cost of meals and rent but are not charged a fixed sum for these services. In addition, they give presents to their brothers' wives and children and occasionally bring meat for the evening meals. Depending upon their relations with sisters-in-law, they may have their laundry done. Otherwise, they wash their own clothes or give them to a laundry man.

School boys who live with their cultivator brothers make no monetary contributions to the household budget. Instead they frequently help to deplete it since they are often clothed and fed by these relatives. On the other hand, they perform all sorts of household chores for their female affines.

Common occupation rather than cohabitation appears to be the significant factor in the social relations between cultivators and kinsmen. Thus, household heads whose younger brothers are noncultivators interact less with these young men than they do with more distant kin who are cultivators. The reason is that cultivators and their younger noncultivator relatives not only have different styles of life, but also different life goals. Moreover, the cultivator household heads know that their noncultivator brothers will leave as soon as money and land can be obtained. These differences and expectations effectively limit any serious discussions on other than purely family matters. But even here, dialogue and concensus is difficult to achieve since the brothers often hold different opinions about family problems. Differences in education and religious affiliation (often a function of mobility) affect the views of many brothers on domestic problems.

Many of the same factors condition the relationships between noncultivator household heads and their cohabiting rural relatives. The nature of these relationships, other than the obligation to provide food and shelter, depends very much upon factors such as occupations, styles of life, and life goals. Apropos of this, it is quite instructive to observe the relations between civil servant household heads and nonliterate relatives in the presence of outsiders. When French is spoken, these relatives are completely left out of the conversation and no attempt is made to interpret for them. But, even when the language is Moré, uneducated relatives remain silent or participate only infrequently. Furthermore, lower-status relatives are expected to bring chairs for the visitors and serve drinks.

The influence of life goals upon kin relations was clearly seen in the discussion of kin terminology usage. This incongruity is even sharper in actual social relations. The urban-born educated children of a civil servant had difficulty adjusting to their father's uneducated sister performing the function of a servant. They could not reconcile the young woman's low modern status with her very high traditional status as father's sister. Perhaps because of this conflict the young girl was being subjected to more abuse than was meted out to other kinsmen in the compound. The household head probably contributed to his sister's dilemma by not treating her as a ward, in the modern sense, but as a little sister in the traditional manner. He was as formal and severe with her as he would have been in the rural area where male relatives shaped the character of women. This meant that men could not joke with young female members in their households after the age of puberty. When the civil servant in Ouagadougou observed the traditional norms with the girl, his children misunderstood his attitude, interpreted it as a servant-master relationship and were as "harsh" to her as was their father.

The plight of this young girl in her urban brother's household highlights the changes in traditional relationships which result from urbanization. Rural people are quite receptive to a request from urban relatives for youngsters to be reared or "civilized" in town. They welcome this gesture as a sign of interest from their prestigious urban relatives, and, unless unwilling to break the engagement of girls to rural men, readily assent to the request. The young people themselves do profit from their urban experiences. For example, one young man sent to be reared by a high-status relative in Ouagadougou learned to speak French and to drive the family's car. Subsequently, the guardian secured a driver's license and a job for his ward. Today the young man is married and lives not far from his benefactor. Many of the girls who come to town under similar auspices eventually marry lower-level clerks and civil servants who prefer to marry "modern" girls who had been reared in town. Both the urban people and their rural relatives manipulate kinship relations to suit their own ends.

The demands of different occupations have an influence upon relations between kinsmen in Ouagadougou. For example, the life of cultivators is highly circumscribed during the planting season. They leave the town early in the morning and return late at night. Some Christian and Moslem cultivators return to Ouagadougou once a week for religious purposes; others, primarily the *Winnam pous'neba* (literally, worshippers of God),[5] stay on their farms during most of the planting period. The result is that unless people visit their cultivator relatives on the farm, they seldom meet during the planting season. During the dry season the situation is different. Cultivators then visit their relatives but complain that intermittent contact leads to divergent interests and estrangement. Interaction between relatives becomes limited to rituals or periods of crisis, but visiting is a bit strained and formal, especially across wide occupational lines.

Differences in the use of time are affecting relations between relatives in Ouagadougou. Except during the planting season, cultivators can visit relatives at any hour. This poses no problem for merchants with fixed business places in the market. Moreover, these visits do not interrupt trading activities. Visiting does not pose too great a problem for clerks working for Europeans, even though both the employer and other customers complain. The situation is different with the civil servants, many of whom do not like to be visisted on their jobs and dislike having their midday siestas disturbed by kinsmen. To make matters worse, they often must return to work before the visitors can talk to them. This upsets the cultivators who will wait since they have the time, but do expect to be able to see

---

[5]There is increasing resentment among Africans over the use of the term "pagan" for believers in the traditional religions.

their important relatives. Civil servants become upset because they dislike situations where they have to be impolite to low-status kinsmen.

Not unexpectedly, clerks and civil servants make fewer visits to extended kin than do the other occupational groups. Yet they are more mobile than all the others, having more bicycles and scooters. It was not uncommon for members of this group to be teased with the term *sana* (stranger) when they took me to visit relatives in the outlying quarters. Often the remark would be made that it took a real stranger to initiate the visit. The standard rebuttal was that the absence of visits indicated no dimunition in affection but was a function of time and distance. Attention would be called to visits of relatives in town. Left unstated was that the persons visited were often members of occupational groups comparable to that of the respondent. It is also true that clerks or civil servants visit relatives similarly employed more regularly than others with different occupations. Of course, personal factors do influence the visiting behavior of all the people involved, but these are the general patterns.

Rituals and ceremonies provide the opportunity for kinsmen in Ouagadougou to visit each other and to provide mutual help. People are still expected to participate in all the important family ceremonies regardless of occupation, education, or income. Yet, here again, the differences of education, occupation, and residence condition how people initiate and fulfill kinship obligations. The rituals introducing babies into the community provide a good illustration: followers of the traditional religion (*Winnam pous'neba*) have no formal rituals, but both Christians and Moslems have naming rituals for their children. In general, low-status persons can attend all such family rituals, but higher-status ones have difficulty attending either because of religious differences or lack of time. For example, when a young Moslem held a naming ceremony for his youngest daughter, his relative, a very influential Catholic municipal officer, could not attend because it was held early on a weekday morning. This official's wife and daughter also could not attend because the Moslem ritual was primarily a man's affair. Some prestigious Christian members of the young man's family did attend the ritual and, contrary to orthodoxy, were provided beer and soda by their host. They were seated with the high-status Moslem relatives and segregated from the ordinary Moslems who came intermittently, offering prayers and congratulations. All the high-status relatives greeted the visitors and, as relatives of the host, they acknowledged the congratulations of the visitors. Nevertheless, the high-status Moslems did not join in the prayers which the visitors offered. Paying no attention to either religion or status, the baby's father followed the Moslem custom of giving grains of millet to all his guests so that they could share these with others and spread the name of his daughter.

Lower-status kinsmen are expected to, and generally do, attend ceremonies and rituals of their prestigious relatives. But again, due to differences in status and styles of life, they do not and cannot fully participate in them. Lower-status relatives participate only differentially in the rather elaborate baptismal and wedding ceremonies of high-status individuals, since these involve church attendance, municipal formalities, and social festivities such as dancing, singing, and drinking. They either perform the appropriate roles of attendants or segregate themselves and depart as soon as they can. Once, when a petty merchant was asked why he did not remain at the wedding reception of a nephew, he replied that he was an old man and left early so that the young people "could enjoy themselves." It was not pointed out to him that other and older relatives, but more prestigious ones, planned to remain until the end of the reception.

High-status people in Ouagadougou sometimes invite kinsmen of equal status for "family dinners." This practice does not exist in the rural areas where people seldom eat in family units except at rituals and are then segregated by sex and age groups. Sunday family dinners in Ouagadougou are quite elaborate affairs and involve the nuclear families of civil servants, politicians, and wealthy merchants. Dependent relatives of the families are not invited, and those who reside with the hosts serve as waiters during the dinner. An interesting commentary upon one such dinner was given by a young student at the *lycée,* who did not attend a dinner to which he had been invited. He explained that the dinner would not be much fun since he would have no one to talk to. What he meant was that at these dinners age and sexual segregation occur as soon as dinner is finished. The young man would have no peers to talk to and could not have joined the older men although he was educated enough to do so.

Except for rather formal occasions, the women among all status groups in Ouagadougou maintain a separate pattern of visiting their relatives. Mossi women have always had a certain freedom to visit their patri-lineages: from the unannounced ritual escape of a new mother to her *babissi* (father and his brothers) where she reared her child until it was weaned, to the periodic "vacations" which a woman spent at her father's compound. Urban women, whether wives of cultivators or of other groups, have generally ceased to "escape" to their own patrilineages after the birth of their children, whether these relatives live within the town or not. The consensus is that this practice cannot be maintained since town men constantly need nonsexual uxorial help from their wives. Similarly, urban women do not formally take "vacations" with urban patrilineal kinsmen. They would be considered worthless wives if they did so. Nevertheless, women freely visit their urban relatives as often as they wish—subject, of course, to the requirements of their households.

Men in town may object to many activities of their wives, but they maintain their traditional silence about visits to patrilineal relatives. Women take great pride in the manner in which they visit urban patrilineal relatives, especially their fathers. When visiting their parents, women cultivators and merchants, including beer sellers, dress smartly and carry the traditional baskets (which rural women use) either on their heads or have these carried by young female relatives. When on such journeys, women even refuse a ride in a car because they desire to have people "see them visiting their *babissi*." Women of higher status have abandoned the head basket as a symbol of filial piety when visiting urban patrilineal relatives. Instead, they use vehicles which indicate the high status of their husbands.

The obligation to aid relatives has tended to mask the emergence of changes in the traditional kin relations in Ouagadougou. For example, cultivators in difficulty ask for and do receive help from higher-status relatives. Clerks and civil servants ask for and receive loans from merchant relatives. Civil servants called out of town for any purpose can and do call upon their brothers' wives, especially lower-status ones, to help in their households while they are away. And relatives contribute to the expenses of ceremonies held by their kinsmen. Thus, one notes myriad examples of kin cooperation and obligations when an inquiry is made into the nature of urban kin relations. Nevertheless, if one has any knowledge of rural kin relations, it becomes quite clear that these differ qualitatively from the urban ones. The latter relations are more specific and more restricted. Whereas a visitor to a rural compound is introduced to all male kinsmen present, the same is not done in an urban household. Indeed, low-status relatives are often passed over when introductions are made, thereby revealing their social position to strangers. This never occurs in the villages.

The relations between people in Ouagadougou and their rural relatives, in contrast to their urban ones, is characterized by great ambivalence. This ambivalence is felt less by the young who, having grown up in Ouagadougou, are cut off from rural relatives, physically, socially, and psychologically. The older people are torn by a feeling of duty toward rural relatives, and a suspicion that they have little to gain from continued reciprocal relations with rural kinsmen.

Relatively high commitment to urban life is one factor that certainly influences the relations between the urban people and their rural kinsmen. Whereas reports from other parts of Africa indicate that the town is exploited by migrants in the interest of the village, the people of Ouagadougou have most of their interests in the town. Ouagadougou was never a Mecca for solitary male migrants who planned to return to wives and relatives in the rural areas. Young men either brought their wives to Ouagadougou, or sent for them, or married women in the town. They do not feel like "strangers" in Ouagadougou, and with the amenities of urban living, do not look forward to returning to the rural areas. Of the 57 cultivators who were asked about their retirement plans, 47 said that they intended to stay in Ouagadougou, 9 did not know, and 1 said that he planned to return to his native village.

One reason why such a large number of persons designated Ouagadougou as a place of retirement is that the tax officials forced them to make a choice. If a man planned to return to his village, he kept his name on the village's tax roll and sent money home to pay taxes. If he planned to remain in

Ouagadougou, he payed taxes to the municipality. People opt for paying taxes in town because it is cumbersome to transfer money to the villages, and they cannot rely on relatives to pay the taxes promptly. Besides, since urban dwellers must have tax receipts and other municipal documents to obtain access to many amenities in the town, they make an "administrative" commitment to urban life. Nonetheless, since only nine cultivators were undecided about the future and only one planned to retire to the country, there is an indication that even the cultivators have a greater commitment to urban life than to rural life.

When cultivators were asked to specify why they preferred to remain in town they gave the following reasons: first, that they had relatives and friends in town and had lost meaningful contact with their rural relatives; and second, that they did not know the children of their rural relatives and feared that no one would care for them if they returned. In contrast, they all felt that they could always get some help from their children and grandchildren in Ouagadougou, and from urban friends. None of these people mentioned the possibility of the rural areas providing "social security" either materially or affectively. Their ties to urban children rather than to rural collateral relatives seemed more important.

Rural people show a greater interest in their urban relatives than vice versa, and they are the ones who attempt to maintain the ties. Male urban cultivators seldom visit their rural villages except for burial and funeral rituals since they seldom have the money to do so. Regardless of how frequently a man returns, he is obliged to take presents for many people: old female relatives must be given bags of salt; old men expect at least tobacco and kola nuts. Often a man does not return home because of involuntary debts to rural kinsmen who, over time, have sent him gifts of food. That rural visitors may have been housed and given gifts to take back home is irrelevant. Rural people whose politeness and hospitality cover a classic understanding of the principle of reciprocity of human affairs are quick to note if visiting urban relatives wish to limit contact by not providing suitable gifts.

The people of Ouagadougou seldom send children to be reared by rural kinsmen in order to have them avoid the "corrupting" urban life. This is in stark contrast to what has been reported for some parts of Africa and even for parts of the Western world. Almost all urban mothers are aware of the medical dangers of rearing children in the rural areas. In fact, it is the rural people who bring sick children to town for medical help and seek lodging with urban relatives. Urban people prefer to keep their children in town so that they can be educated. It is only when they can not get slow-learners or other children admitted to urban schools that some parents send them to the rural areas. In October 1964, a number of cultivators and members of other low-status groups sent children to relatives in Koudougou, Kaya, and other areas because the urban schools were full. They hoped that competition for places would be less in the rural areas and that contact with village school teachers would help their children. What results this will have on the relations between cultivators in town and their rural kin remains to be seen.

The relations between other lower socio-economic groups in Ouagadougou and their rural relatives are similar to those already described for the cultivators. The exceptions are merchants who often use rural relatives as conduits for merchandise to sell in urban markets. Rural people either buy produce and send it to relatives in Ouagadougou or notify them when products are cheap and plentiful. This cooperation benefits not only the urban merchants but the villagers as well. For example, the Commandant of the *Cercle* of Ouagadougou (an official who still exists but whose command area is becoming very small because his *cercle* is being broken up into smaller ones) has been able to use the existing commercial relations between important merchants in town and their rural kinsmen to procure help to build schools.

The relations between the clerks and civil servants and their rural relatives present some of the greatest contradictions. One should, however, hasten to point out that the contradictions are among the older people and their rural kin and not among the younger, Ouagadougou-born. As we have seen, the first clerks and civil servants maintained close relations with their rural relatives; thus, when modern political activity started in the Upper Volta, in 1945, these urban people often used their influence to aid those politicians who campaigned in the rural areas. The urban people and the politicians made many promises and even deposited bags of cement at the chief's house as "proof" of the intention to build schools. Not surprisingly many of the schools were never built. Everyone now recognizes that a fraud took place, but rural people have not permitted their urban relatives to forget the debt, and they seek food and shelter when they visit Ouagadougou.

Today, most of the relations between the high socio-economic groups and their rural relatives (outside of aid in school construction) are quite specific. People regularly send money to their own parents, especially their mothers. The emphasis on the mother is noteworthy. Most urban people are not interested in giving a father money for taxes and the expenses for his other wives. The children of these women are expected to do so. Urban visitors often cause dissension within rural households when they do not share presents equally among all relatives but show preferences for their own mother and her children (*mabissi*). This issue appears to belie the belief of many rural people that there is great household solidarity in the rural areas. Significantly, as soon as developments test the solidarity of the rural polygynous household, it breaks down.

The specificity in relations between urban persons and their rural kinsmen is seen again in their lack of acquaintance with rural extended or affinal kin. Once, when a young female social worker went to a rural area to investigate the background of a juvenile delinquent, a woman in the local market claimed that she had slighted her. The woman declared that since the social worker had a "'white person's' job" (*nansara toumdé*), she had become a white person (*nansara*) and had ignored her. The social worker was upset not only by the abuse, but because she did not know or remember the woman. The social worker felt that the woman (her father's brother's son's wife) should have introduced herself and not stayed aside and become abusive. What neither of these two women realized was that rural relatives more frequently recognize, and take a greater interest in, higher-status urban kinsmen than vice versa.

The celebration of rituals provides the opportunity for both urban people and their rural relatives to do specific things for each other. Conservative high-status Moslems often solemnize marriages in their villages not only because they desire to have rural relatives take part in the rituals, but because they believe that the ceremony is more meaningful there. Similarly, a growing number of high-status persons have started sending the bodies of deceased relatives to rural areas for burial because they feel that it is better to be interred in ancestral soil. Poor transportation had previously made this practice impossible. On the other hand, rural Christians believe that Christmas and other religious holidays are best celebrated in Ouagadougou. They feel that Christmas is a Western institution, whose natural setting is in town. This belief has been engendered and strengthened by such secular aspects of Christmas as family gatherings, gift-giving, and merrymaking. Rural people, even non-Christians, come to town a few days before Christmas and stay with kinsmen until the end of the holidays. One important civil servant explained that he invited both rural and urban relatives to attend midnight Mass because this ritual did not contradict any of their beliefs. He argued that the Moslems recognize Jesus as a prophet, the Christians as the Savior, and that since the traditionalists were not involved in religious controversy, all his relatives could therefore worship together and then go to his home afterward for further festivities.

Higher-status clerks and civil servants may use rural relatives for various purposes, but not as persons to whom to send children for education. They fear that the children would not be encouraged to go to school (a groundless fear in many cases) but more importantly that there would be no one to supervise the education of their children. Clerks and civil servants believe that they must teach their children "culture"— which is viewed as essential for full participation in the modern world. Given these parental attitudes, it is understandable why urban children do not like to visit rural areas and why they are not interested in any but close kinsmen living there. Young people state categorically that there is "nothing to do" in the rural areas and complain of "boredom" after a few days' stay. Even when sent to visit rural areas, they try to live with relatives in roadside villages or in the larger country towns. Most young people ignore the complaints of parents that they ought to appreciate the true life of Africa.

A trend has now started among top-level clerks, civil servants, and politicians in Ouagadougou to build homes among their relatives in the rural conglomerations. So far the reasons for doing this appear to be political as well as social and economic. These men claim that if they lose their jobs or retire, they would be able to live quite comfortably off the produce of their rural farms. Nevertheless, it is doubtful whether these people will really have much interest in the rural areas when they grow older. The chances are that they will retain a great deal of prestige in Ouagadougou even when they retire. Many actual retirees know the workings of the urban bureaucracy better than younger people and are called upon to help both urban and rural persons to deal with it. A visit to the homes of these retired persons usually finds them surrounded by relatives and friends, a very good sign that they are regarded as notables in their urban neighborhoods.

The data presented here indicate that the people of Ouagadougou still attach great importance to kinship and value kin relations, but that these aspects of their behavior are being conditioned more and more by the realities of life in an administrative center with insufficient resources to meet the desire of its population to modernize. The resulting changes in social relations are multi-dimensional and kaleidoscopic, including shifts in kinship terminology from African terms to European ones with concomitant changes in kin relations based on relative age rather than on generation; the emergence of status differences between extended kinsmen; the growth of multi-locality even within the nuclear family; and a greater commitment to urban relatives than to rural ones.

Most people in Ouagadougou are not eager to abandon their traditional social organization—except of course the youth—but they are discovering that these relations are no longer meaningful in contemporary life. Even those persons who are tradition-oriented find that relations with kinsmen are changing. They are not always accessible to kinsmen as in the past; they cannot interact with them at all times and in all places; and even attempted reciprocal exchanges between kinsmen having different social statuses serve to drive them apart. The result is that kin relations in Ouagadougou are losing their generalized and reciprocal nature and are fast becoming specific, intermittent, and manipulative.

CHAPTER IV

Courtship and Marriage

The inability of urban families to control the persons, goods, and services of their members is, in part, cause for the emergence of new patterns of courtship and marriage in Ouagadougou. In fact, in traditional Voltaic societies, procuring a wife was so much an arrangement between heads of families that one cannot talk meaningfully about traditional courtship patterns. Such courting as there was normally consisted of ritual avoidance between engaged couples, or highly structured and carefully chaperoned meetings between them. Elder cultivators in Ouagadougou still insist that the surest way not to obtain a specific woman as a wife is to indicate to potential wife-givers that she is pleasing to the eye. This is done to sustain the ideology that the corporate lineage segments have the *rights in genetricem* to a woman's progeny and to emphasize that a specific man only has *rights in uxorem*[1] to the woman. The result is that, whether or not a man could designate the girl or young woman he wanted for a wife, he could express no overt feelings toward her. It was only when a man had been given a wife that he could pay court to her and give her presents. But even then, he was forced to consider that the young wife was still a minor in his or her father's compound and that he could not be overly friendly with her lest he interfere with or subvert the instructions she was receiving on how to be a wife.

Young people in contemporary Ouagadougou still do not have complete freedom in affairs of courtship and marriage. Cultivators continue to follow the traditional pattern before marriage, and even clerks and junior civil servants are known to marry women recommended to them by their parents.

Since a large percentage of the men who migrate to Ouagadougou from the rural areas bring wives with them, courtship before marriage is not an issue. The exceptions are those men who courted the fiancées or wives of others and ran off with

[1]Cf. Laura Bohannan, "Dahomean Marriage: A Revaluation," *Africa,* XIX, No. 4 (1949), 273–87.

them to Ouagadougou. Of course, the number of men who do so is not easy to discover, but enough of them do so to make the problem of "encouraging women to abandon the conjugal domicile" a major one for the tribunals of Ouagadougou. Courtship is also not an issue when girls or women are sent from the rural areas by family heads as *pughsiudsé* to men in the town. These girls or women simply have to "sit" in the houses of prospective husbands until their marriages are consummated according to the traditional custom.

Tradition-bound family heads in town—and not all of these are necessarily cultivators—find it difficult to maintain the traditional marriage practices and give away girls as wives. Some fathers try to keep the *pughsiuré* ties viable by persuading their daughters to marry men chosen by former benefactors. However, other traditional practices through which wives are obtained, such as friendships involving the giving of economic aid, manual help, and gifts of all kinds, are difficult to maintain in town. Urban household heads, in contrast to those in rural areas, are unable to dispose of the labor and resources of their lineage segments since nucleation of families often prevents this. And in the absence of such gifts and services, marriage partnerships are not viable. Previously, this was clearly seen in the rural areas where the migration of young men to Ghana and the Ivory Coast deprived elders of resources which had enabled them to obtain wives from marriage partners.[2]

Even when urban cultivators are able to maintain friendship bonds with urban marriage partners, they have difficulty persuading female dependents to accept prearranged marriages. One reason for this is that daughters of cultivators who live in town are seldom solely dependent upon their fathers for a livelihood. They often do petty trading and are thus independent enough to refuse husbands they do not like. Again, when a cultivator sends his daughter to school, this very act precludes his making an arrangement for her marriage. Of course, not many fathers realize this and are chagrined when their daughters refuse a prearranged marriage. Some strong-willed fathers do force daughters to marry men chosen for them, but subsequently often regret this act because the girls desert these menages.

[2]Skinner, 1960b, p. 309.

110

A second reason why the traditional marriage pattern is disappearing in Ouagadougou is because little girls are no longer viewed as "little wives" but as children. The institutions most responsible for this changing attitude are the schools and the Catholic church. This is true despite the fact that not all girls in town go to school and a large number of lower-status families are non-Christian. The school plays a role in transforming the little wife into a child simply because it provides an alternate status for her: that of school girl. Even Moslems, who do not send their daughters to school, have to reckon with the fact that girls are no longer simply wives who are small.

Finally, governmental decrees such as the Mandel Decree of 1939 and the Jacquinot Decree of 1951[3] defined the minimum age at which girls in French West Africa and French Equatorial Africa could be married. The law stipulated that a girl must be fourteen years old before being married and a boy sixteen years, but, more important, that the consent of both spouses was required for the validity of a marriage. Subsequent laws raised the minimum age of marriage for girls to seventeen years, but these decrees struck at the root of the Mossi marriage system. Traditionally, girls were married without their consent and sent to live with their husbands when they were quite young, although the marriage was not consummated until they were of age. Now because of these pressures and laws, any urban father who wishes to marry off his daughter against her will is confronted by the school, the Church, and the administration.

The position of the administration on this question was reiterated by the incumbent President, Yaméogo, in May 1964 during a political address to the people of Ouagadougou. He declared:

> As far as the question of age [at marriage] is concerned, the Congress of Banfora, after three days of very animated debate, as you can imagine, has decided to retain the minimum ages of 19 years for the man and 17 years for the woman. Everyone will certainly not agree, but I can say that this decision was not taken lightly. It was only after having weighed most carefully the necessities, the traditions,

[3]Marlene Dobkin, "Colonialism and the Legal Status of Women in Francophonic Africa," *Cahiers d'Etudes Africaines,* VIII, No. 31 (1968), 390–405.

the medical and sociological facts; it was only after having weighed the exigencies of the national standards that we arrived at that decision.[4]

This ruling meant that those urban men who were willing to adhere to the prevailing opinion concerning the marriage of their daughters could find no institutional allies for their traditional views. Moreover, it meant also that the women, who incidentally were really never as subservient as the Catholic church believed, and who had always been hostile or at best reconciled, to the traditional marriage system, were made aware of their new liberties and could react to forced marriages by running away. Now it seems that when girls marry men proposed by male relatives, factors other than overt coercion are at work.

The courtship pattern emerging among the younger members of low-prestige groups in Ouagadougou reflects many of the changes in the town. Young girls selling cooked foods, fruits, or other items establish relations with men in which cajolery, coquetry, and often brazen disrespect are common. Thus, these girls depart from the norms of behavior expected by traditionalists. Those familiar with the public display of respect and subordination of Mossi girls in the rural areas have difficulty adjusting to the behavior of their urban sisters. Again, the young urban girl is more approachable and is less likely to put her hand to the side of her face in embarrassed silence when addressed by a strange man. She is also less likely to respond, "Mam ka mi la!" (loosely, "I do not know") —but literally, "I am only a woman; you should not ask me any questions but address yourself to a man"—in response to a request for information from the stranger.

Lower-status young men in Ouagadougou, whether cultivators, tradesmen, merchants, soldiers, or policemen, now feel free to approach young girls—whether their intentions are honorable or not. (This was frowned upon in the rural areas because, except for girls ritually free to choose their own husbands, girls already had husbands.) These young men now believe that the girls can respond to their charms, if willing and unattached. They are also prepared to disrupt any attachment a girl may already have if she responds to their ap-

[4]*Carrefour Africain,* No. 111 (31 May 1964), p. 2.

112

proaches. And if it turns out that a girl is a *pughsiudga* or has been betrothed without her will and consent, the youths are encouraged to try harder.

Young men are prepared to initiate contact with potential wives on their own because they can no longer depend upon their elders to do so. Most young men in this group are quite prepared to accept the traditional marriage arrangement if the girls are attractive to them. But the ability of elders to make traditional marriage arrangements for their dependents has been considerably reduced owing to their loss of control over the lineage's resources. The young men of these low-status groups in Ouagadougou control their own resources from an early age, and they give gifts to young women who please them.

Most young men use an intermediary to indicate their interest in girls they find attractive. Once this is done, a youth may give a girl small presents or become one of her more zealous clients if she is actively engaged in petty trade. The traditional gift of 44 kola nuts which a young man used to give to a paramour appears to have disappeared, and so has the practice of giving gifts to young women in multiples of 4, the traditional number for women. Young men now prefer to pay court when girls are on their way to market, or selling at the sides of the streets, or while they are sitting with friends or younger kinsmen outside their gates. The practice of going for walks or formal dating has not as yet appeared among low-status young people. Nor, apparently, do young lovers long escape the surveillance of friends and kinsmen who invariably try to regularize the relationship as soon as they believe that it is getting out of hand.

The first step a low-status young man takes in the process of getting married is to seek an intermediary to approach the girl's family. The emissary is commissioned to advise the *yirisoba* (household head or father) or *tuteur* (guardian) of the girl that "X" (the young man) is interested in marrying the girl and that, if there are no objections, the candidate would like to pay him a visit. The *yirisoba* customarily does not give the emissary a direct answer, but tells him to return in about two weeks. During this time, the *yirisoba* or *tuteur* is supposed to make inquiries concerning the character of the man, his family background, his employment, income, and other pertinent matters. When the envoy returns, he is told whether the young suitor may or may not visit the young woman's guardian. Depending upon this answer, the guardian has the opportunity to see the young man and either to accept or reject his suit. If the young man is accepted, he informs his own relatives about his intentions and, if they have no objections, he notifies the girl's guardian that he will marry her. The guardian will usually insist that the engagement period should be no longer than six months. Guardians do profess faith in the good character of the young people but prudently suggest that short engagements preclude those "difficulties" that often cause young men to abandon their fiancées. Once the engagement has been arranged, preparations are made for the wedding.

The courtship behavior of the young people of the clerk and civil servant group is conditioned by the role which modern education plays in their lives. The normal precourtship behavior of young boys and girls at the *lycées, collèges,* and *écoles normales* is to visit and talk, and to go to surprise parties[5] in each other's homes. These are all group activities and there is little individual pairing. The young people are unusually careful about developing romantic attachments. The factors which appear to condition their behavior include: a) the need to obtain a good education and a stable position, and b) that "women never finish" or that "men never finish," meaning that regardless of when a young person wants to marry, a spouse can always be found. Thus, while "love" and "romance" are often given lip service, the young people in this group tend to have a rather pragmatic "no-nonsense" approach to the subject of love, courtship, and marriage. Young men and women, therefore, take care not to become involved until they are ready for marriage. They fear that an unwanted pregnancy would not only result in the expulsion of a girl from school or otherwise short-circuit her educational career, but might also lead the young people to make the often fateful decision to marry before they are economically prepared to do so.

Educated young people view education and the ability to obtain a good job, preferably in the civil service, as important

[5]The origin of the term "surprise party" is obscure and probably represents a borrowing from either America or England. There are no elements of "surprise" at these parties.

Overleaf: Panorama of the city

Top: Woman resisting kinsmen's demand that she return to her husband
Bottom: Children, with birth certificates in hand, waiting to register for school

Top: Republican Guard repelling attack by Mogho Naba's army on Territorial Assembly

Bottom: Changing house types in Ouagadougou

Top: Mogho Naba and officials at Moslem ceremony marking the end of Ramadan
Bottom left: Catholic baptismal ceremony
Bottom right: Traditional religious sacrifice at modern, urban crossroad

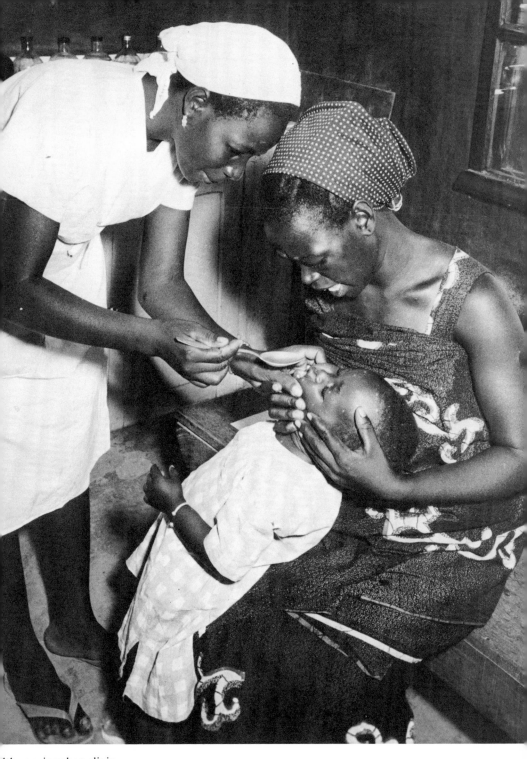

lth care in urban clinic

Top: Roadside vendors
Bottom: Central market

*: Commercial zone

tom: Mother and children preparing cakes for sale

rleaf: View of residential section

criteria for courtship and marriage. As far as could be gathered through interviews, observation, and an analysis of the marriage records of the town, educated girls, without exception, marry educated men. Yet, more than half the educated girls who responded to questionnaires about the importance they attach to education and occupation in potential spouses stated that they would not discriminate against men whose education and positions were inferior to their own. The following are some responses to the questions: "Would you accept a proposal of marriage from a man whose situation was inferior to your own?" and, "If so, why?"

1. Yes, I would accept a proposal of marriage from a man whose situation is inferior to mine because it is not position alone which gives a person value. For me, love is the important factor; position is exceedingly secondary. Of course, I would need a man who could at least feed me and be able to maintain my future household, but I would not refuse to accept a man for my husband because he is a civil servant and not a minister.

2. No, I feel that the man should have a superior position in order to enable him to support his household and because of his need to command it. Otherwise, he would have a certain complex and then it would be his wife who would direct everything in the household instead of there being two of them to do so.

3. I would never accept a proposal of marriage from a man whose situation is inferior to mine. For this I have two reasons: 1) There would always be misunderstandings in our discussions because we would take different positions. 2) I would not like to have a husband who would feel inferior when participating in the activities of my milieu or even in front of me. His pride as a man would be humbled.

4. Yes, I would marry a man who has a position inferior to mine. The diploma does not make the man.

5. I would willingly accept a proposal of marriage from a man who has a position inferior to mine if he fulfills certain other criteria I would like in my choice of a husband. That is to say, if I love him; if there are no problems between our two families with regard to our marriage; if he is healthy; and if he does not have any very bad qualities which could disrupt our communal life.

115

6. Yes! And why not? It is not a superior position which leads to happiness. And I do not feel the need for his position to be superior to mine before trying to make him happy and help him to become a true man.

It is important to note that none of the girls even considered marrying a cultivator, or at least an uneducated man. Such men are simply not thought of as possible mates for educated girls. Moreover, despite the declarations of many of these girls that they would consider marrying a man having an inferior position, their emphasis is on men with higher positions. In general, educated women expect to marry educated men, and it is the man who successfully courts such a woman who is seen as "making the catch." Given the limited number of educated women in the town, many educated men have to settle for women having much less education than themselves.

The young men who were asked the same question about the educational and professional qualifications of potential spouses were quite adamant in their refusal to consider women with superior education and position as mates. The following are some of their responses:

1. To marry a woman who is on my level would be all right; but on a level superior to mine, never! My family would be like a paper boat in a violent current. I say no because my answer is *no!* It is a categorical imperative. The reasons remain inexplicable, but the fact is that there usually are problems in such a marriage which lead to divorce.

2. If it were absolutely necessary, I would agree to a wife who has a situation equal to my own, but not a superior one. Preferably I would like to marry one who has a situation inferior to mine because then I could be more certain that there would be equilibrium in the household.

3. An ideal marriage should hardly concern itself with the situation of the woman. Apropos of this, I read in a newspaper about a woman with a Master's degree who married a tailor who had not even obtained an elementary school certificate. These cases are evidently rare and, as far as I am concerned, it is often necessary to be content with a wife having the same position as oneself, or having an inferior position, because a woman who knows that her position is superior to that of her husband would rarely have a spirit of submission toward him.

116

4. I truly do not foresee any awkwardness if my wife were on the same level as myself, from the point of view of education as well as professional situation. Nevertheless, experience has often shown that in those households where the African woman has the same situation as her husband, the marriage seems to be built on sand. The woman, having just succeeded in receiving her liberation, believes that she has the right to command her husband once she has attained his level.... Recognizing this real fact which could destroy my household, I would prefer to marry a woman whose situation was inferior to mine because the wife is made to obey and be submissive to her husband (see St. Paul).

While these youths are quite emphatic about their desire to marry a woman either equal or inferior in rank to themselves, they still do not consider illiterate women as a possible choice for a wife. Nevertheless, due to the shortage of educated women, many of these men do marry illiterate or semi-literate girls, even though they would prefer literate wives.

Most young men and young women of the clerk and civil servant group do in fact meet their future spouses at one of the numerous surprise parties. A youth shows his preference for a particular girl by dancing with her frequently and by arranging for her to be invited to other surprise parties. Sometimes boys first meet girls at school or at the homes of mutual friends and arrange to have them invited to surprise parties where they are relatively free to talk to each other. When and if the young people feel that they would like to meet each other more often, the youth makes a formal request to the parents of the girl for permission to visit their home. This request seldom comes as a surprise to the girl's parents who have been aware of the young man's intentions either from his talking to their daughter at parties or because of his presence among a group of young escorts taking the girl to the parties.

A surprisingly large number of young women interviewed reported that they had been introduced to their husbands by relatives who specifically had marriage in mind. One young woman, relating how she met her husband, said that she had been in school in Ouagadougou for some time when a relative came and took her to see a provincial chief who was related to them both. The chief scolded her for never having visited him

117

and when she confessed to ignorance of their relationship, he was even more displeased. As to be expected, during the course of the visit the chief asked whether she was betrothed or married (she was then seventeen years of age). She replied that she was still in school and was not interested in marriage. The chief declared that it was dangerous for a girl of her age not to be betrothed or married, adding that he knew a good prospective husband for her. He then asked whether she was Catholic or Moslem. When she replied that she was Moslem, he reportedly said, "Good, I know just the man for you. He is a young civil servant who works in Boussé and he cannot find a nice girl there because all the girls there are Catholic." She reported that she had forgotten the conversation when, weeks later, a young man visited her, stating that he had been told by the chief to look her up.

Even when a young man of this group has been given permission to visit a young woman, the couple is still carefully chaperoned. They continue to go to surprise parties, dances, and the cinema together, but they are accompanied either by friends, relatives, or married couples of their own age. The mother, but not the father, may even ask a man to declare his intentions if it appears that no formal proposal for engagement is forthcoming. This is in direct contrast to rural Mossi areas where women have little say in their daughter's prospective marriage.

The young clerk or civil servant usually writes a formal letter to the girl's guardian requesting permission to become engaged to her. And, unless it is a case where a young man going off for further studies wishes to "tie the girl," that is, prevent her from marrying another, a request for engagement means that a man is ready to marry. High-status people in Ouagadougou, like the low-status ones, distrust long engagements not only because of the danger of accidents to the young woman but, apparently, also because the notion of "engagement" is itself a new idea. Engagement in European terms is distrusted because, while it sanctions close (though not sexual) relations between young people, it provides little legitimacy for a child were a girl to become pregnant. The result of these fears is that engagements usually do not last longer than six months. Only in unusual cases, such as when the man is away at school, are they permitted to last for as long as two years.

Attempts to discover the actual marriage patterns of the

people of Ouagadougou are fraught with statistical and meth-odological pitfalls. First of all, many of the large number of immigrants to Ouagadougou were married before they came to the town. Second, since the traditional Mossi marriage does not include an elaborate ceremony (there are only cere-monial visits by wife-givers to wife-receivers), many marriages escape the notice of most townspeople. They are only brought to the attention of the civil authorities during a census or when a family attempts to obtain official papers. Third, many Moslems, both Mossi or non-Mossi, have regular religious marriage ceremonies, which they view as legitimizing their marriages, and do not register them with the civil authorities. They only ask for "supplementary" marriage certificates when they need them to procure municipal or civil services. The re-sult is that firm data on marriages in Ouagadougou are diffi-cult to obtain and those available must be used with caution.

Marriage

According to the census of 1962, both the ratio of men to women in Ouagadougou and the relatively high percentage of married people in the town appear to be unusual in compari-son to most of the developing towns of Sub-Saharan Africa.[6] Tables XX and XXI show the ratio of males to females in the town and their matrimonial status.

The presence of only 1,859 or 3.2 per cent more males than females in the town in 1962 indicates that migrants who came to Ouagadougou arrived in fairly equal proportions according to sex. The data also suggest that many more family groups migrated to the town than is usual for Africa. The rela-tively equal ratio of males to females in the fifteen and over age group is also significant in terms of marriage. The excess of only 888 males in this group is indeed small when one takes into consideration the large number of male students (with respect to female students) in the secondary schools and the equally large number of young male migrants. The higher incidence of single persons in town to married ones is due to the relatively high proportion—28,591 or 49.5 per cent—under twenty years of age. But 77 per cent of the males twenty years of age and over are married, and, if one considers twenty

[6]Southall, *Social Change,* p. 46.

119

TABLE XX. Ratio of Males to Females among the African Population of Ouagadougou

	Number	Per Cent
Males	29,819	51.6
Females	27,960	48.4
TOTAL	57,779	100.0

Ratio of Males to Females by Selected Age Groups

Age Group	Males		Females		Per Cent of Total Population	
	Number	Per Cent	Number	Per Cent	Males	Females
Under fifteen	11,584	38.9	10,727	38.4	20.0	18.5
Fifteen and over (adults)	17,966	60.4	17,078	61.1	31.1	29.6
Unknown	269		155		.4	.3

SOURCE: "Recensement Démographique de la Ville de Ouagadougou" [Resultats Provisoires], Rép. de Haute-Volta, Ministère de l'Économie Nationale, Direction de la Statistique et des Études Économiques, Ouagadougou, Haute-Volta (June 1962), pp. 10–11.

TABLE XXI. Matrimonial Status of the African Population of Ouagadougou

Status	Males	Females	Total
Married	11,572	14,398	25,970
Single	17,275	12,218	29,493
Widowed	339	1,053	1,392
Divorced	163	98	261
No data (Common-law, etc.)	470	193	663
TOTALS	29,819	27,960	57,779

SOURCE: "Recensement Démographique de la Ville de Ouagadougou" [Resultats Provisoires], Rép. de Haute-Volta, Ministère de l'Économie Nationale, Direction de la Statistique et des Études Économiques, Ouagadougou, Haute-Volta (June 1962), pp. 18–19.

as the average age of women at marriage, then 95.5 per cent of these women are married. If, however, one considers fifteen as the age of marriage of the females in Ouagadougou, then 84.3 per cent are married. Given these figures, one suspects that close to 100 per cent of the eligible women in Ouagadougou over eighteen years of age are married.

Table XXII gives data on the first 50 out of the 278 marriages[7] recorded in the Ouagadougou Town Hall in 1963.

An analysis of these fifty marriages reconfirms, if indeed there is still any doubt, that Ouagadougou is a Mossi town. Furthermore, almost two-thirds of those persons whose marriages were recorded are migrants to the town. Significantly enough, both husband and wife of only seven out of the fifty couples were born in Ouagadougou, and among the migrants, only three couples reported that they both had come from the same region. The majority of those persons who were married in Ouagadougou came from regions different from those of their spouses. Perhaps these figures reflect the traditional Mossi preference for village exogamy; however, given the small percentage of cultivators in this sample, it is rash to assume that common origin, whether from district or village, plays no role in the marriages of urban people.

Given the high percentage of Mossi in Ouagadougou, it is not surprising that most Mossi marriages are endogamous. Indeed, only four interethnic marriages were recorded among the fifty surveyed. In two cases Mossi men married Bobo and Boussance women; in another case a Gourounsi man married a Mossi woman; and in the fourth case, a Dioula man married a Samogho woman. All the other marriages in the sample were ethnically endogamous.

There are apparently a number of structural reasons why

TABLE XXII. Analysis of Fifty Marriages

	Males		*Females*	
Ethnic Group	Mossi	43	Mossi	42
	Other	7	Other	8
Place of birth	Ouagadougou (town)	20	Ouagadougou (town)	16
	Elsewhere	30	Elsewhere	34
Occupation	Cultivator	5	Housewife	47
	Civil servant	9	Civil servant	1
	Domestic	1	Dressmaker	1
	Merchant	2	Clerk	1
	Soldier-police	10		
	Trades	23		
Religious Affiliation	Christian	32	Christian	26
	Moslem	5	Moslem	8
	Traditionalist	13	Traditionalist	16

[7] There were also 461 requests for supplementary certificates.

the ethnic groups in Ouagadougou tend toward endogamy. Occupational specialization, especially that based on trade and commerce with visiting members of the same ethnic group, certainly encourages endogamy. Traders have attempted to retain their traditional family organization which facilitates interaction with their visiting countrymen, but have valued endogamy because it facilitated linguistic continuity. Resident Dioula and Hausa have maintained their native languages for several centuries, and one can assume that they would stop transmitting their languages to children only if trade and commerce with their former homelands ceased to be important. But even in the absence of foreign African trade, occupational specialization leads to endogamy. For example, until quite recently young Yoruba females always worked in the markets under the watchful eyes of elders who prevented noncommercial interaction with non-Yoruba, thereby discouraging intermarriage.

The presence or persistence of certain cultural traits among the stranger groups in Ouagadougou also encouraged endogamy or conditioned the type of out-marriages. The existence of the institution of bride wealth among the Hausa, Songhay, and Yoruba has been an important factor in making these groups endogamous. The Yoruba, having occupation, language, and such customs as bride wealth in common, are almost fully endogamous with few known marriages with other groups in town. The Moslem Songhay are less endogamous than the Yoruba, permitting marriages with coreligionists; the Hausa exhibit the least resistance to interethnic marriages, provided that the spouses are Moslem.

High-status Dahomeans and Togolese seldom married outside their group during the colonial period, and their reputation as *raciste* was as much a function of endogamy as it was of their high civil service status and their Christianity. Those Dahomean and Togolese who did intermarry normally found spouses among the Christian elite of other groups. Almost all the Dahomean and Togolese families now living in Ouagadougou are endogamous and, judging from anxiety over their future in the town, are likely to remain so. Endogamy is apparently also characteristic of the Ghanaians living in Ouagadougou. These people are still so closely integrated within their ethnic community and are so closely tied to their homeland that they do not even solemnize weddings in Ouagadougou. When Ghanaian couples wish to marry, they go to Ghana, obtain permission from their respective families, and marry according to their own traditions.

There are relatively few marriages between Africans and Europeans living in Ouagadougou. During 1964 there were not more than ten mixed couples in the town. Of the three known best to the investigator, two were Mossi army officers who had married their wives in France, and one was a civil servant who had also married his wife in France. By 1969 the number of such marriages had increased to about twenty. Most of these marriages were contracted in France between African men and European women. The year 1967 witnessed the rare marriage between an African man and a European woman solemnized in Ouagadougou, but this couple had met in France. Indeed, it is unheard of for an African man to marry a European woman he has met in the town. On the other hand, there are at least two Frenchmen in town who have African wives.

Racially mixed couples in Ouagadougou attract a certain amount of visual attention and are whispered about (especially by European women), but there are few cases of ostricism either by the Africans or Europeans. And whether or not people approve of the marriages of their relatives to Europeans, they tolerate them. This is significant in view of the comments of African male students that, "The man who marries a European woman risks having his father bring her water to drink," a comment which indicates the fear of fundamental social and cultural conflicts if such marriages were to occur.

Mixed couples encounter little difficulty at social functions. They normally sit at tables with African friends, and while they dance with both black and white persons, European men dance more often with European wives of Africans than vice versa. How much of this is due to the heritage of European dominance is difficult to ascertain.

The survey of the fifty marriages in Ouagadougou did reveal a high rate of what one may call religious endogamy. Only eight cases of interreligious marriages were found in the group. However, there are many indications that religious particularism per se was not the major factor in these marriages. First of all, the juxtaposition of traditional Moslem and Christian names in the register suggests the conversion of many persons prior to marriage. This shows commitment to

123

modern civism, a normal concomitant of conversion to a "modern" religion.

One can even say that Christians tend to be more modern than traditional in their outlook on life, and the fact that, among those sampled, the greatest single religious group was composed of Christians tends to bear this out. The relatively high number of *Winnam pous'neba* who registered their marriages seems to indicate three things: first, that traditionalists in town are dissatisfied with the lack of an elaborate traditional wedding ceremony and now get married in the Town Hall *and* have a wedding; second, that they have no objections to recording their marriages, and, third, that lower-status men believe that registering their marriage will prevent their wives from running away with impunity. On the other hand, the small number of Moslem marriages recorded at the Town Hall appears to be due to the Moslems' lack of concern for the secular recognition of their marriages. Moslems, like Christians, have their marriage and wedding ceremonies, but unlike Christians, many orthodox Moslems view the ceremony at the Town Hall as a "Christian" marriage practice and forego it. Nevertheless, most married people eventually apply for supplementary marriage certificates at the Town Hall since they must have municipal or civil papers.

One surprising feature of this survey of marriages in Ouagadougou is the high incidence of civil marriages among the tradesmen. Members of this occupational group account for only about 20 per cent of workers listed in the census of 1962, but they constitute 46 per cent of all the married men in the survey. One apparent reason for this is that for men to have become tradesmen, they must have lived in town for a long time since it was only there that they were able to learn trades. This means that tradesmen, along with civil servants, are among the most urbanized of the Ouagadougou population. Moreover, their contact with mission teachers and, occasionally with European bosses, probably resulted in a more rapid rate of acculturation than among lower-status groups. Living in town also meant that they knew the importance of civil papers—a trait which has always characterized the French and people under their rule.

The rather high percentage of marriages among government employees (civil servants, soldiers, policemen, and *gardes*) in the survey is quite understandable given their participation in administration and, especially for the civil servants, their willingness to adopt Western values. The pressure on soldiers and *gardes* to legalize their marriages stems from the insistence of the administration that they produce civil papers before obtaining family allotment for their children. This became necessary when the Upper Volta government officials abandoned the easy rule that existed during the colonial period, and insisted that proof of "marriage" and biological parenthood be produced. Formerly, African soldiers and *gardes* could obtain allotments for any of their "children" (often the children of relatives who in the traditional system were their own), and since many soldiers were polygynous as well, scores of children received French Government funds. The Upper Volta Government has not only been regulating the number of children receiving allotments, but has been encouraging soldiers and *gardes*—persons whose values are primarily traditional—to legalize their marriages. The often unstated hope is that these men will remain monogamous.

In general, civil servants take a Western view toward marriage. For many of them, participating in both the civil and religious marriage ceremonies is the only way to take a wife. Even Moslems and polygynist civil servants generally consider the civil marriage as a *sine qua non* for establishing the married state. So strong is the value of civil marriage in this group that even if such men are given additional wives under the traditional system, they tend to legalize these unions. This is done even though no one would condemn nonlegalized unions of this sort as concubinage.

The actual marriage ceremonies of the people of Ouagadougou are related to their style of life, religion, and socioeconomic status. New immigrant cultivators who are sent wives from the rural areas simply consummate their marriages when the young woman comes of age (normally age eighteen or nineteen) without public ceremonies. Moslem cultivators and their male relatives visit the family of the prospective bride on an appointed day, give them the customary marriage gifts[8] (the bride wealth here is purely symbolic consisting, in most cases, of about 1,000 francs—4 dollars), and hold a *sadaqua* (a religious ceremony) to solemnize the actual mar-

[8] Mossi Moslems have adopted the custom of the bride wealth, but it is symbolic among them and is more "religious" than social in nature.

riage. Later that day there may be feasting and drinking depending, of course, upon the resources of the bridegroom and his family. Generally, no civil ceremony takes place and a supplementary marriage certificate is obtained later.

The marriages of tradesmen and lower-level clerks and civil servants are more elaborate and expensive. It is at this level that people begin to have three distinct rituals and ceremonies: the religious ceremony, the civil ceremony, and the wedding reception. The religious and civil ceremonies have no fixed order of priority, especially among the Christians, but the wedding reception is usually held after the other two rituals have been concluded. Among Moslems, the traditional gift-giving and religious ceremony are the same as for cultivators. The civil ceremony and the wedding reception may not take place until one week after the religious ceremony. This delay does not affect the consummation of the marriage, however, because the Moslems consider their religious ritual the most important marriage ceremony. Among Christian civil servants and other high socio-economic groups, the church ceremony "before the eyes of God and the congregation" is the important one, and this must be concluded before the marriage may be consummated. When, for financial or personal reasons, Christians are married at the Town Hall before their unions are solemnized by the church, they are expected to be continent until this is done.

The actual Christian wedding of members of this socio-economic group reveals in all of its ambiguity the problem of syncretizing traditional customs with the requirements of Christianity and modern life. The following is a brief description of a wedding, attended by the author, of a young Catholic carpenter to a young woman of Dapoya II, at the parish church:

At 6:30 A.M. the bride and about five women arrived at the church by taxi and were joined in front of the church by the bridegroom and his friends who had arrived by private automobile. The bride was dressed in a very clean, but frayed, white dress, wore white shoes and a head cover of white satin. The women who accompanied her were dressed in traditional clothes made of imported prints. The bridegroom wore traditional Mossi clothing made of white imported cloth; some of his companions wore European clothes and others, traditional garments. The two groups made no contact with each other. Later, the bride's female companions left her standing at the church door and went in to pray. She stood there nervously waiting for the ceremonies to begin, showing her nervousness and discomfort by placing her right hand to the side of her face, a gesture typical of demure or embarrassed rural Mossi women. A parish priest came out and speaking to her in French, apologized for the absence of the regular priest and asked her for the bridegroom. She did not understand his language and, looking quite embarrassed, turned toward the bridegroom and his friends who then hurried over. The priest asked the groom to step forward and told him that the ceremony would start. Thereupon the priest preceded the group into the church, followed by the groom and his friends. The bride was left to follow the group all alone. The bridegroom's companions did not leave him until he reached the altar, where he was joined by his bride. The marriage ceremony was typically Catholic. When it was over, the couple walked down the aisle together, but without touching each other. Their friends joined them at the door and the men and women immediately separated, milling about for a few minutes. The guests made no attempt to congratulate either the bride or groom, nor were pictures taken. A taxi was hailed and his companion followed in their small car.

This ceremony showed quite plainly the persistence of traditional male-female behavior even within the context of a new institution, the Catholic religion. It also shows that despite the attempts the Church is making to adapt to local culture, its norms for male-female behavior continue to be those characteristic of Western societies. What is also significant here is that these young people had no one in the entourage who was either able or willing to act as a cultural broker and to teach them the norms of Catholic marriage ceremonies.

The civil marriage ceremonies of people in the lower-status groups are relatively quiet affairs. The couples, with their witnesses, go to the Town Hall where they are married according to the laws of the Upper Volta Republic by the Mayor or by one of his assistants. Tradesmen, merchants, soldiers, and policemen normally use witnesses from their professions but sometime choose relatives as witnesses whether these are illit-

erate cultivators or educated civil servants. As of now there
does not appear to be a trend among low-status people to
choose witnesses according to occupational status. This is in
contrast to clerks and civil servants who tend to use literate
witnesses, even if these are foreigners. The secular wedding
celebration of people in this lower-status group is invariably
held on the evening of the civil and/or religious ceremonies. It
is closely modeled on that of the high-status people, but, of
course, it is never as elaborate.

The model marriage for most of the people in Ouagadougou, except immigrant cultivators, is that of the Christian
civil servant. This model is clearly a local variant of French
marriage practices which urban people have intermittently
observed since the time of Governor Hesling. The ability
to adopt such a marriage pattern is, of course, a function of income, religion, and previous marital status. Most high-status
urban Christians like their lower-status coreligionists, consider the religious ritual as the most important part of their
marriage festivities. The banns for these marriages are announced in the local church, but, as in many contemporary
Western countries, these notices are a mere formality or more
properly, a social announcement. The actual religious ceremony is usually held on a Saturday during or after the early
morning Mass. It is becoming more fashionable, especially in
the Cathedral of Ouagadougou, to celebrate the Nuptial Mass
some time between 8:00 A.M. and 10:00 A.M. If one of the
principals is non-Catholic, the practice is to perform the marriage in the rectory and let the Catholic members of the bridal
party receive the sacrament during the Mass afterward.

There is little difference between the actual marriage rite of
prestigious persons in Ouagadougou and that of contemporary
Western Europeans. The bride wears a Western-style white
gown and veil, white shoes, gloves, and so on, and is accompanied by bridesmaids, usually wearing Western clothing.
The bridegroom similarly wears Western formal dress, using
either a white or black tuxedo jacket with formal trousers.
His male escorts either wear comparable clothes or simply
white shirts, black bow ties, and black trousers.[9] When the

[9]In a rather interesting wedding witnessed in 1968 a young educated
couple and their friends wore modern "African" dress and deliberately tried
to "Africanize" the "modern" Catholic marriage rituals. They even invited
traditional musicians and dancers to form two columns between which the

marriage is celebrated during the Mass, wedding guests who arrive before the bridal couple walk into the church and sit in their usual places, women on the right and men on the left. The bride and groom arrive together since he and his escorts call for the bride and her attendants, either at her house or at the house of the dressmaker. They are met at the church door by the priest who then precedes the bridal party to the altar. In contrast to low-status people, the bridegroom holds the arm of the bride, but the ushers do not touch the bridesmaids. Those guests who may have been waiting outside for the party to arrive, then filter into the church, join in the service, and take communion if they so desire. (This aspect of the ceremony is common to all Catholic marriages and needs no further description.) At the end of the ceremony the bridegroom may or may not kiss the bride before they walk up the aisle toward the front of the church to be photographed. Meanwhile, guests mill around congratulating the relatives of the couple even more so than they do the bride and groom, thus showing that they still value the corporate nature of marriage. When the picture-taking is finally over, the couple goes to a wedding breakfast before going to the Town Hall for the civil marriage, if this has not already taken place.

The civil marriage ceremony is important to all high-status groups in Ouagadougou, but is really more important to Moslems than to Christians. For, while the Christian woman has the status of "bride" conferred upon her at the church, the high-status Moslem woman does not really become a "bride" until she goes to the Town Hall to be married in the civil ceremony. Indeed, this is often the first occasion for the Moslem bride to be involved in any of the marriage ceremonies and is therefore the time for her to wear the white veil, the hallmark of a modern bride for all young women, Moslems and Christians alike. Until this time the role of the high-status Moslem woman in the marriage ceremony is not different from that of her lower-status sisters. She, too, does not go to the rural areas for her religious marriage ceremony; she plays no role in the giving and receiving of the symbolic bride wealth; and, of course, she could not look forward to being "married" in the

---

wedding party walked to and from the church for the ceremony. The musicians also played and trilled the traditional greeting in honor of the groom when the couple left the church.

mosque, often considered the "Moslem's church." The Moslem bridegroom also favors the civil ceremony because he, too, can and often does take the opportunity to wear the black tuxedo deemed the most appropriate for modern weddings. Some young Moslems, especially those now returning from universities, have abandoned Western formal wear for a modernized burnoose and a "Sékou Touré" beaded cap. Nevertheless, their brides continue to wear Western-style gowns and veils. All Moslem couples employ Western institutions such as bridesmaids and escorts for the civil ceremony, and these are dressed according to the Western mode, similar to that worn in the religious ceremony of the Christians.

High-status couples naturally prefer to be married by the Mayor of the town rather than by one of his assistants. The legal aspect of the ceremony is quite similar to that employed by mayors in French municipalities. Here, however, the Mayor is often a friend or acquaintance of the young people and usually gives some advice to the married couple and praises their senior relatives for having reared such worthy young people. The witnesses to such marriages are usually literate individuals, the exception being illiterate chiefs or persons with a great deal of traditional prestige. This ceremony, too, concludes with the usual picture-taking and congratulations proffered to the bride, bridegroom, and their relatives. Then the bridal party and guests usually go to the home of a relative or friend of the couple for a nuptial luncheon.[10]

The nuptial luncheon often reveals the social distinction between the high-status couple and guests and low-status relatives and friends, because this is the point at which different styles of life conflict and where different socio-economic statuses among the relatives and guests must be recognized and taken into consideration. The food practices of lower-status or rural relatives are quite different from the ceremonial ones of guests. Rural relatives do not eat the expensive hors d'oeuvres, salads, cheeses, and pastries which are *de rigueur* at such luncheons and are amused that the urbanites eat *nansara dibo* (white people's food). They prefer the more solid traditional food, and the traditional millet beer rather than wine,

---

[10] A feature which has been added since 1964 is that of sticking cotton balls in the ears of the bridal party and blowing car horns as the party leaves the Town Hall.

modern beer, or even soda. Therefore, unless care is taken to provide traditional and separate eating facilities for these people, they leave the reception as soon as food is served and do not return. A problem for lower-status urban relatives is that close kinship alone does not warrant a place of honor at the wedding table. The result is that they often participate in the affair by helping to serve the guests.

A tricky problem at the nuptial luncheon is the seating of male and female guests. Efforts are made to seat European male guests with European women because people know that this is a Western custom. Since, however, the European guests are not always of the same social status, seating them all together is often interpreted as a manifestation of racial prejudice by both Africans and Europeans. To counter this, hostesses often place high-status Africans at the same table with Europeans of comparable status. But since the wives of even the high-status African men prefer to sit by themselves, the situation turns out to be a bit uncomfortable for the Europeans. Another problem here is a generational one. Whereas the younger, French-educated African men do like to sit with their wives, they are embarrassed to do so in the presence of elder Africans who invariably sit with men. The unspoken assumption here is that the old men, true to the tradition that men never sit publically with wives, would consider such behavior of the young as unpleasantly Western. Some mistakes inevitably occur when attempts are made to seat people according to style of life and status. Happily, the social climate at these receptions rapidly becomes so informal that people wander from table to table.

An elaborate wedding reception marks the climax of the marriage ceremony among high-status people in Ouagadougou. This is held in any of a variety of places depending upon the actual position and wealth of the people concerned. The most popular place for such receptions is the Sous-Officier's Mess in the military camp of the town, but others include La Maison des Jeunes and several bars such as Chez Léon, the Buffet Hotel, and recently the Hotel de l'Indépendance. Some prominent men hold receptions in the gardens of their villas. As invitations to such receptions are formally distributed, all except high-prestige guests are expected to produce them before gaining admission.

The cost of the wedding reception, including renting the

"hall," hiring an orchestra, and purchasing food and drink is normally borne by the relatives of both the bride and groom. Sometimes the wealthy parent of one partner may bear the entire cost. Even so, the work of planning the reception, borrowing chairs and other equipment, and cooking the food occupies the time and energies of both families. At times two or even more couples hold their wedding receptions together in an effort to reduce the individual cost. As to be expected, this raises many problems, especially when the guests are of different social backgrounds.

Normally more people attend the wedding reception than either the religious or civil marriage ceremonies. This is especially true in the case of Moslems since their ceremony is often out of town. It is also true for Christians since their religious ceremony is usually too early in the morning for most people to attend. Likewise, few people have the time to attend the civil ceremony because it is normally held during working hours. Thus, except for rural relatives and very old urban relatives, all the kinsmen and friends of the married couple try to attend the reception. This makes the wedding reception the most public of all the marriage ceremonies and the one which, while it brings the most prestige to the couple, costs the most money. Expensive receptions have been severely criticized by the Catholics as a terrible waste of money at one of the most crucial periods in the young marrieds' lives. But, so important is this institution for the social legitimization of marriage that it is doubtful whether it will be abandoned.

The wedding reception starts about 9.00 P.M. Guests arrive before the bridal party and, after showing their written invitations, are assigned seats on the basis of kinship to the couple or social standing. Ordinarily, the higher the social status of the guest, the nearer he is to the bridal table if not actually at it. If any Europeans are invited, they either sit at the bridal table or off by themselves. Drinks are also served on the basis of social status. The table of the bride and groom is liberally supplied with drinks, including champagne, and so are the tables of high-status guests. The tables of the ordinary folk are supplied with beer for non-Moslems, and with soft drinks and fruit juices for Moslems and women. The task of serving is usually performed by bridesmaids and their escorts, but low-status relatives and friends also help.

The arrival of the bridal couple marks the beginning of the

formal ceremony. As they appear at the door, the bridesmaids and their escorts join them and accompany them to their table. Guest then approach and congratulate the couple until the master of ceremonies announces that the bride and groom will begin the dance. The couple dances while the bridesmaids and escorts stand at the side of the dancing platform; later they join them in the second dance. From this point on, general dancing starts and important male guests dance with the bride.

The next important feature of the reception is speeches. Representatives from the families of both bride and bridegroom deliver speeches. They congratulate the bride and groom on choosing each other and encourage them to live worthy and honorable lives. Some speakers add a new note, admonishing the couple to help in national construction and thereby show the world the nature of "Voltaic Man." These speeches really mark the end of the formal ceremony, but the guests dance to orchestral music until the early hours of the next morning. Sometime during the night the couple leaves, but there is little or no attempt to be secretive about this departure. Their main concern is that their guests remain and enjoy themselves. The festivities are enlivened by the distribution of more drinks, fried breads, and roasted mutton.

The institution of the "honeymoon" is not well established among this or any of the other socio-economic groups in the town. The couple may take a few days off from work in order to celebrate their marriage, but, except for students who take their wives away when they resume their studies, there are no regular postmarital trips. Nor are there regular festivities subsequent to the marriage such as "Second Sunday" found in some European-influenced colonial and former colonial areas. There are, however, occasional receptions (*vin d'honneur*) held by friends and influential relatives in honor of the married couple.

The pattern of gift-giving is emerging at the weddings of high-status people in Ouagadougou and represents an interesting convergence of traditional and European practices. European guests to these weddings always bring gifts and some Africans are also beginning to bring gifts. While the giving of gifts by Europeans is part of their traditional custom, this practice by Africans is only partially so. In the traditional system individuals did not give wedding gifts to couples, but families gave gifts to families or to individual spouses. Thus, the help which relatives and friends give during the marriage ceremonies is traditional, as are the furniture and comestibles which both urban and rural relatives give. Indeed, the custom is that when a relative is being married, all relatives and the friends of relatives help. But today when Africans bring gifts to a newly married couple at the wedding, they are acting more in the modern than in the traditional way.

Some members of the high-status group of urban Mossi have elaborated a form of gift-giving from what was a minor part of their traditional marriage practice: the presentation of gifts to a bride by her relatives. For several successive days and nights after the wedding, female relatives of the bride carry her belongings in procession to the home of her husband. Here, they sing, clap, and ululate as they place their bundles in her new room. The implication is that it is the husband's task to furnish the house and provide food for his wife. Then the bride's relatives organize themselves during the late afternoon or early evening of a specific day and go in a final procession to the home of the bride, this time taking her personal gifts.[11] They place these gifts under a shed for all the people to see, and then the bride, her new husband, and his relatives welcome the visitors who sing, clap, and shrill. The bride's brother's wife, her *dakia* (or "joking relative"), accompanies the gift-bringers and "jokes" all the way to the house and afterward in the compound. She, too, brings gifts but in the oldest basket she can find. These include such things as a small piece of soap, a bit of broken pottery, a few grains of locust bean condiments, and a piece of old cloth. The bride takes careful note of all the gifts she receives, and takes a few items such as spoons, plates, and dishes, and gives them to her bridesmaids. Then, the bridegroom is called upon to show his

---

[11] Following is a list of the gifts which a bride in Ouagadougou received from her relatives on Sunday, August 30, 1964: 36 spoons, 8 cups, 59 plates, 2 water goblets, 26 enamel plates, 20 large plates, 1 jar, 3 straw baskets, 10 *pagnes* (wraparound cloths), 3 forks, 13 calabashes, 1 salad bowl, 3 buckets, 1 flour sifter, 5 blankets, 6 silk headkerchiefs, 2 ladles for stirring *saghabo*, 12 baskets, 20 small calabash ladles, 44 large dishes with covers, 16 small dishes with covers, 4 casserole dishes, 2 earthenware pots, 1 Fulani mat, 2 tablecloths, 2 liter bottles of oil, 1 can of butter, 1 ladle for stirring millet, 2 balls of local soap, 2 sheets, 3 brooms, 1 local string bag, 1 basket filled with locust bean balls, 1 locally made iron coal-pot, 12,000 francs to buy condiments (1 old Mossi hat given by the *dakia*).

appreciation to his wife's relatives. He entertains them with food and soft drinks and gives them money. He also summons taxis to take the women to their respective homes when the festivities are over.

This ceremony does not appear to be Mossi in origin, but a practice borrowed from the Hausa or other African groups. It certainly does not exist among the rural Mossi; there the little Mossi bride went to her husband's home long before she even knew how to keep house and was usually taught the womanly arts by her husband's mother and his female relatives. In town, with girls getting married after they have arrived at maturity, this institution for "home building" was easily borrowed by the Mossi from their urban neighbors.

The marriage ceremonies just described represent the goal of most of the young women belonging to the clerk and civil servant social status group. Their chances for achieving this goal are a function of their family background, and the ability of the men they marry to give them this kind of marriage. The problem for some young women, especially the Moslems, is that the men they chose to marry may have other wives and may not wish to undertake such elaborate marriage ceremonies. They are thus deprived of the pleasure of a large wedding and establishing the first menage for their husbands. The Christian girl who chooses to marry a polygynist cannot have a church ceremony, even though she may have the civil ceremony and a wedding reception. Polygyny thereby prevents people of this status group from having the ideal weddings even though they can afford them.

Most married women of Ouagadougou, like many of their rural sisters, prefer monogamy to polygyny. Nevertheless, many of these wives accept the decision of their husbands to take another spouse and thereby find themselves in polygynous households. The census of 1962 does not give data on the number of polygynous households in Ouagadougou; nor does it give any indication of the average number of wives in those households which are polygynous. Some idea about the incidence of polygyny in the town can be garnered from the data (see Table XXIII) on 252 families collected by the Director of Social Servies.

The incidence of polygyny in Ouagadougou must be viewed against the background of the traditional cultures of the dominant Mossi and other groups in which polygyny is the ideal

135

TABLE XXIII. **Polygyny and Occupational Status**

Occupations of Men	Number of Wives					
	One	Two	Three	Four	Five	Six
Cultivators	59	27	3	1	3	1
Tradesmen and merchants	40	11	2	3	1	
Soldiers and policemen	30	22	9	2	1	
Clerks and civil servants	25	7	3			

for men, especially mature men. The primary traditional reason given for preferring polygyny is that the more wives a man has, the better his chances of having progeny and thereby perpetuating his own lineage. As we have seen the Mossi do not have the bride price, but have instead long-term friendships characterized by mutual help and gift exchange—including wives. Therefore, the number of wives a man receives is an indication of his standing in the community and an important index of his relations with his fellows. Second, this ability the head of an extended family or sublineage has to obtain wives for male dependents gives him power over them and reinforces his own position within the local community.

Given this traditional background and the recent influx of migrants to Ouagadougou, it is not surprising that approximately 37.2 per cent of the cultivators in town have multiple spouses. Moreover, since young betrothed women from rural areas are still being sent to join husbands in the town, the persistence of a rural pattern of polygyny among cultivators is understandable. That over 53 per cent of the group of soldiers and policemen is polygynous is also not surprising. These men are quite traditional in outlook and mostly illiterate, but comparatively well off since they work for the government. Thus, of all low-status groups in Ouagadougou they are the most likely to attract many low-status women as wives. The presence of some 29 per cent polygynous households among the tradesmen and merchants shows that these men have fewer traditional links for obtaining plural wives and find it more difficult or inconvenient to have many wives. It is interesting to note that while approximately 28.6 per cent of the clerks and civil servants have plural wives, they are the only group which does not report any more than three wives per household (although there are a few high civil servants and politicians with as many as five wives). The attitude of high-status men toward polygyny is quite complex. They, too, desire children and therefore retain the traditional attitudes toward polygyny. Yet, they desire to have modern and educated wives as well as traditional ones. The result is an initial conflict which is only resolved through time and by taking additional spouses.

The attitude toward polygyny in Ouagadougou, and indeed in all of the Upper Volta, is so mixed that any inquiry about it has to be discreet and circumspect. Since 1962 the Upper Volta Government has been inveighing against polygyny, but even the President of the Republic had to concede in May 1964 that is was "difficult to anticipate unanimity" for his plan to abolish this institution. He said then that he expected resistance from those who feared that ending this institution would destroy their family life, and from the chiefs, those "old feudalists who need plenty of fresh meat to heat their bones." Nevertheless, he felt that "everyone was basically willing to concede that polygyny is retrograde and pernicious for our future generations." He added, "It is not possible to build a young, dynamic society, composed of love and mutual understanding, on polygamy .... We who wish to build a new and strong society must impose monogamy as a rule of law."[12]

The President was right in saying that some chiefs, old men, and polygynists opposed abolition of polygyny, but there are also persons in Ouagadougou who think that the opposition to polygyny stems from an unwholesome belief in Catholic and Western values. There is also the feeling, muted of course, that many officials who publicly inveigh against polygyny are guilty of adultery and concubinage and would be better off with plural wives.

The real difficulty with polygyny for the urban Mossi, as well as for their rural brothers, is that it is still a major cause of marital instability. Moreover, life in town is subjecting this institution to additional strain. For example, male cultivators complain that the main threat to polygyny in Ouagadougou is that women can abandon their conjugal domicile more easily than they could in the rural areas. Because of the changes in the traditional occupations of women, few complaints are heard that polygyny is uneconomical in town. In fact, the cultivators declare that their wives can still cultivate, still go to market, and are even more able to help themselves and their families because of the greater opportunities for petty trading

[12]*Carrefour Africain*, No. 111 (31 May 1964), p. 2.

in the town than in the rural areas. The wives of cultivators interviewed usually disliked polygyny but felt helpless to oppose plural wives. Indeed, they often cooperate with co-wives in caring for children during the planting season, especially when their husband takes one wife to the farm and leaves her children at home with cowives. Often when a wife goes to trade in the market she leaves her children with the cowife responsible for the housework on that day.

Polygynous tradesmen and merchants assert that they do not consider having plural wives either an asset or a liability. The query as to economic liability of polygyny usually brought the response that these wives helped out by cultivating or by trading in the market place. Merchants especially stress the desirability of having children and believe quite firmly that it is better to be polygynous than to have affairs with other women. Interestingly, the wives of polygynous men in this group, like the wives of cultivators, felt that polygyny was "the affair of men" and that women could do little about it.

The attitudes of soldiers and policemen toward polygynous marriages do not differ too much from those of cultivators. Many men said that they were "given wives" and that it was good to have as many wives as one could get. These men deny that they are guilty of the charges, often heard in Ouagadougou, that they are the largest group of wife-abductors in the town—a reputation attributed to the fact that husbands of abducted women are afraid to complain about the police and soldiers—and that women are attracted to them because of their money. On the other hand, a number of these men were heard to admit in court that they did give refuge to wives of others simply because they could not chase away women who came "and sat at their homes." As could be expected, the attitudes of wives of the soldiers and policemen toward polygyny are difficult to evaluate. Their standard replies range from the statement that it is a problem of men and the women could do nothing about it, to an embarrased admission of love for the polygynous husband in question.

The more articulate polygynists among clerks, civil servants, and politicians took pains to justify their actions. For example, it appears to be true, despite the cliché, that some educated men become polygynous because they need a modern wife as well as a traditional one. Persons cite the case of a well-known Catholic civil servant-politician who did his best to "elevate" his wife, but finally gave up in despair and took a concubine. In this case he ignored the censure of the Church in order to have the best possible social life. Many high-status men often cite the desire for children as the reason for polygyny. The only contradiction here is that they are often already fathers when they take additional spouses. Finally, some men simply admitted they fell in love with women other than their wives and married them. That some of these men are also Catholic and are fully conscious of the strictures of the Church against polygyny seems not to have inhibited their polygynous relations. Indeed, it is the polygynist clerk, civil servant, or politician who most aggressively defends the practice and often initiates discussion of this subject with the cautious researcher. Frequently the information is volunteered that the cowives get along well together; that the junior wives consider the senior to be their mentor; and that the wives aid each other with the household work and the children. One high-ranking civil servant who works in the country leaves one wife in Ouagadougou to take care of his school-age children while keeping the other with him.

Conflicting opinions about polygyny are as common among the cowives of polygynous men in this group as they are among the wives of soldiers and policemen. The senior wives of these men are apt to be resigned to having cowives. This is true of the nonliterate senior wives as well as literate senior wives. The nonliterate senior wife can do little about her husband taking cowives because, more than most wives in Ouagadougou, she is financially dependent upon him. Such women have long ceased to cultivate, do little petty trading (except occasionally before the gate), and get almost all money from their husbands. Moreover, these women have little hope of establishing any meaningful marital relations with other men if they sought divorce. Besides, they still fear, and with good reason, that if they were divorced they would lose status among women; lose their status in life; and lose control of all their children over four or five years of age.

The senior literate wives (civil servants) of high-status polygynists do not have the same fear of economic deprivation if they seek and obtain a separation or divorce from their husbands. They have their own salaries, and even if, upon marriage, they had signed a statement at the Town Hall indicating that they wished to pool their salaries with those of their husbands (*ménage à deux*), they could easily break this contract. Nevertheless, they, more than any of the other women in the town, dread the social stigma which would accompany a divorce. They fear also that they would not find an equally good marriage, would be considered a *femme perdue,* and would lose their children. Therefore, these women also accept, however unwillingly, the entrance of cowives into their families. One such woman even indicated, during an interview, that if she discovered that her husband had a "concubine" she would initiate his marriage to the woman. She reasoned that it was preferable to have such a woman in the household where she could see what the woman received from her husband, rather than not know what she and her children were losing to the concubine.

The typical woman who marries a high-status person who is already married usuually gives "love" as the reason for so doing. Nonetheless, one can never discount the possibility that social security or mobility played a role in her decision, especially if her economic position is weak. The decision of an educated and employed woman to enter the *ménage* of a high-status man is also usually attributed to love, but one wonders whether or not it was love alone since love is still so subordinate to status in the marriages of urban, educated women. Indeed, the leading polygynist in the history of contemporary Ouagadougou was a very important man. And most educated polygynists have higher statuses than their most highly educated wives.

Polygyny apparently does not produce many more problems in household arrangements in Ouagadougou than it does in the rural areas. Urban cultivators house their wives either in separate round houses or in separate rooms in oblong houses. The tradesmen-merchants and soldiers-policemen house their wives either in separate small houses in their compounds or in separate rooms in their houses. The clerks, civil servants, and politicians either house their wives in separate rooms in large houses, or, in the case of really high-ranking civil servants and politicians, in separate houses. These housing arrangements permit each wife to be the center of her own household and, except for cooperation in keeping children when another wife is at work, each woman is responsible for her own children's welfare. In one case, a female civil servant whose child was ill could not depend upon her cowives—including one who was a nurse—to take care of it, and she had to cancel an interview to take care of her child. Of course, cowives keep each other's children from time to time and, in the case of cultivators and merchants previously mentioned, women keep each other's children in order to free the cowives to work.

Despite the Mossi ideology that cowives do get along well together, there is ample evidence that rural polygynous husbands had to work hard at keeping peace and harmony in their households. Evidence in Ouagadougou seems to suggest that the task of the urban polygynist is no easier. The presence of cowives of different socio-economic backgrounds in the same house appears to be posing new problems for urban polygynous households. For example, in those households where one wife is a clerk or civil servant, there is a tendency for the working wife only to take care of her own children and leave the other wives to do most of the cooking and housework. One social worker reported that as the only literate and working wife of a civil servant, she arose in the morning at about 6:00 and a cowife brought her and the husband hot water for their toilet. The social worker then prepared water for her child's toilet and prepared his breakfast, but that the wife whose five-day term it was to cook meals served breakfast to all the adults. This wife also prepared lunch and dinner for the entire family. The social worker said that initially she tried to help out, but she could not follow the five-day schedule. Therefore, she gave up all housework except to clean her own room and take care of her child. This woman did not feel that her cowives were her servants and insisted that they were doing only simple household tasks, something they ought not to complain about since they had no incomes. Nor did she feel any obligation to give presents of money to any of her cowives. She insisted that it was her husband's duty to give them money, and a growing problem was that his money often ran short, whereupon she had to help him out. If this is indeed the case, then it is likely that there is built-in conflict where there is disparity in socio-economic status among wives in polygynous families.

Polygyny in Ouagadougou has created few, if any, purely social problems for the families concerned. The cultivators in town, like those in the rural areas, do not interact socially in public with their wives. The same is true of all the other groups in town except very high-status clerks and civil servants. But even here the relations of men and their wives in public are still formal and quite different from the French norms which are taken for a model. High-status polygynous men often take more than one wife to official functions, but these women stay apart, forming a group by themselves, or sit individually with friends or relatives. Their husbands do not sit with them; nor do people find it strange that neither they nor monogamists sit with wives at these functions.

What is true for formal social occasions is even more true for informal ones. Women in polygynous households in all socio-economic groups have retained the traditional freedom of visiting their relatives and family friends. They often appear at weddings by themselves since no one expects them to be accompanied by their husbands.

There are few administrative problems for polygynous families. A man may legally marry as many women as he pleases and have these marriages registered by the Town Clerk in Ouagadougou. Of course, the Christian church does not solemnize polygynous marriages, but Islam does. But since the Christian marriage ritual is only one of the marriage rituals of the urban people, its omission is often unnoticed and does not pose a social problem. Whether or not there is a religious ceremony, polygynists can and do have secular wedding receptions either at their homes or at various places in the town, depending upon their financial means.

The data of this chapter demonstrate that changing attitudes, changing sentiments, and the need to adapt to the exigencies of urban life are encouraging the emergence of new patterns of courtship and marriage in Ouagadougou. Traditional patterns will persist as long as rural cultivators migrate to town and marry female migrants. However, unless migrant cultivators marry girls sent to them from home, they too accept the emerging norms. These include the desire of young men and women to make their own decisions about whom they will marry. Such new practices are being accepted even by low-status men whose attitudes are still largely similar to those of rural people, mainly because they have little choice in the matter.

Male and female civil servants and clerks tend to be quite pragmatic and manipulatory about courtship and their choice of marriage partners. Their main desire is to obtain spouses with the requisite education necessary for remunerative employment, and thereby the income with which to live a modern life.

The tendency of the Ouagadougou people to solemnize their marriages and to register them with the civil authorities is due to the necessity of conforming to the bureaucratic requirement of modern urban life. Indeed, people seek to legitimize their marriage with the state in order to facilitate their family's future access to the amenities of the town. On the other hand, the style of wedding that people have is a function of income, religion, and acculturation to European norms.

Changing attitudes rather than legal prohibition and economic necessity are at present the greatest potential force for changes in the incidence of polygyny among the people of Ouagadougou. Polygynous cultivators, artisans, laborers, and merchants practice polygyny for the usual traditional reasons and seldom are criticized for their marital state. High-status polygynists likewise cite the need for children and the power of emotion as reasons for taking plural spouses. Of course, women in all social categories, low-status or high, generally prefer monogamy, but feel helpless in the face of families who, even today, place them in polygynous households or of husbands who desire plural wives. Even economically independent high-status wives tolerate polygyny since they fear divorce, separation, and loss of children more than the status of plural wife. Given these attitudes and practices, there is very little that the women can do to change their statuses. Changes may come about if the cost of educating children in the town induces men to have smaller families and thereby eliminates one of the traditional rationales for polygyny. It is also possible that the Christian church and the politicians in their joint efforts to Christianize and modernize the town's population may succeed in changing attitudes toward polygyny, or may pass laws abolishing it.

CHAPTER V

Family Life and Status Profiles

Family life in Ouagadougou is conditioned by economic, social, and cultural factors new to the migrants from the rural areas, factors which pose problems even to the better paid members of the elite community. An increasingly difficult problem for the families of cultivator-gardeners is to find a place to live. Table XXIV shows that most of these people live in the outlying wards: Hamdalaye, Nyoghsin, Tampouy, Tanghin, Gounghin, Ipelesse, Sabin, Larhallé, and Zoghona. This is not because they choose to live in areas closest to their peri-urban farms, but rather because these wards are still undeveloped or are in the process of development, and it was in such areas that they could most readily obtain land on which to build houses. They appeal to chiefs for land in the name of the Mossi tradition (that every man should be given land unless he has a bad character and would "spoil the village") and in return give presents to their benefactors.

Those cultivator families who still live in central Ouagadougou (in Kamsaoghin, Bilbalgo, Dapoya II, and Samandin-St. Julien) are mainly older Christians and retainers of the Mogho Naba whose families have had house lots for at least two generations and who prefer to remain near their church and sovereign. However, they too are finding it difficult to live in central Ouagadougou. House lots which formerly had no intrinsic value have now become valuable real estate. Formerly, urban householders paid no taxes, but as soon as the municipality divided the wards into lots, they had to pay some 30,000 C.F.A. (approximately $120.00) for a *permis d'habitation urbain* (a permit to live on a town lot, not a tax on the lot itself). Initially those cultivators who wished to remain in town but had no money divided their lots into two portions, sold the "improvements" on one part (often a small hut, a well, or even sun-dried mud-bricks), and with this money paid for their *permis*. Later on, these cultivator-gardeners discovered that land values in Ouagadougou rose so rapidly that from a strictly economic viewpoint, it was better to sell the remaining half and leave the center of town. The money they received for the "improvements" on their second half was often more than many could have earned for many years and enough to last older people for the rest of their lives.[1]

The families of cultivator-gardeners in Ouagadougou spend more money for houses and furnishings than those in the rural areas. Most of the newer style oblong houses have windows, and there are small windows even in the existing round huts. Doors are more common in Ouagadougou than in the rural areas. They afford their occupants greater privacy and protection from thieves. Most houses also have some kind of blinds and screens to protect the sleeping quarters from prying eyes. On the other hand, bedding has not changed; it consists primarily of Fulani-made straw mats. Occasionally these families possess tables and chairs and boxes for clothing and other valuables; however, the women use small stools rather than chairs for sitting.

Most of the wives of cultivator-gardeners use traditional cooking utensils such as pottery jars, but also supplement these with iron or steel ware. They normally use fireplaces of stones, but a few women have locally made iron coal-pots. Mortars and pestles are still common because the wives of cultivators, like the other women in Ouagadougou, still must remove the husks from the grain by pounding before it is milled. Some poor women who lack funds mill their own grain. On the other hand, the women do not have far to go for water since they have wells in their courtyards. The municipality has installed a few standpipes in town, but these are often very far away from the homes of most cultivator-gardeners. At first, standpipe water was free, but so many quarrels among the female consumers arose that the municipality instituted guards and charged a small fee for water. The resident farmers in town continue to use wood as fuel but have practically abandoned shea butter as fuel for light. Instead, they use locally made or imported kerosene lamps.

Most cultivator-gardeners in Ouagadougou have resisted the municipality's efforts to build and maintain modern sanitary facilities. Their latrines are often just covered pits (when

[1]To illustrate, house plots 25 meters by 25 meters in Dapoya II were being sold in 1964 for from 250,000 F.C.F.A. ($1,000.00) to 600,000 F.C.F.A. ($2,400.00), depending upon their proximity to the main roads.

TABLE XXIV. Occupational Groups and Modern Standards of Living

Residence of Occupational Groups	Occupational Groups						Standards of Living						
	Cultivators	Clerks	Laborers	Traders	Craftsmen	Civil Servants	Radios	Sewing Machines	Motor Vehicles	Bicycles & Motorcycles	Running Water	Wells	Electricity
Bilbalgo	162	10	35	16	94	43	45	10	9	315	100	190	4
Camp Fonctionnaire						66	31	7	5	41	41		47
Camp Militaire							38	2	1	317	91	9	18
Centre d'Apprentissage								2		17			
Cours Normal J. F.							5	2		12			
Dapoya II	370	94	123	110	549	567	385	96	89	1,724	232	305	128
Garde Republicaine and Gendarmerie		1			3	122	34	7		1,457	128	47	112
Gounghin	375	36	60	12	92	22	22	16	4	457	5	393	1
Hamdalaye	44				1					14		4	
Ipelesse	108		17	7	27	8	3	1		63		117	
Kamsaoghin	397	2	50	21	66	23	32	12	6	434	36	521	4
Koulouba			1		113	179	51	18	18	436	98	471	29
Kologh Naba (Col)							10	4		52			
Larhalle	406	23	40	27	95	61	52	14	24	585	2	295	
Lycée National							9	1		63	11		
Mission	44		1		5		5			4			
Nyoghsin	44				1		1			39		16	
Paspanga	86	15	20	10	71	172	63	14	19	351	53	199	28

Prison Civile	166	5	11	12	55	13	5		1	36	2		1
Samandin and St. Julien	503	8	58	36	100	37	42	20	8	430	9	523	11
Sambin	145		23	16	28	17	12	3		215	2	212	1
St. Jean-Baptiste					18		9	5	1	117	70	45	2
St. Joseph	23		14	12	28	14	17	13	1	91	74	19	11
St. Léon	130		25	14	31	57	10	5	2	120	90	50	4
Tanghin	264	7	29	9	48	34	24	10	6	480	3	422	1
Tampouy	307	8	15		12	6	1	3	1	231		115	
Tiedpalogo	102	57	25	75	244	120	71	36	40	377	179	420	38
Ouidi	334	29	55	28	141	100	71	27	15	624	6	764	
Zoghona	355	11	82	31	82	30	16	8	1	505		424	
Commercial Zone	45	6	28	43	61	43	29	10	20	1,457	112	101	26
Residential Zone	112	9	64	24	86		23	4	14	6	42	6	63
Zangouettin	177	13	40	248	258	91	96	30	25	588	247	680	4
TOTAL	4,655	334	816	751	2,309	1,825	1,213	364	590	9,012	1,649	6,428	523
EUROPEANS							246			39	377	9	363
GRAND TOTAL	4,655	334	816	751	2,309	1,825	1,459	364	590	9,051	2,026	6,437	886

SOURCE: Census of 1962.

the cover is missing, young children evacuate near the street for fear of falling into them) and the bathing facilities are small areas fenced either with a straw blind or a mud-brick wall. The municipal authorities are concerned that so many of these sanitary facilities are near wells and fear that epidemics may occur. But they do not have money to build water or sewer systems, and the migrants do not share their concern.

Cultivator-gardeners still use more "local" foodstuffs than "imported" ones. They have been slow to adopt foreign foods, except wheat bread, or change their eating habits (see Table XII). Their morning meal still consists of millet or maize gruel to which only sugar and condensed milk are added. Tea and coffee are seldom used. The midday meal is still not important to newcomers to town, and many are content with a snack of peanuts, roasted or boiled maize, sweet potatoes or, now more frequently, fried cakes. These people continue to eat their main meal at night. This consists of either millet, sorghum, or maize mush (*saghabo*) with either a meat- or fish-based sauce. Rice is sometimes used, but it is still not a staple cereal of this group. Except for Moslems, the cultivator-gardeners drink millet beer whenever they can afford it. The veterans among them buy European beer, soda, and wine when they draw their pensions. Most still chew local tobacco and kola nuts, but the use of cigarettes is increasing.

There has been a substantial modification in the clothing worn by the families of the cultivator-gardeners of Ouagadougou. They spend very little money for new local or imported clothing, but quite a lot for "secondhand materials," most of which are clothing (see Table XII). Some secondhand American clothes are worn by almost every member of these families—from old men who buy heavy coats to keep warm to small children who are given rompers, bloomers, and shorts to wear. Except for the secondhand clothes, the older men continue to wear the traditional garb. Most of the younger male cultivator-gardeners combine both traditional and Western clothing. For formal occasions the Moslems may wear a burnoose, but this is now usually made of imported cloth which is less expensive than local cloth. Catholics and Protestants tend to wear secondhand Western clothes or traditional garb made of imported cotton cloth. Their headgear is limited to the traditional large hats (*zug'peogo*) and cloth skullcaps.

The wives of resident cultivator-gardeners exhibit a complex range of clothing styles. The older ones who sell in the markets or hawk goods along the streets dress in the traditional cloth wraparound skirt with shawls thrown over their unclothed upper bodies. Most of the younger women wear bodices, blouses, and tunics with either long or short wraparound skirts. They tend to use the same kind of clothing on formal or ceremonial occasions, but add headkerchiefs that cover the whole head and not simply the forehead as on workdays. On both informal and formal occasions the younger women wear imported sandals rather than the old-fashioned ones made of automobile tires. The heavy copper and silver bracelets and the copper leg bands, once so popular with rural women (especially the wives of noblemen [*nakomcé*]), are seldom seen in Ouagadougou. These have been replaced by cheap costume jewelry, often made of plastic or of silver-or gold-plated metal. An even more radical change has taken place in the clothing of the children of urban cultivator-gardeners. In contrast to the rural areas, there is little nudity among any urban children. Even small infants wear pants. Moreover, children's clothing is based on Western models. Some of it is imported second-hand from local tailors. Both boys and girls of this group continue to wear Western clothing as they grow older. Girls adopt the blouse and wraparound skirt as they pass puberty, but boys continue to wear ordinary shirts and trousers. It is, however, too early to determine whether this shift in clothing styles will persist to adulthood, since at that period of life African family norms become important, especially for husbands and wives.

The wives of immigrant cultivator-gardeners still kneel when presenting objects to their husbands and efface themselves whenever men other than relatives are present. These women still feel responsible for preparing the husband's meals; washing his clothes; helping on farms (even staying there during the planting season if the farms are far from town); and, through petty trading, procuring condiments for meals. Except for administrative and business reasons, cultivator-gardeners are still rarely seen in public with their wives. Then they usually walk ahead with other males while the women trail behind. Nevertheless, urban life is affecting relations between cultivator-gardeners and their wives. For example, these urban women visit their mothers' homes less frequently than their rural sisters. Gone are the days when wives in polygynous extended family households could visit their parents for weeks on end, knowing that their husbands would be well cared for by cowives or female relatives. Urban women, even in polygynous households, cannot do this since their cowives would object to the additional housework. Also, because of the growing nucleation of urban households, wives cannot count on their husbands' female relatives to substitute for them.

Although the wives of urban cultivators visit their relatives less frequently than rural women, their husbands exercise less control over their movements. Urban women traders can and do stay out late at night without being sanctioned by their husbands. Everyone recognizes that wives try to earn a living, and jealous husbands are advised that their wives would not have to work if they became "ministers." Again, in contrast to rural farmers, urban ones seldom object to their wives going to church or receiving religious instruction from the Catholic church. Urban cultivators usually resign themselves to their wives' conversion to Catholicism. They say that things have changed: "today is the day of women," meaning that women are more free than they were before. Behind this apparent resignation, however, is the recognition of the inability of the women to remain ritually subordinate to the men of their own patrilineages. These men may not be present in town, but even if they are, they may be Moslems or Christians and therefore unable or unwilling to make the traditional sacrifices for female relatives. An equally important factor in the men's resignation is the acknowledgment that the Church is a religious vehicle that permits women to deal with their own spiritual problems. Nor should the pragmatic element here be overlooked: urban cultivators know that it is easier for their Catholic wives to enroll their children in school than for non-Catholic wives to do so.

Cultivators in town are less permissive when their wives seek to attend sewing classes at social centers. They also objected when wives wished to attend the basic literacy courses when these were first established. Not one woman out of the thirty taking instructions in sewing in the town was the wife of a cultivator. In contrast, four out of the twelve girls learning to sew at the same social center were the daughters of cultivators. The wives of cultivators reported that their husbands felt that learning to sew was a waste of time and that it was easier to buy clothes than to make them. The women also reported that their husbands insisted that making clothes was man's work. These husbands allegedly also felt that since they could never buy sewing machines for their wives, learning to sew would simply increase their frustrations. Finally, some of the women revealed that their husbands objected to sewing classes because they believed that the women at the social center spent all their time talking about men and arranging assignations. This charge may have simply masked other objections, but it also reflects the feeling on the part of cultivators that unless women are doing something which engages all their attention, they get into trouble.

It is difficult to generalize about the family life among the middle-status craftsmen, merchants, and lowest ranking clerks and civil servants,[2] given the relatively wide range of incomes, formal education and family compositions of these people. Some of the more prosperous African traders have as many of the amenities of modern life as the medium-level civil servants; and the poorer merchants and craftsmen are as tradition-oriented as the cultivator-gardeners. Nevertheless, the people in this category are better off than the farmers and, economically at least, have less difficulty coping with the material problems of urban life. Significantly, the largest number of merchants, craftsmen, and low-income clerks and civil servants live in Zanguettin, the commercial zone, Dapoya II, and Tiedpalogho, quarters bordering the center of town (see Table XXIV). Thus the merchant families still live in the traditional merchant wards, but more important is the fact that they can afford to live here. Merchant families are spilling into Dapoya II and into almost all the other wards in the town. This is especially true of the younger merchants. The craftsmen and lower-income clerks and civil servants, too, not only prefer to live in the wards nearest their jobs, but they can afford to pay the rents in the multi-room compounds found in Zanguettin, Tiedpalogho, and Dapoya II (see Table XXIV).

Many of the houses inhabited by middle-status families are built of *banco* (adobe) in the oblong Sudanese style with flat roofs. This housing style was originally brought to Ouaga-

---

[2]Low-ranking civil servants and clerks include low-grade policemen, soldiers, messengers, post office clerks, and so on. Normally these persons do not have the qualifications to achieve higher rank.

dougou by prestigious Moslem merchants from other urban areas of the Sudan and is roomier than the traditional Mossi round huts. The outside walls of rooms normally form parts of the walls of the compounds, and the rooms give on to the large and fairly private interior courtyard. The entrance room is called the *zongo*. Some of these houses are plastered with cement, given them the appearance of cement-block houses. Today, many of these interior courtyards are being reduced in size because additional square houses are being built in the compounds. This is due not only to the growth in the size of families residing there, but also because householders build and rent the additional houses or rooms.

The furnishings in the homes of merchants, craftsmen, and lowest-ranking clerks and civil servants are more substantial than those of cultivator-gardeners families. Children and women may still sleep on Fulani-type mats, but the men normally use locally made beds and mattresses. Tables and benches are common in these households, and so are stools. Some families have locally made chairs and, occasionally, imported iron chairs, but women and children seldom use these, preferring to sit on the ground or on the floors. Cooking utensils are increasingly of imported ware, and cooking is more frequently done in kitchens—small, open-faced structures attached to the inside walls. Wood continues to be the primary fuel, but some families have begun to use coal-pots and charcoal. Enamel dishes are seen, but the people have not abandoned the earthenware dishes as containers for sauces. The feeling persists that sauces retain their flavor much better in earthenware dishes than in enamel or chinaware. Mortars and pestles are used for husking grain prior to milling.

Wells for drawing water are still ubiquitous among the families in this category since few of their houses have piped water. The main difference is that many of the wells have cemented openings and covers to keep out dust and dirt and to protect the children. Rubber buckets are used for drawing water from wells rather than the calabashes used by the cultivator-gardeners. In contrast, the sanitary facilities here are similar to those found among cultivator-gardeners. Added elements are walls surrounding the outdoor bathhouses, and galvanized buckets and enamel bath-water containers. The latrines are normally enclosed and the opening made secure against flies and small children. However, in no case are these structures roofed with either tin or mats.

The internal living arrangements in the houses of this social group are still relatively unaffected by urban life. Where the door to the compound goes through a *zongo* (a room built from the front wall inward), this room may be used to house overnight male guests or as the sleeping apartment for the head of the household. Where *zongos* do not exist, the men of the households have their private rooms inside the compounds. Normally, each individual wife shares a room of the compound with her unmarried daughters and younger children. The older boys of the family and other relatives or renters have rooms either in the main building or have separate rooms built into the side of other walls of the compound. Some of the individual rooms are closed off from the rest of the courtyard by small, walled enclosures but this traditional feature is declining. The reason is that now the rooms in these compounds frequently have doors to ensure privacy. This is all the more necessary since the compounds of the middle-status families, in contrast to those of the cultivator-gardeners, tend to be relatively heterogeneous. In Tiedpalogho and Zanguettin, especially, one is likely to find compounds inhabited by unrelated members of the same ethnic group, and even unrelated members of different ethnic groups. There are entire compounds composed of renters, with the monthly rent varying from a few hundred to several thousand C.F.A. depending upon the quality and size of the rooms.

While the families of craftsmen, merchants, and lowest-ranking clerks and civil servants of Ouagadougou have not greatly modified their uses of traditional foods, they have modified their traditional schedule of meals. All the members of some families eat the traditional breakfast of millet or maize gruel. In others, only the women and children use this food while the men buy fried millet cakes from women hawkers for breakfast. A few men buy and drink millet beer even before going off to work. Most men of these families now buy a midday meal at local restaurants or from women who hire young boys to take basinsfull of rice, beans, and stews to work sites. In contrast, the evening meal is normally eaten at home with the family and consists of the customary *saghabo* or rice with sauce. After dinner, some men go to the *dolotière* or send their young children to buy beer. A growing number of men now use cigarettes rather than kola nuts as mild stimulants, but the reasons for this are not clear. Perhaps it is because they can afford to indulge in this modern trait of cigarette smoking.

The clothing of the families of this type in Ouagadougou still runs the gamut from traditional to modern Western. Some men almost always wear Western dress to work, and a few of the older men wear the traditional tunic and pants, but all variations and combinations of these styles are seen. There is also the same variation in formal dress. Even men who are not Moslems wear long burnooses; others wear secondhand Western clothes; and still others wear locally made Western clothing. The older men still wear sandals, but the younger men buy imported shoes. Likewise, only the older men wear the traditional *zug'peogo* or sun helmets; the younger men prefer various types of skullcaps and felt hats.

The clothing styles among the wives of craftsmen, merchants, and junior civil servants and clerks reflect the incomes of their husbands rather than any fundamental difference in taste from that of the wives of cultivator-gardeners. Even the older women appear to have abandoned wraparounds of traditional cloth in favor of those made of the more costly imported prints. The women have also shifted toward wearing imported jewelry and make greater use of plastic or imported sandals than the wives of cultivator-gardeners. They also use multi-colored headkerchiefs instead of the traditional simple piece of cloth. The clothing patterns of the children in this group are closer to Western norms than those of cultivators' children. Since a higher percentage of these children go to school, their Western clothing reflects this fact.

Most of the modern possessions of these families in Ouagadougou are important for their work. Most of the men have bicycles or scooters and a few even own trucks and automobiles. None of these families possess any of the television sets in the town, but many own radios (see Table XXIV). Again, families in this category do not have domestic servants in the usual sense. They do have younger relatives and even unrelated children working about their households, but the element of kinship or fictive kinship governs most of these relationships.

The relations between husbands and wives in middle-status

families (craftsmen, merchants, and lowest-ranking clerks and civil servants) are similar, in their major outlines, to those described for cultivators and their wives. The older wives in this group still efface themselves before their husbands and visitors; and, while the younger wives do not normally join their husbands in entertaining nonrelatives, they are not as retiring as the older women. Many of the young women do have much casual contact with men as a function of their work, but the effect of this on the attitude of their husbands is difficult to gauge.

As long as the relations in the home are good, craftsmen, merchants, and lower civil servants are more tolerant of short-term visits that their wives make to rural relatives. It is not that these women have closer bonds with their rural relatives than do the wives of cultivators, but their husbands can afford to pay for their transportation and, while they are away, their husbands can take better care of themselves. Men of this group, in contrast to cultivators, can afford to buy meals. They also pay to have their clothes washed and pressed by washermen because their wives normally cannot perform these tasks. Conflicts often arise in the households of middle-status families when women are actively employed, especially as traders or as *dolotières*. Because of their trading activities, many women find it difficult to perform all their traditional household roles. For example, in a case which came before the Court of First Degree in Ouagadougou, a mason accused his wife of refusing to cook either his morning or midday meal; of leaving her three-year-old daughter alone at home; and of taking 8,500 francs, his shirts, and his shoes, and running off with another man. The woman rebutted that because she had to leave home early in the morning to sell kola nuts in the market, she could not prepare her husband's morning meals. She added that she was also busy during the day, and therefore could not go home, cook, and take her husband his midday meal. Besides, she added, he had another wife. The judge found it strange that the cowives could not arrange their trading schedules so as to be able to care for their husband. He suggested that the defendant was seeking an excuse to end her twelve-year-old marriage, and ordered that she return to her husband. The woman obviously felt that the pressure of outside work justified her refusal to prepare her husband's meals. The judge felt that she should still perform certain household chores, especially since there was a cowife in the house. Nevertheless, it is true that many men, especially whose wives are traders, buy their midday meals from food-sellers. Many women in such households only prepare morning and evening meals for husbands and arrange to have their clothing washed.

The occupation of *dolotière* often creates problems between women and their middle-status husbands. This job is a marital hazard for urban marriages because it throws women and men together in situations far different from those in the rural areas. There, a beer seller's clients are well known to her husband as well as to her relatives; therefore, social sanctions can easily be applied to any client who tries to exceed the normal seller-client relationship. In town, the *dolotière's* clients are seldom friends of her husband and, more often than not, have higher statuses and earn more money. Again, whereas in the rural areas beer selling usually ends before nightfall, the urban *dolotière* often must work late at night in order to sell all her beer. This creates uxorial problems since a beer seller cannot prepare her husband's meals; sentimental problems because the husband often becomes jealous of clients; and psychological problems since the woman usually makes as much money as high civil servants, and therefore more than her husband.

The men in this group are ambivalent about their wives' participation in new urban institutions. More of them permit their wives to learn to sew at the social centers of Ouagadougou, perhaps in the hope that this will prove valuable for their spouses. In contrast, the non-Christians among them are less willing to allow their wives to join the churches. Unlike the cultivators, these men are too sophisticated about urban life to expect anything but spiritual benefits from their wives becoming Christians. They are not awed by the problems of the town and know how to place their children in school without passing by the *chemin* (the path) of the church. Again unlike the cultivators, they do not fear to combat either the church or the state if these institutions attempt to interfere in their family lives.

Members of this group are starting to differ from the cultivators as far as their public social behavior with their wives are concerned. Not many of these men go out with their wives and families either to the cinema or to dances in the local club-bars. However, a few of the young men take wives riding on bicycles or motorcycles, especially on Sundays when the police normally allow persons to break the traffic laws in this manner.

There is greater ambiguity in the family life of the high-status civil servant-clerk group than among any other status group in Ouagadougou. More than any other group in town, the *fonctionnaires* and *commis* consciously seek to modernize their lives and to adopt those traits considered *civilisé*. Yet, their own traditional values, and the growing recognition of the importance of these traditions, are conditioning the family pattern that is emerging among them. It is therefore too soon to say what type of family pattern will emerge, but when it does, it will probably set the standard against which most family types in Ouagadougou will be viewed.

Civil servant and clerk families live in all but a few of the wards of Ouagadougou (see Table XXIV). The civil servant families in Ouagadougou, as distinct from those of the clerks, have long since spilled beyond Koulouba, the zone especially established for them by Governor Hesling in 1919. When large numbers of civil servants came into Ouagadougou after World War II, the government built the Camp Fonctionnaire for its senior African civil servants, especially those not native to Upper Volta. Those civil servant families, especially the Voltaics, which could not obtain houses either in Koulouba or Camp Fonctionnaire moved into Dapoya II. There they built the type of houses they could afford and improved them as they advanced in status and income. Later, civil servant families moved into such wards as Paspanga and began buying house plots from old veterans and cultivators in Bilbalgo. Subsequently, the younger civil servant families began to drift out to Ouidi, Larhalle, Tanghin, and Zonghona, where land is more readily available. By 1964, they had even started to build houses in Hamdalaye and Nyoghsin, quarters which in 1962 had housed no civil servants.

The residence pattern of the senior clerks' families in Ouagadougou is similar to that of the civil servants except in areas restricted to government personnel. The largest number of clerk families live in Dapoya II, but like the civil servant families, they, too, are purchasing the lots of cultivators who are now moving to the periphery of the town. Twenty-one per cent of the clerks who live in Tiedpalogho and Zanguettin are expatriate former civil servants who elected to remain in Ouagadougou rather than return home.

The housing of the families of civil servants and clerks shows the greatest variation among all the groups in Ouagadougou. Most young married couples of this group who live by themselves in Larhalle, Ouidi, Gounghin, or other quarters normally have two-room or three-room houses of plastered adobe bricks and galvanized iron roofs. A few have cement-block houses. Some families of men in the middle and senior civil service or clerk grades are housed either by the administration or companies, or live in their own houses. Most of the latter represent a synthesis of traditional and Western styles. They have two basic designs: the first is rather large with an oblong floor plan possessing three, or at most four, rooms. The walls are usually built of mud-bricks and plastered with cement; the floor may be of cement or tile, and the gabled roof covered with sheets of galvanized iron. The interior floor plans differ in the buildings, but the norm appears to be a central living-dining room combination which is entered by the main door. This large room is flanked by bedrooms whose doors open into the central room or into the courtyard.

Most of these houses are not located with any specific reference to the geography of the lot. Some of the larger houses are built at the front of the lot, others in the middle, and still others at the rear. The determining factor appears to have been the location of existing dwellings when the main house was being built. Families seldom tore down extant houses or moved while construction took place. The result is that these larger dwellings are usually surrounded by smaller huts or rooms which house adolescent boys or servants. The position of these smaller houses usually determines the location of the sanitary facilities. These range from simple pit latrines surrounded by earthen walls, to substantial outhouses with seats, to modern indoor flush toilets. Bathing facilities vary from water taps or simple showers to elaborate shower rooms with bathtubs and bidets.

The houses of the higher-grade civil servants (and now politicians) are of two types (two-story houses and modern villas) and are comparable to those found in Western countries. In fact, many of them were inherited from former European officials.

158

A higher percentage of the civil servant and clerk families has running water and electricity in their houses than any other African family group in the town (see Table XXIV). Some merchants (in Tiedpalogho and Zanguettin) with high incomes have running water in their homes, but they have less interest in electricity. Small kerosene lamps are apparently good enough for merchants who spend their evenings discussing business in semi-darkened *zongos,* whereas civil servants and clerks need brighter lights for entertaining friends.

The furnishings found in the houses of the civil servant and clerk families are quite varied. Those in the houses of low-grade employees are simple and not much different from those found among craftsmen and merchants. Furnishings in houses of middle-grade persons more closely approach the Western norms. Here bedding ranges from locally made beds, mattresses, and pillows to imported ones. Tables run the gamut from simple ones made out of packing cases to those made by skilled craftsmen of imported mahogany. Benches and locally made straight-back chairs are found, but so are the better made Morris-type chairs with locally made cushions. Floor covering, when it exists, is usually plain or multi-colored grass mats, but Turkish carpets and locally made blankets are sometimes hung on the walls. Photographs of the family and religious pictures adorn the walls, and some families hang European and modern African paintings.

The cooking equipment and utensils of the civil servant and clerk families are also varied. These range from the traditional fireplaces to locally made coal-pots. The latter are still used because most women have no need for the more expensive gas ranges. Either they are quite satisfied with the local cooking devices or have servants to cook for them. Mortars and pestles are also found in these households because grain must be husked before being milled. Even those persons who buy milled flour keep mortars and pestles with which to pound herbs, dried fish, and other foods. Eating utensils, on the other hand, are predominantly European.

The food practices of the *fonctionnaires* and *commis* families are the most varied of all the groups in Ouagadougou. One survey found that food accounted for about 24.8 per cent of the expenses of such families. Breakfast is quite early because the normal day's work begins at 7:00 A.M. Some men and boys have coffee and bread and butter, while others and the women and children continue to eat the traditional morning meal, a millet gruel. Single men simply stop at a roadside tea shop for cups of tea or coffee and bread, but only a small minority buy fried cakes from roadside stands. The mid-morning break for refreshment is a growing institution in the offices and stores of Ouagadougou. Lower-grade individuals buy cakes or fruits from young people who hawk these foods from office to office. Middle-ranking persons go to a *dolotière* for millet beer. Higher-ranked individuals go to local restaurants for beer, soft drinks, grilled chicken, guinea hen, or calves' liver.

All the working members in families of this group go home for the midday meal. This ranges from simple rice and meat stews to such combinations as imported noodles or macaroni with grilled chicken, followed by rice and chicken fricassee, salad, fruit, and cheese. Such meals are sometimes accompanied by wines or soft drinks. The evening meal, served around 8:00 P.M., usually consists of the traditional *saghabo* with meat, chicken, and sauce. Persons with higher incomes add frills to this meal. They may start with grilled chicken, followed by either couscous, rice, or *saghabo,* with okra and vegetable stews, stews of chicken, and then meat or guinea hen. Salads and a variety of fruits are also served and, occasionally, cheeses. Wines are often used, except in the homes of very orthodox Moslems. In general, one can say that the higher the rank of the family head, or the younger and more educated he is, the more French are his meals. Conversely, the lower the rank and the less educated or older the man, the more traditional are his meals. Nevertheless, all meals include items which are traditional and items which are foreign.

The clothing used by the families of the civil servants and clerks is still not standardized, but increasingly it approaches the European norm. Most men wear European clothes to work. Gaining favor among nationalistic men is a local style characterized by long trousers, and an open-necked shirt-jacket with short sleeves. Only rarely do men in these families, even Moslems, wear the long burnoose to work. Characteristically, those few who do are middle-aged men in the higher grades, or very high ranking young men. In contrast, formal and ceremonial dress is highly varied. Men either wear beautifully embroidered burnooses and caps or business suits and both black and white "smokings" (tuxedo jackets) with black ties.

The dress of the women in these families while heterogeneous is more "African" than that of the men. Female clerks and civil servants wear blouses and wraparounds of imported cloth as well as dresses, skirts, and blouses to work. The nonworking wives of civil servants and clerks tend to be more traditional in dress and prefer blouses and print wraparound skirts to dresses. All the older women wear gaily colored headkerchiefs, some elaborately tied. Some younger women eschew the headkerchiefs and go bareheaded exhibiting hair plaited in the many beautiful traditional designs.

For formal dress, some women use modern Sudanese garments, consisting of a long, silk burnoose usually with satin petticoats. Others use a Ghanaian-type formal wear, consisting of a short blouse flared at the bottom and a long wraparound. Still others wear Western-style short or long dresses. On these occasions, the women wear elaborately arranged headkerchiefs or dress their hair either in local or continental fashion. Jewelry consists of expensive gold chains, rings, earrings, and gold bracelets made by Senegalese goldsmiths either in modified traditional styles or in styles copied from the catalogues of European jewelers. Footwear ranges from imported sandals to Western-type slippers.

The everyday wear of the younger people and children in civil servant and clerk families is normally quite Western. Boys usually do not wear the burnoose until they start working; then they prefer dress styles as they see them advertised in *Paris Match* and *Bingo*. Similarly, and for the same reasons, formal dress is always Western. The dress of girls is usually Western, but occasionally they wear wraparounds. Their formal dress is Western and remains so until they approach womanhood when their clothing styles begin to include the traditional garb. As a rule, babies are dressed in the modern style; some of them even wear knitted woolen dresses and booties.

Fonctionnaire and *commis* families possess more of those conveniences (*éléments divers de confort*) necessary for modern life than any other African group in town. Table XXIV shows the items they possess, and in 1964, they and the Europeans owned all of the 200 television sets in town. They also employ a number of household helpers to wash, cook, clean, shop, serve at table, and baby-sit, thus freeing the woman or women in the family for other jobs, including outside work if she is a civil servant or a clerk.

It is difficult to generalize about the relations between husbands and wives of the higher-status groups in Ouagadougou because the wives of this group are so heterogeneous in education and achievement. For the most part, household finances appear to be one of the areas of greatest tensions in these families. The educated wives of such men are usually employed as civil servants before marriage and are expected to continue working after they are married. This is so much taken for granted that when men reply to the question, "What do you expect your wife to do after you get married?" with the response, "Take charge of the household!" this answer would be misunderstood until one discovers that it really means that the wife is expected to "give the orders regarding the upkeep of the household."

The notion that a skilled, educated woman would not continue to work after marriage is foreign to most upper-status men in town. The current rationale for this attitude is that the nation needs the skills of all its people. But even before independence the educated women always worked. It is expected, therefore, that as long as it is possible for women to work, they will do so. The women also concur with this expectation. They point out that they have always worked and would be "bored" if they remained at home. They also declare that any money they earn is needed for the material advancement of their families of procreation, and that they have the responsibility of aiding their families of orientation without their husbands' help.[3] Even the trained wives of important politicians express the desire to continue working, not only for the reasons given, but also because they are quite aware that the exigencies of political life could result in a husband who is a *minister* or *chef de cabinet* one day becoming a simple *instituteur* the next. By retaining their jobs, they seek

[3]On March 22, 1968, the Director of Labor infuriated the ladies of Amitié Africaine (an organization of elite African women and European nuns) by declaring that owing to governmental austerity there would be a moratorium on hiring female civil servants in favor of males. The women violently objected to what they considered "discrimination," claiming that they had as much responsibility in their households as did their husbands and other males.

162

to ensure their families' livelihood if the worst should happen to their spouses.

Because most educated wives of high-status men continue to work, couples have usually subscribed to an institution called *ménage à deux* or *bien en commun*. On or about the time of marriage, they notify the government or other employers that they have decided to pool their resources and that the husband has the right to draw the pay checks of his wife. Very often this arrangement is decided upon while the couple is deeply in love and engaged, and the papers are signed when they get married. Under this plan, the husband and wife are expected to devise detailed budgets allotting money for food, household expenses, savings, pocket change, and even remittances to parents. Initially there is much leeway as to which spouse plans the family budget, and, while there is the inevitable male dominance here, there are families in which the husband takes advantage of the wife's frugality and allows her to plan so as to save money.

The *ménage à deux* is subject to so many strains that it does not survive for long among most couples. Women complain that the older a man becomes the greater is his desire to use the family's money without consulting his spouse. Then, the husband simply gives the wife what he feels she needs to run the household. As the result, she soon feels that she is working for her husband rather than contributing her share to the household expenses. The quarrels which ensue usually involve charges by the wife that the husband married her for "money" and not for "love."

Another strain on the *ménage à deux* is the alleged desire of the husband to take another wife or to engage in extramarital affairs—at least the wife suspects he wishes to do so. When this occurs, wives abandon the *ménage à deux* because they object to helping their husbands support multiple wives. Wives withdraw even when a potential cowife is employed. One suspects that the threat or act of rupturing this arrangement is used by wives to punish husbands who take cowives or have extramarital affairs. The wives involved insist, however, that their main concern is to safeguard the livelihood of their own children which would be jeopardized if the family's income was used to support other wives or strange women.

Still another strain on the *ménage à deux* is the desire of both the husband and the wife to support members of their respective families of orientation. The men charge that their wives give too much support to younger siblings in school or rush to the aid of a mother and, occasionally, a father when famine threatens their rural areas. Women charge that men not only try to do the same thing for their relatives but feel ashamed to inform rural relatives that they must consult their wives before family funds can be spent. Women also charge that rural people try to obtain money from urban sons under the guise of establishing gift-exchanges with other rural families in the hope of obtaining wives for the townsmen. Urban wives insist that their husbands are keenly embarrassed when rural relatives criticize them for permitting the *ménage à deux* to tie up their money and for allowing wives to deny them future polygamous households. This rather complicated charge is difficult to verify but is interesting because it links two strains on the *ménage à deux:* pressure to help relatives and polygamy.

Few *ménages à deux* survive the numerous strains placed upon them. They break up sooner or later, leaving in their wake an almost armed economic truce between husband and wife. Thereafter, the men provide the basic economic needs for their households while the women, like the mothers in the rural areas, use their own resources to give extra help to their offspring. Women even start their own bank accounts and build houses which they rent, and often become economically quite independent of their husbands.

In contrast to the virtual economic autonomy of the educated wives of high-status men, the uneducated and untrained wives of such men are economically the most dependent of almost all the women in Ouagadougou. And while it is difficult to confirm the widely held opinion that these women are more subservient to their husbands than wives with independent incomes, it is certainly true that these women are relatively helpless if abandoned by their husbands. In most cases these women became wives during the colonial period when there were few educated women and when relatively well-paid clerks and civil servants could afford to maintain nonworking wives. Moreover, at that time there was no economic or social pressure for these women to work. In fact, there were few jobs for women and there was social pressure against their working. When, for example, the early group of civil servant husbands were posted to rural areas, their positions there were such that their wives were not permitted to cultivate the fields; nor could these women sell in the market with women who had cultivator husbands. Later when the erstwhile clerks and civil servants became important men and politicians and moved to Ouagadougou, their wives found it more difficult to obtain employment commensurate with their skill and the status of their husbands.

The younger men of high status who do not have educated wives have some of the same problems as do the older civil servants. However, there is evidence that the young wives of these men are attempting to learn economically useful skills. In contrast to the older women, many of these young women while not having the C.E.P.E. (comparable to a grammar school certificate) are not completely unlettered. Many of them work in stores, in shops, and even in bars, although the latter job is still undesirable. Some are also employed in the many dressmaking establishments which are springing up in the town. In fact, such women represent the largest single group of students in dressmaking at the social centers. Thus, of the 18 married women out of 30 who were learning to sew at the social center of Dapoya II, 16 were the wives of civil servants employed in such places as the Town Hall, the Post Office, the Government Printing Office, and the Public Works Department; and 2 were wives of clerks who worked in the private sector, 1 at the bank and 1 for a commercial firm.

The social life of the higher-status married couples is fairly restricted to official functions and ceremonies marking *rites de passage* of their relatives and friends. Given the relatively small circle of high-status couples in the town, these people usually attend all the functions marking official holidays, visits of politicians, and the like. But, unless it is a very important affair where the presence of a wife is *de rigeur,* men of this group do not even bring their wives. When the couple does attend they always arrive together, but they usually separate upon entering a reception unless, of course, they attend receptions given by Europeans. Here, especially, differences in background between husbands and wives are noticeable. Many of the wives remain silent since they cannot speak French well enough to hold conversations with the European women or non-Moré-speaking persons. Moreover, they never dance with their husbands, many of whom have learned modern dancing either in school or while in France.

165

The pattern is not too different when these couples attend such festivities as christenings and weddings. Here the women still sit by themselves, apart from the men. The social climate is more relaxed when the elder couples of this group visit intimate friends or are visited by them. Yet, there is never a free flow of conversation even when Moré is used.[4] It appears that even the most prestigious members of this high-status group adhere to the traditional custom of formal public relations between husbands and wives.

The behavior of the younger members of this high-status group is quite different unless, of course, the wives are relatively uneducated. And since this factor becomes rarer as time goes on, one can begin to generalize about the behavior of the couples where both spouses are literate. Such couples attend receptions together and men often sit with their wives, even though the presence of elder and more prestigious men sitting by themselves does create some uneasiness for the younger men. All except the most conservative younger men dance with their wives at private as well as public affairs. The young people go to the cinemas together and visit friends together as part of their social activities. The social discourse here is seldom strained, but women tend to draw the line at behavior that is considered too Western, or indicates too great a reversal of traditional male-female roles. For example, at a buffet supper line it is difficult to extend the mark of courtesy to a female guest by having her move ahead of the man in front of her. It is also impossible to get a woman to permit a man to bring her a plate of food or return her empty plate to the table even though he is going there. Even those women who have been to France with their husbands do not ordinarily accept this reversal of roles.

In summary, then, social relations between spouses in Ouagadougou are conditioned by occupation, education, and the need to adjust behavior not only to life in an urban setting but to a changing culture. The couples who are most successful are those whose occupational and educational backgrounds are comparable. Where there are differences in education or where the men have risen rapidly in the social hierarchy, the couples encounter more difficulty. However,

[4]Perhaps the presence of a stranger always introduces an unnatural element and thus prevents an observation of the normal pattern of behavior.

166

the growing occupational and educational opportunities for women may well ease the transition of the Ouagadougou people to a modern style of life and reduce conflicts derived from differences in education and culture.

Marital Problems

The sources of marital discord and divorces among married couples of all status groups in Ouagadougou are best treated together because, while all discord does not necessarily lead to divorce, the grounds upon which divorces are sought indicate the nature of the conflicts.

The actual data on the number of marriages in Ouagadougou which fail are difficult to determine since only a minority of couples with broken marriages seek formal divorce. One reason is that the numerically superior Mossi had no traditional divorce procedures. Men repudiated their wives if they stole, were lazy, committed adultery, were suspected of witchcraft, or created problems in the household by quarreling either with cowives or with the wives of their husbands' male relatives. But even under such circumstances men hesitated to repudiate their wives. Most men heeded the injunction that wives were so precious that a man should "close his eyes, close his ears, close his mouth, and keep them." Thus, for the Mossi in Ouagadougou formal divorce is not part of their tradition, and when men repudiate wives, they feel no need to notify the authorities that they have done so. Moreover, unless people have registered their marriages in Ouagadougou or with the authorities at the various administrative offices—*postes, subdivisions, cercles,* or *municipalities*—there is no official record, and they feel free to part if they cannot get along. If marriages were not recorded, formal divorces are never sought.

According to the 1962 census, out of 25,970 persons listed as married, only 261 divorces were reported. Thus, 44.9 per cent of the population of Ouagadougou was married as against 1.5 per cent divorced.[5] Of course, these figures are not accurate. The census collectors certainly missed those per-

[5]"Recensement Démographique ...," p. 10.

167

TABLE XXV.   Data on Forty-two Cases of Divorce in Ouagadougou

Reasons Given for Divorce		Status of Husband	
Abandonment of household	12	Civil Servants	12
Adultery by wife	8	Tradesmen	9
Objection to polygyny	5	Cultivators	8
Lack of respect for parents	4	Soldiers	8
Conflict over wife's job	3	Merchants	3
Mistreatment	3	Policemen and guards	2
Sterility	2	TOTAL	42
Witchcraft and poisoning by wife	2		
Nonsupport by husband	1		
Religious differences	1		
Stealing	1		
TOTAL	42		

sons who were separated from their spouses and those who were divorced but had remarried according to their traditional customs.

Data from 42 verified cases of divorce (see Table XXV) give some idea as to why people obtain divorces in Ouagadougou.

In examining these data, it should be noted that much of the evidence presented at court by the litigants shows multiple causes of marital discord which led to divorce. Thus, quite often when a woman asks for a divorce, claiming mistreatment or disrespect of parents, the husband indicates in rebuttal that it is his desire to take an additional wife which is the real cause for marital discord. Only when the wife gives additional evidence does it become quite clear that her aversion to polygyny is the cause of the demand for divorce. Sometimes couples cite several reasons for seeking divorce and, while in court, give other reasons why their marriages failed. The judges normally select one of the reasons as the dominant cause of marital discord and use it as grounds for granting the divorce.

As would be expected in any population with a Mossi majority, the major cause for divorce is "abandonment of the conjugal domicile." Mossi women have always reacted to marital difficulties by fleeing either to other men or to their "mother's home," which ultimately means the same thing. Mossi women in town continue to desert their homes when they tire of their husbands or resent the treatment accorded them. The reasons they usually gave in court for leaving their

husbands were either that they were given in marriage without
their consent or that they had seen other men who pleased
them. These reasons usually disturbed the Mossi judges who
often scolded the wives and attempted to effect a reconciliation. It was only when this failed, or the husbands accepted
the inevitable, that the women were granted a divorce. The
following case, which came before the Customary Tribunal of
Ouagadougou, illustrates the problem of desertion and
divorce.

Case Number 5

Complainant: Mossi man, forty-three years old, *Wend'pous
neba,* born in Tanghin-Dassouri, living in Kamsaoghin,
cultivator.

Defendant: Mossi man, twenty-one years old, Christian,
born in the town of Ouagadougou, Chief Steward at the
President's Office.

Testimony

Complainant: "I have brought a complaint against this man
because he took my wife, X. She fled three years ago [in
1961]. I brought her back in 1962 but she did not stay at
my house for long. After she left, she was seen at the
house of the defendant. Furthermore, she had asked my
permission to visit her mother who had given birth. I
gave her permission but told her to hurry back because it
was time for the harvest. When I went for my wife at her
mother's house, the latter said that my wife had left that
same morning. I returned two days later and she was not
at her mother's home. My mother-in-law became quite
nervous when she saw me and told me not to come looking for a quarrel again. I told her that she should not
have permitted my wife to leave since she was pregnant
with my child. I am asking the Tribunal to intervene so
my wife will rejoin her conjugal domicile. We were married at the Office of the *Cercle de Ouagadougou* in 1960. I
have the marriage certificate, number 1,929 of 11 December 1960."

Defendant: "If the woman wants to rejoin her husband I
will not oppose her. I only want my child. The woman
came to me in 1962. The child belongs to me."

169

President of the Tribunal (to Defendant): "You say that the woman has been at your house since 1962?"

Defendant: "Yes."

Wife: "My parents gave me to Y. But I do not love him. I will not live with him. I had no [other] reason for leaving him. There was no motive for my departure. My parents did not know that I had left my husband."

President: "Does your husband have millet?"

Wife: "Yes, nothing is missing at his house."

President: "Is he impotent or sterile?"

Wife: "No, he is powerful enough."

The court deliberated and rendered a verdict stating that, since the woman left her husband's house in a state of pregnancy and her husband had asked for her return, she was to return and bring her husband's child along. The defendant was warned against encouraging legally married women to desert their husbands and come to live with him.

During the trial, both the judges and spectators were suspicious that the wife's motive for leaving her husband was impotence or sterility. But when the testimony indicated that this was not the case, the consensus grew that the woman deserted her husband because she did not like to work in the fields and because the defendant was wealthier.

Suspicion of adultery, especially on the part of wives, is the second most important source of marital discord in Ouagadougou, if one judges by the frequency of requests for divorce because of it. As yet, the urban women of Ouagadougou, like their rural sisters, do not accuse their husbands of adultery. They still do not consider that a man can be *guilty* of this act. Of the eight women accused of adultery, three were wives of tradesmen, two wives of soldiers who had borne children from adulterous unions while their husbands were out of the country, and one each the wife of a cultivator, a civil servant, and a policeman. Given the number of cultivators in town and the relatively high rate of abandonment of the conjugal domicile by their wives, it is remarkable that there was only one case of adultery as a grounds for divorce cited for this group. One reason might be that urban cultivators still hesitate to repudiate their wives because of adultery. Another possibility is that urban cultivators, in contrast to other urban groups, are unable to penalize their wives for this behavior and tolerate adultery, albeit unwillingly.

The following case illustrates some of the factors which lead to adultery and the problems it engendered in one family:

Case Number 13

Complainant: Mossi man, thirty-two years old, *Wend'pous neba,* born in Ouahigouya, presently living in Larhalle quarter, ex-soldier but now cultivator.

Defendant: Mossi woman, twenty-eight years old, Moslem, born in Mane, now living in Bilibambili quarter, housewife.

Testimony

Complainant: "When I was away with the army in Algeria, my wife behaved badly and even had a child as a consequence of her infidelity. I would like to dissolve my marriage and I ask for a divorce because I can no longer live with her."

Defendant: "If my husband does not want me, it is better for him to say so plainly rather than question the paternity of his child. I know that the child belongs to him. I remained faithful. As for divorce, he may have it; I will not oppose it."

The Tribunal granted the divorce. The court declared that, "Taking the bad conduct of the wife during the absence of the husband into consideration, it is hereby decreed that the marriage contracted on 7 October 1958 in St. Louis, Senegal, be dissolved."

It is important to note here that the judges granted the divorce because of bad conduct but made no mention of the child which was the product of the alleged adultery. It is also to be remarked that the complainant did not claim the child. This attitude is quite new and characteristic of soldiers, clerks, and civil servants who often refuse to accept the paternity of children born to adulterous wives. These men insist that the judges take into consideration the elapsed time since they had left the country or were deserted by their wives and seek to convince the judges that they could not be the children's fathers if the separation had been more than ten months. One problem here, however, is that in many cases illiterate women do not reckon time according to the European system and often claim ignorance about the onset of pregnancy. This lack of information confuses the issue and often infuriates both judges and husbands. Even when some men are convinced that they are not the fathers of their wives' children, they are often in a quandry as to what to do about it.

While the older cultivators object as strongly as the other groups in Ouagadougou to adultery of wives, they nevertheless still adhere to the traditional view that the husband of a woman is the *pater* of her child. This very often poses a problem for the judges who, today, show a tendency to allow the genitor to claim the child. Nevertheless, when there is any possibility that a woman's child might have been fathered by her husband, the court awards it to him. In cases where the paternity of the child is in doubt, the court may suspend judgement and ask the litigants to reappear in court for the specific purpose of settling paternity. When a cultivator's wife has lived with either a soldier or policeman, or even a junior clerk or civil servant for over a year, the court tends to be quite prudent. If the court awards the child to the cultivator, the latter then would have to spend money to take care of it; but if the court permits the government employee to claim the child, he can claim the valued *allocation familiale* which would enable its mother to take care of it. It appears that in some cases the judges take into consideration the ability of the claimants to the child to provide for its welfare. At least during trials, the judges usually point out that claiming a child implies the ability to support it.

The refusal of wives to live in polygynous households is the third most frequent cause for marital discord and divorce. Most wives complain about mistreatment following the arrival of an additional wife and not about the issue of polygyny itself. The result is that one is never sure whether wives would live peacefully in a household if they were able to get along with cowives and if their husband showed no partiality to any single wife. From other data cited, it appears that women prefer monogamy but would live in polygynous households rather than risk divorce with all of its social consequences. Nevertheless, the fact that polygyny ranks so high as a grounds for divorce seems to indicate that polygynous relations are themselves too brittle to withstand the other pressures of urban married life. The following case illustrates this problem:

Case Number 10

Complainant: Mossi man, forty years old, Catholic, born in Manga, presently living in Zoghona quarter, carpenter.

Defendant: Mossi woman, thirty years old, Catholic, born in Dassouri, housewife.

Testimony

Complainant: "Ever since our marriage, my wife has provoked domestic discord. She has put *gris-gris* [a magical substance] under my bed and in my meals. She even whipped my mother. That was the reason for her first departure for I sent her 'on vacation' to her parents. Upon her return, her behavior had not changed and I found myself obliged to send her back to her parents. Then I visited my parents-in-law to bring clothing to my daughter. My father-in-law told me that I had no daughter in his house. My in-laws whipped me and, as I do not wish to be whipped again, I ask the Tribunal to grant me a divorce and to recover my daughter, who is actually at her grandmother's house, and give her to me."

Defendant: "My husband has taken another wife and has sent me back to my parents. Despite the intervention of friends, he would not listen to any pleas on my behalf. Thus, I left for Dassouri where I now live with another man. He came there to ask for his daughter, R .... I said that I would not give her to him because he could not take care of her. As for the *gris-gris* of which he speaks, I do not acknowledge that as fact. I ask to retain custody of the child until she grows up."

The Tribunal approved the divorce and ordered the defendant to give the girl to her father since she was old enough to leave her mother. It also ordered the husband to pay the defendant 6,000 C.F.A. as compensation for her previous care of the child.

It is noteworthy that the Tribunal did not mention in its judgment the wife's assertion that polygyny was the reason for the marital discord. This pattern held consistently throughout the trials witnessed in Ouagadougou and seems to indicate that the rather conservative judges do not consider objection to polygyny as a valid reason for wives to quarrel with their husbands. They, therefore, seldom take this factor into consideration while deliberating a case, but it obviously influences their decisions. The husband in this case also did not comment upon his wife's charge that taking an additional wife contributed to or caused the marital problems. Thus he, like the judges, apparently rejects polygyny as a valid problem in marital relations. On the other hand, it is quite clear that the wife viewed polygyny as one of the prime factors for the difficulties which arose in the household.

Poor relations between spouses and in-laws are apparently a greater source of marital discord in the town than in the rural areas of Upper Volta. The bride in traditional Mossi society usually arrived at her mother-in-law's compound at an early age and was reared by that woman. This could not guarantee that the two of them would always get along, but they learned to live with each other. Even if conflict did develop between the girl and her mother-in-law, she could not leave her husband's household. The relationship between a young bride and her father-in-law was one of avoidance and the two of them seldom, if ever, came into conflict. On the other hand, while a man did not often see his father-in-law and was respectful toward him, he was always deeply suspicious of his mother-in-law. This woman was always viewed as the *confidante* of a wife, and as someone who hid the wife's indiscretions.

The problem in town is that women never get to know their mothers-in-law in the same way as do their rural sisters, and there are no structural reasons why they should avoid their fathers-in-law. After all, these fathers are seldom involved in their marriage arrangements; nor are their husbands socially or economically beholden to them. Yet the urban husbands are still suspicious of wives' mothers not only because the older women still hide the indiscretions of wives, but also because the lack of long-standing social relationships between families does not inhibit the mother-in-law from helping her daughter desert her husband. Disrespect for parents was mentioned in the previous cases, but this was incidental to the other marital problems which these couples faced. The following is a case of unsatisfactory relations between in-laws that led to divorce.

Case Number 4

Complainant: Mossi woman, thirty years old, Moslem, born in Guiergo, living in Zanguettin quarter, housewife.

Defendant: Mossi man, thirty-five years old, born in Manga, living in Zoghona quarter, ex-soldier.

Testimony

Complainant: "While my husband was in Algeria in 1958, I asked for a plot of land in Zoghona and I built a house. When the house was finished, I invited my husband's father and mother to come to town and live with me. When my husband returned from Algeria, he did not appreciate what I had done in his absence and told me to leave his house. Now that he has chased me away, I have come to ask the Tribunal for a divorce."

Defendant: "What my wife has said about building a house is all true, but I realize that I cannot live with her because she does not respect my parents. I have decided to break my relations with her, and I will not alter my decision."

The Tribunal granted this divorce after a perfunctory attempt at reconciliation.

Neither the woman nor the man discussed in detail the source of the conflict between the wife and her parents-in-law. The suspicion among the auditors in court was that the wife had been indiscreet during her husband's long absence in Algeria, and this led to conflict between her and her in-laws. Since none of the litigants wanted to air these problems in court, the wife's request for a divorce was granted. It should be added that a Mossi father from the rural area might have found it quite intolerable to live at the home of his son and to be, in fact, a dependent of his son's wife. Such an arrangement would never have been made in the rural areas and undoubtedly this was at least one source of conflict between the man and his daughter-in-law.

The problem of working wives has started to plague couples in Ouagadougou, but it appears that when this is cited as the cause for divorce, other factors are also present. When the wives are traders, *dolotières,* or even dressmakers, the evidence suggests that it is not the occupation of these women per se that caused the trouble as much as it is the fear and suspicion of the husbands that their wives are seeing other men. The

175

profession of *dolotière,* with its relatively high income, does present a greater challenge to the dominance of the Mossi man than the occupation of any other group of women in the town. Indeed, the only other women who earn as much as *dolotières* are civil servants, but their husbands are also civil servants. The inability of cultivators and tradesmen to control the activities of their *dolotière* wives leads to misunderstanding and divorce. The following case dramatizes the *dolotières'* marital problems.

Case Number 2

Complainant: Mossi woman, twenty-five years old, *Wend'-pous neba,* born in Lougsi, *dolotière.*

Defendant: Mossi man, thirty-one years old, *Wend'pous neba,* born in Ouagadougou, employed as a *garde republicaine.*

Testimony

Complainant: "One year ago I left my husband as the result of a quarrel and went to Lougsi. He came and took me back just for the sake of appearance, because he has continued to beat me. He does not support me. As I was given to him by my parents according to the traditional system, and as he has since given me back to them, I have come to ask the Tribunal to dissolve the marriage officially so that he will no longer be able to accuse me of having abandoned the conjugal bed. He has accused me of being sterile. I ask for my liberty through this divorce."

Defendant: "Everything my wife has said is false. All I know is that my wife sells *dolo* late every night and when I reproach her, she refuses to comprehend. Every time she goes to visit her family she does not want to return, and each time I am obliged to go in pursuit of her. The last time she returned, she secured the marriage certificate in order to ask for a divorce. Despite the efforts the judges made when we came here on 25 April 1963, to get her to agree to a reconciliation, she has refused to be reconciled. Because she has this unreconciliatory attitude, I ask that the divorce be granted."

Judges: Whereas the Tribunal has been unable to effect a reconciliation between the two spouses, ...

Whereas taking into consideration the Mossi tradition which conforms to the stipulations of Article 6 of the Law of 3 December 1931 which applied to the ruling of this litigation, that when the husband of a household perceives the infidelity of his wife, divorce can be granted, and taking the wishes of the interested parties into account, . . .
On these grounds, the Tribunal, ruling with the right to appeal, decides that the marriage contracted on 16 January 1960 is dissolved; and orders that mention of this divorce be made in the margin of the Suppletory Marriage Register for marriage number 63 of 16 January 1960."

Mistreatment or the inability to live amicably ranks as the next most serious source of marital discord among Ouagadougou couples. Mistreatment as such is something that Mossi women in the rural areas do not have to tolerate, especially if and when it is proven that they are not at fault. When a rural woman complains of mistreatment, she is granted asylum by her patrilineage until it can be ascertained who is at fault. A guilty woman is scolded and made to rejoin her husband. On the other hand, if the husband is at fault, he is deprived of his wife's uxorial services for a certain period. He is also warned that future mistreatment would result in his wife not being returned to him and that he might even be beaten by her male relatives. The Mossi woman in town does not usually have such safeguards and often must seek surcease from the court. The judges appear to be aware of this situation and not only scold a husband for mistreating the "mother of his children" but usually grant a speedy divorce to a mistreated woman. The following case is illustrative.

Case Number 3

Complainant: Mossi woman, twenty-eight years old, Moslem, born in Bere, now living in Tiedpalogho quarter.
Defendant: Mossi man, thirty-five years old, Moslem, born in Yako, resident of Zanguettin quarter, porter.

Testimony

Complainant: "Since my husband and I have been married, we have continuously had misunderstandings. He beats me frequently. One day he beat me so severely that I died [lost consciousness]. Besides, he lacks respect towards

177

my parents. I cannot tolerate such a relationship any longer. Purely and simply, I request a divorce."

Defendant: "It is true that we quarrel and fight, but I have never declared my intentions to abandon her. She has hailed me before the Commissariat de Police on two occasions, demanding a divorce. We were sent away when I did not consent. But now, since she is insisting upon a divorce, I am asking her to be patient until my children grow old enough; then she can leave."

The Tribunal scolded the husband for continually mistreating "the mother of his children" and, after failing to reconcile the couple, ordered that their marriage (Number 55 of 2 November 1955, promulgated at Ouagadougou) be dissolved. The Tribunal also granted the mother custody of the children until they were old enough to join their father. The president of the court enjoined the man to support his children and warned him to leave the children's mother alone. The defendant's dilemma was that, despite bad relations with his wife, he wished to retain her in order to keep his young children. Interestingly enough, he would not have had this problem had he lived in the rural areas. There a man would have simply chased away a wife with whom he could not get along and asked his other wives or his extended family to take care of his offspring.

Sterility is a source of difficulty between husbands and wives in rural areas and continues to be a problem for them in town. Traditionally, if a woman had no children it was deemed to be clearly her fault, and she was either repudiated and sent home or remained a pariah in her husband's household. Of course, many sterile men never suspected their true condition since, when young wives failed to conceive, older women frequently advised them how to procure a child *for* their husbands.

In Ouagadougou, a barren woman is often repudiated and divorced, especially if she resents her husband taking an additional wife. Urban Mossi still believe that people should have children and when a wife is barren, the husband is expected to take another wife. Likewise, a woman is not blamed by townspeople if she leaves a sterile husband or even gets a child for him. The difficulty is that now husbands, especially noncultivators, have adopted the principle of biological parenthood and have discarded the traditional Mossi custom of sociological parenthood; they charge wives who bear other men's children with adultery and seek divorces since they will not accept such children as their own. Likewise, some women, having succeeded in bearing children with other men, seek divorce from their sterile husbands so that they can live with the fathers of their children. Many tradition-minded husbands contest such divorces, claiming the parenthood of these children. The irony here is that often the judges heed their plea and refuse to grant divorces to the women, but insist that the children be given to their genitors when they come of age. The following case illustrates the new problems of sterile men and women:

Case Number 12

Complainant: Mossi man, forty years old, *Wend'pous neba,* born in Guirgo, now living in Ouagadougou, cultivator.

Defendant: Mossi man, forty years old, *Wend'pous neba,* born in Toudou, now living in Ouagadougou, cultivator.

Testimony

Complainant: "My wife was persuaded by her close relatives to leave me and to marry ... [the defendant]. This happened four years ago and I have sought in vain to get back my wife. As a result, I ask to be reimbursed for all those expenses made on her behalf."

Defendant: "I have been falsely accused of having given ... [my relative] to another man. I have witnesses to prove that I did no such thing."

Witness: [the man who took the wife of the complainant]: "It is true that ... [X] told me that the woman is married; but he said that if she wants me, he could ask for nothing better because she has indeed left her husband and does not want to return to him."

Wife: "It was my desire to have a child that caused me to leave my husband. I lived with him for several years of married life and I had not had even one pregnancy. But as I have gotten a child by the [witness] and I am pregnant again, I will never leave him."

The Tribunal made a *pro forma* attempt to reconcile the parties, but, failing to do so, judged that the defendant had indeed conspired to alienate the affections of the wife of the complainant. The president of the court ordered that both he and the "new husband" of the woman pay the complainant 15,400 francs, a sum held to have been spent by him on his wife. Interestingly enough, the court made little attempt to encourage the woman to return to her husband. The judges seemed to be convinced that the husband was sterile and noted that the woman had visible proof of her own fecundity.

Accusations of witchcraft and poisoning have always caused marital strife and repudiation in the rural villages, and it is therefore not surprising that these also cause problems in Ouagadougou. Witchcraft is greatly feared by the Mossi people, as it is by most Africans, since it is frequently used as a threat against a member of the family. So great is the fear of witchcraft in a rural community that, when a man does not repudiate a wife accused of it, he and she are often expelled from his family. In Case Number 10 (see above), the husband accused his wife of putting magical substances (the Moré word for both a witchcraft potion and for medicines is *teeme*) not only under his bed but also in his food. And as usual, the accusations of witchcraft were linked to other problems. The court granted the divorce in that case, but characteristically did not deal with the accusation of witchcraft. Formerly, a person convicted of witchcraft in Mossi country was either executed or driven out of the village and district. Today, in town, the "witch" or poisoner, if found guilty, is jailed by the legal authorities. Moreover, when either a husband or wife is suspected of attempts to poison or bewitch the other, divorce is granted.

Stealing is as much a cause for marital discord in Ouagadougou as it was in the rural areas. Stealing by rural wives (theft by men is no cause for marital discord) reflected upon a man's ability to provide for his family and impaired social relations both within the household and the community. At the same time, thefts in the rural areas seldom came to the attention of the chiefs. Men sanctioned wives who stole and repudiated recidivous ones. Stealing is viewed in much the same way in Ouagadougou. A man's ability to provide for his wife is still questioned if she steals. The difference here is that cases of theft are more likely to be brought to court since urban women are more apt to steal from strangers than from relatives. The result is that urban men are more likely to divorce thieving wives since there is usually more scandal.

180

Nonsupport and religious differences are the only two causes of marital discord found in the survey which appear to be solely a function of urban living. "Nonsupport" is seldom, if ever, a reason for divorce in the countryside because women cultivate both communal holdings and their separate plots and thus earn their livelihood. Of course, not all rural men assiduously prepare their wives' fields prior to cultivation, with the result that women have difficulty earning extra funds. Again, not all men in the rural areas readily provide clothing for their wives or give them the small presents which keep them content. When this happens, a woman either complains to her husband's kinsmen to urge him to mend his ways or returns to her family and remains there until her husband relents. However, in none of these circumstances does the charge of "nonsupport" apply. In contrast, women in Ouagadougou really can charge their husbands with nonsupport. If a man does not provide land for his wife to cultivate in the peri-urban area (only exceptional women can themselves obtain land from chiefs) and if he does not support her, then she is placed in an impossible economic position. Of course, as wives of cultivators with a tradition of self-support, many women may eke out a living by petty trading or by competing with little girls as water vendors in the markets. The neglected, unskilled wives of junior clerks and civil servants can do no such thing and are truly in an untenable position. The status of their husbands precludes their hawking goods in the market, and, since cultivation is unthinkable for them, they are left destitute. Their only recourse is to charge their husbands with nonsupport and sue for divorce.

Differences in religious affiliation are also seldom a cause of either marital discord or divorce in the rural districts; and when this issue is raised, there are usually other factors involved. Thus, some rural Mossi fathers who had promised their daughters to friends reneged on their promise when they converted either to Christianity or Islam, claiming that they could not give their daughters to nonbelievers.[6] The real reason was often that they wanted to give the daughters to their new coreligionists. Marital discord also developed between rural Christian and Moslem husbands whose tradi-

---

[6]Elliott P. Skinner, "Christianity and Islam among the Mossi," *American Anthropologist*, LX, No. 6 (December 1958), 1,107.

tionalist wives insisted upon visiting diviners either in the hope of curing some disease, resisting witchcraft, or worse, securing help in witchcraft. In these cases, however, one could blame fear of witchcraft more than religious differences per se for the marital problems. In contrast, religious differences do often cause major dissension within some Ouagadougou households. Many women simply feel that they have such need for the comfort or community of the church that they are willing to risk marital conflict and divorce by becoming converts to Christianity against the will of their husbands. Of course, the church does not encourage women to neglect their husbands, nor would it sanction divorces which result from this problem, but since it cannot control the actions and feelings of non-Christian husbands, divorces often ensue.

Childbirth and Childrearing

Life in Ouagadougou is beginning to effect a subtle but growing change in the childbearing and childrearing practices of the town's inhabitants. People still place a high value on having children. In fact, sterility and barrenness are more likely to lead to divorce in town than in the rural areas because of family nucleation, the decline of polygyny, and the increasing value of biological parenthood.

According to the 1962 census, the one to five year age group was the largest in the population, numbering 8,119 children and representing 14.1 per cent of Ouagadougou's population. The 10,599 women counted had given birth to 16,125 sons (of whom 12,365 were alive) and 14,065 daughters (of whom 10,406 were alive), During 1961, 3,706 women had borne 2,214 sons (of whom 1,909 were living) and 2,155 daughters (of whom 1,882 were still alive).[7]

Judging from the 1962 census, infant mortality in Ouagadougou continues to be very high, amounting to 132 per 1,000 (13.8 per cent of the boys and 12.7 per cent of the girls). However, the women's belief that it is easier to rear children in Ouagadougou is borne out by the fact that infant mortality in rural Upper Volta during this same period was 174 per 1,000. Indeed, inquiries reveal that the wives of cultivators view migration to town as a boon to childrearing. They assert that: 1)

[7]"Recensement Démographique ...," pp. 10–13.

the facilities for confinement are better in town than in the
rural areas; 2) that there are more dispensaries and clinics in
town than in the rural areas to care for sick children; 3) that
the town's water is safer and cleaner than water in the rural
areas; and 4) that ailing or orphaned children in town survive
much better because they are given milk and other food products. Almost every woman in Ouagadougou knows of some
sick child, orphan, or set of twins which had been brought
to Ouagadougou so that they would have a better chance to
live.

Despite the fact that the Ouagadougou women feel that it is
safer to bear children in town, few of them seek prenatal care
unless complications arise. This is as true among educated
women and wives of educated men as it is among illiterate
wives of low-status husbands. Women of all social statuses
still tend to perform their domestic chores or to pursue their
occupational activities until time for their confinement. When
a group of elite women in Ouagadougou discussed the dating
of maternity leave, there was no agreement. Some preferred
maternity leave beginning six weeks prior to confinement and
continuing for eight weeks after parturition; others wished to
work until the date of actual confinement and have fourteen
weeks' leave afterwards.

The practice of going either to the hospital or to one of the
maternity centers to have a baby is steadily gaining ground
among the women of Ouagadougou. Almost all the wives of
high-status men have their babies in the main hospital of the
town, and an increasing number of other mothers go there or
to the maternity clinics. During the calendar year 1964, approximately 5,204 babies were delivered in the main hospital.
The professions of the fathers of the first 65 infants born there
in 1964 are listed in Table XXVI. According to these figures,
the cultivators in town made as much use of the hospital's
obstetrical services as any of the other groups in town. In fact,
the percentage of their hospital use is about equal to their percentage in the population. The same appears to be true of the
other status groups in town.

In general, women give fairly obvious reasons for the steady
rise of their use of the maternity wards in the hospital and
clinics. Most of them are convinced that mothers receive
better medical care and that babies born there have a better
chance of surviving than those born at home. This could have

183

TABLE XXVI. Professions of Fathers of a Sample of Children Born in the Main Hospital of Ouagadougou (1964)

Profession	Number
Cultivator	26
Civil servant	9
Soldier	6
Laborer	5
Chauffeur	4
Cook	3
Merchant	3
Mechanic	2
Carpenter	2
Painter	1
Electrician	1
Deputy (politician)	1
Male nurse	1
Unemployed	1
TOTAL	65

been predicted. What was unexpected was that both women and men (especially cultivators) desired to have babies delivered in the hospital and clinics so that their births could be automatically registered, thus providing the children with the birth certificates so necessary for attending school.

Despite the growing recognition that the municipal health services are good, quite a number of women, especially the wives of cultivators and other low-status men, still hesitate to use them. Sometimes women and their husbands object to the strict rules governing sanitation. But the most hated regulation is the one which controls visiting. People reject the rule that relatives and friends of parturient women should not visit them whenever they can or wish to do so. Some women complain sarcastically that the Africans responsible for making or maintaining the rules are *nansaraba* (whites or Europeans) and lament the introduction of the ways of the *nansaradin* by the nurses and midwives. The latter respond that they are doing what is best for the women and state philosophically that with "evolution" and *civilisation* the women, especially the wives of cultivators, will understand.

Higher-status people value the medical attention in the maternity wards of the hospital and clinics as well as the social recognition granted when their children are born there. Radio Upper Volta always announces the birth in a hospital or clinic of a child of high status in the following manner:

> Mr. X of [here the name of the service or business] and Madame, have the joy of announcing to their relatives and acquaintances, the birth of their [nth] child, a boy [or girl] at the hospital [or maternity] ... [name of place] on [day and month]. Mother and baby are enjoying perfect health.

Such news broadcasts are eagerly listened to by the population of the town and help to foster a feeling of community among the high-prestige groups. They also serve to maintain kinship bonds between townspeople and their rural relatives. Conversely, the births of children of high-status persons in the rural or smaller centers are also broadcast on the radio in the capital. Needless to say, the births of ordinary persons—merchants, tradesmen, and cultivators—are not broadcast unless, of course, these births are spectacular in their own right.

Only very high-status women provide layettes for their unborn babies. If these mothers do not bring clothes to the hospital for their infants, they usually have them sent as soon as the child is born. The wives of cultivators and other low-status women feel, like their rural sisters, that it is folly to buy clothes for a child before it is born since it may not live. Thus, it is only when the child of low status is ready to go home that clothes are bought and brought for it. These differences in dealing with babies among status groups tend to persist after the children are taken home. Low-status women tend to rear their children in the traditional manner. For example, such children sleep near the mother on a grass mat. Higher-status parents normally buy locally made or even imported cribs for their children.

Health facilities for children in Ouagadougou consist of three municipal dispensaries and one run by the Catholic mission. These provide different types of immunization for the children. In addition, there are five social service centers at which infants, up to about two years of age, are weighed, given simple medical care, and referred to dispensaries and hospitals if their state of health warrants it. Nowadays, urban mothers of all status groups eagerly bring their children for immunization against such diseases as smallpox, diphtheria, typhoid,

185

and measles which, in the Upper Volta, is especially virulent. Women are so anxious for children to be vaccinated that they appear at the dispensaries quite early on the morning that the shots are to be given, even when they had been assured beforehand that enough vaccine was on hand. The day of the week does not make any difference either. Women are as content to come to the dispensaries on Sundays as on any other day.

The use of the social service centers for child care, while fairly extensive, is not as universal as that of the dispensaries. Table XXVII indicates the occupations of the husbands of 320 women who brought babies to the social service centers of Bilbalgo, Kamsaoghin, Ouidi, and Paspanga during the month of October 1964.

Here again, the wives of cultivators were the most numerous users of the social service centers. Their numeral superiority to other groups in Ouagadougou should, however, not obscure the importance of this type of behavior. Many of these women had trouble rearing children before migrating to Ouagadougou and actively seek advice in raising subsequent children. Some young mothers, especially those with first children, distrust the traditional knowledge of child care and go to the center to learn modern child care methods, or the "civilized" way. Some of these women believe that since a child born in town is "civilized," it must be cared for in a "civilized" way. They normally refuse help with their children from older women who live in their household, preferring to visit the *teeme-dogo* (house of medicine) and learn modern child care from the social workers there.

TABLE XXVII.   Use of Social Service
Center for Baby Care by Occupational Groups
(Ouagadougou, October 1964)

Occupation of Husband	Number of Babies
Cultivator	114
Soldier, policeman	101
Tradesman	52
Civil servant, clerk	46
Merchant	5
Clergy (Protestant catechist)	1
Unemployed	1
TOTAL	320

A significant number of the wives of police and military men bring their children to the health center because of three factors: 1) many of them are young, illiterate, relatively lonely, and they seek modern care for their town-born babies; 2) the medical officials at the several military camps and *gendarmeries* encourage the wives of their men to take children to the social service centers rather than seek pediatric services at the camps; and 3) these women use the social service centers because they consider them a service provided by the municipality and the Republic for their employees, among whom are their husbands. Thus, in a way, the use of the center legitimizes a woman's connection with the government, and with the high-status women.

The wives of tradesmen assert simply that, "It is good to bring children to social service centers." Thus, it appears that these women consider the social service centers to be not only an institution of the town but also of a new and modern way of life which they seek to share. One suspects that the fact that their husbands are engaged in trades related to modern life is one of the contributing factors to the view which these women have about such institutions as the health center.

The health and municipal authorities are often disappointed by the relative failure of the literate wives of civil servants and clerks to bring children to the social service centers. When these centers were being created, the Mayor of the town voiced the hope that those persons who understood their purpose would patronize them and encourage their less educated sisters to do likewise. This did not happen. One reason for this was that many educated women believe they know as much about pediatrics as the social aides who work there. Morever, many literate women distrust the competence of the social aids who, for the most part, have inferior academic backgrounds to many high-status women. They prefer to buy books on pediatrics and care for their own babies.

When high-status women do visit the social service centers, they behave and are treated quite differently from lower-status women. They usually know the nursing aides or get to know them quite easily. Thus, when they arrive, they shake hands with the personnel of the center and are given or take seats. They do not stand quietly in the doorway like low-status women, nor do they greet the aides by putting cupped hands to chests and standing or sitting in line. Moreover, high-status

187

women seldom have to wait their turn; their babies are treated shortly after they arrive. These women help the social aides undress and weigh their babies and the social aides, for their part, usually fuss over the babies.

The wives of merchants and female merchants seldom bring babies to the social service centers. These women claim they are too busy in the market to do so. The Hausa and Yoruba women have the poorest attendance record at the social service centers. Not one Yoruba woman brought her baby to the social service center of Kamsaoghin in 1964, even though this establishment is quite close to their homes. One social aide conceded that the Yoruba women, like most women in commerce, have little time to visit the centers, but pointed out that they are also the most reluctant to become involved with "the affairs of the whites."

The belief of many women—not only the Yoruba—that the social service centers are instruments of socio-cultural change, or *civilisation,* as it is called in Ouagadougou, is basically correct. The centers are interested in modern pediatrics and in helping mothers to adjust to the urban environment. Yet some of the personnel still believe in the efficacy of certain traditional practices. About 90 per cent of the babies observed in the health centers wore some kind of protective amulets: traditional ones, consisting of bracelets made of three metals and various types of animal material; Moslem ones, consisting of Koranic verses covered with leather; Catholic ones consisting of various types of medals and crosses; and imaginative combinations of all of these. None of the social aides ever attempted to dissuade mothers from placing these protective devices on the children. Even when fairly large leather chains containing packages of Koranic verses interfered with weighing children, the social aides said nothing. In reply to the researcher's query, one aide remarked that as long as the amulets did no harm to the children, they were tolerated. She added, parenthetically, that any help they might give is appreciated. Of course, it is difficult to determine how much, or how little, faith these workers place in the efficacy of the amulets.

There are, however, several traditional pediatric practices which the social aides are trying to persuade urban mothers to abandon. One is their constant use of enemas to facilitate defecation in children—a practice found among the Mossi,

Gourounsi, and Bobo—which is said to be related to the difficulty young children have of evacuating the residue of sorghum and millet gruel. The problem is that many mothers
start the *lavage* (washing or enema) as soon as a child is born
and continue this practice through the nursing period, even
though the child is nourished with milk only. The result is that
children become so accustomed to the enema that they are unable to defecate without it. The social aides have tried with
little success to root this practice out. Some young mothers
are willing to abandon this practice, but their older female
relatives resist and complain. Social aides are also trying to
stop mothers from placing medicine (*teeme*) on the fontanels
of infants. The mothers believe that the sunken spot on the
top of a child's head indicates poor health and use *teeme* in an
effort to raise the fontanel.

There have been slight changes in the feeding of children
among different status groups in Ouagadougou. The social
service centers had little difficulty persuading mothers in town
to accept bottles and nipples and to use different types of preserved milk. This trait-complex is being adopted so widely
that some social workers are complaining that it is unwise for
all mothers to prefer canned cow's milk to their own. The
reason for this is not difficult to understand. Commercial milk
companies, such as Nestle, Galliasec, and Guigoz, display
advertisements all over town showing African women with
healthy babies and promising the same to all mothers whose
babies use their products. Second, many women cultivators
are impressed with the fact that high-status women, whose
babies are considered by all the town's women to be the best
cared for, use the bottle. (A corollary of this, according to
the social aides, is that low-status women use preserved milk
because by so doing they feel and become *un peu civilisé*.)
Third, working mothers, especially civil servants, use bottled
milk because, although they are released from work to nurse
their babies, they have to leave milk home to tide the infants
over until they get there.

More difficult to ascertain is the suggestion of some social
aides that women used bottled milk instead of relying on
breast milk to get around the lactation sexual taboo. The
traditional belief is that every baby arrives in the world with its
own milk supply and may die if its mother spoils the milk by
resuming sexual intercourse, and possibly becoming pregnant.

189

The problem in town, however, is that monogamy taxes the ability and willingness of both husbands and wives to observe the lactation taboo. Consequently, it is believed that both husbands and wives try to shorten the period of abstention and use bottled milk in order not to endanger the baby's health when sexual relations are resumed.

One difficulty faced by low-status women who would like to change the feeding habits of their children is the cost of doing so. Some even have difficulty practicing the dietary rules which the centers recommend for sickly babies. Many cultivators, tradesmen, and military men consider preserved milk a luxury and refuse to give their wives money to buy it. The centers try to help underweight children by using surplus U. S. milk distributed through an American Catholic welfare agency. At the same time, they encourage the women to persuade their husbands that growing children need additional milk. The danger in illiterate women using bottled milk is that they often impair the health of their children. Many of the mothers do not take proper care of the bottles and nipples and honestly do not understand the need for all the fuss and bother. If pressed to clean the bottles and nipples, they do so, but consider such demands to be idiosyncracies of the *nansaraba*. The aides, for their part, lament the resistance of the women but keep on trying.

Social aides encounter difficulties persuading low-status women to add certain types of foods to the diets of children. Many urban Mossi women still refuse to give their children eggs and powdered dry fish. Some women also believe that meat is bad for children or that the *kissigou* ("totemistic") affiliations of husbands prevent their children from using certain foods. The centers try to cure dietary difficiencies by giving the children vitamins, but limited budgets preclude much help.

The social service centers in Ouagadougou play an important role in the care and feeding of orphans and twins. Most groups in the Voltaic culture area do not like orphans, especially those whose mothers died in childbirth, and some may have formerly even permitted orphans to die. Although the Mossi people did not permit orphans to die, they did distrust them. The orphan in Mossi society used to be accused of having a "bad head" or of "killing his mother," and was believed to be a bad influence in the community. Therefore, unless some woman took pity on the orphan, or the co-wife of its mother decided to serve as a wet nurse, an orphaned child had difficulty surviving. Twins in the Voltaic area often received the same treatment. The Mossi considered them to be strange beings, inveterate tricksters, and custom impelled the mothers of twins to beg for gifts in the villages and market places. There are old reports that in many Voltaic areas, and even Mossi country itself, twins were often killed. Today no citizen of Upper Volta believes that twins are still killed or allowed to die, yet they continue to view them as strange beings. Christians in the town do not even call twins by their traditional term, kinkirsi, but refer to them as camba yibo (literally, two children).

One result of this apprehension about both orphans and twins is that people in the rural areas often send them to Ouagadougou to be given milk and to be cared for by the social service centers. Sometimes a cowife or daughter of the dead mother is commissioned to bring the orphan to Ouagadougou and stay there until the child is weaned. At other times, the orphans are given to strangers or to priests who place them in the care of parishioners or the centers. The result is that the orphan population of the social service centers is quite high. Out of 75 children treated at the center of Bilbalgo during one day, 15 were orphans. The number of twins found in the social centers is also quite high, and for the same reasons. People either bring twins to the town because they feel uneasy about them or because it is easier to get milk for them there. In some cases it is difficult to separate one reason from the other.

There have been some changes in other areas of childrearing among urban women. The wives of cultivators continue to allow their children unlimited access to the breasts, but some high-status women now retreat from the main room while breast-feeding their children. This frequently causes some comment and joking between husband and wife or among the guests as to whether the mother is "adopting the 'bad' habits of the Europeans." The traditional permissive attitude toward bowel control has not changed and very young children defecate wherever they are. High-status women out visiting with children simply change the child's diaper while continuing their conversation. Older children are encouraged to go outside or near the street for these purposes. The rationale for this is the fear that an unsupervised child may fall into the toilet pit. The health authorities and the municipality are opposed to this practice and plan to prohibit it by law. These authorities, especially the former Mayor, while quite conscious of the problems involved in socio-cultural change, feel that not only the health of the children would be improved by a ban on such practices, but that the municipality would be a cleaner and better place in which to live.

Municipal and health authorities concerned about the health of children have made it possible for young boys to be circumcised in the urban hospital. This has resulted in the disappearance of the institution of the *bongo* (circumcision lodge) from the town. There is, therefore, no formal institution for the boys to learn traditional lore, and they must either pick this up from older relatives or remain ignorant of it. Perhaps because of the absence of the circumcision lodge and its training, or because boys are circumcised at a much earlier age than in the rural areas, some young male children walk about naked after they are circumcised. It would have been unthinkable in the rural areas for a boy to do so, since after circumcision he is considered a man.

The health authorities have no provisions for the clitoridectomy of girls. The reason is that this operation is not only foreign to French medical practice but is against Western mores and encounters the subtle opposition of the Christian churches. The result is that this practice is seldom discussed and is a source of embarrassment for many urbanites. Nevertheless, the practice of clitoridectomy is still universal, at least for Mossi girls, and elder kinswomen threaten to abduct their young female relatives and have the operation performed if parents hesitate to do so. Young parents seldom resist, partly because they still believe in the practice, and the young girls are taken to the houses of older practitioners where the operation is performed. Whether this practice can survive urbanization and modern female education is still problematical. Already some girls who grew up in France with politician fathers have not had this operation, and modern mothers may not wish their daughters to be operated upon by old women who lack medical knowledge.

Data presented in this chapter indicate differences in family life and status profiles among the people of Ouagadougou. It is clear that occupation and income levels have an influence on where most of these families live, the types of houses they live in, the type and amount of modern "elements of comfort" they possess, the type of clothing they wear, and the food they eat. These factors are also related to relations between husbands and wives in the families of cultivator-gardeners, the middle-status groups, and the high-status civil servants and clerks. There is a net deviation from traditional social and cultural patterns among the Ouagadougou population as income and education rises: the higher the income of the families involved, the more modern (*civilisé*) or European is their behavior. The more educated the members of the family, the more changes from the traditional norms are encountered. The behavior of the older high-status clerks and civil servants reveals a greater synthesis of traditional and modern features. Most of these people were born and reared in the rural areas. Some of them married women less educated than they were and only later in life did they achieve high status. Interestingly enough, many of these persons show a marked tendency to become more traditional in dress as well as behavior as they grow older. There is a parallel tendency of women in all status groups in Ouagadougou to Africanize their clothing as soon as they achieve the childbearing stage. It is also at this stage that the high-status women dissolve the *ménage à deux*. The reasons normally given are that their husbands contemplate polygamy or its equivalent, and that they need money to take care of their own children.

The change in family life in Ouagadougou is as much a conscious manipulation of new social and cultural elements in the town as of urban life itself. The reason that European-type traits predominate among the young and educated—and this is true for mothers with "civilized" urban-born children as well as for young families—is that these people consciously strive to behave in a manner that they consider most efficient in the town. The cultivator-gardeners in town make fewer changes in behavior because they are not involved with most of the modern institutions in Ouagadougou. The younger clerks and civil servants adopt more European and modern social and cultural patterns because they desire to participate in the more important aspects of town life, and these are the most modern.

Yet it appears that once people have achieved their goals, whether they are high-status women who start childbearing

193

or young men who have become ministers, they find little reason to continue to manipulate their social and cultural environment. Very often they refrain from doing so in the name of nationalism or traditionalism. Part of the dialectic here, however, is that in the process of manipulating their social and cultural environment in order to succeed in the urban environment, their behavior is permanently changed. The resulting pattern, more than a synthesis of the old and the new, portrays the volition of the actors. Moreover, as the various occupational and income families establish regular patterns of behavior, the social categories now found in Ouagadougou will undoubtedly harden into social classes. The nature of these classes and their attributes would of necessity reveal the process of their development.

Wedding of civil servants

CHAPTER VI

Ethnic Interaction and the Role of Associations

The numerical superiority of ethnic Mossi in contemporary Ouagadougou has served to mask the importance of the strangers in the early history and development of the town. As late as the end of World War II, the disparity between the two groups was not great. In 1945 there were more than 5,000 foreign Africans in a total African population of 17,800, only slightly less than one-third of the population. By 1962 the percentage of African strangers had declined to 23.5 per cent, amounting to only 13,578 in a total African urban population of 57,779 persons.[1] And, given the fact that only 5,078 are non-Voltaic strangers (such as Hausa, Malinke, and Yoruba) in contrast to 8,500 Voltaic strangers (Gourounsi, Boussansé, Bobo, Samogo, etc.), it is clear that the percentage of the traditional strangers in Ouagadougou has declined significantly. The number of traditional strangers in the 1964 Ouagadougou population of over 100,000 is unknown but, given the massive in-migration of rural Mossi, it is clear that the strangers are becoming demographically insignificant within the town.

The people of Ouagadougou take pride in their hospitality to strangers, citing the historical presence of foreign traders and teachers in the town. Nevertheless, a gradient can be perceived in the way the contemporary Mossi majority views the strangers in its midst. As would be expected, the Ouagadougou Mossi hold the Mossi of the other kingdoms in high esteem, subject only to the normal chauvinism found in any local group. The people of the town, especially the Mossi, subscribe to the almost universal belief that the Mossi from the northern region of Yatenga are touchy and haughty. The townspeople attribute these same negative traits to the Gourmantche of the brother kingdom of Fada N'Gourma. There is general praise for the cleanliness of the houses and persons of the Bobo and Gourounsi women. The Mossi attitude toward the Gourounsi men is conditioned by the fact that the

---

[1]"Recensement Démographique ...," pp. 10, 13.

Mossi were still expanding and absorbing the Gourounsi when the French arrived. Mossi often jokingly refer to the Gourounsi as their *ligidi* (meaning money), implying their status as individuals to be sold as slaves. The joking relationship between Mogho and Samogho is more nearly symmetrical. Both groups declare that their two ancestors quarreled over the bones of a dog, and this quarrel still continues. However, there are no rituals or ceremonies in which these joking relationships are dramatized.

In contrast, the Mossi of Ouagadougou have little esteem for the Fulani, even though the latter have lived in the town and in the Upper Volta for centuries. Mossi delcare that the Fulani have always considered themselves to be cleverer than other groups and have always attempted to get the better of the persons among whom they lived. To the traditional distrust of the farmer for pastoralist is now added the dislike of the Fulani attempt to capitalize on their Caucasian traits, valued by the French during the colonial period. The Fulani for their part, concur that they are clever and affirm their Caucasian origin. However, they insist that the Mossi dislike them for not originally having been cultivators and feel that urban Mossi should abandon this traditional prejudice especially toward those Fulani who have settled in the town. But the problem here is that the urban Fulani, especially the females, are now the butt of a new stereotype—that of soldiers' companions. During the heyday of the military presence in Ouagadougou, certain legendary amatory relationships developed between a number of Fulani women of Bilibambili and soldiers stationed in the town. These relations are still celebrated in songs on fete days by the young men of the town.

The Dioula and Hausa are the most esteemed of all stranger groups in Ouagadougou. These groups are the oldest strangers in town and in the past contributed much to Mossi life, being involved in the realms of trade, Islam, and Koranic studies. Moreover the Dioula and Hausa integrated themselves into the life of the town. There are few resident Hausa or Dioula who do not speak Moré or other Voltaic languages. Furthermore, for generations these groups have intermarried with the Mossi, including members of the royal house. The Yoruba, who came under the auspices of the Hausa, have inherited a share of the latter's goodwill among the Mossi. Both Yoruba men and women are viewed as honest and hardworking. The Yoruba women are held to be especially morally correct and are said to present few problems for their own families or for the other groups in the town.

The town's inhabitants are ambivalent about the Songhay and Djerma of neighboring Niger. The men of these two groups are held in high esteem as traders and hard workers, but the women are disdained for their activities as itinerant prostitutes catering to lower-status migrants.

The Senegalese are distrusted by the inhabitants of Ouagadougou. People believe that the Senagalese men (women are rarely considered here) are notorious contrabanders and gold smugglers whose illegal entry into the town and country should be controlled, since they allegedly contribute nothing to the country. The gold and silver smelting activities of the Senegalese are appreciated, but people believe that they must be watched carefully lest they cheat their customers.

The Dahomeans, Togolese, and Ghanaians are the most unpopular stranger groups in Ouagadougou. The Dahomeans and Togolese are especially resented because of their association with the previous French administration and because they held clerical jobs to which many of the local educated people aspired.[2] People still recall with displeasure the alleged arrogance and superior attitudes of these strangers whose better education and "culture" led them to want to keep the "locals in their place." The result has been the persistence of stereotypes about the Dahomeans and Togolese and prejudices detrimental to them. For example, the people of Ouagadougou still believe that these strangers should not be trusted since they use their intelligence and accounting ability to manipulate records and commit forgeries. They also believe that these strangers continue to be extremely *raciste* and that they try to obtain employment for their fellow countrymen at the expense of all the others. Furthermore, they accuse the Dahomeans and Togolese of exploiting the country by sending money home as a retirement fund. But most dangerous of all is the local belief that these strangers, despite being good Catholics, still practice many of their traditional

[2]Cf. Skinner, 1963, p. 318; cf. also Herschelle S. Challenor, "Expatriation, Discord and Repatriation: A Study of Dahomeyan Strangers in French West Africa as a Problem in the Colonization and Decolonization Process." Unpublished Ph.D. dissertation, Faculty of Political Science, Columbia University, New York, 1970.

religious rites, including gruesome human sacrifice, to increase their intellectual and other powers.

It was these stereotypes and prejudices that led the officials of Upper Volta to repatriate the Dahomean and Togolese civil servants as soon as the country became self-governing. Moreover, the persistence of these beliefs continues to create unpleasantness for those strangers who remain in the town. For example, one night in 1964 there was a wild rumor in Ouagadougou that the Dahomeans had tried to sacrifice a child. Investigation showed the following had taken place: a Dahomean clerk allegedly saw a young Mossi boy loitering around his household and asked him whether he wanted a job as a "boy," that is, a young helper in the household. The child accepted and the Dahomean took him to his house to sleep, then locked the door and went off to the movies. Sometime during the evening the child awoke and, finding the door locked, started to cry. The landlady heard the boy's cries and, recalling rumors that Dahomeans used children in rituals, raised a hue and cry and alerted the Municipal Councilor of Tiedpalogho. The official summoned policemen who broke into the house and freed the boy. Here they found typewriters and other office equipment believed to be stolen. They waited for the Dahomean to return, and, suspecting him to be part of a criminal ring, forced him to take them to the home of other Dahomeans in Dapoya II. The sight of police and soldiers bearing sub-machine guns invading the homes of Dahomeans in the quarter frightened the local people. They then spread rumors that the Dahomeans were responsible for killing those missing children whose disappearance had been announced over the local radio but whose reappearance was never made known.

No one knows what the future of the Dahomeans and Togolese in Ouagadougou will be. Almost all the civil servants were fired, and so were many in the private sector as their employers feared the accusation of favoring foreign employees over "nationals." The French Government and commercial establishments still employ some Dahomeans and Togolese, especially as bookkeepers, and various English-speaking foreign embassies have hired them as clerks. The Togolese, especially, have been recruited for the clerk jobs because many of them learned English in Gold Coast schools.

But whether these people can continue to work at these jobs is difficult to predict, for, in addition to the growing competition of educated Voltaics for the white-collar jobs, their non-citizen status is beginning to affect the social status of their families.

Whereas the townspeople envy and fear the Dahomeans and Togolese, they distrust and have contempt for many Ghanaians. This is interesting since the Ghanaians have only recently arrived in the town in any appreciable numbers. The urban people charge that many Ghanaian men are criminals and that most of the women are prostitutes, and highly professional ones. Like many stereotypes, these do have a certain factual basis. Some Ghanaian men have indeed been arrested for antisocial activities, especially for some of the more spectacular thefts in town. And many Ghanaian women are prostitutes. Nevertheless, it is also clear that the negative attitude toward the Ghanaians has a linguistic basis (the Ghanaians do not even have a European language in common with many townsmen); a cultural basis stemming from the colonial period; and a political basis which is the result of a long feud between ex-Presidents N'Krumah and Yaméogo. It remains to be seen whether the good relations between the successors of the ex-Presidents will help ameliorate relations between the Ouagadougou people and the Ghanaian strangers.

Independence and modern politics have affected the status and role of the African stranger groups in Ouagadougou. The birth of the Upper Volta Republic had an adverse effect on the Dahomean and Togolese strangers, many of whom were dismissed from their clerical jobs and sent from the country. The other African strangers were affected less by these changes. The greatest change so far involves the relationship between the strangers and citizens of their homelands. The notables of stranger groups can no longer provide many services for, nor give aid to, their visitors. First of all, strangers can no longer enter the country freely, and their hosts must ascertain that they have necessary passports and identity cards. Moreover, the stranger elders must make sure their visitors are not fugitives from justice nor *agents provocateurs* of neighboring African states. The stranger elders must provide the visitors with the civil documents so important for living in Ouagadougou, and these are not always easy to obtain. Indeed, the difficulty of getting such documents often provides stranger notables with ready-made excuses for withholding or withdrawing aid from visitors, especially if the latter appear to be "parasitic." Thus, the birth of the modern nation-state has modified the nature of relations between the African strangers and their visitors by making it possible for the stranger community to insist upon visitors fulfilling certain specific requirements before they are welcomed. Any failure to take the precautions which are important to the whole town is dangerous since it can jeopardize the total nexus of relations between the strangers and their hosts. Despite these new problems, however, the strangers can and do help bona fide visiting countrymen. For example, a prominent stranger Malian family was able to obtain permission for a relative from Mali to obtain a delicate eye operation (which could not be performed in his native country) even though ex-Presidents Keita and Yaméogo were at odds. The Malian stranger had such good relations with the local community leaders and politicians that he was able to overcome the interstate problems.

The relations between the Ouagadougou people and the dominant European (French) group have always been different in kind from those with the African strangers. First of all, the Europeans at one time represented a conquering group. Now they are a high-status one. Because of this, the Europeans never had to cater to the wishes or inclinations of the indigenous groups as did many of the African stranger groups. The Europeans conquered a society which had its own status hierarchy, based on the right of conquest. The military and therefore status superiority of the Europeans was acknowledged quite early during the colonial period and accepted until independence. Even today, the tradition of European racial and cultural superiority still affects the behavior of most resident Africans and Europeans.

The number of Europeans (primarily French) in Ouagadougou has never been large. There were 15 whites in town in 1912 and the number never rose to more than 400 before World War II. After the war, the European population in the town increased rapidly so that by 1951 there were 1,500 of them. However, by 1962 there were only about 1,347 in the town. Of this number there were 709 men to 638 women, a reflection of a trend toward the in-migration of European families rather than of single men so characteristic of the colonial period.[3]

Although it had the power and opportunity to do so, the European population of Ouagadougou never fully segregated itself physically from the African population. The first European officials settled in the area once occupied by the former palace of Mogho Naba Wobogo, and the missionaries built their mission not far distant from the new royal palace. When Governor Hesling laid out the commercial, administrative, and educational areas of the town, those Europeans who were associated with these various functions lived in or near their places of work. The teachers lived in a quarter near the schools, and the administrative personnel lived in the residential area between the administrative center and the educational center or in Koulouba, directly behind the main colonial government offices. Today, Europeans still inhabit these areas, but they are also found in a small area surrounding the Town Hall, in Dapoya II, Gounghin, Bilbalgo, and in a section of Zoghona (really La Rotonde quarter) near the new administrative buildings of the government, and the area now being developed for industrial purposes.

In spite of residential propinquity there is little contact between the local population and the Europeans outside purely economic, administrative, and academic activities. The reasons for this are complex but interrelated. First, there is the heritage from the colonial period, a heritage which, in the Upper Volta and especially for the Mossi people, was one of forced labor and hardship both at home and in the neighboring colonies. And, while the local people normally do not show animosity toward the Europeans, they have not quite forgotten the past and prefer not to have any more to do with the Europeans than is necessary. Second, most higher-status Europeans with whom the educated African group must work were colonial civil servants and still retain colonialist attitudes of racial and cultural superiority (the two factors are inseparably linked despite disclaimers to the contrary). Moreover, since the Upper Volta Government still needs the Europeans' services, the latter can and do retain these notions of racial or cultural superiority. The European prefers to consider these attitudes as a form of class snobbishness or

[3]"Recensement Démographique . . . ," p. 10.

201

ETHNIC INTERACTIONS

"pride." But these attitudes have led to unfortunate unpleasantness. As late as 1960, a number of European hotels
and bars would not use the same glasses for their African and
European patrons. European officials and sales people often
tutoient members of the African elite class. In 1964, the
foremost African intellectual in Ouagadougou was rudely insulted when he asked the owner of a hotel whether she knew
the location of the room of two visiting researchers who had
asked to see him.

Despite independence, most Africans in Ouagadougou display an inferiority complex when dealing with Europeans.
Many Europeans claim, and with some validity, that it is difficult to meet Africans socially. They say that whereas Africans honor formal invitations from the French community,
such as to receptions given at the French Embassy, they seldom accept invitations proffered by ordinary whites. And,
when they do honor such invitations, they do not reciprocate.
The Europeans understand some of the reasons for what they
consider to be the negative social behavior of their African
colleagues but they still resent it. One obvious reason for
the lack of African social reciprocity is shame. Except for
ministers, the housing and living conditions of most Africans
are so different from those of Europeans, even those with the
same education and jobs, that the Africans feel ashamed of
exchanging social visits. Again, except for a few well-known
African couples in the town, African women normally do not
accompany their husbands when the couple is invited to visit
a French home because they are not fluent in French and are
unacquainted with formal European social behavior. People
express the hope that as more Africans build modern homes,
and as many more African women learn French and European
social customs, there will be a change in the pattern of
interaction between Africans and Europeans.

Africans who do entertain Europeans treat them quite differently from African guests. The fact that the Europeans
are "strangers" as well as guests accounts in part for the
great solicitude shown them. Moreover, the tendency for
Africans to invite only Europeans of similar or superior social rank confuses the issue as to whether ethnicity or politeness plays the dominant role in these relations. Normally
when Africans invite Europeans to weddings, parties, receptions, or dances, they place them either at the head table or at

separate tables and give them the best food and drink they have to offer. They are quite solicitous over the comfort of these guests and try to ensure that they have a good time. On the other hand, if the Europeans fail to dance or depart soon after the refreshments have been served, the Africans complain and make perjorative comments about the customs of the *nansaraba, les toubab,* or *les colons.*

The lack of meaningful social contact between the Africans and Europeans in Ouagadougou is underscored by the relative absence of intermarriage between the two groups. During 1964 there were no more than five mixed married couples in the town. Of the three well-known to the investigator, two were Mossi army officers who had married their wives in France, and one was a civil servant who had also married his wife in France. Whether or not the relatives of men who married European women approved of the marriages initially, they tolerate them, as do the Europeans. At social functions where mixed couples sit at tables with their African friends, there normally is social interaction between them, especially between the European wives of Africans and Europeans. As far as could be ascertained, there is only one case of marriage between European men and African women in the town, even though one's attention is drawn to liaisons between several such couples. The Mossi declare that there has never been a case of concubinage or cohabitation between a Mossi woman and a European man, and when evidence to the contrary is produced they readily admit the existence of this "unfortunate" case, but insist that it is "the exception that proves the rule."

The European community in Ouagadougou is far from monolithic and homogeneous. It is, rather, more diverse now than it was during the colonial period. During that time most of the Europeans, aside from the Lebano-Syrians, were in the administration, the mission, or were higher echelon representatives of the large commercial houses. There were very few lower-class Europeans (*petits blancs*) in the town; and the French soldiers stationed in Ouagadougou were marginal to everyone. With independence and the development of Ouagadougou, many more middle-class French technicians and their families arrived in town and, to serve their housekeeping needs, many lower-class Europeans came also. All of these French nationals are linked together through the

French Embassy, but socially they form their own groups. And, given the end of colonialism, the Europeans no longer have the stimulus to group together socially against the colonized people. In 1964, the Ouagadougou jail had one of its few European prisoners, a journalist accused of fraud. This fact scandalized the local people who could not understand why the French Embassy did not go to the rescue of its "person." Apart from two Frenchmen who brought some presents to the prisoner, his only benefactors were the African jailers who gave him the run of the prison, even allowing him to go outside, and African social workers who "felt sorry for him because he had no relatives in Ouagadougou."

There was no opportunity to obtain meaningful data on the Lebano-Syrian community in Ouagadougou. As far as was observed, this group is still fairly homogeneous and endogamous, and, although some of the younger Lebano-Syrians have been interacting with both Africans and Europeans, there is little expectation on the part of Africans that the integration of this group is possible. Nor is it clear, judging from the entrance of Africans and Europeans into the retail business, what the economic future of this group is. There is, however, no overt antagonism between the local population and the Lebano-Syrians and, unless this changes, they may be permitted to conduct their trade.

Associations

The Mossi and stranger groups in Ouagadougou apparently had little need for many of the voluntary associations characteristic of the populations of many emerging African towns.[4] The dominant Mossi group in the town had its traditional chiefs and political structures which provided a fairly effective organization for what was still not a complete urban life style. And the Mossi from outside the Ouagadougou kingdom and the various stranger groups were apparently quite satisfied with the functions of their *vieux,* as their elders were called. Thus, few associations developed and those that did were designed to serve purposes other than those normally associated with voluntary associations in African towns.

[4]Kenneth Little, *Some Contemporary Trends in African Urbanization,* Melville J. Herskovits Memorial Lecture (II), Northwestern University (April 20, 1965). Evanston: Northwestern University Press, 1966, pp. 85ff.

One voluntary association among the Mossi which has a long history in Bilibambili ward is the *nam*. For the traditional Mossi the concept *nam* means, "That force of God which permits a mere man to rule over other men."[5] Thus it represents such attributes as sovereignty, authority, and legitimacy. The term is associated with *naba,* the word for chief, the "father *ba* of the *nam*." Within Ouagadougou, an organization called the *nam* arose among young Mossi men; it was maintained for the sole purpose of doing good work. Thus, if an old woman or an old man needed a hut repaired, a field cultivated, or grain harvested in the outskirts of the town, the young men of the *nam* got together and did these tasks. The *nam* is not a *sisoga* (a cooperative work group) since its members do not help each other with chores.

The history of *nam* in Bilibambili is lost in time. It may once have been an agricultural association of Mossi youth. Today, however, its functions are purely philanthropic and recreational. The head of the *nam* is called the Yung'Naba (literally "Night Chief"), a title which is equivalent to Mogho Naba, but since that title is forbidden to any man other than the king of the Ouagadougou Mossi, the title Yung'Naba is used. The person named Yung'Naba must be kind, wise, considerate, jovial, and helpful. He is usually elected from among his generation and retires when his generation moves into the more serious affairs of life. The Yung'Naba is assisted by a number of young men (33 according to informants, but this is doubtful since multiples of three are used for any number associated with Mossi men) who take any vacant chiefly title they prefer. Thus there is the Manga Naba, the Tema Naba, the Tengkodogo Naba, the Baloum Naba, the Nobéré Naba, the Kam Naba, and so forth. There is apparently no relationship between the origin of a young man and the title of the *naba* he chooses. Again, there are no functions which are assigned to specific *nanamsé* in the association. Any person could be asked by the Yung'Naba to perform a specific task for the organization or can volunteer to do it. For example, as *chef de propagande* in the organization, the Kam Naba has the duty to summon his fellow chiefs whenever there is a meeting of the group either for recreational purposes or voluntary work.

[5]Skinner, 1964b, p. 13.

There are few requirements for membership in the group. Any young man from the ward who wishes to join can do so provided he is able to buy enough millet beer to entertain the other members on the day of his elevation to the *nam*. An inquiry into the status of *nam* members showed them to be both Ouagadougou-born Mossi and immigrant Mossi. They are primarily illiterate tradesmen and laborers; a few of them are cultivators, a number of whom consider themselves to be unemployed because they have no noncultivating occupations.

The members of the *nam* have little contact with either the traditional or modern elites in the town, but, like most persons forming an organization, they had to have a sponsor. They succeeded in being sponsored by the Municipal Councilor of their quarter, and they elected him their honorary treasurer. However, this official took almost no interest in the *nam* and placed little value on his association with that organization. This was perhaps beneficial to the *nam* because it continued to be viewed as a nonpolitical organization. And, unlike most organizations that existed before the efflorescence of and politicization of associations during the years between 1958 and 1960, the *nam* continued to function even after the revolution of 1966. The problem for the *nam,* however, is that it may not be able to adapt to rapidly changing Ouagadougou. One wonders whether future migrants from the rural areas will participate in such a recreational institution modeled as it is on a traditional institution, the chieftainship, which has encountered difficulty modernizing itself.

The *gumbé* is another association in Ouagadougou that is old as asociations go in the town. This organization appeared in Ouagadougou during the early years of World War II, having either come from the Ivory Coast via the French Soudan (Mali), or, as is claimed by some of the present members of the *gumbé* in Ouagadougou, brought to town by young Mossi labor migrants who had seen it in the Ivory Coast.[6] The *gumbé* apparently reached its climax in the town between the years 1956 and 1958, when there were six *gumbé* groups in various wards. Besides Koulouba, which was the first quarter in which it developed, *gumbé* groups existed in Tiedpalogho, Bilibambili, Paspanga, Dapoya II, and Ouidi. These groups were

[6]Cf. Claude Meillassoux, *Urbanization of an African Community* (Seattle: University of Washington Press, 1968), pp. 116–30.

autonomous, but the group in Bilibambili had close relations with the one in Koulouba and they often planned activities together. After 1958 the *gumbé* disappeared from Ouagadougou, only to reappear in November 1964 again in the Koulouba ward. Although the author attended several meetings of the new *gumbé*, most of the data were gathered from interviews with past officers and members of the organization.

As described by its members, the *gumbé* is an organization of youth formed for the purposes of recreation, mutual aid, and for educating the youth in such matters as public service and obedience to parents and authority. The *gumbé* members pride themselves on the fact that their organization has always encompassed members of all the ethnic groups in the town. The majority of the members of the revived *gumbé* are Mossi, but there are youths from all the other groups in the town with the number of Dioula members only slightly lower than that of the Mossi. Another characteristic of the *gumbé* is that, while it is "multi-confessional"—that is, it has members from all the various religious groups in the town—there is still a decided Moslem tinge to the organization. The *gumbé* does not meet during the holy month of Ramadan, nor does it permit any alcoholic beverages to its members. On the other hand, the *gumbé* is more modernistic than the average Moslem association and has always included a substantial number of girls among its members. Thus, during 1958, the *gumbé* in Koulouba quarter had 120 male and 69 female members. Moreover, the female members of the *gumbé* were actively included in most of the affairs of the group.

The *gumbé* has always had a well-organized structure, table of organization, and clear-cut functions. Its officials include a president, vice-president, secretary-general, secretary-general-adjunct, commissioner of finances, commissioner of police, and police attached to the president. There is also a female president and vice-president, but no other female officials. Although there apparently are no age restrictions on membership in the *gumbé*, most of the members are persons between the ages of twelve and thirty, since younger persons are unable to pay dues and older people are too busy with affairs of their own. A prospective member of the organization is usually proposed by a member and is invited to attend a Monday night meeting where he or she is either admitted or rejected. Persons are only rejected for reasons of bad character, and since such persons are normally known to the youth of the ward they are seldom proposed for membership in the first place.

Each member of the *gumbé,* except the president, pays monthly dues based on rank within the association. Thus, the vice-president pays 500 francs, the secretary-generals 300 francs, other officers, such as the commissioner of police, 200 francs, and ordinary members 100 francs. However, owing to "unemployment" and other problems causing financial embarrassment among the youths, the association does not insist that all of its members pay their dues every month. Because of his responsibility, the president does not pay dues. The feeling is that his service to the organization is enough.

As one of the aims of the *gumbé* is to instill obedience in the young people, discipline within the organization is quite strict. Members call each other comrade and no one is permitted to call the officers by name; they are addressed by their titles. Again, discipline is maintained at the affairs of the *gumbé* (perhaps discipline is overstrict since it is ritualized), and violators of the rules of the *gumbé* or those persons guilty of misbehavior are summoned to the Monday meetings of the association where they are judged and, if found guilty, fined. Acting as another stimulus for discipline among the youths of the *gumbé* is their fear that adults and other authorities might misunderstand the aims and activities of the organization. The older people in the town, especially the Mossi, mistrust the interaction of young males and females in the organization and believe that they associate together for immoral purposes. This fear is due to the fact that traditionally the Mossi never permitted close public relationships between young males and young females. Furthermore, the older people fear that the modernistic tendencies of the organization will lead to a breakdown in the traditional moral system.

The Catholic missionaries, too, dislike the fact that many members of the *gumbé* are Moslems and therefore beyond their spiritual control; and they mistrust mixed dancing without the sponsorship of adult persons. So strong was mission opposition to the *gumbé* that when the young Christians of St. Léon ward organized a *gumbé* and had their first public dance, a Catholic priest went to the meeting, took off his belt and chased the participants away, exclaiming that "the devil is routed!" In the face of such apprehension on the part of many townspeople, the *gumbé* members are especially careful in the relationships between the males and females in the group. The president and his officials quite carefully chaperone the young girls who attend the meetings and dances of the *gumbé* and provide escorts to take the girls home when these affairs are over. Ironically, the *gumbé* members now criticize the Christian and other non-*gumbé* youths about immorality at the various "surprise parties" and dances following weddings and baptisms.

The most publicized and best known activities of the *gumbé* are the open-air dances held on Saturday and Sunday afternoons and on the various holidays. For these performances the members gather in the street before the house of the president where they place benches forming a square. The president, major officials, and the musicians are usually seated at the side of the square backing on the president's house and the young people segregate themselves by sex on the other benches. The policemen of the *gumbé* make sure that order is maintained on the benches, seat girls and visitors, and chase away the numerous young children who try to fill the benches and disturb the members. All the members of the *gumbé* are recognizable by their dress or insignia. The president and the men wear shirts and long trousers, both of which have fringed sides resembling those worn by American cowboys. The men wear either a version of a western hat or a military-style overseas cap. When the latter are worn, badges indicating the rank of the wearer are pinned on them. The policemen normally do not wear this type of dress but use regular pants and shirts, overseas caps, bandoliers, and belts, the latter often decorated with red, white, and black, the colors of the Republic. The girls most often wear what has emerged as "modern" African dress, wraparound skirts and blouses. The skirts are usually made out of imported cotton prints and the blouses may be of the same cloth or of white cotton cloth. In any event, what with similar headkerchiefs, the young women can be said to wear a kind of uniform during the dances.

There is now a standard pattern of music, singing, and dancing associated with the *gumbé*. The musical instruments consist of a large drum called a jazz, small square drums (really boxes covered with skin) called tambours, rattles, and gongs. The musicians beat a rhythmic pattern, changing the rhythm from time to time, and stopping at intervals to tighten the skins on the drums by heating them over a fire. The singing is usually done by young women who sing through a "micro" in a high falsetto the numerous *gumbé* songs which have been transmitted from the Ivory Coast and Mali. The words to the songs are usually in Dioula, but occasionally the singers use Moré and even French. The dancing is also stylized in the *gumbé* pattern, with young men and women dancing solo or at times dancing with each other, either in bodily contact or separately. When the youths dance separately, they usually compete with the musicians in an attempt to see whether they or the musicians can dance or play rhythmic patterns which the other cannot follow. After each dance, or when a dancer has stopped dancing, he or she goes before the president and either salutes or curtsies in respect. The organization furnishes water for thirsty members and may even provide soft drinks when the treasury is full. Neither modern alcoholic beverages nor the traditional millet beer are permitted.

During the heyday of the *gumbé* in Ouagadougou there were other social activities in which the young people participated. For example, almost every Saturday morning the young men of the *gumbé* accompanied the young girls to the pools at the northern part of the town in order to entertain them while they did their weekly washing. This activity ceased when the *gumbé* was deactivated and has not recommenced since there are now standpipes in the various quarters for such purposes as washing clothes.

In addition, the members of the *gumbé* performed social as well as political functions for the politicians during the height of the campaigns for political offices between 1956 and 1958. They were engaged by individual politicians to drive around the town in vans, singing the praises of the men and their parties. And they were often used to sing songs of welcome for "high personalities" arriving either by train or by air. Indeed, some members of the *gumbé* consider this political function of "activating the masses" so important that one cannot help wondering whether the fact that the Upper Volta was having elections in 1965 was not the major factor in stimulating the president of the *gumbé* to reactivate the organization. True, he did not receive the presents, such as a small car, which certain politicians had previously promised him, but the fact that he entertained hopes for the future was seen when, on New Year's Day 1965, he led his group in singing the praises of influential politicians and the Mayor of the town. Even if he does not get anything for himself, he at least hopes to receive some aid from the administrative authorities in the town to buy instruments for the musicians and costumes for the members of the organization.

One further aim of the *gumbé* is to provide mutual aid for its members. However, owing to the fact that the association was being activated, there was no opportunity to witness what this aid amounted to. During its heyday, the *gumbé* provided material aid for those of its members who got married either to other *gumbé* members or, since there was no pattern of endogamy, to strangers. An even more important aid provided at this time was that referred to as "organizing joy" or festivities for the young couple. The *gumbé* also provided assistance to those of its members who were ill or out of work and were especially helpful during funerals, a period of sudden and great expense. *Gumbé* members also sought out the members of foreign *gumbés* and gave them any help they could; for, as the president said, "It is important for strangers who visit Ouagadougou to be able to return to their homelands and declare how kind the youths of Ouagadougou are and how well they get along with each other. When this happens, people in the foreign areas will not hesitate to welcome the young people from Ouagadougou to their lands."

Besides the *nam* and the *gumbé* there were very few so-called voluntary associations in Ouagadougou prior to the end of World War II. Even the *nam* and the *gumbé* are very specialized types of associations since their recreational, and in the case of the *gumbé,* modernizing activities are especially geared to the youth.

Politics was responsible for the rise and fall of most of the associations which appeared in Ouagadougou at the end of World War II. About 1946 civil servants and clerks from the region of Koudougou, who felt that the representatives of the Ouagadougou Mossi such as Messrs. François Bouda, Joseph Conombo, and Joseph Ouedraogo were too prominent in the political life of a reemerging Upper Volta colony, formed an Association des Originaires de Goungweogho to fight for their interests. Despite the terms of its constitution, which stated that the organization was to provide social and material aid, it quickly became moribund when its members not only failed to pay dues but lost interest as soon as people from their respective areas gained some political power. Little effort was made to form new associations until the passage of the *loi-cadre* in 1956 enlarged the political arena in the Upper Volta territory and stimulated practically every possible group in the town of Ouagadougou to organize for its own advancement. One "group" which now saw itself being severely challenged for leadership consisted of the major politicians of the Ouagadougou kingdom. On December 12, 1957, they formed the Association des Originaires de Zoundiweogho [Cercle de Ouagadougou], with headquarters in the town of Ouagadougou. Characteristically, it declared that its objectives were: "1) The grouping in a fraternal union of the people originally from Zoundiweogho. 2) To provide mutual aid among them and defend their common interests." An explanatory note appended to this declaration stated that the association, "Is a fraternal grouping of people originally from Zoundiweogho organized for mutual aid and to defend the common interests of its members. All persons originally from that region, whether domiciled there or living elsewhere and regardless of religious or political affiliation, may join this association." Nevertheless, this association, like its predecessor, the Association des Originaires de Goungweogho, was purely a political instrument for certain civil servants and politicians and never did anything except mobilize the people of Zoundiweogho for political purposes.

There were a fairly large number of associations like those mentioned above during this period. For example, an association known as Regroupement des Originaires du Cercle de Kaya in Ouagadougou had as its objective "mutual aid among themselves and the defense of its members." The purely political nature of this association is seen from the fact that its honorary president was a well-known politician from that region. The Union Fraternelle des Peulhs [Fulani] de la Ville de Ouagadougou had as its objective to provide mutual aid and to strengthen lines of friendship and brotherhood among its members. The Association des Originaires de la Subdivision de Zabre at Ouagadougou gave slightly different aims as its *raison d'être*. It wished to group persons from Zabre "in a sentiment of solidarity," and, aside from safeguarding their interests, wished to ameliorate conditions in the home area economically, morally, and culturally as well as socially. But here again, the real aim of these associations was political mobilization.

Other groups in Ouagadougou were not to be left out in this drive toward formal association. Various religious, educational, secular, sports, and occupational groups were formed: the Jeunesse Étudiante Chrétienne Feminine (J.E.C.F.) of Ouagadougou; the Moslems of Ouagadougou also organized Communauté Musulmane de la Haute-Volta: Siège Social—Ouagadougou; and the Protestants in Ouagadougou organized an Association des Educateurs Protestants de Haute-Volta. Not to be outdone, the secularists formed the Fédération Voltaique des Oeuvres Laiques and gave as their objectives to make known and to defend the ideal of secularism against the growing identification of the government with the Catholic church. The sport associations included the "Mimosas" club, organized to "create and to maintain relations, especially sportive, between all of its adherents residing in Ouagadougou; and cultural groups such as the Association Sportive et Culturelle de Ouagadougou dite 'Amitie Africaine' came into existence for the purpose of "the development and expansion of the personality of the young girls and young women by physical, family, social, cultural, and artistic education." Occupational groups such as the Syndicat des Petites et Moyennes Entreprises de Haute-Volta were founded to protect their members' interests against the large companies and enterprises; and parents' groups organized themselves in such associations as Association des Parents d'Elèves de l'Enseignement Libre de la Haute-Volta to facilitate the education of their children.

The stranger groups in Ouagadougou also formed their own formal associations, but here the stated aim was self-protection against what they feared would be a difficult period once greater political power was given to the local inhabitants. Thus there came into being the Association Fraternelle des Originaires de la Côte d'Ivoire in Ouagadougou which had as its objectives to come to the material and moral aid of its members in case of necessity, and to entertain its members by organizing recreational, cultural, educational, and artistic affairs. The Soudanese formed L'Amicale Soudanaise de Ouagadougou and the Senegalese in Ouagadougou, the Ressortissants du Fouta Sénégalaise. The hard-pressed Togolese formed the Association de la Jeunesse Togolaise in Ouagadougou to protect their goals and jobs.

Since most of the associations which emerged in Ouagadougou between 1956 and 1960 had a partisan political basis, it is not surprising that the Conseil de Gouvernement of the Upper Volta, fearing trouble, asked the town's young people to form Le Comité d'Entente de la Jeunnesse à Ouadougou representing all the youths of the town. The Council warned them that,

> the time of divide and rule is not entirely past; that is why you are being asked to form a committee. Its job will be to make our ideas known, to discuss them openly so that this discussion will cast the necessary light on issues pertaining to the construction of that country we wish to have. We have the desire and the courage to do this, but we lack the means. It is still evident that it is the Government toward which we must turn, certain that it will understand us.[7]

There were, however, many persons in the town, as elsewhere, who were concerned that the proliferation of associations did not auger well for the town and its inhabitants. People did acknowledge that it was good to create "a true fraternity, or more exactly, groups of fraternizations, each one desiring to bring its brick to the construction of the Africa of tomorrow."[8] But it was also pointed out that the formation of Originaires from one place or another was divisive in that people who normally had little in common joined together, and those with the same training formed different groups, often in opposition to each other. One young man warned that one night a phantom had come to him in a dream and said, "Soon you will see the creation of an association having as its objective to determine the capacity for lactation of Zulu grandmothers in South Africa."[9]

The fact is that each one of the associations which arose in Ouagadougou was striving to get one of its members associated with each political party and to obtain an important position for him on each party's slate. This plan boomeranged when the political parties themselves fused, fissioned, or abol-

---

[7]*Bulletin Quotidien,* 15 April 1959, p. 10.
[8]*Ibid.,* 12 July 1957, p. 10.
[9]*Ibid.,* 12 December 1957, p. 8.

ished themselves, leaving the associations in limbo. Then, when in 1959–60 the U.D.V.-R.D.A. finally won its struggle for political supremacy in the town and territory, many associations, such as the Union des Jeunes de Regions Sindoises, were banned by the Minister of the Interior and of Security and the other associations disappeared. Ironically, the informal associations of strangers, and even the regional Mossi groups, which had been overshadowed by the formal associations reemerged in Ouagadougou. They, rather than the more formal associations, continue to provide the mutual aid so important to townsmen and to groups coming into the town.

The one association among Europeans in Ouagadougou which has mutual-aid functions is the Amicale des Bretons. This group, composed of natives of Brittany, meets at least one Sunday a month for dinner and supports those of its members in need of material or spiritual help. However, the Bretons and their association are not taken seriously by the other Europeans in town who accuse them of "regionalism." They declare that wherever two or three Bretons are gathered together they found an *Amicale*.

The local branch of La Croix Rouge Française, founded in 1955, was the only voluntary association in colonial Ouagadougou to be patronized by the important Africans and Europeans in the town. A report of June 1956 stated that there were 400 members of the group in the capital and that it had started to perform charitable work. During the Christmas season of 1956, Madame Bourges, wife of the Governor of the colony, led a group of women in the distribution of kola nuts, cakes, and cigarettes to 340 ill persons in the hospital; and on January 12, 1957, the same group distributed 200 garments to small children at the social centers around town. The Red Cross also inaugurated a number of new social service projects in the town. It organized festivities for children on Mother's Day; established a nursery for the children of working mothers, especially the children of African and European elite women; and, in 1958, began the first courses in life-saving and first aid in the town.

With independence, the control of the now Upper Volta Red Cross passed into local hands, but Europeans continue to be members of it. The only problem which developed was a competition for the leadership of the organization between the wives of the traditional elite and modern elites. This was resolved in favor of the modern elites, and the Red Cross did not suffer when many of the organizations which had sprouted for political action were disbanded. As a matter of fact, the Red Cross was declared a national utility and as such beyond the boundaries of partisan politics; at least this was the hope. By 1964, the Red Cross was still functioning in Ouagadougou and had established meaningful relationships with foreign groups from which it received some aid. For example, at a meeting of its national council on October 22, 1964, in Ouagadougou, the organization heard reports on the journeys of its members to Europe, and acknowledged correspondence and gifts from Red Cross groups in West Germany, Canada, Poland, Finland, the Netherlands, the U.S.A., and Japan. It also planned elections for a committee for the Junior Red Cross within the parent organization.

The Lions Club of Ougadougou was founded only after independence. Like the Red Cross, it has the support of the government. In 1964 it had 21 members, including such influential Europeans as the manager of the Banque de L'Afrique Occidentale (B.A.O.), and a number of Africans, including an important professor at the *Lycée,* the former Secretary of Defense of the African and Malagasy Union, and the Mayor of the town. The organization, whose work includes giving charity to such institutions in the town as the hospitals and social centers, has in the past been chaired by both Africans and Europeans. During 1964 its chairman was an African who maintained close contact with the group in Dakar, the regional headquarters for the Lions in this part of French-speaking Africa. The Ouagadougou group has established contact with the parent organization in the U.S.A. and Voltaic visitors to America have been received by the locals there. The only problem facing the local branch in Ouagadougou is a financial one since many of the African members find it difficult to make as substantial contributions to charity as their European opposite numbers.

The status and role of the strangers in Ouagadougou have always been a function of the political organizations. The traditional strangers such as the Hausa and Dioula, linked as they were to the Mossi political hierarchy, did not change either their status or role during the colonial period. In contrast, the Dahomeans and Togolese ignored the sensibilities of the indigenous population. The latter accepted domination by the Europeans because they were conquered by them, but resented many of the other groups that arrived in the train of the Europeans. The nature of the resentment varied according to differences in socio-cultural institutions and language, and with decolonization the more resented strangers were expelled.

The voluntary associations in Ouagadougou functioned more as political mobilizers than adaptive mechanisms for social and cultural change. True, the *nam* and the *gumbé* served traditional and modernizing youths in Ouagadougou in the manner described by Little. However, voluntary associations in town did not proliferate until elite Africans saw the opportunity and possibility of achieving ultimate political and economic power within the town. Once this had been achieved, the voluntary associations either withered away or were banned. Even the Red Cross and the Lions Club of Ouagadougou now operate under the aegis of the political elite.

President of the Republic greeting resident foreign diplomats

217

Education

Ouagadougou has become an important educational center, and an increasing number of its inhabitants view the schools as conduits to modern life. Formal education in Ouagadougou really began with the arrival of the first Moslem traders. Mogho Naba Doulougou (c. 1783–1802) permitted the first Imam to open a Koranic school in the capital. According to Dim Delobson, "Naba Sawadogo, who succeeded his father, Doulougou, sent his children to the Koranic school. Many of them obtained a fairly good education there, and the eldest son, who later succeeded to the throne under the name of Naba Koutou, even became a *marabout* [a learned holy man]."[1]

Modern education, per se, was introduced by Catholic missionaries shortly after they arrived in Ouagadougou on June 25, 1901. The then resident officer, Captain Reuf, "asked the Fathers to open a school, and he interceded with chiefs to send their children. The missionaries happily took up this task."[2] Early the next year, a new commandant, Captain Dubreuil, recruited 29 children (mainly orphans) and sent them to the missionaries. The latter employed Mr. Badre, a Soudanese interpreter, to teach them French. By July 1902, there were 93 pupils in the school, divided into two classes: 30 in one and 63 in the other. Among them were 39 boys from noble families, including the sons of 4 of the 5 provincial governors (the Kamsaogho Naba, being a eunuch, had no offspring), and the children of many courtiers. To the amusement of the teacher and pupils, the sons of the Bend'Naba (the court's chief musician) appeared for the first day of classes bearing their miniature drums. The other pupils were 36 peasant sons, 16 ex-slave orphans, and 2 adults. The administration recruited additional boys, and by the end of the year there were some 173 pupils in school. But now 91 of them were the sons of peasants, 53 *nakomcé* (noble boys), and the rest either ex-slave

---

[1]Delobson, *The Empire of the Mogho-Naba*, p. 101.
[2]Baudu, p. 17.

children or adults. The recruiting zone was also extended. About 72 of the 173 pupils were natives of Ouagadougou; the others came from such distant places as Beloussa, Boussouma, Kipirsi, Koupéla, and Léo. The mission housed 18 *nakomcé,* 16 orphans, and 4 peasant boys and prevailed upon the chiefs and parents to provide food for the children.

The pupils in Ouagadougou followed a curriculum which had been developed for all the schools in Upper Senegal and the Niger Basin. This included arithmetic, French, gymnastics, sports, carpentry, gardening, and weaving. But the big problem for the school and its teachers was the irregular attendance of many pupils. On some days as many as 13 pupils were absent. We are told that "this was due to the fact that parents did not feel pressed to bring their children to school, and the children decided not to attend. Fathers and sons did not perceive, and would continue to ignore for a long time, the importance of the instruction given at the schools. Only gradually was this recognized. The parents preferred to have their sons work in the fields because they were able to see the results of work done there. 'What can our sons bring to us by going to school?' asked the parents. This question constituted an obstacle and explained the position of parents."[3]

But if the parents were scornful of education for their sons, they actively opposed attempts to educate their daughters. Nevertheless, in 1902 the administration and mission were able to recruit some 24 girls (many of whom were "orphans"). In contrast to the boys, the girls were instructed in Moré rather than French, and spent most of their time learning to weave carpets.

Even before the African parents became reconciled to the compulsory education of their children, a battle broke out between the administration and the mission about goals and the nature of this education. The administration's policy was clear: "In the Soudan, we are faced with a population which we have conquered militarily; now its *intellectual and moral conquest* is our objective. It is necessary then, to try to draw the people to us, to indoctrinate them completely, to take away their traditional esprit, and to impose our particular stamp on

---

[3] "Education catholique en Haute Volta," anonymous manuscript in archives of the author, p. 3.

them."[4] Some administrators expected the schools to produce civil servants and modern traders, but the idealists felt that it was an error to consider such materialistic goals as being the principal aims of education. The latter believed that "the schools are created to spread our civilization, to instruct the natives about the rights and duties of individuals in society, to discover for some of them the splendors of philosophy, science and history, and to lead all to respect and to love our beautiful French homeland."[5] The administrators also expected the missionaries "to teach the French language to the young natives and the manual arts which are absolutely absent in the country and crucial for its exploitation."[6] Unfortunately the missionaries heeded an older injunction: "Go ye therefore into all Nations baptizing them in the name of the Father, the Son, and the Holy Spirit," and this brought them into conflict with "Caesar."

The early church-run public school in Ouagadougou had the misfortune to have been supervised by several anticlerical administrators. The more anticlerical the administrator, the greater the difficulty for the mission and the school. Whereas the first administrators in 1901–1903 gave the Church a subvention of 1,200 francs per annum for the school, the subsequent administrator in 1904 discontinued it. The unstated reason was that the administration did not want the pupils to receive religious instruction. The mission, for its part, pleaded that it was not using the schools for proselytism. The clerics pointed out that of 173 pupils in school in 1902 only 58 (18 *nakomcé*, 12 peasant boys, 19 orphans, and 9 catechists) were voluntarily receiving religious instruction. Moreover, the mission insisted in its report to the administration in 1903 that "these children [the pupils] promise to become, if not scholars, at least useful men in their country. They will know how to speak, read and write our language well enough to be qualified interpreters between French administration and the Native authorities."[7]

Apparently the declarations of the missionaries did not improve Captain Lambert's dim view of mission-run schools.

---

[4]Denise Bouche, "Les écoles françaises au Soudan à l'époque de la conquête, 1884–1900," *Cahiers d'Etudes Africaines,* VI, No. 22 (1966), 246.
[5]*Ibid.,* p. 250.
[6]*Ibid.,* p. 246.
[7]Baudu, pp. 26ff.

On December 26, 1904, he announced that Ouagadougou had received 3,000 francs to build a public school. A few months later, on May 6, 1905, he "gave orders to parents to cease sending their children to the Mission school, and ordered that those already there be recalled. The Chief of Komsilgha recalled his two sons and a son of his page. At the formal invitation of Captain Lambert, the Baloum Naba sent to get his two children the same night."[8] Moreover, the Commandant threatened to quadruple the taxes of those parents who refused to withdraw their children from the mission school. Finally in 1910 the administration forbade the mission to teach anything but religious subjects in their now strictly clerical schools.

Despite intermittent anticlerical outbursts, the administrators in Ouagadougou had to modify their opposition to the mission schools because they did not have enough money to provide secular schools for the children of Ouagadougou, and because they realized that it was impossible for the clerics to teach Christianity without imparting Western or French values. Caught in this contradiction, the administrators contented themselves with restricting the privilege of granting diplomas to the secular schools. Thus, until after World War II many highly educated youths in the mission schools had no recognized diplomas—a *sine qua non* for any government employment. This meant that unless brilliant pupils at the mission schools opted for the priesthood, their best hope was low-paying clerical jobs. Those pupils with secular ambitions were constrained to attend the public schools.

As soon as the people of Ouagadougou realized that modern education was more than the children's equivalent of "forced labor," they actively sought to put their children into school. Their problem then, as now, was insufficient money to provide schools for all children desiring an education. The problem became so acute that in June 1942,[9] when Governor-General Boisson visited Ouagadougou, he invited the Apostolic Vicar, Monsignor Thévenoud to increase mission education. The chief administrator authorized subvention to the mission schools provided that they increased the number of pupils and recruited and upgraded teachers. The mission agreed to open

[8]*Ibid.*
[9]Baudu, pp. 220ff.

more classes, but lack of funds still prevented many children in Ouagadougou from attending school. The budget for Upper Volta in 1953–54 provided primary education for only 11,542 pupils in 270 classes scattered throughout the whole country. The next year the number of primary school pupils increased to 13,126 in 316 classes; some 12,324 students attended various types of secondary schools. Alas, these numbers represented only about 5.2 per cent of the school-age population of the country.

The people of Ouagadougou had a disproportionately large number of schools during the post-World War II period as compared with the rest of Upper Volta, but these still were not sufficient for the needs of their children. The *Bulletin Quotidien* for October 4, 1956, stated: "As far as the primary schools of the town of Ouagadougou are concerned, it has been necessary now, as in other years, to limit the recruitment [of pupils] because of the lack of space. This is as true for boys as it is for girls. At the end of its recruitment, La Salle [a Catholic boys' school] reported that it had accepted 132 pupils thus making an effective total of 640 (boys). The girls' primary school has passed the effective total of 328 in the classes CPI to CM2 [primary grades]."

School facilities in Ouagadougou have improved since 1956, but the shortage of classrooms still persists. The 1962 census showed a school-age population (ages six to fifteen) of 11,000 children representing some 19.1 per cent of the town's population. Of these, approximately 6,500 or 59.1 per cent attended some sort of primary school. This figure is quite high given the fact that only 6.0 per cent of the children in Upper Volta were attending school at this time. (The figure is 10.5 per cent if the 4.5 per cent in rural education classes are counted.) By 1963 the school-age population of Ouagadougou had increased to 12,250; the total number of pupils had also increased to 7,053, but the actual percentage of children in school had declined slightly to 57.6 per cent. At the beginning of the school year 1964–65, there were 30 primary schools in the town with 134 classes.[10] However, the authorities admitted that these would still be insufficient. The situation in the town would have been

[10]In 1964–65 there were 9,238 pupils in the primary schools of Ouagadougou, or 70 per cent of all eligible children. By 1967 there were some 9,818 pupils in 43 schools having 179 classes. However, by this time the overall population of the town had reached 110,000. It was estimated that

worse had the Catholic and Protestant missions not provided schools for their converts and some non-Christian children.

One important reason for the low percentages of pupils in school is that classroom construction has not kept pace with the need for additional space. This is due to the continuing inability of the government of Upper Volta to provide enough money for schools. The demand for modern education is vastly greater than the ability of the government to meet it. Secondly, Ouagadougou is growing so fast that the existing shortage of schools continues to be exacerbated by increasing immigration. Of 102 lower-grade pupils (ranging in age from ten to fifteen years) interviewed in one Ouagadougou school, 32 were native born whereas 70 were born elsewhere. Thus the municipality was having to provide schooling for twice as many immigrant children as for those born in the town.

Given this relative shortage of schools and classrooms, there is intense competition for the available places, and parents use every available means to get their children into school. The events which took place during school registration in 1964 show the keen competition for schooling and the selective factors which determined who was admitted.

During July and August 1964, parents were already being urged by the local radio to provide their children with the necessary inoculations and civil-status papers for the coming school year. Early on the morning of Monday, September 22, 1964, over 100 children, led by their parents, appeared at the school in Bilbalgo ward to seek admission. When the school authorities arrived (these include the teachers, the municipal councilor for the ward, and the Baloum Naba) they told the parents to produce their children's papers and declared that only those children born in 1957 or during the first four months of 1958 were eligible for admission. This announcement was greeted with grumbling, and about ten parents took their children home. One man complained that, whereas the school was intended for children from the Pedaogo, St. Julien, and Bilbalgo wards, the school could not even accommodate those eligible from Bilbalgo alone. The officials then conferred and explained that they could enroll only 32 boys and 20 girls for the new term. They indicated that the 40 boys and 50 girls

---

there were 88 students for every 1,000 inhabitants, and that about 21 per cent of school-age children attended school.

223

who passed their exams the previous year were continuing in school and that 8 boys and 5 girls who had failed the past year were being allowed to repeat. This information caused consternation and a general stampede among the parents, and each tried to get his child as close to the front of the line as possible. The parents also tried to catch the eyes or the ears of the teacher, the municipal councilor, or the Baloum Naba.

Those parents who had the foresight to get letters of recommendation for their children from employers or supervisors showed these to the school authorities and had little difficulty getting their children enrolled. One man who was able to get his boss, the Director of the Labor Exchange, to accompany him and his child to the school had the boy enrolled. Those parents who had no influence with the authorities were less fortunate. They complained that the school was "like a *douane* [customs house]; those who have money pass." The least fortunate of all were women who could get no males to accompany their children to school. These women stood aside in tears not daring to push their way into the mass of men. Very few of them did succeed in getting their children into school. It was said that some of these women, although traditionalists, had tried to get their children into Catholic schools which had registration the previous June. They had slept outside the schools to be first in line when the children were registered, but were largely unsuccessful since their children were rejected in favor of Catholic ones.

As we have seen, in Ouagadougou, as in most communities, there is unequal access to the schools—even the primary ones. African civil servants and politicians have no difficulty getting their children admitted to schools. Even the rule limiting access to schools in the various wards to resident children is often violated for the benefit of the elite.

The children of very high-status Africans and those of resident expatriates go to two special schools. One is L'Ecole Privée, a private school run by French women, and the other is L'Ecole Pilote, a public school supported in part by French Government funds. The latter school has been criticized for catering to elites and for failing to include African subject matter in its curriculum. However, the country's need for French technicians and the corresponding responsibility to provide adequate schooling for the children of these people has so far prevented a concerted attack on what is considered the principle of elite education at L'Ecole Pilote. One should add also that many Africans aspiring for political leadership avoid criticizing the school in the hope of enrolling their children there if they do gain political power.

The schools in Ouagadougou, like all the schools in Upper Volta, follow the French curriculum. Children generally enter both public and private primary schools between the ages of six and seven. This course of study lasts for six years and is divided into three stages: preparatory courses 1 and 2; elementary courses, 1 and 2; and intermediary or middle courses, 1 and 2. The emphasis in the initial stage is on learning French (a new language for the majority of the children), reading, writing, and arithmetic. Later, geography, history, natural sciences, art, and physical education are added. In the parochial schools, religion is also taught.

During the last two years of primary school those students with above-average performances may take examinations for either secondary or vocational schools. However, at the end of the sixth year, or after finishing what is popularly called CM2, every pupil must take a standard examination. If successful, he is given a C.E.P.E. or *Certificat d'Etudes Primaires Elémentaire*. However, because so many pupils lack fluency in French at this time, less than half of them pass this examination. Of the 1,702 pupils who took this examination in Ouagadougou during 1967, only 755, or 44.35 per cent of them passed. This meant that more than half the pupils did not obtain this basic certificate without which no pupil can hope to continue in school or apply for even the least important salaried position. Influential high-status persons often arrange to keep their unsuccessful children in school, have them repeat CM2, and retake the examination. If this fails, parents may even send their children to distant towns or villages in order to have them repeat the examination until they pass. This is, incidentally, one of the few reasons why Ouagadougou parents send children back to the rural areas during their educational years.

Not all those people who receive the C.E.P.E. go on to secondary schools. Only those students who do well on the C.E.P.E. examinations and pass the more difficult examination for entrance into *sixième* are admitted to the public secondary schools. Those children who are not admitted to the public secondary schools and whose parents can afford it are sent to private ones. Less fortunate students have to look for work. In 1966, some 5,172 of the 10,134 pupils in Upper Volta who took the C.E.P.E. exam passed, and of these only 1,666 or 32.2 per cent were admitted to secondary schools.

There are now a variety of secondary schools in Ouagadougou with a substantial number of students. This is in marked contrast to 1953 when there were only 194 students in the Collège Modern et Classique, a school which had evolved out of the Ecole Préparatoire Supérieure, the most advanced school in the town. However, due to the imprecision caused by the development of the specific schools, it is not always possible to determine what level of education is offered at the various secondary schools. The public lycées in Ouagadougou include the state-supported Lycée Philippe Zinda Kabore and Lycée Technique, and the town's own Lycée Municipal. Of these three only the Lycée Zinda Kabore is really a lycée in that it prepares a large number of students for the *baccalauréate.* The Lycée Technique plans to prepare students for this diploma in the future, but so far its students only receive the *brevet* and diplomas on that level. The recently created Lycée Municipal has also not yet attained the level of *lycée* since its first students have only reached the *quatrième.* The plan is to add new classes each year over the next three years until the students reach the *terminal* class and are thus eligible to take the "bac" examination. The other public secondary school in Ouagadougou is the Ecole Normale Supérieure which prepares students for the "bac" in education.

There are a number of public secondary schools in Ouagadougou which regularly prepare students for the different varieties of *brevet.* The Cours Normal des Jeunes Filles trains girls for the teaching course. If at the end of four years (3ème) they successfully pass the examination for the B.E.P.C., they receive one year of professional training and can be appointed assistant teachers in the primary schools. However, the Cours Normal in Ouagadougou is scheduled to be closed and its functions fulfilled by the newly created Collège d'Enseignement Général de Ouagadougou. The latter establishment is coeducational and prepares students for the B.E.P.C. but, unlike the Cours Normal, these students are not specifically directed to teaching. Successful students in this school can take examinations to enter the 2ème class in the various lycées or the Ecole Normale Supérieure. Nevertheless, the hope is that most of the students in this "short" cycle—that is below the "bac"—will go to work.

The Ecole Militaire Préparatoire, now called Le Prytanée Militaire de Kadiogo, is the secondary school in Ouagadougou which trains boys for a military career. Those who successfully pass the B.E.P.C. may take exams to enter the various lycées or écoles normales or for entrance to the Ecole Militaire at Bingerville in the Ivory Coast.[11]

There are presently four private secondary schools in Ouagadougou. The Collège Notre Dame de Kologho Naba is a Catholic school for girls, and the Collège de la Salle is the boy's equivalent. The Collège Protestant de Ouagadougou is a boys' school, while the Collège Laurent Ghilat is a coeducational and nondenominational school. These four schools are called *collèges* because they are small and prepare students primarily for the B.E.P.C. However, both La Salle and Kologho Naba have prepared a limited number of students for the "bac" and plan to prepare all students for this degree in the future. The Collège Protestant de Ouagadougou and the recently established Collège Laurent Ghilat both hope to follow suit.

There is a definite prestige gradient among the secondary schools in Ouagadougou. The Lycée Philippe Zinda Kabore is the most prestigious of the secondary schools in the town. It is commonly referred to as the *Lycée* and its students are considered the only bona fide *lycéens*. First of all, the school's renown is based on the belief that academic qualifications are the sole criterion for admission. Conversely, the ability to pay is the important criterion for admission to the private secondary schools. Second, people believe that the future elite of the country is formed at this school, and the students of the other *lycées* are held inferior to those at the *Lycée*. Third, and perhaps most important of all, is the belief that the *Lycée* provides the best education and gives the students the best chance to pass the "bac." People also point to the fact that the *Lycée* always has a large number of qualified teachers. In 1964 there were 5 Africans and 42 Europeans teaching there, whereas the private *lycées* have fewer qualified teachers.

The *normales* schools in town are less prestigious than the *lycées* and *collèges*. They are designed to train teachers, and

[11]This school prepared its first *baccalauréate* candidates in 1968–69.

227

the teaching profession, especially on the primary school level, is considered one of the least rewarding of elite occupations. Indeed, both *lycée* and *normale* school students fear the prospect of teaching in rural schools. They declare that, whereas their nonteacher colleagues have a good chance of remaining in urban centers and of working in air-conditioned offices, the newer teachers are sent to the "bush" where they have no electric lights, no running water, and poor food. Young men have little esteem for the *normales* schools because, in contrast to female teachers who can get urban appointments if they marry urbanites, male teachers can be posted to rural schools and kept there. Young male teachers believe that once this happens, they are stuck in the rural areas unless they go to France for further studies or use their influence with politicians or high-prestige relatives to secure teaching positions in town. The inability, until recently, to get more than the *brevet* at the *normales* schools (only in rare cases were professional aptitude certificates [C.A.P.] given) did not help their prestige. It is possible that the establishment of the Ecole Normale Supérieure and the granting of the *baccalauréate* in education may increase the prestige of these schools.

The vocational secondary school in Ouagadougou is the least prestigious of all. The belief is that the students of the Lycée Technique (evolved out of the Cours d'Apprentissage and a Collège Technique) are drawn from the ranks of the less qualified holders of the primary school certificates—students who were refused admittance to the *lycées* and *normales* schools.

Students from the *lycées* are known to refer to those at vocational schools as a *collection des ânes* (bunch of blockheads), and teachers at *lycées* endeavor to get failing students to work harder by threatening to send them to the *poubelle* (garbage can)—a derisive term for the Lycée Technique. The valuable training that this school provides in the building trades and secretarial and commercial fields seems not to have raised its status. There are, however, a number of changes in sight. One is that the Lycée Technique plans to prepare its students for the technical "bac" rather than limit them to various types of *brevets* and professional aptitude certificates. Second, the Upper Volta Government is currently emphasizing the importance of technical and vocational training for the development of the country, and, as will be seen, a larger number of youths are indicating a desire to enter these fields. Meanwhile, the technical school in Ouagadougou has so little prestige that students interested in technical fields prefer to study at a *lycée*, gain the coveted "bac," and later specialize in France. And until the technical and vocational schools in Ouagadougou begin to grant the "bac," that magic key to *fonctionnaire* status and economic success, they will not gain prestige. Even so, it will take a shift away from "fonctionnairism" where diplomas hold sway, to professionalism, where ability is the criterion for economic advancement, before the students change their present attitudes toward education.

Despite the overwhelming interest in the prestige of schools and levels of diplomas, students do favor certain professions and might have gone into them had other things been equal. A questionnaire filled out by 82 students in the *deuxième* (11th year) of the *lycée* provided the data on professional choices given in Table XXVIII.

The results of this survey showed a preference for those professions popularly believed to be most useful for the "economic development and modernization of the Upper Volta."

TABLE XXVIII. **Professional Choices**
of Students

Professions	Number of Students
Professor or teacher	25
Doctor	16
Engineer	12
Agronomist	7
Nurse (all girls)	4
Ambassador	1
Ambassador's secretary (girl)	1
Director of school	1
Lawyer	1
Midwife (girl)	1
Pediatrician	1
Technician	1
Veterinarian	1
Agronomist or engineer	1
Bailiff or technician	1
Doctor or deputy	1
Doctor or lawyer	1
Professor or agronomist	1
No response	4
TOTAL	81

229

Education was the occupation preferred by most students because it was held most vital to the Voltaic population and because most of the respondents were actually from the *Lycées*. (It should be pointed out, however, that the choice of teaching as a career refers only to teaching at the secondary school level and in the large towns. *Lycée* students have the same aversion to teaching in rural primary schools as do the students in the *normales* schools.) The students show the same bias in favor of other "modernizing" professions such as medicine, engineering, and agronomy, which were chosen in that order. As far as agronomy is concerned, only time will tell whether many students will in fact choose it as a career because, although agriculture is the base of Upper Volta's economy, students have resisted associating with the soil.

Except for the bunching of girls in their choice of nursing as a potential career, the *lycée* students did not show a marked preference for any but those occupations listed above. The lack of interest in law is probably due to the relatively low prestige of this profession in Upper Volta. Most of the African lawyers in Upper Volta are in fact civil servants, and the non-African lawyers in town work mainly for European businessmen. The only real surprise in the survey is the absence of any preference for the career of deputy or parliamentarian. The possible reason for this is that in 1964 these occupations had fallen into disrepute. They were so impermanent that they did not afford the economic security so valued by the educated person in Upper Volta. As a matter of fact, prior to the revolution of January 3, 1966, low-ranking civil servants used political power to overcome barriers which formerly prevented them from advancing to high civil service positions. In some cases, this meant asking for or seizing the opportunity to take exams for senior posts.

Given the importance of education for success in contemporary Upper Volta, it is not surprising that the students in the Ouagadougou schools are quite serious, work hard, and present few disciplinary problems. Moreover, since the students do not have housekeeping chores at their schools, they can devote full time to their studies. The teachers in the *lycées* are impressed by the zeal of the students, but say that they have such poor study habits that they must work much harder than comparable European students to obtain the same results. Indeed, at one time the government attempted to house all African secondary public school students in dormitories in an effort to improve their study habits. In 1964, some 600 *lycée* students of a total of 800 (including 200 girls) were *internes.* These came either from rural homes or from modest urban homes. Most of the 200 *externes* were the children of African and European civil servants and technicians whose urban homes were deemed adequate and whose parents were judged able to supervise their homework. Later, with increased enrollment and a general economic austerity in the country, this system was modified. An attempt was made to assign most public secondary school students to establishments close to their homes so that they could live there. In addition, dormitory space was made available only to those students who lived out of town. In 1967, Lycée Philippe Zinda Kabore had 669 male *internes* and 283 *externes,* and 89 female *internes* and 12 *externes.*

No provision was made for dormitories in the newly established Lycée Municipal. This underscored the pledge of the municipality to create the school primarily for the townspeople. As was to be expected, however, many rural parents did succeed in getting their children admitted to the Lycée Municipal and boarded them with relatives in Ouagadougou.

Whether *internes* or *externes,* the primary goal of the students in the *lycées* and *collèges* of Ouagadougou is to pass their exams. And like students everywhere, when given the opportunity, they choose the easiest course of studies. For many students in the *sixième,* the problem is whether to take the classical program including Latin or the modern program which does not include it. Most students, left to themselves, choose the modern, because they find Latin difficult, old-fashioned, and irrelevant. Indeed, the only students who take the classical program are those whose grades are excellent and who are persuaded to do so by teachers. If these students fail Latin, they are then permitted to shift into the modern program. In 1967, only 203 students in the Lycée Philippe Zinda Kabore and 34 in the Lycée Municipal took the classical program. In contrast, 1,101 in Lycée Philippe Zinda Kabore and 141 in the Lycée Municipal followed the modern program. Significantly, none of the students in the private secondary schools in town took the classical program. Thus, out of the 2,178 students in Ouagadougou who had a choice of the modern or the classic programs, only 237 or a little over 11 per cent took the classic.

Only slightly more than half the secondary school students in Ouagadougou successfully pass the *brevet* examinations, representing the first "cycle" of secondary school studies. In 1963, some 413 boys and 68 girls took the examination and 228 boys and 50 girls passed it. The figures for 1964 are given in Table XXIX. It should be noted, parenthetically, that the students in public and private schools in Ouagadougou (55 and 57 per cent respectively passed the examination) did as well, but no better than, the students in the other school districts. Table XXX gives figures for all the students in Upper Volta taking this examination from 1951 to 1967.

It should be noted also that the girls did much better than the boys on the B.E.P.C.-B.E. examination: 67 per cent as against 56.2 per cent passed. One possible reason for this is the higher selectivity among girls than among boys: only the most promising girls are encouraged to acquire advanced diplomas. Another reason is that the girls may simply be brighter than the boys. At least, this is the opinion of many elite women in Ouagadougou when they use these figures to protest unwarranted discrimination against women.

Judging from data collected in Ouagadougou and those

TABLE XXIX. **Results of B.E.P.C.-B.E. Examination in Ouagadougou, 1964**

Public Schools	Taking Exam		Passing	
	Males	Females	Males	Females
Lycée Philippe Zinda Kabore	180	23	94	14
Lycée Municipal	—	—	—	—
Lycée Technique	74	6	27	—
Ecole Militaire	35	—	25	—
Ecole Normale	—	—	—	—
Cours Normal des Jeunes Filles	—	32	—	13
Private Schools				
Collège de la Salle	41	—	34	—
Collège de Kologho Naba	—	34	—	19
Collège de Ouagadougou	27	—	21	—
Collège Laurent Ghilat	—	—	—	—

N.B. These figures do not include non-Voltaics; nor do they include 222 outside candidates for the B.E.P.C. Of the latter, 46 passed the B.E.P.C. and 5 passed the B.E.

TABLE XXX.   Results of B.E.P.C.-B.E.
Examinations in Upper Volta, (1951–67)

Year	Students	Passing	Per Cent
1951-52	89	55	61
1952-53	105	48	46
1953-54	147	57	38
1954-55	185	64	34
1955-56	201	77	38
1956-57	253	118	45
1957-58	301	167	55
1958-59	335	214	63
1959-60	350	253	72
1960-61	373	205	54
1961-62	381	278	57
1962-63	585	425	72
1963-64	700	399	57
1964-65	899	466	51
1965-66	1,305	684	52
1966-67	1,643	912	55

SOURCE: *Statistiques Scolaires,* Bureau des
Statistiques Scolaires, Direction Générale des
Services (Ministère de l'Éducation Nationale),
Rép. de Haute-Volta, 1966–67, p. 20.

drawn from official sources, only about one-third of those students who pass the *brevet* examinations continue their education. One reason for this attrition is that many students, especially those in the *normales* and technical schools go off to work. However, even many eligible students in the Lycée Philippe Zinda Kabore and Ecole Militaire do not enter the *deuxième.* For example, in 1967 only 167 out of 187 eligible in the Lycée and only 22 out of 34 in the Ecole Militaire continued. The reasons given for dropping out included problems at home and within families, boredom with continued schooling, and leaving the town or country.

Students continuing their education toward the "bac" still face the problem of specializing in the courses taken in the classical or modern programs, or switching to those for which they have shown a certain aptitude. The choice is often left to the professor who takes into consideration the relative performance of the students in the various courses. But, from the *deuxième* on to the *terminale* class, the students must concentrate in either philosophy, experimental sciences, or mathematics.

At the Lycée Philippe Zinda Kabore in 1967, 44 out of 85

233

or 51.8 per cent of the students in the *terminale* classes chose the philosophy program which included French and modern languages; 27 or 30.6 per cent chose the experimental sciences, and 17 or 19.4 per cent chose mathematics. At the Ecole Normale, 34.4 per cent opted for philosophy; 50 per cent for experimental sciences; and 15.6 per cent for mathematics. It should be noted, that mathematics is considered by the students as the most difficult subject matter. Indeed, a breakdown of the courses chosen by the Upper Volta students who successfully passed the 1967 exam showed that 53.27 per cent took philosophy, 26.71 per cent experimental sciences, and 21.05 per cent mathematics. These percentages are surprisingly close to those given for the subject matter chosen by the *terminale* classes at the Lycée Philippe Zinda Kabore.

Actually preparing for the "bac" exam is as traumatic for the students in Ouagadougou as it is for those in France. Indeed, the attitudes toward the examinations came with the first exams from France. Today the exams are prepared at the University of Abidjan, but they are deemed the equivalent of those prepared in France, and the student still retains his fear of them. The difference now is that, since 1966, the so-called "second" part of the *baccalauréat* exam has been eliminated and the students have only one period of anxiety.

The students in the Upper Volta *lycées* used to do significantly worse on the examinations for the first part of the "bac" than on examinations for the second part (see Table XXXI). The obvious reason for this is that only those who successfully passed the first part were allowed to take the second. However, since the second part of the "bac" was eliminated, only about one-third of those students who took the combined examination passed. In 1967, of the 321 students who took the *baccalauréat* examination, 158 were from Ouagadougou. Table XXXII lists the results.

The Ouagadougou students did significantly better than all the others in the country who took the *baccalauréat* examination. With a percentage of 41.8 passes to a national average of 38.94, they accounted for about 50 per cent of all those passing the examination. The result shows clearly that the public school students perform relatively better than the private school ones. It also shows that the "lower-status" *normaliens* did much better than the *lycéens,* this being true for boys as well as for girls. The *lycéens* rationalize this differ-

234

TABLE XXXI. Results of Baccalauréat Examinations
in Upper Volta (1951–67)

Year	First Part of "Bac"			Second Part of "Bac"		
	Students	Passing	Per Cent	Students	Passing	Per Cent
1951–52	55	28	51.1	1	0	0
1952–53	70	25	35.5	3	3	100
1953–54	87	33	37.9	—	—	—
1954–55	91	21	23.1	3	1	33.00
1955–56	109	32	29.5	13	11	84.00
1956–57	121	17	14.2	15	12	80.00
1957–58	134	60	44.8	36	20	55.00
1958–59	189	69	36.7	34	22	64.00
1959–60	125	74	59.1	51	27	52.00
1960–61	172	65	37.9	78	25	32.00
1961–62	192	105	54.9	96	64	66.00
1962–63	162	81	49.9	99	62	62.00
1963–64	252	104	41.2	122	76	62.00
1964–65	327	145	44.4	137	67	52.00
1965–66				195	67	34.00
1966–67				321	125	38.39

SOURCE: *Statistiques Scolaires,* Bureau des Statistiques Scolaires, Direction
Générale des Services (Ministère de l'Éducation Nationale), Rép. de Haute-Volta,
1966–67, p. 20.

TABLE XXXII. Results of Baccalauréat Examinations
in Ouagadougou (1967)

School	Taking Exam		Passing Exam	
	Males	Females	Males	Females
Lycée Philippe Zinda Kabore	82	10	37	3
Ecole Normale	19	3	10	2
Collège de la Salle	18	—	2	—
Collège de Kologho Naba	—	26	—	8
TOTAL	119	39	49	13
		158		62

SOURCE: Personal communication from the Ministry of Education.

ence by citing the relative difficulties of the subject matter; but
given the rather pragmatic student approach toward degrees,
it would be surprising if many more students did not choose
the Ecole Normale in the future.

The students in Ouagadougou consider passing the "bac" as
the major event in their academic lives. They still share the
memories of their fathers and older brothers about the days

when even the most intelligent African in French Africa could not present himself for that examination. Thus the students who successfully pass the examination are given parties by relatives and friends to *arroser* (pour libations on) their success. Those who fail the examination in June repeat the process in October. And if they fail again, they are permitted to repeat (*redoubler*) the *terminale* class provided their record has been good, and their failure was not too disastrous. For example, 37 students at the Lycée Philippe Zinda Kabore were permitted to repeat the *terminale* class in 1967. Students have been known to repeat the *terminale* more than once, but generally after a second failure, they are not permitted to register at school. They can still retake the examination, but as an external student (*candidat libre*).[12]

It is normally quite difficult for external students to pass the *baccalauréat* examinations. One reason is that students who have failed go to work at jobs for which they had qualified on passing the *brevet* and have little time to study. Second, students out of school find it difficult to keep abreast of the curriculum upon which the examination is based. Some students take correspondence courses in an effort to keep up with the work, but the lack of direct contact affects their performance on the examinations. For example, in 1967, only 9 of the 54 external students who took the examination passed, a percentage of 18.5, about half as low as the country's average.

Almost all of the students of Ouagadougou who pass the *baccalauréat* examination continue their education. Formerly they were sent to France since there were no institutions of higher learning in French Africa. Today, except for the recently established Institut de Formation Pédagogique, the Upper Volta still has no institutions for higher education, and most continuing students leave the country. The difference is that they do not all have to go to France, because French-affiliated universities have opened at Dakar (1957) and at Abidjan (1961), and a number of students are sent there. Where a student goes to study depends as much upon his aptitude as upon the judgment of the Ministry of National Education. However, other factors such as family connections and ethnicity are believed to play a role in the selection process.

[12]Only a few students who fail have the means to pursue their education at a private instution in France.

Indeed, every year the announcement of the destinations of scholars is sure to be greeted with disappointment and cries of *combine*—meaning favoritism.

Most students prefer to go to French universities even though there are theoretically no differences between those universities in France and those at Dakar and Abidjan. However, almost everyone believes that the diplomas and certificates granted in France are superior to those granted in Africa, and that students educated in France acquire a "culture" not available in Africa. Moreover, the students and their parents hold that, since French technicians still determine where a returned graduate will work, it is better to have "French" diplomas, which are respected by these men, than "African" ones. The result is that students, if given the opportunity, will choose a course of study they do not particularly like at a French university rather than choose a subject they really desire at an African university.

Given these attitudes, it is not surprising that the students have established a hierarchy among universities and establishments of higher education: those in Paris first; those in the French provinces second; the University of Dakar third; the University in Abidjan fourth; and the Institut de Formation Pédagogique in Ouagadougou last. Moreover, the general belief is that those students with connections are sent to France, and those less favored are sent either to Dakar or Abidjan. Nothing could convince the brilliant Upper Volta-born son of a Malian father and a Voltaic mother that he was not discriminated against when he was sent to Dakar instead of Paris. The Ministry of Education hopes that in time the universities in Dakar and Abidjan will gain in stature in the eyes of the students, thereby making its task easier. However, until that day comes, most students in Ouagadougou will prefer to study in France.

In 1964–65, of some 257 (19 female) Voltaic students in establishments of higher education, 148 were in France, 61 in Senegal, 45 in the Ivory Coast, and 3 in the U.S.A.[13] Table XXXIII gives the figures on the distribution of Voltaic students for 1966–67.

[13]*Statistiques Scolaires,* Bureau des Statistiques Scolaires, Direction Générale des Services (Ministère de l'Education Nationale, Répresentative de Haute-Volta), 1964–65, p. 35.

TABLE XXXIII. Voltaic Students in Establishments of Higher Education (1966–67)

| Specialties | Upper Volta | Countries* | | | | | | | | | | | |
| | | France | | Senegal | | Ivory Coast | | U.S.A. | | Other | | Total | |
	Male	Male	Female	Male	Female	Male	Female	Male	Female	Male	Female	Male	Female
Agriculture		6										6	
Architecture & arts		2										2	
Commerce		12	2									12	2
Engineering		11		5								16	
Dentistry		2		1	1							3	1
Law and economics		6		19		25				2		52	
Letters	10++	12	4	17		26	2					65	6
Medicine		9	1	12		7						28	1
Pharmacy		3	1	4	2							7	3
Political science		2	1									2	1
Sciences and mathematics		21		24	5	30						75	5
Veterinary medicine		7										7	
Divers		9	2									9	2
TOTAL	10	102	11	82	8	88	2			2		284	21

SOURCE: *Statistiques Scolaires*, Bureau des Statistiques Scolaires, Direction Générale des Services (Ministère de l'Éducation Nationale), Rép. de Haute-Volta, 1966–67, p. 35.

*France provided most of the scholarships for 206 students. The Upper Volta provided scholarships for 53, and other countries provided scholarships for 37 students.

++These ten students were at the Institut de Formation Pédagogique in Ouagadougou.

Personal choice and aptitude as well as employment possibilities in the civil service and the wishes of the Minister of
Education are reflected in the decision of the students to follow
various careers. The decision of the minister can be crucial to
a student's future, especially if he insists that a student should
take a certain course "in the country's interest." If, per-
chance, the student objects, the minister has the right to refuse
him a government-derived or controlled scholarship. For example, in 1964, the Minister of National Education refused
students the right to take courses in political science and jour-
nalism, stating that these two courses were more "political
than academic" and not in the country's best interests. In
1968 the minister prevented a student with independent means
from going abroad to teach and study a subject he did not approve of by invoking an old and relatively little-used decree
which controlled "the departure of Voltaic students to foreign
countries."[14] Thus, unless the government agrees, students
cannot even pay their own way to foreign universities to pursue the course of study they desire.

There is a certain congruence between the specialities pur-
sued by Voltaic students in institutions of higher education
and the responses of *lycée* students of Ouagadougou when
asked about career preferences (see Table XXVIII above). In
response to the questionnaire, the highest number of *lycée*
students (25) indicated the profession of "Professor or
Teacher" as first choice. The highest number of graduate
students (161) are studying letters, sciences, and math, spe-
cialties which lead to a teaching career. The second highest
number of *lycée* students (16) preferred medicine, but this
profession ranks third in number of students (28) pursuing it.
The study of engineering was chosen in third place by the
lycée students and ranks fourth among professions being
studied by the university group. The biggest surprise was that
law and economics which few *lycée* students (1) indicated an

[14]The minister declared, "It is certain that this measure had not been well
received, but I had no choice at the time when I am seeking fifty or so teachers for the *lycées* as for the *collèges....* I believe that the students
have understood the importance of this act, for I have told them what the
realities are and have asked them to act like the great 'revolutionairies' as
they are accustomed to saying. For from now on all responsibilities will be
shared by the whole nation." (*Bulletin Quotidien,* 18 September 1966, pp.
2–3.) The law used was Ordonnance No. 40, Pres/MF/DOM/ of 13 August
1959 which stipulates that exit visas are necessary for ordinary passports.

interest in were actually being studied by the second highest number of university students (52). The reasons for this are unknown. It may be that when the *lycée* students were surveyed in 1964, the professions of law and economics had lost prestige because of the unpopularity of the existing national government and thus the students reacted against them, whereas they regarded these professions more realistically when they graduated. It is also possible that the *lycée* graduates selected these two subjects after the fall of the Yaméogo Government in the belief that they could help the country modernize. However, this facile assumption could be called into question by comparing the *lycée* students' positive response to agronomy with the small number of university students actually studying this important subject. The Voltaic students may pay lip service to the importance of agronomy for developing their country, but they have not yet lost the well-known repugnance of the educated classes in francophone Africa toward agriculture. There is still a great conflict between the needs of Upper Volta society (Ouagadougou and the other urban centers excepted) and the attitudes of the students. The country is still largely rural, but the students, until now, have been inevitably urbanized while being educated. They, therefore, find it difficult to use their educational skills outside the urban area or to aid the people in the rural areas.

A growing number of educated people are challenging the whole educational system of Ouagadougou and, indeed, of contemporary Upper Volta. Some people allege that there is a "rupture, and indeed a net divorce between the primary school in particular, and life in the society."[15] And this is held to be as true for the urban children as it is for those in the rural areas. A number of critics blame the country's retention of the French educational system for this impasse. When Upper Volta became independent, it signed a cultural convention agreeing to recruit French teachers, if any foreign teachers were needed, in exchange for France's reciprocity in granting Upper Volta students unlimited access to its institutions of higher learning.[16] The critics maintain that Upper

[15]Personal conversation with Dr. Joseph Ki-Zerbo, Inspector de L'Academie dans Le Ministère de l'Education Nationale, 1968.

[16]According to Article 2 of this agreement: "The Republic of Upper Volta agrees . . . to give to the French Government the right to recruit teaching personnel, to give all facilities to this personnel and likewise to the per-

Volta made a mistake in opting for an educational system conceived by Frenchmen for French society and point out that even the French realize that this system is inadequate for the modern world.[17] The more radical critics accuse the Upper Volta Government of "submitting to cultural neo-colonialism" by maintaining "the predominant position of the French language and culture in the educational system, and of continuing the practice, after independence as before, of not *forming medium or superior cadres.*"[18] These critics also lament the lack of a determined effort to "Africanize" the educational system; the omission of subject matter from anglophone areas in Africa; and the failure to teach the children about the African's conception of man and the universe, subjects coming under the heading of *négritude.*

Some African educators in Ouagadougou, while recognizing the deficiencies in their educational system and the need to adapt it to the realities of contemporary African life, cite historical, practical, and economic reasons for their plight. They point out that only close cooperation with France has enabled them to give their young people access to the vast store of Western knowledge. Indeed, each year France does give Upper Volta substantial aid in the form of books and school supplies. And without France's technical aid, Upper Volta would have had, and would still have, difficulty staffing its higher schools. For example, in 1964 there were only 5 African teachers out of a total of 47 teachers in the Lycée Philippe Zinda Kaboré, and of 213 male and 68 female teachers in the higher schools of Upper Volta in 1967–68 only 67 were African males and 5 African females.[19] Of course, this is as much due to France's willingness to help as it is to the inability of Upper Volta to lure its own people home. In 1967 there were at least 17 Voltaics with teaching qualifications in France or working at more remunerative jobs elsewhere.

---

sonnel of the corps of inspectors and juries of examinations and competitions to accomplish their mission." Article 8 states that "to assure solidarity in the field of education with the French Republic as much as to enable its own people to gain access to French institutions, the Government of the Republic of Upper Volta declares its wish to coordinate the education given in its educational establishments with that given in corresponding ones in the French Republic." *Jeune Volta,* February 1967, p. 12.

[17]*Ibid.,* p. 10.
[18]*Ibid.,* p. 12.
[19]*Statistiques Scolaires,* 1967–68, p. 76.

Many Upper Volta school officials insist that it is simply not true that they have failed to introduce African subjects into the school curriculum. They declare that they have done their best, despite the lack of suitable material available for the schools. Moreover, they point out that they are striving to adapt education to the milieu of Upper Volta, especially education in the rural areas. What the school officials do not like to admit, however, is that both conservative French and African teachers resist and resent change or adapting the curriculum to the African environment. These teachers believe—and some government officials share their views—that the time is not propitious for Africanizing the curriculum. They fear that to do so would jeopardize the attempt to maintain proper standards in the schools. The upheaval in French educational circles during 1968 has shaken the faith of the conservatives, but inertia and bureaucracy may well delay any radical changes in Upper Volta's educational system.[20]

A much more serious charge of those who would change the basic educational system in Ouagadougou is that the present system is too costly for the job it does. They point out that the state cannot afford to devote 18 per cent of its national budget to educate only 10 per cent of the school-age population. Speaking before the XIV Congress of the National Syndicate of African Teachers in Upper Volta, Mr. Ghilat, President of the National Association of Parents and Students declared:

> All education should lead to an end; therefore, it should be adapted to the conditions of life and livelihood of a country. Nevertheless, we have observed that, since our independence or, more correctly, since about three years ago, our diplomas have no value. The C.E.P.E. and the B.E.P.C.

[20]A recent editorial in the Upper Volta weekly, *Carrefour Africain*, entitled "For a School That is Adapted," suggested that the teachers be "retrained if the educational system would be adapted to the country." The editorialist lamented that the children "especially those in the towns" do not know the difference between a goat and a pig, and between millet and sorghum. He would even return the "school to the fields," suggesting that the colonial school system, which insisted that each school keep its own fields, was not completely wrong. He concluded: "It is high time that our revisions and our educational methods take into account our needs and especially our means. Without these conditions *sine qua non*, we will roll like a bouncing stone on an incline towards disaster." *Carrefour Africain*, No. 363–64 (5–12 April 1969), p. 1.

242

which formerly used to guarantee social mobility and good employment now lead nowhere in Upper Volta since there is no employment. Thus while we produced some 15,000 students with certificates and 2,896 with *brevets,* during the three years 1966, 1967 and 1968, 1,600 of them have nothing to do, the others having remained in school to continue their studies. What has become of these graduates? And what will become of them? What are they good for? They are neither useful to this country, which does not know how to employ them; nor to their relatives who do not know what to do with them; nor to themselves, because they know how to do nothing. Here, then, is the product of our schools in Upper Volta. Here is what we have attained by maintaining the status quo and by not evolving.[21]

The issues of the high cost of education in Upper Volta, and its relevance to the society, have sparked a long-dormant but now potentially dangerous controversy between church and state over subsidies to parochial schools. The ordinary people in Ouagadougou were not involved in the early conflict between the administration and the mission over education. It was an "affair of the whites." However, they did appreciate Governor-General Boisson's decision in 1942 to resume subvention to mission schools. In fact, the progressive members of the local community were only too glad to send their children to any school available. Both the Church and the administration were to gain. The Catholics produced the largest percentage of the elites in Upper Volta, and the administration was able to recruit many parochial school students as clerks. Government aid to parochial schools did not become an issue in Ouagadougou and in Upper Volta until the post-World War II years when both Moslems and traditionalists demanded education for their children, but demanded education without Christianization. They inveighed the budding politicians who were seeking their votes to provide more public schools. The politicians pressed the claims of their constituents only to be told by outgoing and church-oriented colonial administration that there was not enough money for public schools, nor enough qualified teachers to staff these schools. The people rejected the response of the government, pointing out that the Catholic schools continued

[21]*Ibid.,* No. 329, 10 August 1968, p. 5.

to receive subsidies and were being permitted to employ teaching personnel without required diplomas.[22] A temporary compromise was reached when the government built a number of badly needed public schools between 1956 and 1960, but the issue of private schools versus parochial schools was only covered up, not solved.

The problem of subsidies for schools arose immediately after Upper Volta gained independence. A grateful government started a policy of expanding public education in order to compensate those parents who had voted for it and who were demanding more education for their children. The Catholic church, susceptible to the same pressures as the government—to meet the need for education—endeavored to open more schools. The problem, however, was that the government did not have enough money to build its own schools and to subsidize those being built by the Catholics. A conflict between church and state arose in 1964 over the level of subsidies and created a crisis of conscience for President Yaméogo, a Catholic convert and a former student in the Catholic seminary at Pabré. He "accepted his responsibility" and promulgated a degree in which the old formula of granting the Church a subsidy for every school built was changed to one which stated that "the maximum sum total of the subsidy [for parochial schools] is determined each year as a function of the budgetary possibilities [of the state], and the objectives of the Development Plan."[23] The Church grumbled, but reduced the rate of increase of its primary school pupils from 15.2 per cent per year in 1959–60 to only 3.2 per cent in 1965–66. However, and perhaps because of the previous large number of primary school pupils, the Church was not able to reduce the increase of secondary school students below 8.4 per cent.

The government's reduction of subsidies for Catholic parochial schools did not satisfy all the critics of these schools, however. The president of La Ligue Voltaique des Oeuvres Laïques (Voltaic League for Secular Action), a Moslem, speaking before a teachers' group in 1964 criticized what he considered then to be "an excessive interest of the 'Higher-Ups' on behalf of religious education—an interest which manifests

[22]Skinner, 1958, p. 1,117.
[23]*Jeune Volta,* April 1968, p. 14.

itself by the state contributing enormous sums to it."[24] The speaker charged that there was officially sanctioned discrimination against non-Catholic pupils. He declared: "In Upper Volta there are 70 per cent pagans, 23 per cent Moslems, and scarcely more than 6 per cent Christians. The maximum level of school attendance attained is only 10 per cent of the school-age population. The breakdown in percentages of those being educated is as follows: young Christians 5.5 per cent; young Moslems 2 per cent; and young traditionalists, 2.5 per cent. Here then is a republic which permits a certain group of its children, or its citizens, to have a better chance of being educated and with the involuntary contribution of others. When this state of affairs is reached, the only possible and just solution should be to abolish the subsidies pure and simple; to refuse to divert public funds from their logical purpose; and to secularize and nationalize the establishments in question. The efforts of the government would have a direction and no one could complain."[25]

The Church did not reply to its secular or Moslem critics, preferring perhaps to deal with the greater threat, the state. However, later events were to show that the Church was smarting from these attacks. The Church did feel compelled to respond to a proposal of the austerity-minded military government to grant it a subsidy of only 298,365,000 C.F.A. toward a total school expense of 622 million C.F.A. in 1966–67. It declared the subsidy was too small and threatened to close its schools at the end of December 1967 if it did not receive more government aid. Interestingly enough, the Catholic church did not attack the law upon which the subsidy to the private schools was based, nor did it challenge the impartiality of the military. What the bishops did was to send a letter demanding special treatment in compensation for the early achievements of Catholic education. They rejected all charges of discrimination and calumny heaped on their schools, stating that they have always accepted all children "without discrimination as to race, religion or social class." The bishops further criticized all those who felt that it was "a crime to

[24]Triande Toumani, "Message du Président de la Ligue Voltaique des Oeuvres Laïques." Travaux du Xe Congrès du Syndicat Nationale des Enseignants Africains de Haute-Volta (Koudougou, 8–11 July 1964), pp. 69–73.
[25]Ibid.

have left a place for God in our schools." And, adopting one of the favorite postures of their detractors, warned against "the false friends of the Upper Volta, who, by the means of fallacious arguments, would like to keep this country in the last position in the caravan of nations. Neo-capitalists of all kinds have a great interest in maintaining the stagnation of our country, and thereby maintain a choice reservation of ignorant and illiterate laborers without professional qualifications who would be doomed to shameful exploitation by conscience-less people."[26]

It was only after the Minister of Finance declared publicly that there was no discrimination against the Catholic schools, and that, in fact, "a pupil in the private [school] receives for his upkeep a sum of money 3.5 times greater to one in the public [school]" that the Church discussed the economic situation. The clergy disagreed with the minister's figures, rebutting that "a pupil receiving a private education costs the state only 9,000 C.F.A. whereas a pupil receiving public education costs it 1,300 C.F.A."[27] At this impasse, both the government and the Church sought the good offices of influential persons in Ouagadougou and a compromise was reached. The government agreed to pay the debts of the parochial schools for the year 1967–68 provided the Church opened no more schools without the specific permission of the government. Moreover, the government implied that future subsidies for parochial schools would still be based on budgetary possibilities. The Church reopened the schools and a crisis was narrowly averted, but the problem remained unsolved.

The church-state controversy broke out afresh in Feburary 1969. At that time, the bishops of Upper Volta, meeting under the chairmanship of Paul Cardinal Zoungrana, Archbishop of Ouagadougou, declared that "the Church deems that its duty is to hand over to the government the responsibility for the educational activities of which it had assumed charge, hoping thereby to bring peace and tranquility to all concerned." The bishops acknowledged that "the subsidies accorded Catholic education are important," but denied that by offering to surrender the schools to the government they had any intention of trying to sabotage the school system or create more difficulties for the state. They even held out the possibility that per-

[26] *Jeune Volta,* April 1968, p. 4.
[27] *Jeune Afrique,* No. 431 (7–13 April 1969), p. 28.

246

haps the Church would try to cooperate with the government in the field of education, provided a new formula could be found. However, they insisted that under the present circumstances, the Church was no longer able to support the cost of its schools. Thus did the Church endeavor to solve the problem once and for all time.

It is not now, in 1970, clear whether, in fact, the Catholic church in Upper Volta will or can relinquish its important role in education. These schools have served the Church well, especially in creating and sustaining a ruling Christian elite. Nevertheless, it is also true that many members of this elite have not been as faithful to the Church as the bishops would have wished them to be and were willing to sacrifice the interests of the Church to political expedience or for economic benefits. For example, the qualified African parochial school teachers, and supposedly good Catholics, demanded the same salaries and other perquisites as their colleagues in the public schools. Also, most Catholic parents prefer to send qualified children to public primary and secondary schools rather than send them to the parochial schools and spend the little extra money that even scholarship students in these need. A concomitant of this is that the Catholic secondary schools have gained the reputation of being a sanctuary for elite children not bright enough to be accepted in the public schools.

Perhaps all of these factors have convinced the Church that its basic mission is no longer being served by its schools. For one thing, these schools can no longer be used as important vehicles for proselyting of Moslem and traditionalists children because these children can go to public secular schools. Second, the Catholic church in Upper Volta is neither faced with, nor needs to combat, a government or ideological movement determined to undermine the faith of its adherents. Thus it can afford to wait and see whether it can effect another compromise with the state that would enable it to continue parochial school education in Ouagadougou and in the rest of the country.[28].

The Protestant school officials in Ouagadougou have not been a party to the conflict between the Catholic church and the state over government subsidies. One reason for this is

[28]There were reports in June 1970 that the Church had relinquished the primary schools to the government and that secondary parochial schools would be placed in the hands of foreign Catholic lay orders.

that the Protestants have not yet lost their fear, engendered during the colonial epoch, that they are at best only tolerated. They still act as though it is a privilege for them, as American and French Protestants, to be able to have schools in town. Second, because the colonial French Government made it so difficult for American missionaries to qualify as teachers in Upper Volta, the Protestant schools are few in contrast to those of the Catholics. Moreover, the Protestants were never able to demand subsidies from the administration and relied upon foreign support to run their schools. The prevailing view of the Protestant school officials is that they would gladly continue to accept whatever help the state can give and try to do their best for the children of the town.

Like the Protestants, the Moslems in Ouagadougou have not taken part in the controversy over government aid to parochial schools. The Moslem elites have always been against such aid in principle because they felt it provided the means whereby the Catholics could recruit young Moslems and young pagans, and under the guise of educating them, convert them to Christianity. They have, therefore, always expounded the notion that the government should rationalize the schools so that all children could have equal access to modern education. Conservative Moslem parents have especially resented the absence of an all-girl secondary school in Ouagadougou for their daughters. They complained that their daughters were exposed to immorality at the Lycée Philippe Zinda Kabore and even at Le Cours Normal which, although reserved for girls, shared common classrooms with the *Lycée* boys. And because of the possibility of conversion, they did not want to send their daughters to the Catholic girls' college.

While many people in Ouagadougou may not agree with the desire of some Moslem parents to have all-girl schools, many of them criticize the state of education for girls. The percentages of girls in both public and private schools have always lagged behind those of boys. Today, girls make up 32 per cent of primary school children; 25 per cent of those in secondary schools; and only 7 per cent of the students in the advanced institutions. The reasons for this disparity are as complex as they are difficult to overcome. Initially the Church, the administration, and Voltaic parents all were reluctant to educate the girls. The Church preferred to educate boys because it wished to produce catechists and priests. The administration favored the education of boys because it wanted clerks and auxillaries in the persons of the sons of chiefs. Parents ferociously opposed the recruitment of their daughters for school because this disrupted the girls' prearranged marriages and deprived the families of their domestic and agricultural services. And, when the girls were recruited for school, they were initially taught in Moré and trained to work in the Catholic-run carpet factory in Ouagadougou. Parents naturally believed that their daughters were being taken to join the ranks of male forced laborers. Of course, one deep and often unstated fear of Voltaic parents was that their daughters who "had been taken by the Europeans" to Ouagadougou would become as morally loose as the young ladies who frequented the military camp near Bilibambili. Some parents feared also that their educated daughters would marry without their consent. When some of the girls in the carpet factory (who, according to the Catholics became the foundation of Christian families) actually did this, those parents felt that their worst fears had been confirmed.

Over the past two decades there has been a marked shift in the opinion of the Ouagadougou people in favor of more education for girls. One reason for this is that the first generation of educated Ouagadougou girls did not run wild; instead, they were sought as wives by the first group of well-paid local civil servants. Many parents, noticing the comportment of the daughters of Christians and ex-soldiers who attended school, were encouraged to "send their daughters to the Sisters." Second, a number of girls persuaded their own parents to send them to school. The life histories of a number of women in Ouagadougou revealed that as girls, with younger siblings on their backs or in tow, they watched with envy the Sisters teaching the other little girls to play games and asked to be sent to school. Third, many urban parents finally realized that education often brought as great economic benefits to girls as it did to men. The mothers in Ouagadougou noted with amazement Dahomean women working at the hospital and in offices around town and realized that their daughters could do likewise. They also discovered that educated women civil servants not only had money to contribute to their families of procreation, but could spare money for their families of orientation, and especially their mothers. (We have seen how this latter practice was one of the factors making for the breakup of the *ménage à deux*.) Today, many parents send their daughters to school because they are convinced that bright girls should be given as great an opportunity to gain an education as any boy.

Despite an appreciable increase in school attendance among girls, they still have difficulty getting an education. Some urban cultivators continue to balk at educating their daughters, preferring these girls to hawk vegetables in the markets or along the streets. Second, many girls are simply too old to attend primary school when they migrate to Ouagadougou and therefore miss the opportunity to obtain a formal education. Third, girls are still discriminated against in the recruitment of children to attend school. We have seen how in Bilbalgo ward the teachers and notables preemptorily limited the number of places available to girls. And finally, many socially conscious parents in Ouagadougou are simply dissatisfied with the kind of education their daughters receive.

The major complaint against the education given girls is that it is irrelevant to the African setting. Female African school teachers complain that no attempt is made to subject the school girl to parental control, with the result that all sorts of moral problems arise. Illiterate mothers are not encouraged to act as a stabilizing force for their daughters since they are held not to understand the world of the school. The tendency is, therefore, for these mothers to confer the task of character formation in their daughters to the schools. The latter are expected to act *in local parentis* to see that their charges do not come to grief. The difficulty here is that the school cannot supervise the girls either during vacation or after they complete their education. The head of a female secondary school in Ouagadougou wrote: "It is indeed striking to note that the accidents which oblige us to dismiss a young girl are less frequent during the school year than during vacation. Of course, the majority of the girls exposed to this kind of accident are secondary school students and boarders. However, the virtues of our young girls are protected less by school regulations than by scholarly activities. If the mammas gave their grown daughters less leisure, they would read less dangerous literature, would dream less, and would behave better."[29] A more serious

[29]*La Voix des Enseignants,* No. 22 (1968), Ouagadougou, Répresentative de Haute-Volta, p. 20.

criticism of the education of African girls is that the attempt is made to acculturate them according to European standards, whereas even the most highly educated African women, by force of circumstances, return to African ways as they grow older. Girls may act like *petites Européennes* but, as they marry and create their own nuclear families, or are absorbed in the lives of their husbands' families, they must be prepared to accept many of the traditional African norms. We have seen that educated matrons prefer to wear African clothes. But even young educated African wives must be prepared to accept impromptu and extended visits from their kinsmen and those of their husbands. They must also be prepared to tolerate the behavior of husbands who, later in life, retreat to the all-male world of African men and who, though Christian, may wish to take younger and often illiterate wives. We have noted that one problem of educated Upper Volta women is that they must learn to treat these women as cowives rather than as domestic servants. Of course, the difficulty in modifying the education of the girls, and of boys too for that matter, is that the schools' curricula are still French, and that the French teachers consciously or unconsciously provide European models for life styles. The possibility for change will only come with the Africanization of the curricula, the availability of more African teachers, and a psychological change among school officials who have physical but still not ideological control of the schools. There is an already marked difference between the comportment of the girls at Le Cours Normal des Jeunes Filles, directed by a very militant African woman, and the girls at the other schools. The modernized African hair and dress styles of the *normaliennes* is symbolic of their deeper commitment to modernize African values to serve the people of contemporary Ouagadougou.

The emergence of a class of secondary school educated girls in Ouagadougou has stimulated discussion about higher education for women. In 1969 young women composed only 7 per cent of all the Upper Volta students receiving higher education. Both the administration and parents resist granting scholarships to girls for higher education, despite the fact that girls have out-performed boys on examinations (see Table XXXII above.). Government officials declare it does not pay to educate women since they get married and, if they become civil servants, must be granted long maternity leaves and lactation recesses. Poor parents do not encourage their daughters to continue their education since with a *brevet* the girls can receive specialized training and enter the job market. Many girls place matrimony before education, despite the fact that the higher the diploma a girl has, the more money she will earn when she marries and inevitably goes to work. The reason for this attitude is simply that in order to get a higher education, Ouagadougou girls must go to France and there the chance of meeting a qualified potential spouse from Upper Volta is quite limited. In France they also face competition for Upper Volta men from white as well as from black women, and so far they have not been as successful as their foreign competitors. *Jeune Volta*, a publication of General Union of Voltaic Students, recently congratulated its members who were married in France. These included an Upper Volta student with a Masters of Science degree who married an Upper Volta woman studying dressmaking; an Upper Volta man with a diploma in law married to a French woman studying to be a laboratory technician; an Upper Volta man married to a French woman; and an Upper Volta man married to an African nurse at the Moslem mosque in Paris (but it is not clear from the name whether the young woman is from Upper Volta or a neighboring country); an Upper Volta veterinarian who married a French teacher at the Paris mosque; and an Upper Volta veterinarian who married a midwife from Upper Volta. Note that not one of the Upper Volta women appears to have obtained the *baccalauréate* diploma. *Jeune Volta* impartially wished all the "young and new households its heartfelt congratulations and best wishes for happiness and joy."[30] Ironically, the two most educated women in Upper Volta declare that the educated Upper Volta men do not really know what to do with the better educated women. They accuse these men of wanting the best of often contradictory African and European worlds and resent having to make a final choice between them. Meanwhile the debate about higher education for women goes on. The elite women, like their counterparts in Western countries, insist that they should not be discriminated against because of their valuable and necessary function in perpetuating the species. The men, for their part, insist that educated

[30] *Jeune Volta,* February 1967, pp. 36–37.

women simply take away jobs that should properly go to "heads of households."

There are other equally pressing educational problems in Ouagadougou: how to provide further education for working adults; how to provide low-level commercial training; and how to curb illiteracy. A major complaint of the civil servants is that the lack of educational opportunities during the colonial period prevented them from realizing their full potential. Thus, when in 1959 the officials of the emerging Upper Volta nation-state thought about future cadres, they authorized the establishment of the Ecole Nationale d'Administration (E.N.A.). The aim of this school was "to assure the rapid training of an important number of civil servants capable of rendering immediate service to the new administrations of the country."[31] Ninety civil servants were chosen at random, that is, without competitive examinations, to go to the school for six months and of these 77 received C.A.P. diplomas. In 1961, the school started accepting only those civil servants who had passed their entrance examination, and to date, some 107 of these have received certificates.

Partly as a result of its origin and partly as a result of its function to train local career civil servants, the E.N.A. is not viewed in the same light as its homologue in France. True, its program is rich, seeking as it does to accomplish four main tasks: produce civil servants; improve their skills; develop their capacity for the fields of research and information; and help in the general development of the country. However, most secondary school students consider the E.N.A. to be a place one goes for another chance in life. It is not judged as the kind of school to which hopeful and young students should go. In other words, most young students in Ouagadougou view the E.N.A. as a "vocational" school for adult civil servants. It enables one to step back on the academic ladder and receive more specific training for better paying jobs.

A growing number of influential persons in Ouagadougou are creating private institutions to help those persons who for various reasons were not able to take advantage of educational opportunities at either public or parochial schools. At one

[31]"Ecole Nationale d'Administration," Ministère du Travail et de la Fonction Publique, Répresentative de Haute-Volta, 1961, p. 13.

time the Catholic mission did provide evening classes for migrants too old to attend regular schools and for urban-born persons who did not go to school. However, this school posed many ideological and financial difficulties for Catholics as well as non-Catholic students. Finally, in 1957, a group of young educated men, primarily Mossi, formed an organization, known as Entraide Culturelle Voltaique Association de Lutte contre l'Analphabétisme (E.C.V.), to fight illiteracy. They desired, above all, to help both illiterates and school dropouts obtain the elementary school certificate. They opened classes staffed by volunteer teachers in any available space and in 1958 presented 10 pupils for the exam. Only one of these pupils passed, but this did not discourage either the teachers or pupils. Every year since then pupils have been presented for the certifying examinations. The high point came in 1966 when they were able to present 28 candidates of which 18 received certificates. By 1968, the E.C.V. had expanded its activities to eight of the quarters of the commune and even held classes in the suburbs. By then 30 volunteers were giving lessons to 1,036 pupils, including girls. The municipal authorities, who had always favored the literacy campaign but who could give no help, finally granted the association a plot of land in the school zone. Here, in 1968, a school was erected with the help of visiting American and Canadian students and with contributions from local business groups and foreign embassies. At the inauguration of the school, the association expressed the desire to wipe out illiteracy among the young people of Ouagadougou and thereby help them adapt much more effectively to urban life.

Another volunteer group in Ouagadougou, the Jeunesse Ouvrière Chretienne Féminine (J.O.C.F.), has also endeavored to reduce illiteracy among migrant girls and to help female school dropouts. In 1963 the organization made a survey which disclosed that a large number of urban girls were unemployed because they had no education. The survey also showed that many of these girls exhibited a real and dangerous lack of concern for their future and often a complete lack of initiative. Once married, these women looked to their husbands for everything, not knowing how to maintain a house, take care of a baby, vary the meals, or keep their fingers occupied. The members of the J.O.C.F. concluded that such a state of affairs "rapidly provokes misunderstanding, disputes,

254

and even, alas, divorce."[32] The next year, 1964, the organization devised a plan to help the young women of Ouagadougou adapt to the urban environment. First, they persuaded Catholic nuns and African and European women to volunteer to conduct classes in dressmaking, knitting, crocheting, weaving, ironing, cooking, and domestic science for all girls, adding French for the illiterate ones. Second, they had to encourage the young women to attend classes and to pay a nominal fee of 500 F.C.F.A. ($2.00). As to be expected, a few townspeople took the same jaundiced view of this center as they did of the sewing classes at the social centers. Nonetheless, the enterprise was so successful that the leaders decided to build a larger establishment. They secured a plot of land near the market of the Mogho Naba (*Nab'Raga*) and both male and female volunteers erected the building. The new center was inaugurated in 1969 and some 72 young women, between the ages of fourteen and twenty-two, were recruited. Eleven of them had elementary school certificates, 25 had finished elementary school but had no certificates, 20 had some elementary education, and 6 were illiterate. The J.O.C.F. is so satisfied with the progress of the center that it plans to open others in the other quarters of the town.

The latest attempt of the townspeople to provide education adapted to modern life was the founding of Centre Privé d'Etudes Commerciales. The prime mover in this venture was the former head of the Upper Volta Foreign Trade Service. This young man became alarmed at the inability of the intelligent and ambitious youths to master the elementary skills of bookkeeping, stenography, typing, and salesmanship, despite costly correspondence courses. He had also previously chafed at the relative absence of these skilled persons for the private sector, despite the growing inability of the government to employ additional civil servants. His decision to found a school to train youths with the *brevet* in commercial skills and to increase the competence of those persons similarly employed in the private sector was welcomed by the Ministry of National Education and gained the support of the local Chamber of Commerce and at least one foreign embassy. The school was inaugurated on March 20, 1969, with 100 students divided into two classes. Forty of these were regular day stu-

[32] *Présence Voltaique*, No. 18 (April-May 1969), p. 4.

dents who paid 30,000 C.F.A. ($120.00) per year. The school has both African and European teachers and graduated its first group of students in 1971.

A number of international organizations are also working to improve the skills of the urban population or are planning to do so. These include the International Labor Office which trains a number of girls as typists and young men as craftsmen. The French Government has provided a technician to help the young artisans increase their skills in the arts and crafts with the intent of providing tourist goods. The efforts here are designed to prepare the groundwork which would enable the local people to train these young people or provide the structure through which they can be trained.

Given the importance of education as the passport to the good or better life, it is easy to understand the concern the people of this nonindustrial town have about it. A group of persons met in 1958 and founded an Association des Parents d'Elèves (A.P.E.), "grouping the parents of children in all the schools in the Commune." The association, like all those founded during that period, was viewed as having political aims. Nevertheless, it has endeavored to be apolitical as well as nonsectarian and multi-ethnic, devoted only to the task of helping the community, the students, and the schools. Since 1958 its members have served on the councils of administration of the Lycée Philippe Zinda Kabore, Le Cours Normal des Jeunes Filles, and the Centre d'Appentissage. They have served on the council for the distribution of scholarships and also helped the government resolve disciplinary problems on a number of occasions. In 1960, among other things, the associations's members served on a panel for movie censorship and in 1965 addressed themselves to the vexing question of equitable recruitment of children for the local schools. The year 1968 was an especially hectic one for the association: it took part in the discussion between the government, the Church, and the people on the issue of subventions to parochial schools, coordinated efforts to get better equipment for the school in the commune; sought for a loan scheme whereby parents could pay part of the education for their children; and made a study of government proposals for educational reforms in Upper Volta.

The most difficult tasks of the A.P.E. have been mediating problems between students of specific schools and between

students and the government. It helped the government resolve two touchy disciplinary problems in 1958; in 1965 it
intervened to help settle a student strike at the Ecole Normale; it heard reports, in 1966, from Voltaic students about
their problems at the Universities of Dakar and Abidjan; and,
as will be seen, tried to mediate in the confrontation between
the government and the students of the Institut de Préparation
aux Enseignements Supérieurs de Ouagadougou (I.P.E.S.).

All reports indicate that the A.P.E., like similar institutions
the world over, has more difficulty mediating between the students and the government than it ever had during the colonial
epoch. During that brief period (1958–60) the A.P.E. did conceive of itself as an advocate of students dissatisfied with a
foreign colonial regime and its resident agents. This changed
somewhat during 1960 and the early part of the postindepen-
dence Yaméogo regime, when some of its members received
political appointments and thereby surrendered their role as
intermediaries between the students and the government. Later, when most of them lost their connections with the administration, the A.P.E. again started to function as an advocate
of the students. In 1964 many A.P.E. members were overheard criticizing the Minister of Education for his arbitrari-
ness in distributing scholarships. The association also criticized
urban parents for not taking an active role in the education of
their children and lamented the seeming inability of rural children to get to the capital for higher education.

After the revolution in 1966, A.P.E. members were severely
criticized by students who accused them of opportunism during the former regime and of playing the same game by too
readily agreeing to the new military government's austerity
program—especially in education. The students declared
that they should not be asked to observe austerity by the
A.P.E. or "any member of the older profligate generation."
Moreover, the students disdained any help or guidance from
people whom they felt did not understand the contemporary
youth and modern education.

The students in Ouagadougou have always felt that they
represent the future elite of the country and, as soon as they
became numerous enough, attacked the outgoing colonial regime and later their first African government. Their first important tilt with the government took place in 1958 when they
struck in anger over the death by heart seizure of a girl attend-

ing the *Cours Normal*. They accused the European headmistress of arrogance and racism for refusing to help even though warned of the girl's plight by an African monitress. The European headmistress was finally replaced by an African one, but the students did not feel that the incoming African government was firm enough in this case. The result was that students started to snipe at the government.

By 1962 student attacks on the government had become quite vitriolic. The Union Générale des Etudiants Voltaiques (U.G.E.V.), through its organ *Jeune Volta,* accused the Yaméogo regime of all evil, of being a lackey of neo-colonialism and a supporter of Western imperialism and the racist regimes of southern Africa. The government responded that the students were the offspring of the "Marxist and communistic" Fédération des Etudiants de l'Afrique Noire en France and banned copies of *Jeune Volta* from the country. President Yaméogo himself took offense and when the U.G.E.V. held its annual conference in Ouagadougou in the summer of 1962, and blasted the government, he went to the conference, lambasted the conferees, and prohibited any future meetings in the country. Nevertheless the U.G.E.V. did not disband and continued to keep a critical eye on events in Upper Volta. Thus, *Jeune Volta* declared, in December 1965, that the "Public should be informed that the latest Presidential elections in Upper Volta [October 3, 1965] were nothing but an immense fraud and a ridiculous performance." The journal had a presentiment that matters would erupt and cautioned its members: "But patience; a sovereign people always has the last word. All of these measures can only emanate from a fearful man, afraid of the rising conscience of the people, afraid of having abused power, and of not having been capable of assuming its responsibilities. Every dictatorship has its moment of truth—In Upper Volta, too, that hour will sound one day."[33]

Jeune Volta's appeal to the students for calm and patience was as much related to their own activities as to the behavior of the government. The students in Ouagadougou had struck for the second time in October 1965 in support of some girls who had been banned from classes for four and five days because they contravened dormitory rules. This strike was halted momentarily when the A.P.E. appealed to the students

[33]*Jeune Volta,* December 1965, p. 9.

by radio to accept mediation. When negotiations broke down, the strike resumed and was only brought to an end when the government cracked down and expelled twelve strikers. The government's action was resented by the students, the A.P.E., and most people in town. Many of the latter admitted that the students had gone too far and should have permitted the A.P.E. to negotiate with the government. But more than this, they lamented that the government's action had probably blighted twelve young lives. The consensus was that the youngsters could never obtain jobs in the civil service and that explusion from school was a lifelong punishment. The suggestion that these youths could find employment in the Ivory Coast was rejected as being equivalent to exile.

The students were to have revenge on the Yaméogo Government when they rallied to the call of labor leaders on December 20, 1965, and January 3, 1966, to participate in a "general strike" until the regime fell. The students also went on a hunger strike. They were still smarting from the expulsion of the strikers and from the sanctions which deprived them of free weekends from October to Christmas, and the decree which stipulated that "During the vacations of Christmas and the New Year, they [the strikers who were not expelled] shall be taken in charge by the National Army.[34] They precipitated the fall of the government by hurriedly organizing in their schoolyards on the morning of January 3, 1966. Bearing placards reading "Bread," "Water," "Democracy," they paraded to the Place d'Armes. The rest is history.

The students have been skeptical about the policies of the military government they had beseeched "to take power." But, like most of the people of Ouagadougou, they were willing to grant it the opportunity to restore fiscal and budgetary sanity to the country. The government, for its part, sought to alleviate the grievances of the students, especially those of the students affected by the crises in the universities in France, Senegal, and the Ivory Coast. This circumspection came to an end when, in December 1968, the students in Ouagadougou challenged the authority of the government over the stipend for scholarships.

Beginning in October 1968, the students at the Institut de Préparation aux Enseignements Supérieurs de Ouagadougou

---

[34]*Ibid.*, p. 7.

refused to accept their scholarships unless given the same stipends as those given to students in France and other foreign countries. The latter received a monthly allowance of 22,500 C.F.A., and a yearly clothing and school supplies allowance of 50,000 C.F.A., and 12,500 C.F.A. respectively. The students in Ouagadougou held that they needed the same stipend as students in France because: 1) the Institut had neither a restaurant nor a dormitory at which they could get food and shelter at student rates; 2) high postage rates made books more expensive in Upper Volta than in France; and 3) they needed the same amount for clothing as those students in foreign countries. The students decided to force the government's hand by calling for a strike and a boycott of the first trimester examinations scheduled for December 17, 1969.

The government—quite conscious of the result of student-induced crises all over the world, and remembering the Ouagadougou students' role in the December-January revolution of 1965–66—took the threat quite seriously. The President of the Republic held an extraordinary Cabinet session and decided upon a compromise. The government offered the students the same monthly stipend as that received by those studying in foreign countries; 30,000 C.F.A. for clothing instead of the 50,000 C.F.A. demanded; and 10,000 C.F.A. for school supplies instead of the 12,500 C.F.A. that the students wanted. The Minister of Education, appealing to the "civism and good sense of [the] youth," told them that their demands were outrageous given the plight of the country's poor people and cautioned them "against accepting bad counsel." He advised the students to accept the government's offer and to resume classes after the year's end recess. He also warned that they would have to accept the consequences if they refused these terms. He said that, if faced with a boycott, the government would find itself obliged to envisage "the closing, pure and simple, of the Institut de Préparation aux Enseignements Supérieurs."[35]

The government's conciliatory attitude placed the students in a difficult situation, especially since they received little or no support from the population in Ouagadougou. The cultivators in town could not get seriously excited about the problems of unmarried students getting 50,000 C.F.A. per month when

[35]*Carrefour Africain*, No. 349 (28 December 1968), p. 2.

most of them earned less than 10,000 C.F.A. per year. Nor would domestic servants and other service employees, who seldom gained more than 20,000 C.F.A. per month, support the students. But even the civil servants were hostile to the strikers. Most of these civil servants had just gained some surcease from heavy income taxes and patriotic contributions which had drastically reduced their take-home pay, and therefore strongly criticized the students' attitudes. They asserted that, whereas the students in Europe had to buy winter clothes or freeze, the students in Ouagadougou could well do without fancy suits. They also complained that the students in town did not, in fact, pay for food or lodging but boarded and lodged with relatives, often poor persons. Thus, when the people in Ouagadougou were brought face to face with the possible effect of the elitist demands of the students on their resources, they refused to support them.

The conclusion here is that as soon as the people of Ouagadougou realized that modern education, introduced by the missionaries, provided the means of upward mobility they readily adopted it. Initially, they opposed the education of girls, but today they are as anxious to educate their daughters as their sons. Urban people now use all sorts of stratagems to get their children into school. Some give their non-Christian children Christian names so as to get them into the town's parochial schools. Others seek places for their children in rural schools — the only reason why Ouagadougou children are sent to the country areas. Most of the students in school choose academic programs because these afford the best opportunity for employment, good salaries, and high prestige. They show less interest in technical studies which until quite recently were of little economic and social benefit to them.

The problem in contemporary Ouagadougou is that the diplomas, which in the past guaranteed a good job and a bright future, no longer do so. The government has not emphasized technical education because there are no manufacturing industries in the primarily administrative and nonindustrial town. It has started to de-emphasize education by reducing subsidies to religious schools and by imposing austerity on the students. The result is disappointment for many parents who now fear for the future of their children, and resentment from a rapidly modernizing population.

CHAPTER VIII

Recreation and Entertainment

Most of the modern recreational activities in Ouagadougou were first introduced to African school children by European teachers and administrators. Thus the sports, games, entertainments, and intellectual endeavors were strongly linked to European education and associated with very tangible benefits. Therefore, it took some time before the ordinary people in town could view them in strictly recreational terms. This is quite understandable since the recreational activities in traditional Upper Volta cultures were quite different from European ones and were anchored in a different cultural context.

The ceremonies at the court of the Mogho Naba[1] provided the formal entertainment and recreational activities in precolonial Ouagadougou. However, it was the market place, especially on the day of the big Friday market,[2] that afforded regular entertainment for most people in aboriginal Ouagadougou. Then everyone wore his or her best clothes and paraded about the market place for all to see. Men gathered around the *dam* (beer) sellers where they were entertained by *griots* and where they were often joined by women, especially by a class of free women called *iodrhe*. The songs sung by the habituees of the beer shed were quite ribald. Lambert, writing about Ouagadougou in 1908, gives the following words of a song:

> Leave me alone. Leave me alone Bila [name of a man]. If it is beer [that you want] my mother will get it for you. If it is kola nuts, my father will go to Salaga and buy them for you. [There followed a long list of all the things that Bila could wish except an amorous embrace. And the song finished thus:] But if there is another thing [that you want]. No! Leave me, I am tired.[3]

If the adult recreational activities in the market could be

[1]Delobson, "Le Mogho Naba," pp. 386–421.
[2]The big Friday market was held every 21 days, after 7 three-day markets; cf. Skinner, 1962.
[3]Lambert, "Le Pays Mossi."

262

ribald, those of the younger people were more innocent. Young men and women flirted with each other and arranged rendezvous. The younger girls formed rings near the market place and danced the *kidiga* (a dance in which two girls danced in the middle of the ring, circling each other and clapping their hands, and then suddenly turned their backs to each other and bumped buttocks) to the accompaniment of handclapping and a solo sung by an elder woman. Boys either looked on or danced the *taraki,* a dance favored by young Moslems. Groups of professional dancers danced the *waraga* to the accompaniment of drummers, and individual drummers often followed merchants or wealthy men about the market, singing praises in honor of their ancestors. Women were normally excluded from the latter activities, but noble women, especially the daughters of chiefs, often gave presents to *griots* overheard chanting royal genealogies.

Ceremonies surrounding *rites de passage* and religious festivals did provide entertainment for people in the town.[4] Among the Mossi traditionalists, birth and marriage ceremonies took place within the extended families, but festivities at initiations and funerals involved friends as well as neighbors. On the other hand, both stranger and Mossi Moslems celebrated births and marriages publicly. All the youths of the town, Moslem and non-Moslem alike, participated in the Moslem festival known as *Zambende.* At night the boys decorated themselves with masks and paint and sang before the homes of the inhabitants in return for small gifts. Moslems of all groups were often joined by their non-Moslem neighbors to celebrate the "Feast of the Sheep" *(Tabaski* or *Aid-el-Kebir)* and the feast *(Id-al-Fitr)* at the end of the fast of Ramadan. These festivities, like those at important Mossi ceremonials such as funerals, included exhibitions of horsemanship and horse racing by and between notables. However, wagering on the results of the races was not originally part of the pattern. Notables were content to relive the memories of the past in contests which recalled their previous roles as cavaliers in the armies of Kombemba and Mogho Nanamsé.

Horse racing was the first modern recreational activity to develop in Ouagadougou. Initially, the French organized races in an area behind the military camp between Bilibambili

[4]See Yamba Tiendrébéogo, *Contes du Larhalle* (Chez Le Larhalle Naba, Ouagadougou, 1964).

263

and Nemne—still known as Cosa (from the French *champ de courses*) to the older people. These activities were transferred to the Hippodrome area behind the Governor's palace, now part of the Quartier de la Rotonde. In its heyday, horse racing was truly a community pastime. Banners over the main streets announced the meets. Races were held about once a fortnight and several times during major holiday periods. The Governor or other important French officials were the patrons on Bastille Day (July 14) and Armistice Day (November 11)[5] and often sponsored the meets. On such days, the stands would be crowded with both European and African officials and their ladies, members of the clergy, the Mogho Naba and his courtiers, and members of the business community. The ordinary people milled about the stands or mingled in the crowd. On other days, businessmen would be the patrons and, in the absence of notables, the ordinary people occupied the stands.

Most of the race horses were owned by the traditional nobility: the Goungha Naba, the Ouidi Naba, and the Larhalle Naba; and by a migrant from northern Mossi country named Diallo. These men, or their agents, canvassed the entire country for fast horses, bought them, and brought them to Ouagadougou to be trained as race horses. The horse owners also provided the jockeys, most of whom were Boussansé youths who had migrated to Ouagadougou from the Tenkodogo area. There was no organized betting at the races. When Europeans sponsored the meets, they gave money to winning jockeys and to the owners of successful horses. Horse owners wagered on their horses, and spectators wagered against each other on their favorites. The stands were often enlivened by the behavior of one or two racing fans. The banter and humor of these men, their extreme partisanship, and their behavior when they won or lost added to the pleasure of the spectators.

The decline of racing in Ouagadougou during the early 1960's is attributable to many factors. One is that the African parliamentarians who replaced the Europeans after independence were not racing fans. Second, the modern Mossi elites have no interest in horse racing. They view traditional horse racing as the pastime of rural and uneducated people, and modern horseback riding as being too *toubab,* that is, too European. Besides, they could play no role in this sport except

[5]Archives of the Centre Voltaique de la Recherche Scientifique, Ouagadougou.

as spectators since only traditionalists were interested in horses and riding. Thus, there was no opposition when the municipality decided to create a new residential ward, La Rotonde, where the Hippodrome stood and transfer the race track to the outskirts of town near ancient Ouagadougou. So far the town's officials have done little to develop a new race course except to clear a track. They have plans to build stands in the area, but as late as 1969 nothing had been done. The horse owners who exercise their animals on the new track lament what appears to be lack of interest in their sport.

While the educated people in Ouagadougou declined to take an active interest in horse racing and considered horseback riding too "colonial," they quickly became and remained avid soccer fans. Soccer (football) was brought to Ouagadougou by the French and taught to boys in the parochial and public schools. Two clubs—L'Association Sportive Voltaique and L'Equipe Militaire de L'Armée Française—were founded in the 1920's, but, unfortunately, little is known of their membership or organization. Soccer, like all sporting and nonsporting activities, declined in Ouagadougou when the town ceased to be the capital of the dismantled Upper Volta colony. The administrative and commercial population of the town departed and with them the participants and supporters of the major sporting activities.

The rebirth of the Upper Volta in 1947 and the redesignation of Ouagadougou as its capital opened a new era for sports in general and for soccer in particular. One reason for this was the arrival in town of many civil servants, the cadre of the new colony, who promptly organized sporting clubs. Second was the presence in Ouagadougou of a French sport enthusiast, one M. Mallet, who worked at the Upper Volta treasury and stimulated the civil servants to form clubs. By 1951 a number of Dahomeans and Togolese (then a majority of the civil servants) and one or two Voltaics formed a club called the Modèle Sport. The following year Abbé Ambroise, an African priest of the Ouagadougou parish, organized a club called Charles Lwanga after the Uganda martyr. In 1953–54 a number of soccer clubs and associations were founded. Among these were L'Equipe Nouvelle, Champions des Sports, Cercle Athlétique de Ouagadougou, and the Association Sportive des Commerçants de Ouagadougou.

The early soccer clubs in Ouagadougou faced a number of

problems, including the bane of all sports, financial support. The clubs in Ouagadougou, like those in all of French Africa, were given minimal support by their members. They sought support from businessmen and especially from the colonial administration. This practice was due to several factors: a) the Africans learned quite early that the French would provide the means for them to play "European" sports: and b) the Africans used the requirement that they register their clubs with the colonial administration to apply for official help. Moreover, the wits among the Africans reasoned that since they were supported by M. Mallet, "who worked where the money was," they saw no need to support their own clubs. For example, in 1954 the administration gave the Charles Lwanga association 40,000 C.F.A. But even the Association Sportive des Commerçants de Ouagadougou, which ostensibility was founded by Lebanese businessmen to support sports in the town, received an official subvention of 30,000 C.F.A.

These subsidies, small as they were, had a nefarious effect on the clubs. The availability of even limited financial help from the government caused disagreements within the clubs about how the money should be spent. This often led to the resignation of members who, consciously or unconsciously, sought government help by forming new clubs. In other words, the availability of financial support led inevitably to an intolerance of internal stress within the clubs. Closely linked to tensions created by the struggle for control of the clubs' finances was the problem of ethnicity or "race" (which means the same thing in Ouagadougou). Initially, the Voltaic civil servants eagerly cooperated with the Dahomeans and Togolese (called collectively, "Dahomeans") in the formation of the Modèle Sport Club. Later, the economic and status rivalry which developed between the Voltaics and these strangers in the civil service was transferred to the playing field. A number of Voltaics resented having a club in Ouagadougou controlled by senior Dahomean civil servants. In 1955 they accused the strangers of *racisme* and broke up the club. Those Voltaics who resented the act of the rebels founded a club called the Alliance Sportive de Ouagadougou, while the rebels formed a soccer club known as the Racing Club. As if to show that they were only against Dahomean *control*, members of the Racing Club invited persons from all the different ethnic groups in Upper Volta then living in Ouagadougou to join, and this membership pattern persists to the present day. In contrast, the Dahomeans never again recruited Voltaics for their clubs.

Another major source of instability in the early soccer clubs in Ouagadougou was their large and peripatetic civil servant membership. These men were always subject to transfers by a French colonial regime naturally more interested in its administrative needs than in soccer clubs. Again, individual civil servants were always taking exams for promotion, and success in them usually led to transfers to higher positions, normally in a different country. The effect of all this on the clubs was a floating membership, and often when key individuals departed, the clubs floundered or disintegrated. In a few instances the transfer of key members led to the fusion of clubs. In 1954, when many of the members of *L'Equipe Nouvelle* were transferred, the remainder joined the Charles Lwanga Club. And when, during the next year, 1955, both the Charles Lwanga and the Racing Club lost a number of members because of administrative transfers, they fused to form the Jeanne d'Arc Soccer Club. On the other hand, administrative transfers often did bring good soccer players to Ouagadougou. Some important French colonial officials were even suspected of using their influence to get good soccer-playing civil servants assigned to Ouagadougou and thereby procure personnel for the teams they supported. In 1956 it was widely believed in Ouagadougou that M. Mallet, who directed the Centre Athlétique de Ouagadougou, "imported" civil servant soccer players when he organized L'Etoile Filante Soccer Club.

Civil servants were important members of the early soccer clubs in Ouagadougou because, as a European sport, soccer was initially taught only in the schools, and its best players, as well as its early fans, were educated persons. In other words, soccer was an elite game. Later, the game diffused to the ordinary people, often through boys who had been dismissed from school. Many of these persons became skillful players, but they could not become members of the elite soccer clubs. Finally, these sportsmen were organized by Abbé Ambroise, who being unable to recruit civil servants for the Charles Lwanga club, took these youths instead. Then when later the Charles Lwanga fused with other clubs to form the Jeanne d'Arc Club, soccer in Ouagadougou lost its essentially elite civil servant nature. Thereafter, all the clubs were composed of civil servants, commercial clerks, students, and ordinary workers. And, by 1956, the organization of the soccer clubs in Ouagadougou had crystalized into its present form. The clubs shifted their activities from the old Stade Grivat built on the mission compound to the Stade Municipal constructed under the aegis of M. Mallet.

The formal organization for competitions of soccer clubs in Ouagadougou during the 1950's resembled that in the rest of French Africa, and indeed of France itself. The clubs in the town competed for the championship of the district, meaning the championship of Ouagadougou. They competed against each other and against clubs in the other districts, such as Bobo-Dioulasso, for the championship of Upper Volta, and the so-called *Coupe Mallet* (M. Mallet was the first president of the Ouagadougou soccer district). Finally, an "all-star" Upper Volta team competed against teams from the other territories for the championship of French West Africa (*Coupe de L'Afrique Occidentale Française*).

The contests between the local teams did not create too much excitement in the town. Most of the spectators knew the players on opposing sides and were not too partisan in their attitudes. Contests between teams of the Ouagadougou district and those from other Upper Volta districts were more lively. Migrants in town were expected to, and did, support teams from their home districts, much to the amusement, but often to the chagrin, of the autochthonous population. Contests between teams from Upper Volta and those from the other colonies created more excitement. There were few intercolonial matches during which there were not angry exchanges between the local people and the countrymen of the visitors. The author's journal for February 12, 1956, has the following brief statement: "Later in the day I went to a football match and perversely rooted for the team from Abidjan. The visitors won. Most of the officials in the town were there, including the Governor, but a fight broke out between the spectators. The 'up and coming' elites looked embarrassed." A similar record for September 1, 1956, states, "Heard about a fight in the municipal stadium between the Dahomean team and a local football team. The Dahomeans were accused of being 'racists.'"

The organization of football in Ouagadougou changed as Upper Volta proceeded toward independence. In November

1956, the Ligue de L'Afrique Occidentale Francaise, which was a member of the Fédération Française de Football and to which the Upper Volta clubs belonged, broke relations with the former Metropole and became an autonomous member of the Fédération Internationale de Football. Dakar still remained the focus for football in A.O.F., but now each territory, such as the Upper Volta, was stimulated to take charge of the development of football within its boundaries. The Voltaics held a meeting and Maxime Ouedraogo, who was not only a football fan but also a politician, took charge of football in Ouagadougou. However, before this reorganization could get started, the French West African Federation broke up and, in October 1960, the soccer players of a now independent Upper Volta created the Fédération Voltaique de Football linked directly to the Fédération Internationale de Football. They made the two former districts, Ouagadougou and Bobo-Dioulasso, headquarters for the Est-Volta and Ouest-Volta leagues respectively and placed them in control of all football activities in their regions.

The character of football in Ouagadougou did not really change once political independence had been achieved. The teams still sought support from the government and businessmen, but now instead of M. Mallet being the animator, the players chose politicians such as Lompolo Koné, the first Foreign Minister of Upper Volta, to play this role. The pre-independence clubs continued their activities, but some changed their name. L'Equipe Militaire de L'Armée Française became L'Equipe du Premier Battaillon de Haute-Volta. Civil servants still dominated, but they were joined by clerks of the private sector, tradesmen, and even unemployed but expert football players. Multi-ethnicity within the clubs continued and became even more marked as additional numbers of rural Voltaics migrated to Ouagadougou.

One new development—accepting patronage from specific ministers—created problems for the clubs. Some of the clubs sought and received help from ministers whose reputations were subsequently enhanced by the success of their teams. This would not have posed a problem had the political supporters of a minister not supported his team so vigorously that they sought to intimidate referees who penalized their heroes. The result was that fights often broke out between the supporters of politicians who were patrons of opposing teams.

269

The situation was made more difficult by the impermanence of ministers, since their enemies and those of their teams sought the first opportunity after ministerial changes to taunt their opponents. In other words, the politicization of the clubs that took place when they tried to gain economic support from politicians militated against good sportsmanship. Backed by politicians, some teams thought themselves invincible. For example, the Union Sportive de Ouagadougou was suspended for two seasons, 1963–65, and prohibited from playing any teams in the Federation because it refused to accept the verdict in a disputed championship match against L'Etoile Filante de Ouagadougou.

The fall of President Yaméogo, and the accompanying nation-wide austerity, have had an effect on the soccer clubs and their members. Government subventions were so drastically reduced that players had difficulty procuring equipment for training and competition. It was difficult to get footballs, and almost impossible to get government transportation for teams to visit neighboring towns. Attendance at games also declined, thus reducing this source of economic support for the team. But more important was the growth of unemployment among the non-civil servant players. Managers could not get people to train who were demoralized and "hungry," even though the latter state did not really often exist.

By 1967 the situation had become so critical that one player, Soumaila Traore (nicknamed "Insurance" because he could be depended upon in any game), felt constrained to address an open letter to the President of the Republic, to the ministers, directors, and heads of services, and to employers in the private sector. He declared:

> With exceptions of those passions which lead to disagreeable chauvinistic demonstrations, no effort should be spared to place the Upper Volta in the highest ranks of the next international sporting events. Therefore, I would plead with you that each time one of your employees is selected by the Secretary of State for Information, Youth, and Sports, to defend our colors and is asked to go into training for an international match, please examine his request with the maximum of good will. It is a problem of the question of national honor and I do not doubt that you are determined to do what is necessary to support these young sportsmen

270

who have the heavy responsibility of defending the honor of our country.... Upper Volta football is rich in middle quality players; they should be supported, and sustained by the government.[6]

The Upper Volta Government did accede to the request of the players and asked that football players in Ouagadougou and in the other areas be given leave to improve their techniques and to participate in contests on all levels. However, when the national team was successively beaten by Algeria, Mali, and the Ivory Coast, the local paper accused the team of suffering from "a detestable inferiority complex which does not permit them to do anything on the field but limit the damage."[7] The paper concluded that "it is true that the public should support its team. It does not remain less true that the team also must give some satisfaction to its public by some show of victory." Unfortunately, the malaise in the team continued and, as a result of a disagreement within the Federation, Upper Volta did not participate in the All-African *Coup* during the 1968–69 season.

In addition to organized "semi-professional" soccer clubs, there are clubs in the various quarters, schools, and government services which compete under the auspices of the various government ministries or independently. Among these, the element of sportsmanship is more highly developed and the spirit of amateurism predominates. The element of jocularity can be readily observed in "friendly" matches between two teams of civil servants "Les Abeilles" (The Bees) and "Fly-Tox" (an imported insect spray). The members of "Fly-Tox," who worked at the Information Service, had acquired such sobriquets as "Pepper," "Caterpillar," "Lightning," "Black Dragon," "Express," and "Amarillo," overpowered and defeated "Les Abeilles," much to the amusement of the spectators. One commentator remarked that:

[Les Abeilles] came to the match with the sound of an Italian claxon replacing the noise of a hive; but the honey makers departed in complete disarray. They had confused Fly-Tox and Nectar .... "Fly-Tox" utilized a dose of anesthetic against the "Abeilles." Next time a deadly dose will be used. Now ... a piece of advice to the "Abeilles." Flee from "Fly-

---

[6]*Carrefour Africain*, No. 255 (11 March 1967), p. 6.
[7]*Ibid.*, No. 257 (25 March 1967), p. 6.

271

Tox" because it is toxic. Seven goals to four, that is too much![8]

The attitude of the players in contests such as the one between the "Abeilles" and "Fly-Tox," and at those between "Veterans" (retired players), is understandably different because little of importance is involved. Tension does increase as the level of competition rises, so much so that citizens of Ouagadougou have felt constrained to decry publicly the attitude of members of important teams. Thus, Martin Kabore wrote an open letter to the local paper complaining that "the football fields, a place where young people play, should not be a battlefield where issues of all sorts are settled [and where] shocking things happen." He appealed to all parties concerned—the referees, the players, the spectators, the clubs, and the directors—to improve the sport.

The soccer players in Ouagadougou should have little difficulty getting support from both municipal and national governments if the economy of the town and country improves. There is ample psychological support for a game in which Africans and peoples of African descent are doing so well at the international level. The legendary exploits of Péle, the Afro-Brazilian, are well known, and the activities of African football players in France are closely followed. In July 1968, in an article entitled "Honor to Black Football Players," the local paper reported that "Five colored football players have taken a very active part in the triumph of three clubs. Keita, the Malian, and N'Dombé, the Cameronian, at Saint-Étienne [Champion of France, 1968]; Frank Fiawoo, the Togolese, with the Batia [Club]; and Kanyan and Charles, with The New Caledonians, Ajaccia."[9] The often unstated hope is that a football player from the town or the country may, in time, gain international stature with all the personal rewards and national prestige that it would bring.

If football in Ouagadougou evolved from a sport of civil servants to one in which all types of persons now play, bicycle racing has always been for everyone. Indeed, cycle races are the most popular sport in the town and attract the greatest number of spectators. One reason is that cycling itself does not require much more than strength and stamina, and not, for

[8]*Ibid.*, No . 174 (22 August 1965), p. 6.
[9]*Ibid.*, No. 327 (27 July 1968), p. 8.

272

example, the skillful technique of the soccer player. A second reason for the popularity of cycle racing is that the rewards are large and immediate. This fact is of great importance to the cyclists, most of whom are low-paid workers, and an attraction to the equally underpaid masses who get a vicarious thrill out of seeing their heroes win. Another factor in cycle racing's popularity is that the people do not have to pay to see it.

The first bicycle races in the capital were sponsored by the colonial officials as part of the morning festivities on Bastille Day. However, the sport was deprived of its patronage and practitioners when Ouagadougou lost its administrative primacy to Abidjan and Bobo-Dioulasso. As a matter of fact, Bobo became and remained the Mecca for the cyclists from Ouagadougou until the mid-fifties, long after Ouagadougou had regained its capital importance. During the colonial period, on the morning of Bastille Day, the senior French officials would officiate at the races, distributing trophies and as much as 5,000 C.F.A. ($20) to the winner, a very large sum in those days. European businessmen, especially those selling bicycles, added prizes to those of the colonial administrators and later sponsored their own cycle meets. The object here, of course, was to advertise the various brands of bicycles—a worthwhile venture in a country in which bicycle riding was becoming customary.

As Upper Volta proceeded to independence, the emerging governmental institutions began to sponsor meets and provide prizes. Thus we read in the *Bulletin Quotidien* for January 22, 1956, that the Comité Territorial du Cyclisme and the Vélo Club de Ouagadougou had been asked by the Conseil Générale to organize the *Grand Prix Cycliste* to be a run over a distance of some 120 kilometers.[10]

Cycle racing has changed very little over the past years. Most cyclists belong to the Vélo Club de Ouagadoubou, an association organized primarily to facilitate the meets. This club, like most sports clubs in Ouagadougou, is multi-ethnic in composition, but it reflects the overwhelming Mossi percentages in the town's population. Nevertheless, the Mossi have not always been champions. In 1966, the best cyclist in the Vélo Club de Ouagadougou and the champion of Upper Volta was Bakary Ouattara a Dioula from the Bobo-Dioulasso

[10]*Bulletin Quotidien,* 22 January 1956, p. 5.

region. In contrast, Tiga Tassembedo, a Moaga, and also a member of the Vélo Club de Ouagadougou, was national champion in 1969. As such, both Bakary Ouattara and Tigo Tassembedo are viewed as champions of Ouagadougou, even though there are no races for the championship of the town per se. Cyclists from all municipalities (Vélo Club de Kaya, Vélo Club de Bobo, etc.) are invited to meets throughout Upper Volta, not only to enhance competition, but also to advertise the products of the sponsors and provide cyclists from every region with the opportunity to win money.

Most cycle races in town conform to the same pattern, whether sponsored by the Ministry of Information, Youth, and Sports, by the French Ambassador in honor of Bastille Day, by gas and oil companies (such as BP, VOLCY, Texaco, and Total), by the Société Voltaique d'Equipement or by SOVI-MAS, a store which, among other things, sells bicycles. The only difference is the location of the *tribune d'honneur.* Usually it is placed on the Avenue de'L'Indépendance, but sometimes it is in front of the sponsor's store. However, regardless of the sponsors and the location of the *Tribune d'honneur,* government and municipal authorities are invited to attend. For example, at the meet of the Société Voltaique d'Equipement held on Sunday, January 26, 1969, the director of the society and his deputy were joined at the table of honor by two inspectors from Youth and Sports and the Larhalle Naba. Often present is the Mayor of the town or his deputy, providing an element of municipal support.

The cycle races in Ouagadougou are often quite long, sometimes covering a distance of between 104 kilometers and 120 kilometers. In the 104 km. race, the cyclists make 40 laps of a circuit of streets some 2 kms. 600 m. long. And in the 120 km. race, they cover 12 laps of a course 10 kms. long. The organizers and prestigious spectators take advantage of the number of circuits (laps) to augment the prize money. Thus individuals may give a "prime" of several hundred to several thousand francs, or some other prize, to the winner of a specific lap; or the sponsor or a spectator may offer a sum of money to a specific cyclist "to encourage him." This gesture can be the means whereby people boost themselves, or honor or ridicule a participant, because the benefactor's name is announced by the speaker and so is the amount of money offered the cyclist. When a large sum is offered to a winning candidate, the spectators applaud, but when a ridiculously small sum is offered to a losing candidate to "encourage him" the spectators roar with laughter.

The cyclists of Ouagadougou, like the soccer players of the town, are known to the public by amusing sobriquets. Thus, Tiga Tassembedo is called "The King of Sprint," Joseph Zongo, "The Gorilla," Mohamoudou Passere, "The Strongest Man of the Day," Norbert Nabole, "The Little Lion." Not only are these men known, but their numerous fans keep a record of how much they win in the same way that people in other countries keep track of the athletic prowess of their heroes. Thus cycle fans know how much of the 71,000 C.F.A. was won by each of the ten finalists in a race, from who won the first prize of 20,000 C.F.A. to who received the last prize of 1,000 C.F.A. Some of the more dedicated fans keep track of how much of the total "prime" prizes (often as much as 30,000 C.F.A.) individual winners receive. They sometimes wager against each other on the chances of their favorites, thus attempting to obtain more than a vicarious thrill on the outcome of a race.

The cyclists in Ouagadougou, like the football players, do aspire to mobility and many leave the town when more rewarding opportunities present themselves. A large number of Voltaic cyclists are members of the national teams of the Ivory Coast. Curiously enough, these men are not regarded as Voltaics but as Ivorians and thereby subject to any opprobrium shown to these foreigners. The reason for this, of course, is that people recognize that sport migrants, like other migrants, go where the opportunities are better and do not blame them for this. Second, cycle fans believe that at international meets officials pay less attention to the origin of participants than to national colors, thereby making it irrelevant to Voltaics whether they are beaten by a native of their own country living in the Ivory Coast or by a native Ivorian. On the other hand, it is equally true that any Voltaic who made a name for himself outside the continent would be claimed by and held in highest esteem by the people of Upper Volta.

Boxing is the third most popular sport in Ouagadougou. The first club in town, the Boxing Club de Ouagadougou, was organized in 1955 by young men who not only liked the sport but who sought to earn money from it. They therefore invited M. Aubaret, the president of the Chamber of Commerce, to be

275

its honorary president and asked a number of European and mulatto civil servants, as well as business and professional men, to serve on its board of directors. This club was subsequently disbanded and gave rise to two others: the Ray-Sugar Club de Ouagadougou, and the Renaissance Club de Ouagadougou. Both of these clubs are now members of the Fédération Voltaique de Boxe, which groups clubs from the other urban centers in the country.

All the boxing matches take place in the Maison du Peuple, a building constructed for meetings of the R.D.A. political party but subsequently transformed into a public hall for the people of the town. The usual sponsor of the bouts is the Fédération Voltaique de Boxe, but normally the merchants in the town act as cosponsors, contributing prizes of money to the victors. For example, the following firms, Société Peyrissac, Sovolcom, Sovimas, Marc-des-Champs, Camico, Pharmacie Nouvelle, and Attie Assad, were listed along with the Upper Volta Government as sponsors of an International Boxing Tourney that took place in Ouagadougou on May 7, 1969.

With very few exceptions the boxers in Ouagadougou are not civil servants. When not in training most boxers are employed as taxi drivers, bicycle repairmen, and motor mechanics. Their perennial problem is to find enough time and money to train as boxers. The Ministry of Youth and Sports does provide some help with training, the trainers being primarily employees of the ministry, but it provides little financial help for the boxers. Thus the main source of money for the boxers is what they gain as prizes during fights.

There is much more partisanship among the fans at boxing matches than at cycle races and even football games, a fact that may be attributed to the nature of the boxing contest itself. This partisanship is not readily apparent when the local teams compete with each other. Nevertheless, certain boxers like Ouattara Keletigui—known as "La Panthère Noire" (The Black Panther)—from Bobo-Dioulasso, do have a large number of fans among the resident Bobolais, and they usually support him against all opponents. Partisanship is stronger when local or national boxers compete against those from Niger, Nigeria, and Ghana and strongest against the Togolese and Dahomeans. At almost every boxing match between the Upper Volta boxers and those from Dahomey and Togoland that

276

took place in Ouagadougou during 1968, the spectators threatened the personal safety of the visiting referees. Nevertheless, in almost no case did they threaten the boxers. The referees bore the brunt of their partisanship.

In general, there is a good deal of sociability at the boxing matches. In contrast to football and cycle racing, men bring their wives and children; mothers with nursing infants bring them along; and there is a great deal of visiting during the match. Boxing, much more than any other sport in Ouagadougou, also attracts a large number of the Lebanese, both males and females, and a fair number of Europeans. These people attend because they like the sport, and also because, as part-sponsors, they give money to individual boxers during the bouts "to encourage them." Businessmen may give each boxer in a match as much as 2,500 C.F.A. ($10.00) to encourage him, in addition to the prize given to the winner. African spectators give much less to the boxers to encourage them and are highly partisan in their donations. Thus people, including small children, give money to support boxers who are obviously winning for Upper Volta. Very few local people give anything to foreign boxers, and apparently Upper Volta boxers receive the same treatment when they go visiting.

The boxing bouts themselves are not long, normally lasting three rounds of three minutes each for "amateurs," six rounds of three minutes for "neo-professionals," and eight rounds of three minutes each for "professionals." The boxers may be well-dressed, wearing the colors of their teams or countries, or they may have nondescript uniforms and even lack boxing shoes. The boxers of the Ray-Sugar and Renaissance Clubs do place a greater emphasis on appearance, a practice which contributes to the economic problems of the clubs.

As is to be expected, the competence of the boxers differs, but there is an emphasis on technique, and the spectators shout encouragement, give advice, or heap ridicule on the boxers during the match. There is generally great appreciation when the boxers are really "mixing-it-up" and corresponding displeasure when the contestants appear to be evading each other. There is not much appreciation for the efforts of the referees to ensure clean boxing, since most spectators fear that referees may aid boxers who are in difficulty by halting the fights on the pretext of breaking clinches or warning about low blows. The

277

result is that many referees have to be as concerned about the mood of the spectators as they must be about the nature of the fight. Everyone, and apparently including the referee, prefers the fight to end with a knockdown, and the fans shout for the kill when a boxer appears to be getting the worst of it. Woe to the referee who attempts to award a TKO when a boxer is still standing and when it is not clear to the spectators that he is badly hurt. The summoning of a doctor to verify the gravity of a wound does mollify the crowd, but so marked is the fear of *combine*—meaning trickery—that people prefer the fights to continue until the victor is clearly known. Inclusive fights are judged by a committee composed of civil servants from the ministry and officials in the Fédération de Boxe.

In contrast to soccer, cycle racing, and boxing, those sporting activities generally known as *athlétisme*—high jumping, track, javelin and discus throwing, basketball, handball, volley ball, and so on—are not highly developed in Ouagadougou. As a matter of fact, *athlétisme* per se did not attract much attention until about 1956 when about thirty athletes of three clubs in Ouagadougou held a meet at the municipal stadium. Nevertheless, by 1959, the following athletic clubs in town were recognized: L'Université Club de Ouagadougou, Le Club Sportif de la Jeanne d'Arc, Mimosas, Club Olympic de la Salle, and Essor Ouaga. In addition to these, there were the sporting clubs of the army, and police, and the *gendarmerie*. Unfortunately, most of these clubs were ephemeral organizations started by enthusiastic sportsmen, and they quickly folded for lack of popular and financial support.

Almost all the athletes in Ouagadougou are or were students or members of the armed forces or forces of public control stationed in the town. This is understandable since only the schools and the military and police organizations have the money and technique to provide training for athletes. Moreover, most of these athletes cease active participation in sports unless they are employed by the Ministry of Sports or join either the police force or the army. Given these circumstances, it is not surprising that *athlétisme* per se does not attract a large public unless there are special events. For example, in 1965 there was a great deal of athletic activity in Ouagadougou because Upper Volta had been invited to send a team to the All-African Games at Brazzaville, and the preliminary selection took place in the town. As to be expected, most members

278

of the national team, except the cyclists and boxers, were students, policemen, gendarmes, and soldiers. However, the Upper Volta team was not very successful, winning only one silver and one bronze medal in judo. Both medalists were residents of Ouagadougou who had migrated from the Bobo region to become members of the para-military Compagnie Républicaine de la Sécurité. They both had steady incomes, time for training, and professional instruction from a Frenchman.

The relative lack of success in the Brazzaville games caused some embarrassment and led to numerous appeals to sportsmen and sportswomen of the town to help the government field a good team. An editorialist said that, "It is utopic to constantly wait for the government to subvene entirely all variety of sports."[11] This sentiment soon passed, however, and today the local inhabitants blame the former government and the general austerity for the little emphasis placed upon sports from 1966 to 1969.

Entertainment

Although the *nam* and the *gumbé* did provide entertainment for their members, they were multi-purpose associations which had more serious functions than making merry. Entertainment in its modern form first became popular with the educated people of Ouagadougou, especially the younger ones. These persons quite early showed an appreciation for Western music and dancing as a form of entertainment. Despite valiant efforts, the Catholic hierarchy was not able to prevent the emerging African elite from adopting these Western habits. The priests complained but failed to "rout the devil" when he appeared in the guise of the *gumbé*; they were even more powerless when he appeared in their own Western dress.

The first Western dances in the town were organized by the French colonial administrators and businessmen at the military messes and later at the Volta Club. The local Africans could not attend, but they observed the behavior of their rulers, and many of them, especially the school boys, practiced the dances and learned the songs and dance tunes. The people of Ouagadougou first saw African dancing in a Western

[11]*Carrefour Africain,* Nos. 170–71 (25 July and 1 August 1965), p. 1.

manner with the arrival of Senegalese, Dahomean, and Togolese civil servants. Interestingly enough, they considered this dancing to be comparable to the *gumbé*, and when they began to dance in the Western manner, they considered this form of entertainment to be the elite *gumbé*.

Initially, modern dancing among the Africans in Ouagadougou took place at their homes during the celebrations of weddings and baptisms. These were, of course, Christian *rites de passage,* but the non-Christian elite friends of the principals also participated in them. The only musical instrument used then was an accordian played by one Prosper Tapsoba, a Moaga who apparently learned this skill at the mission. Later, by about 1951, the Ouagadougou Africans held receptions and dances at a bar owned by one Jean Baptiste, a Mossi civil servant in the quarter of Koulouba. Apparently, it was here that the first modern musicians in Ouagadougou developed. Soon trap drums, played by a man named Baba Barry, were added to the accordian. A Soudanese (Malian) called Antonio then brought a saxophone and trumpet to Ouagadougou and joined the local musicians. The reason for Antonio's arrival in Ouagadougou is itself indicative of the cosmopolitan nature of the town at that time and of the nature of the acculturative processes taking place. Antonio was taught to play the saxophone and trumpet by a Frenchman in Bamako. Later he joined an orchestra called L'Harmonie Soudanaise in Bamako but left that organization to found his own band, called Symphonia. This band used to play for dances and other festivities organized by civil servants in that town, and during one of these dances he made the acquaintance of an "African" doctor originally from the Ivory Coast. Later this doctor was transferred to Ouagadougou and when he decided to marry, he invited Antonio to play at his wedding.

Music in colonial Ouagadougou, like many other "Western" activities, was affected by the fact that most of its practitioners were civil servants and therefore subject to transfers. Thus, Prosper's group began to break up when its "batter," Baba Barry, was transferred. Then, in 1952, Antonio with the remainder of Prosper's group organized L'Harmonie Voltaique. With the exception of Antonio, a barber by profession, almost all the members of this orchestra were civil servants. And, reflecting the nature of the civil servants in Ouagadougou at that time, these musicians came from various colonies in

French West Africa. The music, dancing, and dancers in Ouagadougou during the 1950's were truly cosmopolitan. The orchestras played a wide variety of music: waltz, rhumba, samba, swing, fox trot, beguine, mamba, march, calypso, and high-life. The origins of the dancers were as varied as the music to which they danced, but they were primarily civil servants.

There were four bars in Ouagadougou during this period where Africans organized dances: Chez Léon, Eloi's Bar, the Tropic Bar, and the Volta Bar. The Tropic Bar, run by a Senegalese woman, catered to the same clientele as the Volta Bar, namely, the middle-and higher-level civil servants. Chez Léon and Eloi's Bar catered to lower-level civil servants and ordinary people. The music in these two places was not as varied, and, even when Antonio's band played there, he played fewer European dance tunes. However, it was here, rather than at the Volta and Tropic Bars, that the younger immigrants learned to dance. Crowds of them sat ringing the walls surrounding the *piste* and watched the dancers. Occasionally they danced to the music, but outside the walls. It was these youngsters who became the dancing public of Ouagadougou when the non-Voltaic civil servants departed.

After independence, the character of music and dancing in Ouagadougou underwent subtle changes. The general politicization of all institutions in the town extended even to this form of recreation. Now the youth groups of the political parties, such as La Jeunesse Voltaique du R.D.A. de La Commune de Ouagadougou, organized dances.[12] The result of this politicization was that many foreign Africans began to leave the town, and as a result dancing activities were affected. The Volta Bar closed when its Guinean owners returned home. But even when, as in the case of the Tropic Bar run by a Senegalese woman married to a Voltaic, the foreigners did not leave, the departure of foreign civil servants forced these establishments to close.

The exodus of foreign civil servants also affected the orchestras. About 1962, there was a crisis in L'Harmonie Voltaique caused by the departure of the music-playing civil servants ("placed at the disposition of their governments") and charges that the Mossi were "racists." Antonio, himself a non-Voltaic,

[12]*Bulletin Quotidien,* 2 November 1964, p. 9.

decided to form a new orchestra,"Antonio avec ses Cha! Cha! Cha! Boys," and hired musicians from Ghana, the Ivory Coast, and, of course, Ouagadougou. Unfortunately, the foreign musicians were not happy with conditions in the town and returned home. Antonio became disgusted, abandoned music, and returned to full-time barbering. However, by 1964, he was able to collect about him a number of Voltaics and strangers, and he recreated his Cha! Cha! Cha! Boys. Meanwhile, L'Harmonie Voltaique recruited all local people and became the first orchestra in Upper Volta to have no strangers as members. This orchestra had many more civil servants than Antonio's, and its members, being younger, were more responsive to the newer musical trends in Africa. L'Harmonie Voltaique was strongly influenced by Congo's (Brazzaville) O.K. Jazz Orchestra which visited Ouagadougou during the Union Africaine et Malagache meeting in 1963, and played pachangas in the "Congolese" style. The result is that their music has become more popular, even though it is less varied than the music of Antonio.

The dances in contemporary Ouagadougou reflect the ethnic composition of the town. Most of the people at them are Mossi, most of them are young, and most are civil servants or students. The sponsorship and locale of the dances are also different from what they were in the colonial period. Most dances are now organized by such groups as the Red Cross and Sport Federations and are held at the Army Junior Officers' Mess or at the Town Hall. A few of the Sport Federations hold dances at the Hotel de L'Independance, but the cost of doing so prohibits most organizations from using those facilities. The owners of such bars as La Croix du Sud, Chez Léon, and Africana Bar have continued to organize dances, and their clientele has not changed from being mainly junior civil servants or ordinary workers.

There now is a new kind of bar in Ouagadougou such as the Clabash d'Or, the Princesse Bar, the Ricardo Bar, Chez Michel, and the Scotch Club. These are incipient night clubs featuring dancing as well as other entertainment for civil servants "out-on-the-town," white visitors to Ouagadougou, and many local "ladies of pleasure." These bars or clubs have also started to host foreign itinerant orchestras and performers. For example, in October 1968, the Princesse Bar featured Rochereau et L'Orchestre African Fiesta National du Congo

Kinshasa. The Scotch Club, owned by whites, presented twice nightly during May, June, and July 1969 such artists as Jacques Berty (guitarist and songster of the Paris cabarets), Marla Heredia and Lily Llores, Spanish dancers, Maria Aranda, Chanteuse des Iles, and Argl Damiani.

It appears now, in contrast to colonial times, that there are no dancing enthusiasts in the town. Previously, groups of foreign civil servants regularly sought out dances every week end as a means of recreation. Today people do attend dances when they are organized, but a dancing crowd per se seems to have disappeared. The reasons for this, of course, are that the local people do not have as great a need for distractions as did the foreigners since they are at home; moreover, they have less money to spend. The price of admission to dances now is 500 C.F.A. ($2.00) per couple, and 300 C.F.A. for single persons, and only civil servants can regularly afford this.

Most dances are all-night affairs, normally starting about 9:00 P.M. and terminating at dawn. There is usually a *table d'honneur* reserved for distinguished guests, while ordinary people sit at tables with friends. Normally dancing does not begin until the guest of honor arrives, makes a speech, and dances with the chief hostess. The "march" or "slow" (fox-trot) always used for this first dance is as much a concession to the age of the guest of honor as to the decorum he is expected to maintain. From this point on however, most dance music played is generically "Congolese," even though the words sung may be Kikongo, Bambara, or Mossi. A number of the songs satirize the former President (whereas before they praised him); others honor the new President, and a growing number make social commentary upon government and local affairs. Since the dance tunes have only subtle differences, it is easy to enjoy oneself once the basic pattern is learned. However, dancers do enjoy the "Twisse" and the "Madison," but view these as the dances of Black Americans. Ghanaian high-lifes are also played but not as regularly as they were during the colonial period. Waltzes, marches, tangos, and fox trots are occasionally played, but more out of politeness or deference to older Africans or to European guests than for enjoyment.

A new and intriguing development in Ouagadougou during 1969 was the use of traditional dance steps and music, such as the Mossi Waraga, at the dances. This usually occurs during the playing of a cha-cha or pachanga with the orchestra gradually shifting into the traditional rhythm. The dancers, for their part, have no difficulty "shifting gears" since the partners do not touch for the cha-cha and pachanga, and the traditional dances are solo performances. No one could provide adequate information about this development, but it may have come about in several ways. It is possible that the orchestras simply added these traditional rhythms to their repetoires in order to please audiences in the smaller towns. Or it may be that the orchestras and public in Ouagadougou are now psychologically so secure that they can utilize traditional music and dance steps at Ouagadougou dances.

Most dances in the town are relatively informal. Men wear Western business suits, a shirt, jacket, and pants combination, or African ceremonial garb. Women wear either Western or African dress. Those participating drink everything from fruit juices to champagne, but the normal drinks are soft drinks and beer. People can usually buy brochettes of mixed meats, roasted poultry, or barbecued lamb, and occasionally fried breads and cakes are available. All of these comestibles and drinks are sold by young female and male members of the organization sponsoring the dance. These young people are also the ones who sell "surprise" packets, some of which do contain "prizes" but most only pieces of paper bearing bits of wisdom. Young people are also used as "floormen" in the game of *Tombola Américaine.* This game is really a device for raising funds and despite its name, *Américaine,* it is quite different from anything seen in the United States. First of all, an official offers to auction a bit of handicraft and the bidder makes an offer of, let us say, 100 C.F.A. He pays the money but before the auctioneer repeats that he has bid 100 C.F.A., someone may bid 200 C.F.A. but in fact only add 100 C.F.A. to the previously bid 100 C.F.A.; this really makes the total bid 200 C.F.A. The first bidder loses his 100 C.F.A. and the auctioneer repeats that he had been offered 200 C.F.A. and normally another person would offer 300 C.F.A. when in fact he only pays 100 C.F.A.—and so on. The raffle finally comes to an end when no one offers any more bids. Thus, the auctioneer collects thousands of francs for an object valued at only a few hundred francs, and the individual participants in the auctions do not spend more than a few hundred francs

284

apiece. On the other hand, the choice of the winner is not haphazard. She or he is usually the person who has made several bids, thus showing either generosity or an interest in the object or both. Or the winner may be a high-status person to whom the gathering would like to give a gift. When the time comes for the winner to be chosen, people refrain from bidding more money than the honored guest, or the auctioneer counts so fast that no one has the opportunity to make a further bid.

Movie-going is an important recreational activity for many persons in Ouagadougou. These include the young illiterate and semi-illiterate youths, and both African and European civil servants, clerks, and businessmen. Most middle-aged cultivators, domestics, tradesmen, and merchants in town have never been to a movie and would not use their money to do so. In contrast, many migrant and local-born youths, if the police are to be believed, would do anything to go the movies—even steal. Clerks and civil servants and Europeans are not motivated by the same desires as the youth to go to movies, but they do provide an adequate public so that certain types of films can be shown profitably in the town.

There are two movie theaters in town, the Nader-Ciné and the Olympia. These are fairly large structures whose areas of cheaper seats are uncovered. The more expensive seats and the projection facilities are covered with galvanized iron. The screen itself is a white painted concrete structure; at the foot of the screen and extended a few rows toward the rear are concrete benches. This area, appropriately called *la place des indiennes* (after the whoops its excited, youthful habitués make during Wild West films) contains the cheapest seats (or places on the concrete benches) costing, normally, 40 C.F.A. The middle part of the cinema, the "second class," is larger than the "pit" and has wooden seats priced at 75 C.F.A. The third or "first class" is the largest of all and possesses individual chairs (the last few rows are the most comfortable and most often used by high-status movie-goers), normally costing between 175 and 200 C.F.A.

As one would expect, there are important sociological and psychological distinctions between the persons who regularly sit in the three areas of the cinema. The *indiennes* or the people who regularly go to the pit are by far the most interesting in their reaction to the movies. Emile Kargougou[13] has published some observations on this class and divides them into two groups: a) the neophytes, visitors from the country districts taken to the movies by friends or relatives, and newly arrived immigrants; and b) the habitués of the cinema who include the underemployed youths, the members of youth gangs, and the hustlers in the markets who carry parcels for shoppers or transport goods for merchants. Kargougou believes that the neophytes have difficulty making sense out of the rapid succession of scenes which flash past on the screens and focus on specific objects as the speed of horses, the prowess of a man, and so on. He suggests that it takes several visits before the neophyte begins to understand the movies. In contrast to the neophyte, the habitué goes to the movies every chance he gets. Movies become a passion for him and in time he may become a "commentator." The so-called "commentators" are sharp or fairly literate individuals who not only go to the movies "to see, but also to make themselves heard." These persons often see the same movies several times and give a running commentary on them in the vernacular interspersed with French, improvising as they go along so as to command the attention of their auditors. The most competent commentators are designated by the title *vieux* and are respected by their auditors. These youths identify with certain actors and are not above giving their heroes advice in times of danger. Thus, a commentator seeing that his favorite is about to be ambushed may jump to his feet and cry out, "Look out, there is somebody behind you!"

The preferences of the *indiennes* are well known to the managers of the Nader-Ciné and Olympia who try to satisfy their tastes several times each week. During the week of November 2 to November 8, 1964, the Nader-Ciné presented such films as *Le Héro de Babylone* with Gordon Scott as "Hercule," *L'héritier d'Al Capone,* and *Rocambole,* described as "thrilling adventures and legendary exploits of a great hero. Dynamic is 'Racombole'...." Other films of interest to the *indiennes* are *Le Forgeron de Bagdad* (The Smith of Bagdad) billed as "a Hindu super-production with dances, battles, bravery, and all

[13]Emile Kargougou, "Le Cinéma en Haute Volta: Comportement et goût d'un public Africain," *Voix Voltaiques,* I, No. 4 (January–March 1969), 40–44.

the magic of the Orient"; *L'arsenal de la Peur* (Arsenal of Fear), said to have "little-known events of the war in Greece, violent action depicting authentic episodes, and boundless suspense." By 1969 the *indiennes* were seeing *Bonnie and Clyde, Alvarez Kelly,* and *L'équipe Sauvage* (The Savage Team) starring Marlon Brando, Lee Marvin, Mary Murphy, and Robert Keith. They were also seeing *Les Titans, Les Gladiateurs, Goliath contre l'Hercule Noir, La Guerre des Monstres, L'invincible Spaceman,* and *Le Jour le Plus Long* (The Longest Day). Kargougou, like most elite in Ouagadougou, is unhappy with this fare for the *indiennes,* believing that the youngsters get a warped view of the world, of history, and of life. The belief is supported by attempts of the *indiennes* to "relive the films." The Inspector of Police in the town told me that he had noticed that whenever a spectacular type of robbery was shown in a film, several young men attempted to imitate what they had seen.

The clientele of the second-class seats in the cinemas in Ouagadougou, representing as they do more literate individuals and a good percentage of women, are more sophisticated about the films. Of course, like the *indiennes* they enjoy the spectaculars and they identify with the heroes, even when these heroes mistreat "Africans." They once applauded when in a film Robert Mitchum knocked down an African who had inadvertently released a leopard from a trap, much to the annoyance of the elite sitting in the first class. There is a comparable emotional response to religious films, especially by the female clientele. Many of these women wept when they saw *The Little Miracle of St. Camille,* thereby indicating not only maternal concern but possibly an identification with Catholicism.

The audience in the first class are mainly French-speaking Africans and Europeans. They are also persons educated enough to try to follow English dialogue in many films. As has been stated, the prices for first class seats range from 175 to 200 C.F.A., but for special performances the prices may be as high as 300 to 500 C.F.A. Elite taste in movies is quite different from that of the ordinary movie-goers, and people scout the movies by driving past them at about five P.M. to see what is playing. Indeed, cinemas show the appropriate films for these people on Wednesday and Saturday nights, and, as is to be expected, the *indiennes* stay away unless the particular films also interest them. These films are the usual "A" rated ones dealing with romance, espionage (*policiers*), comedy, and religion. Superior movies attract large crowds in the first class, and it is as difficult to obtain seats to see such films as *The Ten Commandments, Maldonne pour un Espion,* and *L'Obsédé,* as it is easy to get seats when films of the *Hercule* cycle are shown.

There are laws in Ouagadougou prohibiting minors from seeing certain films, and the Association des Parents d'Elèves does participate in the municipality's board of censors. Nevertheless, there is no evidence that the Association, the municipality, the national government, or religious leaders have objected to the "new mode" in films. One suspects that the local leaders are hesitant about imposing cultural prohibitions on the French community which, by definition, is the largest consumer of these specific imports. Second, most Voltaics feel that they are unqualified to judge or determine French tastes; and third, the local authorities fear the charge that they are against any "culture" in this "culture-less" town. The result is that such movies as *Benjamin,* with their rather bold themes from the local standpoint, are shown in Ouagadougou. Nevertheless, it is true that when such a movie is shown, it is often done for special purposes and attracts a primarily European audience. Thus, in 1969, *Benjamin* was shown as a benefit for the Lions Club and the first-class seats, costing 500 C.F.A. per person, were filled with Europeans. Only about 10 Africans were present among the 500 or so persons who viewed that film, and these included the African "intellectuals" of the town. Very few persons, that is Africans, were interested enough in the film to pay the relatively higher price for the second-class seats and the place des indiennes was almost deserted. Kargougou holds that risqué films in which nakedness is portrayed do not have the same impact on Africans that they do on Europeans. "To say that style of clothing is the function of a country or of a given season is a truth of the Pallice. One knows that in Africa the heat permits the wearing of more or less summary clothing. This is why films prohibited to those of less than 18 years, such films as *Liane, Le Repos* of Brigitte Bardot or of Jeanne Moreau, have no effect on the African spectators of the third class."[14]

One form of recreation which has become adapted to life in Ouagadougou is radio-listening. This has been made possible

[14]*Ibid.,* p. 44.

by two developments: the desire and the necessity of the Upper Volta nation-state to have a radio broadcasting service in its capital town, and the development of inexpensive transistor radios. Until just before independence there was no radio station in Ouagadougou and only a few electric lines to provide power for the rather costly short-wave radios. The only persons who owned radios were Europeans, high-level African civil servants, and foreign Africans for whom the radio was a means of keeping in touch with their respective homelands. Those Africans who lived in quarters without electricity used car batteries to provide the power for their sets. One problem was to keep these batteries charged, especially if the owners had no vehicles. The other problem was to pick up the stations in Africa, especially Radio-Dakar with its political news from the Federations capital and from France, and music of various kinds.

The inauguration of Radio Haute-Volta on October 26, 1959, coinciding as it did with the development of relatively inexpensive transistor radios, gave the people of the city access to a new form of entertainment. One must say entertainment because, except for a few minutes of news in the various African languages every day between 5:30 and 6:30 P.M., music broadcasts are the most important radio programs for the town's inhabitants. Most of the townspeople are not interested in the rest of the programing which is in French. But so strong is the emphasis on French as the idiom of broadcasting (some 83.5 per cent of the time) that programs specifically directed to the ordinary inhabitants of the town are often in this language. For example, during the agricultural production campaign of 1969, the people of Ouagadougou were bombarded several times daily with the slogan: "Protégez vos semences." This was indeed a bit curious since crop cultivation is prohibited in the town and the broadcast range of the long-wave transmitter in Ouagadougou is not strong enough for reception by small transistors more than 15 kilometers from town. Moreover, at the time the broadcasts were transmitted, the peasants had been in the fields for hours. The only conclusion that could be drawn was that either there were arrangements for the "bush" telegraph to get the messages to the peasants or that the urbanites were being involved ideologically in the production campaign.

The only two programs of great interest to the non-French-

289

speaking Mossi majority in the town are the "La Soirée du Larhalle Naba" and "La Voix de L'Islam." The former is a variety show in Moré featuring the Larhalle Naba who not only recites traditional tales, teaches proverbs, and gives a running commentary on the clash between the traditional and the modern, but also features singers, dancers, and drummers. The Voice of Islam, a religious program, is important because it cites the names of those persons in Ouagadougou and in Ghana and the Ivory Coast who have contributed (*baraka*) to the mosque in honor of friends, or in thanksgiving for restored health, the birth of children, the successful completion of business enterprises, or safe arrival after a journey. Both people at home and those with short-wave sets on the coast can thus get news about each other's activities. As would be expected, these two programs are the favorites of the older people, both illiterate and literate, but, except for the young intellectuals who place a "cultural" value on the Larhalle Naba's program, the youths are not interested in them. The illiterate and literate youths prefer the programs of Western or Congolese music. This preference has distressed some people who lament that "The youth do not know [the traditional music] or, rather, they only like French stars: Dalida, Johnny Halliday, Françoise Hardy, etc.—witness the success of the radiophonic program called 'Listeners Choice.'"[15] The young people like this show not only because of the music, but because it permits them to dedicate records to each other, whether they are in Ouagadougou or in the rural areas, or even outside the country. Another reason for its popularity is that the show enables the young people to keep up with their peers throughout the world, especially the Western world. Interestingly enough, this is now easier than it was just a few years ago. At one time, say in 1956, it took about one year for American records to diffuse from France to Upper Volta. In 1964 the time was about three to six months. By 1969 there was almost instantaneous diffusion of songs, and, in contrast to several years ago, these songs now come translated into French.

In contrast to radio, television, first introduced in Ouagadougou in 1963, is still a very limited form of entertainment for most of the town's inhabitants. In fact, because there were

[15] *Afrique Nouvelle*, No. 94 (25–31 August 1966), p. 14.

only some 200 to 250 television sets in town, owned by senior government officials and wealthy Europeans, the austere military government stopped transmission when it took over from Yaméogo in 1966. Television transmission was not renewed until February 1969 and was limited to two days a week (Wednesday and Saturday) from 5:00 P.M. to 9:00 P.M.

In the early days, that is between 1963 and 1966, almost no attempt was made to adapt French television to local conditions. For example, field notes on the programing for the evening of November 12, 1964, noted: a performance by the ballet troupe of Rose Aimée (little European and mulatto girls) which danced classical ballet, followed by an exhibition of the Charleston by Rose Aimée herself. There followed a Hausa tale using cartoon figures and accompanied by Hausa music. This show, sponsored by UNESCO, was quite good. The news came next and included news clips of the Soviet Union's October Revolution and the army of Cambodia. The patrons of the Ricardo Bar who witnessed the TV program were noncommittal about the ballet, but were surprised by the quality of the Cambodian army. To the layman, the television technique was only fair, but the female announcer was judged quite beautiful. Interviews during this period revealed that, while people were interested in the foreign programs, they much preferred "La Soirée du Larhalle Naba." This was especially true of the crowds of little boys who sought out every TV set in town to view the Larhalle Naba's troupe. For this group, at least, once the novelty of the TV wore off, the foreign programs held little interest for them because they had seen much better at the movies. In contrast, most people in town knew the Larhalle Naba and his troupe, and while they were familiar with the skits, songs, and dances, they got a thrill out of seeing familiar persons on the TV screen.

Television in contemporary Ouagadougou has not changed too much from the early days, except that there is less money to pay for programs. Greater use is now made of programs provided by the various embassies in the town, and, of course, from the French television services. The program for Saturday, June 21, 1969, included a documentary on "Marjorque"; a short feature demonstrating the versatility of a rubber canoe; this was followed by the news, and the program terminated with a number of short subjects such as dances, acrobatic feats, and the like. The Larhalle Naba and his troupe have

291

performed several times on TV since the resumption of transmissions, but by the end of 1969 they had not been given a permanent slot in the weekly program.

The popular appreciation of the performance of the Larhalle Naba's troupe on television is quite similar to the reaction of the African sophisticates to *African* theater. As it is commonly known, African Theater first began among the students at the Lycée William Ponty in 1937 and was fairly well developed when the first Upper Volta students arrived at that school in the late 1930's and the 1940's. A decade later, plays based on African themes had diffused to the Upper Volta and were performed by students in the Collège Moderne et Classique in Ouagadougou. For example, in the mid-fifties two important plays were performed in Ouagadougou; one was *Da Monzon,* depicting the tragedy of an ambitious queen, and the other, *Doudadou,* showing the fate of a headstrong young man who turned *gris-gris* (magic) his father had given to him to use against other boys on the father himself.

The African Theater in Ouagadougou, as in the other areas of French Africa, was given structural support by the Governor-General of the West African Federation who in 1953 authorized the establishment of cultural centers in every territory. The next year, 1954, he sent circulars to all the eight territories, including Upper Volta, establishing the procedures by which plays should be performed and the rules for competition between the theatrical groups from the local levels up through the territorial and federal levels. These procedures included, among other things; the stipulation that the plays could not last more than one-and-a-half hours; that only 25 actors could perform in any one play; that, while the main language should be French, songs and such things as salutations could be in the vernacular languages; and that the jury should be composed of a certain number and class of persons, i.e., representatives of the Institut Français d'Afrique Noire, representatives from the Service de la Jeunesse et des Sports, and des personalités africaines.[16] In June 1955 many students and civil servants from Ouagadougou went to Bobo-Dioulasso to witness the semi-finals of the *Coupe Théâtrale des Centres*

[16]Bakary Traore, "Le Théâtre Modern au Mali," *Présence Africaine,* No. 3 (Paris, 1965), pp. 164–65; cf. Bakary Traore, "Le Théâtre Negro Africain et ses fonctions socialiques," *Présence Africaine,* Nos. 14–15 (Paris, 1957), pp. 180–201.

Culturels de L'AOF in which the Ivory Coast defeated Niger. The Niger troupe had presented Nigerian songs and dances plus two comedies, *La Chèvre* and *Des Maries*. In contrast, the Ivorians performed a very African dance entitled the *Fin d'initiation chez les Adiokrou;* a dream, *Kwao Adjoba;* a comedy entitled *Les Prétendants rivaux,* and concluded with *L'invocation à Zeroë Outou, Génie Baoule*. In August of the same year Fodeba Keita brought his "Ballets Africains" to Ouagadougou, thereby reinforcing the trend toward African theater. Two years later, the theatrical group from Banfora defeated all opposition at the cultural center in Ouagadougou for the Upper Volta cup with its presentation of *Le Paysan Noir,* an adaptation from a book by Robert Delavignette. And, in 1959, the same Banfora group again defeated all the groups at a competition in Ouagadougou with its performance of a play entitled, *Soumaloue,* written by Lompolo Koné, who later became the first Foreign Minister of Upper Volta.

The interest in African theater generated by the performance of so many troupes in Ouagadougou led to the founding of a local theatrical group called Arc-en-Ciel in 1958. The next year this troupe performed a play called "Amour ou Coutume" written by Mr. Sulla Djem, a Malian who later became his country's minister to the European Common Market. Arc-en-Ciel became so successful that an official of the still nascent Ministry of Youth and Sports in the Upper Volta, Mr. Sebastian Ouedraogo, asked Mr. Félix Boyarm, a youth with long-term interest in the theater, to found a group for the Maison des Jeunes at Ouagadougou. However, before this theatrical group could become fully established, the task fell to a Malian, Mr. Boubacar Dicko. Boyarm went to Europe to study, and when he returned a conflict developed between Dicko and himself over the relative merits of French plays as against African plays or what Boyarm called "realistic" plays. Dicko allegedly became quite upset over the preference of the troupe for plays such as *Trait d'union* by Boubou Hama (later to become President of the National Assembly of the Niger Republic) and the play entitled *Le Trône Sanglant de Boukary Koutou*. Apparently the conflict was too deep. Boyarm and a number of actors left the troupe and, with the support of the Larhalle Naba, Professor Joseph Ki-Zerbo, and playwright-politicians Lompolo Koné and Moussa Sawadogo, founded the Troupe Nyennega. Boyarm's attitude toward the theater was indicated by the name of the troupe, Nyennega, in honor of the mother of Ouedraogo, the culture-hero of the Mossi people. Despite the Mossi bias, however, the troupe recruited both Mossi and non-Mossi actresses and actors and people from different occupational groups: civil servants, teachers, nurses, office workers, and students in the various secondary schools of the town.

The conflict between the partisans of French theater and of the "national" African theater "heated up" when the Upper Volta Government established a committee to organize the-atrical programs for the country's independence celebrations. The Africans at the Maison des Jeunes and the European technical counselors at the presidential office allegedly wished to import a French troupe. The Africans in the Troupe Nyen-nega protested, mobilized political support, and persuaded the government to authorize the performance of a local play writ-ten by Moussa Sawadogo. This play, *La Fille du Volta* drama-tized the life of Princess Nyennega. It was performed against the background of the reservoirs of the town in the mode of *Son et Lumiére* and was judged a great success by almost everyone in town. Robert Pageard, who witnessed a per-formance of the play, called it "an original piece, fresh and animated, marking a most lively addition to the national life, past and present."[17] He considered the play to have been "an important step in the history of Voltaic Letters." The Presi-dent of the Republic was reported to have been so pleased with the play that he authorized the troupe be given 50,000 C.F.A. ($200.00).

African theater in Ouagadougou achieved its apogee during the years 1961–64. Different troupes performed such plays as *L'Oracle* by Moussa Sawadogo, dealing with the conflict and interregnum attending the death of a Mogho Naba; *L'Avare Moaga* (The Greedy Mossi Man), a comedy written by Ouamdégré Ouedraogo; *Kango,* another play by Sawadogo treating the royal history of the Mossi Kingdom of Yatenga; *La Mort de Chaka* written by the Malian, Syedou Badian (1961); and a number of humorous skits. However, in 1964 both troupes, the Maison des Jeunes and Nyennega, en-countered financial and personnel difficulties. The govern-

[17]Robert Pageard, "Théâtre Africain à Ouagadougou," *Présence Afri-caine,* No. 39 (Paris, 1961), pp. 250–53.

ment did not continue its subsidies after the troupes had visited most of the larger conglomerations. The Nyennega troupe could not even get money to perform *La Fille de Volta* in Mali and neighboring countries and could not go on tour for lack of funds. Moreover, once the Ouagadougou elite had seen the plays, there was no public able to support the theater. The problem of personnel was due to the success of the plays. Some of the youthful actresses, especially the heroine of *La Fille de Volta,* had attracted the attention of the more important politicians in the town, and the resulting scandals led many parents to withdraw their daughters from the troupes. As one wit observed, the parents did not wish their daughters to become *Filles des Voltaiques.* Finally Mr. Boyarm, who worked at the Town Hall and had the confidence of many people in Ouagadougou, left the troupe for another course of study in Europe. The new director could not solve either the personnel or financial problems, and the fall of Yaméogo, bringing with it austerity, effectively stifled the budding theater in Ouagadougou.

Between 1966 and the beginning of 1969 there were few theatrical performances in Ouagadougou. The Troupe Nyennega ceased its activities altogether, and the actors of the troupe of the Maison des Jeunes performed only skits as part of "cultural" evenings at the Maison du Peuple. The French Embassy did book touring French troupes at the Franco-Voltaique Cultural Center, but aside from members of the government, a few interested African intellectuals, and school children, most of the audience was European. African interest in the theater in Ouagadougou did revive in early 1969 with the advent of the African Festivals of Arts in Algeria. Students at the teachers college performed a play by Aimé Cesaire treating the plight of Patrice Lumumba, but this attracted little attention from either the public or the government. There was no encouragement to send these students to the festival. More interest was aroused as a result of a visit to Ouagadougou on May 9–10 of the Troupe de L'Institut National des Arts D'Abidjan. This troupe gave a brilliant performance of *Monsiuer Thogo-Gini,* a comedy by Bernard B. Dadie. Subsequently, on May 22–24, the Théâtre Daniel Sorano de Dakar performed the tragedy entitled *L'Exil D'Albouri* and a comedy, *L'Os.* Both of these plays drew overflow and appreciative crowds at the National School of Ad-

295

ministration and at the Maison du Peuple. There is, thererfore an indication that, under certain circumstances, the educated people of Ouagadougou can be encouraged to attend the theater. The hope of the board of directors of the somnolent troupes of the capital is that with the stimulation of the Ivory Coast and Senegal, the Upper Volta Government will give them the necessary support and encouragement.

The tendency to look to the government for help is still strong among the civil servants. On the other hand, there are some indications that the military government's austerity has induced the civil servants and other elites in Ouagadougou to try to fund their own cultural and recreational organizations. In December 1966 a group of people in Ouagadougou[18] led by Mr. Lompolo Koné (the Director of the National School of Administration, former Foreign Minister, playwright, and graduate of the Lycée William Ponty) organized the Cercle D'Activités Littéraires et Artistiques de Haute-Volta (C.A.L.A.V.) with the aim of "presenting the values of African culture at the Convention of Civilizations and of Peoples."[19] With this goal in mind, the group planned to stimulate the cultural growth of the country by discovering and developing hidden talents. It wished to enlighten those who were ignorant of Africa's intellectual potential. But beyond this, it wished "to unite the young authors and artists with their elders—the peasant artists and poets with those who had been influenced by European culture—and to encourage the peasants and urbanites to work side by side to raise mountains of enthusiasm." During 1967, C.A.L.A.V. organized conferences and competitions at which juries examined some 45 poems, 15 novels, 3 plays, 100 paintings and pieces of sculpture by 8 painters and 5 sculptors, and judged the performances of 5 theatrical groups, 17 traditional dance groups, 8 African musical ensembles, and 3 modern dance orchestras. In 1968

[18]These persons included Sonde Augustin Coulibaly (journalist), Felix Boyarm (secretary at the Town Hall), Mamadou Kolla Djim (teacher), Roger Nikiema (television speaker, journalist, and author), Abdoulaue Derme (teacher), Sotigui Kouate (clerk and playwright), Adama Konfe (professor at the *Lycée*), Julien Ouedraogo (inspector at the post office and painter), Abdoul Karim Bokoum, Michael Compaore, Karim Laty Traore, Sekou Tall (Inspector of Primary Education), the Larhalle Naba (traditional chief and author), Father Hebert (sociologist).

[19]*Visages d'Afrique,* Revue bimestrielle, Première Année, No. 1 (Ouagadougou, Haute-Volta, 1967), p. 1.

the organization had a comparable record in the arts and sponsored lectures at the Franco-Voltaique Cultural Center.

The birth of C.A.L.A.V. prompted the revival of the Association Voltaique pour la Culture Africaine (A.V.C.A.)[20] in 1967. This organization was founded in 1962 as a local branch of the Paris-based Société Africaine de Culture (S.A.C.) but its activities were circumscribed by the Yaméogo regime which feared its leaders. Apparently, the political factors that led Mr. Yaméogo to proscribe the A.V.C.A. are still present or there would have been no reason for the early A.V.C.A. members not to have joined the C.A.L.A.V. Indeed, the programs of the two organizations are quite similar. In an introduction to the first number of its organ, *Voix Voltaiques,* the directors of the A.V.C.A. lamented that the Upper Volta with its imposing group of intellectuals (for such a small country) has not contributed more to contemporary African culture. They believed the reason for this was that "culture is often minimized, indeed mistrusted in our country. But, and indeed, especially in a poor country that must develop in all aspects, culture must not be regarded as a luxury. It is a necessity and a repository; a vital need, and a national good."[21] The directors felt that the columns of their publication should be "open without reservations to all who have something to say about African culture, and also about French and Universal Culture.... There are too many problems in the realm of culture which face our country, and which ultimately touch so many dimensions of our African and Voltaic community for interested groups of young and old intellectuals not to use the *Voix Voltaiques* as an instrument."[22]

The activities of the A.V.C.A. and the C.A.L.A.V. have led to a veritable efflorescence of Upper Volta's traditional cultures and to a dialogue between the people and intellectuals of all ages within Ouagadougou. However, on the popular level the C.A.L.A.V. has been more successful than the A.V.C.A. It

[20]The members of this organization include Emile Kargougou (Director of Rural Education), Ignace Sanwide (teacher), Bakary Coulibaly (civil servant), Darsalam Diallo (teacher, former minister), Joseph Ki-Zerbo (Professor of History), Aly Pascal Zoungrana, Laurent Ghilat (civil servant and director of a secondary school), and Gilbert Ilboudou (Professor of English).

[21]*Voix Voltaiques,* I, No. 1 (April–June 1968), 1–2.

[22]*Ibid.*

has encouraged the Larhalle Naba, who has always been interested in Upper Volta's history and traditional cultures, to
reorganize his troupe and to seek out and bring good dancers
from the rural areas to Ouagadougou. This action has stimulated the elites in the rural districts to rebuild their troupes
with the result that during the years 1967–69 more traditional
dance troupes performed in Ouagadougou than ever before.
As to be expected, the urban environment has started to infl-
ence the troupes and their performances. Already their costumes are being regularized and modernized and the performances geared to the esthetics of the urban elite and foreigners
who are now the significant "others" whose approbation is
sought, if not exactly asked for.

The A.V.C.A. has also shown an interest in traditional
dancing, but here the effort has been to create a national ballet
to represent Upper Volta in foreign countries. In September
1968, the folkloric section of the A.V.C.A., working in con-
junction with the Paris-based S.A.C. and the Municipality of
Ouagadougou, sent the Troupe Naba Niandfo (named after
the first Mogho Naba to settle in the town) to Loudun as a
gesture of friendship to Ouagadougou's French "twin" city
and from there on to Paris. The "Mayor" of Ouagadougou
(really head of the special delegation that runs the town), who
acted as master of ceremonies during the trip, apologized to
his French audiences for the modifications in the dress of the
maidens and youths, but assured them that the sacred and
secular songs and dances they were seeing were as authentic as
those encountered in the rural villages of Upper Volta. The
audiences were reportedly delighted with the troupe, and the
laudatory reports from France pleased the people of Ouagadougou. One reporter wrote: "Never have we felt so much
pride and admiration. Thanks to the talents of the young girls
and young boys of the Troupe Niandfo we were able to witness
a performance of very great quality and a thrilling spectacle
which renewed in us the reality of our national culture, of its
vitality, its value and its warmth."[23] Nevertheless, the fear was
expressed that "this cultural treasure was now seeking refuge
in the remote area of the country, there to die slowly but trag-
ically to the profit of an erroneously perceived and badly defined emancipation." The reporter defended the traditional

[23]*Carrefour Africain,* No. 340, 26 October 1968, p. 5.

cultures, but felt that they had to evolve so as to provide the nation with the necessary force and dignity, and regretted the "absence of a national cultural program" in Upper Volta. He declared that "All neighboring countries have National Theatrical Troupes and try to ensure a veritable cultural development thanks to the modern means of communication by radio and television. In Upper Volta, there is a 'no-man's land in this domain."[24]

On the other hand, a number of persons who accompanied the Troupe Niandfo to Loudun and Paris, witnessed what they considered to have been emotions of shame among their comrades living in France when faced with aspects of their traditional cultures. One reporter said that he met people for whom "the wearing of a boubou, or any attachment to aspects of traditional culture is judged *a priori,* retrogressive and degrading....During the performance at the Embassy [of Upper Volta in Paris] I saw a student-comrade in a corner, affected by the performance, gesticulating miserably, his body taut, his spirit empty. You realize that he is a partisan of the assimilation of the masses. Please listen to me! I am not a partisan of a despotic static culture, condemned indubitably to degeneration. We believe that if a man is a product of his past, then, in the same way, the future of a society is based on its past, and the traditional values possess riches whose rational exploitation confers force and dignity to the nation."[25]

Many of the leading intellectuals of Ouagadougou are or used to be as negative toward elements of African culture as was the young student in Paris. In a rather revealing article, one of the leading radio and television personalities of the town confessed his former shame of his fellow African man and of African culture. He was the seat companion of a European woman traveling from Marseille to Africa, and although they exchanged confidences enroute, he was unable to answer her query as to whether he liked the *balafon* music they both heard while disembarking at an African airport. Long afterwards he declared: "I helped those who would destroy me by sometimes rejecting with horror those things which today I desire to see considered. During that period I participated in the merited punishment of that African who, to use a re-

[24]*Ibid.*
[25]*Ibid.,* p. 4.

doubtable expression of the pupils of my generation, 'carried the symbol.' I never used to feel at ease except in white company. I visited my village as seldom as possible. I 'blushed' when I was called Black or African. In a word, I was dazzled by my pretence—I would say of my chance—more than the child who leads his cow (a cricket) to the stream (a line of water) .... However since that time, I have recognized that I was oxidized in Westernizing myself. This is because I recognized in myself that feeling of frustration, of negation for which I do not blame myself, however. And having discovered better reasons for pride I now reject these feelings with supreme contempt."[26] In other words, this man, by admitting his *négritude,* was able to "feel himself, himself."

Indeed, *négritude,* whether admitted or not, is one of the main themes of the intellectual, artistic, and literary endeavors of Upper Volta writers, whether living in Ouagadougou or elsewhere. This has been as true of the older men as the younger, and for the most "traditional" as for the most "modern." Thus Yamba Tiendrébeogo, the Larhalle Naba, published *Contes du Larhalle,* a book containing tales and proverbs "mirroring" Mossi customs; whereas Nazi Boni, teacher and politician, wrote a novel, *Crépuscules des Temps Anciens,* depicting the society of the Bwa people of western Upper Volta and their resistance to French conquest. Joseph Ki-Zerbo, Professor of History and Geography as well as an essayist and politician, has finished the first volume of *Le Monde Africain Noir,* a history of Africa, while a young journalist, François Bassolet, wrote *L'Evolution de la Haute Volta (1890– 1965)* in which he discusses the political history of the Upper Volta from French conquest until the fall of Yaméogo. Lompolo Koné, an "old boy" of Lycée William Ponty, sportsman, and former Foreign Minister wrote a play *La Legende de Telli Soma* retelling chiefly ambitions and warfare in ancient times, while Moussa Sawadogo, a politician and administrator, dealt with aspects of Mossi history in two plays, *La Fille de la Volta* and *L'Oracle.* And Augustin Coulibaly, a very young man, wrote the play, *Les Rives du Tontombili* about the daily life of a peasant boy.

The articles published in both *Voix Voltaiques* and *Visages*

[26]Roger Nikiema, "Le Folklore: Une Force," *Visages d'Afrique,* Deuxième Année, Numéro Speciale, 1968.

d'Afrique likewise reflect a concern with Africa's traditional culture, but they also attempt to deal with the problems of Africa's present. One finds articles dealing with "Les mangeurs d'âmes" juxtaposed with one on "L'inadaptation Sociale et Délinquance Juvenile en Haute-Volta" and one on "Les rites de initiation pays Mossi" followed by others entitled "Apropos de Martin Luther King" and "Plantification et Sous-Development."

The data provided in this chapter show that the people of contemporary Ouagadougou, whether cultivators, laborers, domestics, craftsmen, or civil servants, now have at their disposal many types of recreational activities from which to choose. The older urbanites and civil servants adopted European recreational activities introduced during the colonial period as an aid to mobility but are now using such activities as soccer to relate to their African neighbors and even to peoples and states outside Africa. The civil servants, especially, are now interested in using borrowed European art forms and recreational activities to present new ideas about old Africa, its traditional cultures, and the struggle of Africa's man to redeem his cultural heritage. They desire to influence the lives of the people of Ouagadougou and to present these ideas to the people of the world. Here the theater and television are the vehicles chosen, but the theater-going public in Ouagadougou is still not large and there are too few television sets to justify maintaining a television system. Nevertheless, these modern recreational forms are destined to remain in Ouagadougou, if only because they represent the symbols of modernity and satisfy the desire of the urban population to belong to the contemporary world.

CHAPTER IX

Religion

Ouagadougou is a "Christian" town in which the majority of the people are Moslems. This paradox stems from the domination of the town's major institutions by a group of Westernized and Catholicized civil servants and politicians. The traditional rulers who defended the town against Islam lost out not only to European interlopers but subsequently also to an African generation trained primarily by Catholic priests. Mogho Naba Kougri, the current representative of sovereigns whose power was supported by the traditional religion, perhaps in reaction to the Catholics, became a Moslem. The result has been that both Islam and Christianity are now ascendant within the town; and the retreating traditional deities receive oblations at the foot of modern "stop" signs.

The actual number of adherents of the various religions in the town is difficult to determine since each denomination claims more members than it can possibly possess. Table XXXIV lists the religious affiliations of the population, according to the census of 1962. In 1964–65 the various religious groups in the town claimed larger numbers of adherents. The Catholics claimed 32,000 adherents (22,000 Christians and 10,000 catechumen), the Moslems claimed 50,000 followers

TABLE XXXIV. **Religious Affiliation in Ouagadougou**

Religious affiliation	Number	Per Cent of Population
Moslems	30,253	52.3
Catholics	19,394	33.6
Traditionalists [*Wend' pous neba*]	6,569	11.4
Others (including free-thinkers)	846	1.5
Protestants	717	1.2
TOTAL	57,779	100.0

SOURCE: "Recensement Démographique de la Ville de Ouagadougou" [Resultats Provisoires], Rép. de Haute-Volta, Ministère de l'Économie Nationale, Direction de la Statistique et des Études Économiques, Ouagadougou, Haute-Volta (June 1962), p. 14.

of Islam, and the Protestants reported 1,800 church members within the town of Ouagadougou. The traditionalists and some of the "Others" have no interest in recording their numbers; and only the next census will indicate how many of such persons there are in the town.

It is ironic, but prophetic, that the Moslems represent the largest religious group within the Mossi capital of Ouagadougou. The Mossi, especially those of the northern kingdom of Yatenga, had incurred the wrath of both Mali and Songhay from A.D. 1328 onward by expanding into the Bend of the Niger, sacking Timbuktu, and threatening other Sudanese entrêpots.[1] Subsequently, both Mali and Songhay invaded Mossi country with the aim of conquering the country and converting the people to Islam, by the sword if need be. The Mossi resisted the *jihads* and remained faithful to their ancestors, while both Mali and Songhay were destroyed.[2]

The Mossi rulers of the seventeenth and eighteenth centuries apparently took a kinder view of Islam. They permitted Moslem traders to establish communities in Ouagadougou and in other parts of the country. About 1780, Mogho Naba Kom I, whose mother was a Yarsé, gave Yarsé traders permission to establish communities in such important trading areas as Dakay (Sagbatenga) near what is now the Ghanaian border, and during the subsequent reigns of Sagha I and Doulougou, the Yarsé traded and built mosques in Ouagadougou and the outlying districts. Mogho Naba Doulougou, allegedly imitating his kingly relative, the Gambaga Naba, ruler of the Dagomba, finally appointed the first Moslem Imam at court.[3]

Although Doulougou permitted the Moslems to build a mosque in Ouagadougou—a mosque which was still standing in 1967—and appointed an Imam at the palace, he expressly forbade his eldest son, Sawadogo (1802–34) to become a Moslem. Like many Mossi rulers, he believed in the traditional religion's efficacy in supporting and protecting the country and its political organization. Nevertheless, Sawadogo persisted in his adherence to Islam even when he became Mogho Naba. Subsequent Mogho Nanamsé abandoned Islam until

[1]As-Sadi Abderahman, *Tarikh As-Soudan,* trans. O. Houdas (Paris, 1900), pp. 16–17.
[2]*Ibid.,* pp. 121–23.
[3]Delobson, *The Empire of the Mogho-Naba,* p. 205.

303

Koutou (1850–71) received the *nam*. This ruler was described as being "truly a Moslem" but, interestingly enough, "All [his children] except his eldest son, who succeeded him as Naba Sanum, were sent to Koranic schools even though none did any serious work there since they were more interested in becoming naba."[4]

After the reign of Naba Koutou, all the rulers of Ouagadougou remained traditionalist until Mogho Naba Kougri became a Moslem in 1960. Nevertheless, the Mossi rulers did continue to have Moslem councilors at court and usually attended Moslem religious ceremonies. They thereby added Islam to the other institutional supports for their regimes. Yet, from some of the evidence available, it appears that the rulers of Ouagadougou discouraged Moslems from worshiping publicly. Tauxier, quoting Lambert, stated that "prior to French occupation, Moslems were forbidden by the Mogho Naba to say their prayers (*kella*) publicly. They merely recited their rosary (*seki*) silently."[5]

French conquest not only weakened the ability of the Mogho Naba to stop the public worship of the Moslems, but enabled the Moslems in Ouagadougou to champion the cause of the Mossi against the foreigners. Lambert reported that the Moslems told the defeated and demoralized Mossi of Ouagadougou that "as soon as all the blacks become Moslems, the whites will leave."[6] It is probably only a coincidence that the number of Moslems in the capital increased considerably over the years, but in the end the French did surrender political control to black men.

According to the census of 1962, Moslems outnumbered all other religious groups in 20 of the 34 town census tracts.[7] The large number of Moslems in Dapoya II is due not only to its size, but also to the presence of many Moslem traders (Dioula and other Mandingo) who had moved there when their former quarter was suppressed. Similarly, the large number of Moslems in both Zanguettin and Tiedpalogho is the result of the movement into these two new wards of those Hausa and other Moslem teachers who did not care to move to Dapoya II. The high proportion of Moslems in Hamdalaye is due to the cir-

---

[4]*Ibid.*
[5]Tauxier, pp. 585–86.
[6]*Ibid.*, p. 792.
[7]"Recensement Démographique...," p. 35.

cumstance that this quarter was developed primarily by members of the Tijaniyya sect of Islam who make up almost its entire population. Hamdalaye has thus replaced Mwemne as the foremost Moslem quarter in town (Mwemne, itself, has lost its preeminence because the construction of the railroad dispersed its population). The only area in the town for which no Moslems were reported was the Mission quarter. Moslems were found in all of the "Saint" quarters, an indication that Moslems either had households there or that Moslems lived in the households of their Christian and traditionalist relatives.

Despite the lack of exact relationships between residence, occupation, and religion in Ouagadougou, it is possible to draw some conclusions from these factors when they are taken together. A large number of the merchants who live in Zanguettin, Dapoya II, and Tiedpalogho are Moslems; and Moslems account for more than 50 per cent of the inhabitants of the commercial zone. In fact, the two wealthiest African merchants in Ouagadougou (both Mossi) are Moslems, and they live in the commercial zone. Again, almost all the cattle buyers and butchers in the markets of the town are Moslems and so are the goldsmiths and other skilled artisans in the town. The indication that less than 25 per cent of the inhabitants of Camp Fonctionnaire and less than 50 per cent of the persons in Zone Scolaire are listed as Moslems supports the well-known fact that the Moslems in town (probably because of their early distrust of Western and, very frequently, Christian education) are underrepresented in the clerical and professional fields.

Most members of the Moslem community in Ouagadougou, especially the male merchants, are recognized by their long burnooses, skullcaps, and, occasionally, their turbans. Some of the older Moslem men have never worn European clothing and evince no desire to do so. In contrast, most of the laborers who are Moslem wear typical European work clothes and are only recognizable by the skullcaps they habitually wear. Civil servants who are Moslem mostly wear Western clothes without the skullcap and don Moslem clothing only when they go to mosque or on ceremonial occasions. In the latter case, they are often indistinguishable from their Christian colleagues for whom the long burnoose and cap are the garb of "Africans."

Ordinarily the clothing of female Moslems is no different from that of Christian and even traditionalist women of nonelite status. On festive occasions, however, these women, too, wear the long burnoose characteristic of Malian and Senegalese women.

As one would expect, it is in the area of ritual and belief that the Moslems stand out sharply from the people of other religious groups in the town. There are now over 36 mosques in Ouagadougou, including the ancient mosque in Mwemne (built at the time of Mogho Naba Doulougou but now abandoned) and the Grand Mosque, built in 1953. Most of the other mosques in the various quarters are rather small structures of *banco*, frequently plastered with cement. There are several mosques in such quarters as Dapoya II, Zanguettin, and Tiedpalogho, with each mosque being the place of worship of a specific ethnic group. In Dapoya II there are two mosques—one used primarily by Dioula, Fulani, and Moors, the other by Mossi Moslems. Zanguettin has mosques for Hausa, Yoruba, and Mossi Moslems, but there are no rules enforcing or encouraging such segregation, and friends belonging to different ethnic groups do occasionally worship in each other's mosques. Nevertheless, ethnic ties and the use of common languages are strong inducements for people to worship in ethnically homogeneous mosques. Of course, ethnic segregation is usually abandoned for the Friday prayer when most Moslems go to the Grand Mosque.

The mosques in the various wards of Ouagadougou are autonomous entities, founded by the local residents who then elect Imams to lead them in prayers. The Moslems insist that the Imams are not like priests; that they are not usually full-time specialists (unless, of course, they are also Koranic teachers) and are not paid. They allegedly differ from their coreligionists only in knowing the Koran and in being "upright men." Moreover, the Imams do not have to report to any superior about the affairs of the local Moslem community.

Despite the absence of hierarchy, since the time of Mogho Naba Doulougou, Ouagadougou has always had a Grand Imam who not only has had great prestige among the Moslems but also represented the Moslem community at the court of the Mogho Naba. The present incumbent of this office, El Hadj Raghian, a relative of the Mogho Naba, is of Yarsé origin and still heads the ancient community of Mwemne. He is commonly believed to be well versed in the Koran and is also considered to be a good politician. Nevertheless, he does

encounter opposition in the Moslem community of Ouagadougou from persons who declare that he is "not authentic."
These people charge that he was imposed upon the community
by the Mogho Naba who wished to establish a hereditary
Imamship when, according to many, a hereditary Imamship is
contradictory to Koranic law and Moslem practice. Moreover, the detractors of the Imam, while acknowledging
Raghian's education and political astuteness, complain that he
is not as upright as an Imam should be. Nevertheless, the
Grand Imam presides at the Friday prayers and leads the
major religious festivals in Ouagadougou, and is an important
personage in the Moslems' organization in Ouagadougou.

Despite the autonomy claimed by the various Moslem communities in the town, they found it necessary to form an association, the Moslem Community of Ouagadougou, in 1951,
and this later became a branch of La Communauté Musulmane de la Haute-Volta with headquarters in Ouagadougou.
The prime movers for this organization were Moslem civil
servants who, in the face of the strength of the Catholics, felt
that they had to protect, preserve, and propogate their religion. According to the "Declaration of Association," their
desire was,

> To develop among Moslems a pure and precise Islamic con-
> science. To unite all Moslems of both sexes in order to
> permit them to understand each other and to help each
> other both morally and religiously. To rid Islam of all cor-
> rupt practices and influences prejudicial to it and to combat,
> by all appropriate means, the fanaticism, superstition, and
> exploitation of the credulity of the Faithful; to organize
> trips to Mecca; to obtain official recognition of Islam's holy
> days; and to follow the precepts of the Koran.[8]

Within the Ouagadougou community itself, a subcommittee
of the national association was created and twenty notables—
one from each of the larger wards—were elected by popular
vote to form the committee of directors. This committee
elected a president, vice-president, secretary-general, and a
whole slate of administrative officers. These were assisted by
technical councilors among whom were the Imams, *kadis,* and
walis of the town. During one period, all three of the influen-

[8] *Bulletin Quotidien,* 8 June 1963, p. 9.

tial Moslems in Ouagadougou held office on both the national and community level: El Hadj Ousmane Sibire, a wealthy merchant, was president of the national association; El Hadj Hamidou Ilboudou was president of the subcommittee of the Ouagadougou Moslem community; and the Grand Imam, El Hadj Raghian, became the most important technical councilor for the Ouagadougou group.

The creation of the Moslem Association in Ouagadougou did have an effect on the lives of the Moslems there. One of its first acts was to undertake the building of the Grand Mosque for Friday prayers. The committee wanted to build it on a plot of land in the Zone Commerciale so that the Moslem merchants who formed the most influential group in the community would find it easy to attend prayers. The colonial officials of that period refused to permit the establishment of a mosque in the commercial area and suggested that the Grand Mosque be built in Mwemne, the ancient Moslem ward. The Moslems objected to this, because the railroad had truncated Mwemne, and decided to force the issue. After a Friday prayer, all the Moslems marched down to the *cercle* office to press their demands; the administration capitulated, and the construction of the mosque was authorized. Money for building the mosque was collected from the Moslems in the town, and from wealthy Voltaic Moslems in Accra, Kumasi, Abidjan, Bouaké, Niamey, and Zinder.

The Ouagadougou branch of the Moslem Association has influenced other aspects of the lives of its members. For example, certain problems of litigation involving conflicts between Islamic law and French colonial law which were beyond the competence of local Imams are now channeled more effectively to the Imamate and the officers of the association for adjudication and resolution. The Moslems were also able to insist upon certain standards for the teachers of Koranic schools; obtain help with international visas and accommodations for pilgrims; and secure the recognition of the major Islamic holy days by the administration as well as permission to hold communal prayer on these days in public places.

The religious practices of the Ouagadougou Moslems do not differ too much from those of most Moslems in Upper Volta.[9]

[9]Elliott P. Skinner, "Islam in Mossi Society," in I. M. Lewis (ed.), *Islam in Tropical Africa* (published for International African Institute by the Oxford University Press, 1966), pp. 350–73.

Early every morning, in every quarter of the town, Moslems and non-Moslems alike are awakened by the local muezzin's call to prayers. On the margins of some wards, it is possible to hear several muezzins seemingly chanting in unison their summons to the Faithful. During these prayers all Moslems make the ritual declaration of the faith: "God is One." Most of them know and recite the other articles of Islam: that God (Allah) is the creator and disposer of the universe; that Mohammad, though human, was a prophet of God; that Mohammad's Koran is a holy book; that angels are messengers of God; and that there is a Day of Resurrection and Day of Judgment with punishment and rewards for sinners and the Faithful respectively.[10]

It is quite difficult to determine the adherence of most Moslems to the other practical duties of Islam (*amal*), and one normally has to accept their own statements about their actions. For example, one cannot really know how many persons give alms or *zahat* to the indigent or to their local communities, although they have ample opportunities to do so, especially on Fridays when students at the Koranic schools, the *garibous,* go begging from house to house. Again, it is always difficult to know whether persons really observed the *carême* or month-long fast during Ramadan. Merchants in the markets, laborers, such artisans as jewelers and smiths, all tend to restrict their daytime activities during this period, and some of them sleep late to avoid extra exertion. And all business activities come to a stop at sundown as their practitioners hasten to break the fast. The impression is, however, that many of the Moslem civil servants do not fast during this period, and, of course, little children and invalids are not expected to do so.

Many more Moslems in Ouagadougou now consider it possible to make the *Hadj* or pilgrimage to Mecca before they die, although in some ways this has become more difficult. Pilgrims can no longer simply take off and hope to get to Mecca by way of Ghana, Nigeria, Niger, Chad, and points east by walking, seeking free transportation, or stopping to work and earn money along the way. The "route is now barred" to pilgrims in that they have to obtain travel vouchers, exit and entrance visas, innoculations, and show that they have enough money for travel before they are permitted to leave the town

---

[10]Cf. J. Spencer Trimingham, *Islam in West Africa* (Oxford: Clarendon Press, 1959), pp. 68ff.

and enter foreign countries along the way. On more than one occasion the Moslem Association in Ouagadougou has had to obtain identification papers for some of their co-religionists who had been living in Mecca or in one of the countries along the way and who had to have these papers before they could return home.

On the other hand, many more pilgrims from Ouagadougou now make the *Hadj* than in the past. For one thing, there is more money available, and the Moslem association charters flights for pilgrims from Ouagadougou and other places in Upper Volta, thus reducing the plane fare. For another, the Upper Volta Government provides adequate travel documents. Some of the wealthier merchants and civil servants in town have not only made several pilgrimages to Mecca, but a number of them have taken their entire families along. By 1968 there were hundreds of persons in Ouagadougou who had made the *Hadj,* including several older women. Indeed, the religious leaders in Ouagadougou are seldom seen without the distinctive headdress of the *Hadji;* and merchants, civil servants, and other persons, including women and children, wear the *Hadji* gold headband at formal ceremonies.

The Moslems of Ouagadougou normally worship together at the Grand Mosque on Fridays and on the great religious festivals of Islam. At midday on Fridays the Grand Mosque and its outbuildings are packed with worshippers from all the wards of the town and often also from the surrounding areas. The size of the congregation has made it necessary for the Imam to use a loudspeaker so that his message may be heard; and, on Friday evenings, he broadcasts his message to those in Ouagadougou who are unable to attend the mosque and to those Moslems within listening range of Radio Upper Volta. Older women also attend this Friday mosque, but are segregated from the men. The only Moslems who do not customarily attend are young women, little children, and members of the Tijaniyya sect for whom Friday is no holier a day than any other.

All Moslems in the town gather to celebrate the two great feasts of the Islamic year; the feast that breaks the fast of Ramadan (*Id-al-Fitr*)—called *Karem Salla* (small prayer) by the Hausa and *No-Lokre* (detaching the mouth) by the Mossi; and the important feast of the *Aid-el-Kebir,* the "feast of the

310

sheep," called *Tabaski* by all the Moslems in Ouagadougou and said by them to be "a celebration in memory of Sidna Ibrahim who was asked by God to sacrifice his eldest son, Ishmael." Since the Great Mosque is too small to hold all the worshippers, the festivals were formerly held in a clearing east of the Auto Gare. They are now held at the Place d'Armes. Both important ceremonies are presided over by the Grand Imam of Ouagadougou. He arrives walking under a great umbrella and is escorted to the prayer ground by holy men, violinists, and drummers. During the ritual he is assisted by other important Moslem leaders of the town. There is much celebration after the grand prayers of Ramadan, and dancing and other festivities continue in the several wards of the town for about one week afterward. On the day of the *Tabaski,* the Grand Imam sacrifices a white sheep before all the Faithful. Later in the day, Moslem families sacrifice either sheep, cows, or goats for their own celebrations; but they prefer to use sheep if they can afford to do so.

The other important festivals among the Ouagadougou Moslems are the New Year celebration (*Al Muharram*), which they call *Zambende,* and *Mouloud,* the birthday of the Prophet Mohammed. In contrast to both the *Karem Salla* or *No-Lokre* and *Tabaski,* there is no public ceremony for the New Year festival. At one time the Moslems used to throw colored water and burning stalks on passersby, but this practice has all but disappeared. Now small boys, disguised in masks and painted all over, roam the town at night dancing and singing in return for small presents. Formerly, also during this festival, young boys used to go to their mothers' brothers' (*yasenamba*) compounds; if they did not receive "productive" presents from these relatives, such as female chickens, goats, sheep, or even cows, they were allowed to seize any property found there. The following year these sisters' sons *(yagensé)* took the off-spring of the animals back to the *yasenamba* compound where they were given additional presents. The Prophet's birthday, *Mouloud* (called *Canne* by the Ouagadougou people) is becoming more important than *Al Muharram*. Formerly this festival was celebrated privately by the Fulani and the Setba Moslems, but now all the Moslems regard the *Mouloud* as comparable to the Christians' Christmas. They celebrate the "eve" of *Mouloud* in the same way that the Christians celebrate Christmas

Eve with feasting and dancing. In addition to these festivals, Moslems in Ouagadougou hold ceremonies, called *sadaquas,* in connection with important *rites de passage.*

The Moslems of Ouagadougou have always provided training for their children in numerous Koranic schools. Delafosse records that at the turn of the century there were approximately 42 Koranic schools with about 230 students in the town.[11] And Tauxier, writing about the same period, states that Ouagadougou had about 33 Koranic schools with approximately 358 students.[12] Unfortunately, neither Delafosse nor Tauxier tells anything about the nature of Islamic studies in the town at that time. The 1926 census reported that there were 70 Koranic schools and 4,000 Moslems in Ouagadougou, and the census of 1944 reported that there were 240 Koranic schools and approximately 25,000 Moslems there. But it is clear that these figures referred to the *Cercle* of Ouagadougou and not the *ville* (town). It was only in 1956 that a report appeared giving an estimate of the number of Koranic schools in Ouagadougou-*Ville* at that time. Mathieu reported that some 66 of these schools existed in the town.[13] Of these, 27 were taught by Mossi teachers (*karemsam'damba,* pl. *karemsamba*) and 39 by strangers: 22 Yarsé, 6 Hausa, 5 Fulani, 2 Marka, 1 Gourounsi, 1 Dagari, 1 Marince (Songhay), and 1 Boussansé.

Most of the teachers (called *marabouts* by the French) have had some sort of scholarly training in the Koran as well as in Moslem precepts and laws. The knowledge of these men varies greatly and one is never quite sure whether their renown is a function of their education or their piety. There is no overall body controlling the competence of the teachers, but at the end of six years of training a man is examined by a number of older teachers and, if judged competent, is "certified" by them. Thereafter he is free to do as he wishes. The six years of training is considered sufficient to enable the man to be literate in Arabic, and to know how to read the Koran and interpret it, but few of the *karemsam'damba* acknowledge

[11]Maurice Delafosse, *Haut Sénégal-Niger* (Paris: Larose, 1912), III, 193.
[12]Tauxier, p. 793.
[13]M. Mathieu, *Notes sur L'Islam et le Christianisme dans la subdivision centrale d'Ouagadougou,* Cercle d'Ouagadougou (Haute-Volta), Paris, 1956, p. 27 (Mémoire 2,619 du Centre des hautes Etudes d'Administration Musulmane, Paris).

a ready, speaking knowledge of Arabic. The Yarsé are still considered to be the best Koranic teachers in town, and the Fulani teachers are renowned for their brilliance. The Mossi teachers are not considered too "strong," a fact no doubt linked to their relatively recent venture into this field.

There is a wide variation in the number of children (*karem camba*) attending the various Koranic schools in Ouagadougou. The average size school appears to have about eleven pupils among whom there are never more than two girls. Many of the children attending the schools come from the families of the teachers and from the neighborhood, but a number of teachers recruit pupils from the rural areas. In some cases, rural parents send their children to Ouagadougou to study with teachers judged more famous than those in the rural regions. In other cases, urban-based teachers "beg" their rural kinsmen and former neighbors to send children to them.

Classes for the children of the Koranic schools are held mainly in the open air, and most frequently on the sidewalk in front of the master's house. During inclement weather, classes meet either in the *zongos* (a reception room at the front of many compounds) or in the homes of the teachers. The masters of the larger Koranic schools have regular classrooms which also serve as dormitories for resident pupils. The pupils learn by reading aloud from wooden slates upon which they write Koranic verses or upon which these verses are written. Normally, the teacher pays attention only to the more advanced pupils, and these are entrusted with the education and discipline of the younger ones.

In general, classes in the Koranic schools are held for only part of the day. Some pupils then return home while others go into the town to beg for alms.[14] For most youngsters there is no ceremonial graduation from Koranic schools. They simply drift off into adult life and stop attending when they start working. The few youngsters who attend Koranic schools after their regular classes at the public schools stop attending as soon as they become more involved in modern educational training.

The educated elite of Ouagadougou, Moslem and non-Moslem alike, are disappointed with the Koranic schools. One major criticism of these schools is that the children learn

[14]*Carrefour Africain*, No. 12 (8 July 1962).

the Koran by rote only, learn little else about Islam, and not enough Arabic to communicate with the people of the Arab world. Perhaps as a result of this criticism three Koranic schools, called *medersa,* were established in 1963: one in Dapoya II, the second at the Central Mosque, and the third at Tiedpalogho. These *medersa* do teach Arabic, and the masters in them include such well-known leaders as El Hadj Idrissa.

The Koranic school teachers and the Imams, as the main Islamic leaders, are those persons responsible for the sectarianism among the Ouagadougou Moslems. Most of these men belong to the Qadiriyya and Tijaniyya, the two main sects or *tariquas.* The Qadiriyya sect is not only the oldest in the town, having been introduced by early Moslem traders, but it has the largest number of adherents. Qadiriyya Moslems control the Imamate of the town and some of the largest mosques among the Hausa population. Adherents of this sect are, however, said to be fairly lax about their faith. The Tijaniyya, introduced to West Africa by El Hadj Omar, represent a smaller group, and, in contrast to the Qadiriyya, are considered to be so devout that they border on fanaticism. Known locally as the people of the *onze grains* (eleven beads, in contrast to other Moslems who are called *douze grains* or twelve beads), they are said to be so strict that they do not tolerate any deviation whatsoever from the formal orthodox Moslem code. They forbid smoking and drinking *dolo;* eating the meat of pigs, dogs, and rabbits, or of any animal which died naturally; making sacrifices to ancestors; or taking the widows of fathers. Tijaniyya Moslems also insist that their wives become practicing Moslems, and if they refuse they are sent back to their relatives. Quadiriyya Moslems and other people in Ouagadougou are scandalized by the refusal of many devout Tijaniyya to shake the hand of any but their Moslem coreligionists and by their unwillingness to share food, utensils, and sleeping materials with members of other groups. Moreover, the Tijaniyya do not attend the Friday mosque because they do not believe that Friday is holier than any other day. And until two years ago they even refused to join the other Moslems in prayer on the major Islamic holy days.

There are also three Imams in the Kamsaoghin and Bilbalgo quarters of Ouagadougou who are leaders of small congregations of the reformist Hamallist movement, but so far their influence has not been felt by the other Moslems in the town. As of 1964, there were no known followers of the Ahmadiyya modernistic movement in the town, although the activities of this group are well documented for other parts of Mossi country and the Upper Volta. There are Moslem Imams in Ouagadougou who do not adhere to any sect.

The majority of the Moslem population in town is not concerned with sectarianism and is ignorant of the differences in doctrine and dogma among the sects. Many Western-educated Moslems, among whom are several officers of the Moslem Association, refuse to take sectarianism seriously, contending that "all paths to God are valid." They are, therefore, generally impatient with what they consider to be the dialectics of the *marabouts*. Even many Koranic masters appear not to know too much about the origins of the sects and the main differences in their doctrines. Thus, when one Hausa Koranic school teacher was questioned about the origins of the *tariquas*, he declared that they date back to the time of the Prophet Mohammad's nephews. One nephew, Hassan, was said to have founded the Qadiriyya, and the other, Hosein, the Tijaniyya. (The fact is that the Qadiriyya dates from al-Mukhtar b. Ahmad (1729–1811) and the Tijaniyya to Ahmad b. Muhammad al-Tijani (1737–1815).

The Moslem Association of Ouagadougou is unable to do very much about those Imams and Koranic teachers who misuse their religion. Although the officers of the association, their technical councilors, and the Imams know about the existence of "charlatans" who, in the guise of Moslem Imams, vend charms and cures about the town, they can do little except bring these men before the court of public opinion. One such "charlatan" was encountered in Ouagadougou selling a brown powder and cigarettes wrapped in paper bearing Arabic script. He told the gathering that the powder was good for everything and that the cigarettes were especially recommended for chest colds. He also advised those persons who were buying cigarettes, at 100 francs a pack, to smoke one in the early morning and another late at night for best results. Several policemen walked over to the crowd to see what was going on, but they took no action against the "curer." The presence of such men in Ouagadougou is displeasing to the regular Moslem community as a whole since it hurts their image with the Christians who continue to accuse even regular

315

Moslem Imams of dealing in talismans and "cures" of dubious value. Members of the association sadly admit that even if they could control or sanction the activities of questionable Moslem teachers and holy men in Ouagadougou, they would be helpless against those itinerant preachers and healers who cater to recent migrants.

There is no official information about the rate of Moslem migration into Ouagadougou or of the percentage of the population that converted to Islam after their arrival in town. Of 103 noncultivator migrant families queried about their religion before coming to Ouagadougou, 49 or 47.6 per cent reported that they were Moslems; 41 or 39.8 per cent reported that they were Christians, and only 13 or 12.6 per cent that they were traditionalists. Among 78 cultivator migrant families interviewed, 37 or 47.5 per cent reported that they were Moslems, 28 or 35.9 per cent that they were traditionalists, and only 13 or 16.6 per cent that they were Christians. The data on the religious affiliation of the migrants suggest that there is a high correlation between the religion of the migrant and the strength of certain religions in the areas from which they had come. Thus migrants from Kombissiri and Ouahigouya, important Moslem areas, are invariably Moslems, whereas migrants from Saponé and Koupéla, important Christian centers, are invariably Christians.

There is some, albeit inconclusive, evidence that the Moslems are not as successful as are the Christians at winning converts among migrants to Ouagadougou. For example, among the 13 *Wend'pous neba* noncultivator migrant families in the sample, 3 reported conversion to Christianity after they had arrived in town, whereas only 1 such family reported conversion to Islam. There was, in addition, 1 family which converted to Christianity but left the church, and 1 family which converted to Islam but subsequently joined the Catholic church. Among the 28 traditionalist cultivator migrant families queried, 9 reported conversion to Catholicism and 8 to Islam.

The Moslems in contemporary Ouagadougou make little or no provision to satisfy the religious needs or socio-religious sentiments of young women. Whereas Catholic girls have elaborate first communions and spectacular church weddings, the Moslem girls have nothing of this sort. There are very few non-Christian girls who go through the public schools of

Ouagadougou without seriously considering conversion to Christianity, especially Catholicism. Traditionalist girls have no difficulty becoming Catholic since they simply "follow" their peers to church, agree to be catechumen, and are later baptized. Moslem girls are similarly drawn to Catholicism, but are usually refused permission to join the Church. Moslem parents have tried to counter this attraction of Catholicism by demanding the establishment of an all-girl *lycée* which, they hope, would attract more Moslem girls who could group together and not be attracted to Christianity through friendships with non-Moslems. They also favored the female *lycée* as a means of preventing contact between their daughters and non-Moslem men who form the largest group in the coeducational *lycées* in Ouagadougou. Generally, once an educated Moslem girl marries a Moslem man, she usually abandons any interest in Christianity. If she remains interested in religion, she may say Moslem prayers within the confines of her home. This type of religious behavior is not satisfying to some young women, however, and they resent having to wait until the onset of the menopause to go to the Friday mosque. But even here they are carefully segregated from the men.

The younger Moslem elites in Ouagadougou recognize the dilemma for Islam in a town whose major educated group is Christian and where the symbols of modernity are considered Christian as well as Western. They believe that modern Western education is ill-adapted to the local environment, inimical to Islamic precepts, and results in alienating the educated Moslem youths from their religion. These persons complain that when Moslem youngsters study Western Christian or secular philosophy they often become atheists, or at best, agnostics. They do not think this would happen if the youngsters were taught Islamic philosophy. The elites also believe that Western-educated Moslem youths have many more conflicts with uneducated Moslem parents than do educated Christian youths with equally illiterate Christian parents. For example, Moslem parents object strongly when their children drink wine, since they view this practice not simply as the acquisition of French dietary habits, but as a rejection of Islamic law and custom. Moslem parents regard the desire of young people to choose their own spouses not as a function of education but as the adoption of Christian values and a rejection of Islamic teachings. The Moslem elite of Ouagadougou hopes that through the work of such organizations as the Ligue Voltaïque des Oeuvres Laïques they can change the Christian, and especially Catholic, orientation of modern education and help young Moslems enter the modern world as Moslems and not as Christians. They would like Ouagadougou to continue to modernize, but not to be Christianized.

Catholicism

Christianity came to Ouagadougou in June 1901 when Father Templier, a Catholic missionary of the Pères Blancs (White Fathers) established a post there. The missionaries initially were quite cautious in seeking converts. They made little effort to convert the young pupils who were sent to them to be educated by the Commandant of Ouagadougou, nor the orphans, lepers, ex-slaves, and other unfortunates who gathered around the mission.[15] It was not until the Reverend Father Joanny Thévenoud arrived in the capital on November 11, 1903, that the drive was begun to implant Catholicism, especially among the Mossi of Ouagadougou. His first efforts were frustrated by anticlerical administrators. Moreover, some of the Mossi chiefs, such as the Kamsaogho Naba, were hostile to Catholicism. Many of the pupils recruited by the administration were withdrawn from the mission, as were the slave children.

Father Thévenoud smarted under this opposition and awaited the opportunity to change this sentiment. His chance finally came in 1908 when a revolt broke out in Mossi country. The administration asked the mission for the services of interpreters, and Father Thévenoud seized the opportunity to place the administrators in his debt. He rationalized that, "The role of the Mission does not include becoming involved in political questions, but it does not believe that it can refuse the services requested of it in these circumstances where the lives of the missionaries are as compromised as those of the other Europeans."[16] According to Baudu, "Father Thévenoud, primarily a Man of God, did not see in that affair anything but the advantages and progress the Mission could get

[15]Baudu, p. 17.
[16]*Ibid.*, p. 44.

318

out of it."[17] Thereafter, Father Thévenoud was to take every opportunity and use every ruse to advance the cause of the Catholic mission. When, in 1908, famine also broke out in and around Ouagadougou, he published several articles criticizing the local administration for allowing the people to suffer. These articles not only attracted the attention of the Minister of the Colonies, but also attracted help for the mission from the French people.

By 1912, the Catholic mission in Ouagadougou had some 200 Mossi converts, among whom were several women as well as entire families. The eight Soeurs Blanches (White Sisters) who arrived in Ouagadougou at this time (the first white females the Mogho Naba and his people had ever seen) were given the task of evangelizing Mossi women. The schools opened by the Fathers had by this time produced their first graduates. Baudu states: "Several young men, former pupils of the Pères, were engaged as interpreters or writers in the offices of the *Cercle* of Mossi country. This could be viewed as showing confidence in the educators who taught them and, at the same time, as an index of the diminution of that distrust which had so long surrounded these men."[18]

In 1914, Father Thévenoud and his assistants baptized 341 Christians, but a number of persons in Ouagadougou complained that the missionaries had replaced the chiefs as impressors of young children. The missionaries did not deny this charge. In fact, they felt that such techniques were necessary. The missionaries even suggested that some parents would prefer to give their children to the Church instead of to the Mogho Naba. They quoted with approval the statement that one man made to a missionary: "Thy word is the word of God, how can I refuse something to God? You want my son, take him, he is yours. If the Mogho Naba had asked me to give my son to him to become his *soghoné* [page] I would have refused to give him up. But to you, man of God, never. God will give me more children."[19]

A number of Mossi notables accused the Fathers of recruiting Mossi girls to serve as *pughsiudsé,* that is, using girls in the same way as chiefs, who often gave wives to men with the ex-

[17]*Ibid.*
[18]*Ibid.,* p. 62.
[19]*Ibid.,* p. 38.

pectation that these men would honor, obey, and pay tribute and surrender daughters to serve as future *pughsiudsé*. The White Fathers did not deny this either. Bounoil declared:

> A Mossi who is unable to acquire a wife by traditional means must either remain unmarried or seduce another man's wife ... they must choose between celibacy and immorality.
>
> Such a state of affairs creates many problems for the missions, especially since the system is recognized and sanctioned by the colonial authorities. ... Young native Christians are obviously placed in a very awkward position. Their conversion angers their parents, who refuse to give them a wife; neither will their friends bestow a daughter upon them, because they know that they will not receive one in return, since a Christian may not give a daughter in marriage to a pagan.... Consequently, unless the missionaries help them to find a wife, they must remain unmarried—a very discouraging prospect![20]

So single-minded was Father Thévenoud in his desire to convert the people of Ouagadougou to Catholicism that he ignored all of the accusations leveled, then and later, against the mission and sought every opportunity to establish and maintain good relations with all those who could aid him in his task. He cooperated fully with the administration to recruit men and material during World War I, but also tried to help chiefs who had run afoul of the administration. Thus in January 1917, he interceded with the administration at the request of the Mogho Naba whose brother, the Djiba Naba, was accused of exploiting the people. "The Djib-Naba was released, and the Mogho Naba came to thank the person who had efficaciously helped him in his misfortune. The lines woven between the Mossi and their apostle became stronger and stronger."[21] But Father Thévenoud did not hesitate to use his relations with the administration to humble chiefs, such as the Nobéré Naba, who refused to deliver grain or other commodities to the mission.

When Governor Hesling arrived in Ouagadougou in 1919 as head of the New Upper Volta colony, he sought the support

[20]Joseph Bouniol, *The White Fathers and Their Missions* (London: Sands and Company, 1929), p. 160.
[21]Bandu, p. 73.

of the mission. In April 1920, he named Father Thévenoud Member of the Council of Administration of the Upper Volta. True to his vocation, the missionary declared:

> My presence in the Council could only place the Mission in a good situation in the eyes of the Europeans as well as in the eyes of the civil servants, merchants, and natives who are there. The Mission is on the best terms with the present governor who had already been accustomed to ask my opinion on important questions. It is clear that now they depend upon us, and upon our endeavors, and this indication of sympathy will not do us any harm. Should we not profit from it for the good of the Mission? I would believe so.[22]

Among the benefits that the mission received from the new administration was the expansion of the carpet factory which had been opened in Ouagadougou by the White Sisters. "The administration ... having financed the Mission's construction of a beautiful roofed building, busied itself furnishing it. The Commanders of the *Cercles* in Ouagadougou and Koudougou sent a hundred or so little girls, who were quickly acclimatized and trained." When this factory reached full production, it employed 238 girls ranging from eleven to twenty years of age. This factory was also viewed by the missionaries as a "nursery of excellent Christian women, companions of catechists, and true collaborators of their husbands. During 1925 and 1926, 45 of them were married to Christians, establishing religious homes, the foundation of a developing Church."[23]

The Catholic church in Ouagadougou also took advantage of a sympathetic administration to increase its activities on other fronts. It sought to consolidate its hold on its converts and to create an African clergy; it also endeavored to secure the promulgation of a series of laws ameliorating the position of the women in Upper Volta, especially with regard to their right to choose their own husbands; it promoted higher education in Ouagadougou when it opened the Petit Séminaire (Little Seminary) at Pabré for the graduates of its urban school; it opened additional dispensaries; and, in 1927, it sponsored the Association of Catholic Mossi Men (Association Catholiques des Hommes Mossi) to stimulate secular activities

[22]*Ibid.*, p. 81.
[23]*Ibid.*, p. 123.

among Christians and non-Christians alike. On December 8, 1930, the Catholic church founded the congregation of the Black Sisters of the Immaculate Conception with seven novices, an event which Father Thévenoud, now a monsignor, hailed as marking a significant step in the evolution of the Mossi woman.

The Church also established chapels and catechists in the peri-urban areas of Ouagadougou such as Saba, Tampouy, and Zaghtuli, from which Christians journeyed every Sunday to Ouagadougou to join their urban brethren in worship. The mission also permitted Father Goarnisson, a doctor, to accept the government's request to educate medical personnel for the "Autonomous Service of Trypanosomiasis." This activity brought many non-Catholic-educated Voltaics under the direct influence of the missionaries, and some of these were subsequently converted to Catholicism. Also converted at this time were all the children of the Baloum Naba, the traditional chamberlain of the Mogho Naba's court. The administration was so pleased with the cooperation of the Church that, in 1932, it gave Monsignor Thévenoud the *Légion d'Honneur*. This honor was muted, however, by the news that on January 1, 1933, the Upper Volta was to be suppressed as a colony and Ouagadougou to cease being a capital.

The Catholic church was disappointed by the eclipse of the town but remained silent and devoted to its mission. Yet, it reacted vigorously when its own activities were threatened. In 1934, Mr. Dim Delobson, a non-Catholic civil servant and Mossi historian whose two fiancées had been converted to Catholicism, led a number of chiefs in an attack on missionary activities. On August 16, 1934, a number of chiefs met at the office of the Commander of the *Cercle* of Ouagadougou and testified before an Inspector of Administrative Affairs, appointed to inquire into the following charges:

1) that Christian Africans do not obey the chiefs; refuse to pay taxes, do *corvée* work, or accept military service.

2) that Christians create problems for the population by taking women and girls who do not belong to them.

3) that the Fathers oblige people to come to catechism and refuse to respect the rights of parents to prevent their children from attending.[24]

[24]*Ibid.*, pp. 166ff.

The chiefs stated that they resented these acts on the part of the Christians and the missionaries and requested the administration to tell the priests that they should not advise people to refuse to do communal labor. Moreover, they demanded that the missionaries restrict their activities to religion.

The missionaries replied that many of their Christian converts did in fact misunderstand that they could obey God, their parents, and the civil authorities at the same time. One missionary pointed out that the cause of the difficulty was the statement of Jesus in the Gospel according to St. Matthew that, "He that loveth father or mother more than me, is not worthy of me" (X:37). He insisted that the missionaries always told their catechumen that they should obey their parents and should be prepared to suffer reprisals from their parents—such as the denial of meals—for the sake of their faith. The Commission of Inquiry scolded the mission and reaffirmed the rights of the people to go to church or not, as they saw fit. It also told the people, through their chiefs, that, in contrast to the other Europeans, most of whom were government officials, the missionaries had no power over them. The missionaries neither liked nor agreed with this decision which they considered anticlerical, but they accepted the dictates of the administration.

The Catholic church survived these attacks of Mossi elite and chiefs and again won the favor of the administration by its full cooperation during World War II. Once again the missionaries responded as Frenchmen, and at the end of the war their status began to rise again as many of the mission's converts and ex-pupils entered politics.[25] The Union pour la Défense des Interêts de la Haute-Volta (U.D.I.H.V.), the first modern Mossi political group, was composed primarily of educated young Mossi Catholics, such as François Bouda, Joseph Conombo, Christophe Kalenzaga, and Joseph Ouedraogo. Other politicians included such ex-seminarians as Maurice Yaméogo. The growing power and prestige of all of these men added to the luster of the Church, and the Church was not slow to exploit it. Thus, when these young African Catholics invited Father Goarnisson to join them in the general council charged with preparing administrative structures for the recreated Upper Volta Colony, the Church willingly granted him permission to do so.

[25]Skinner, 1964b, pp. 179ff.

The Catholic church was fortunate in having Catholic converts in all political parties and even among the traditional chiefs struggling for power against commoner politicians. There were even Catholics in the radical Rassemblement Démocratique Africain, a federation-wide political group said at that time (1946–50) to have been under Communist influence. Fortunately also for the Church, religion never became an important campaign issue in Upper Volta, even though a few Moslem-dominated parties did arise and compete for power. When, in 1960, the political dust settled, M. Maurice Yaméogo, an ex-seminarian, emerged as President of the Upper Volta Republic.

The Catholic priests in Ouagadougou were among the first Catholic missionaries in Africa to make a determined effort to produce an African clergy. The program started in the 1930's, and during World War II the Church accelerated its drive toward Africanization. The first Voltaic priests (all Mossi) were ordained in Ouagadougou on May 2, 1942, and on February 29, 1956, one of these priests, the Abbé Yougbare, became Bishop of Koupéla, and the first African bishop in all of French Africa. The enthronement ceremony took place in Ouagadougou, to the delight of the town's Catholics, whose satisfaction was only tempered by not having their own bishop. Finally, in April 1960, another from the group of first priests, the Abbé Paul Zoungrana, a native of Ouagadougou, was named to the archbishopric of the town. He was later to be named cardinal, becoming in the process the first West African so honored.

As soon as the Vicarate of Ouagadougou (later the Archdiocese) had ordained its first African priest, it endeavored to increase its activities in the town. The mission which had been established in Kologho Naba (Ouidi) became a full-fledged parish and assumed control over the Catholics and chapels in Ouidi, Larhalle, and Tampouy, as well as in the peri-urban districts of Bazoule and Tanghin-Dassouri. The Dapoya II mission was also transformed into a parish church with its own abbé, but the Catholics in Gounghin, Nimne, Koulouba, Tiedpalogho, Samandin, and Bilbalgo remained under the control of the Cathedral Diocese.

The number of missionaries and clerics of the Catholic church has increased dramatically over the years, and, although there are African clergy in control of the Church and its activities in Ouagadougou, the bulk of the 100 or so clerics there are still whites. Thus, at the parish church of Dapoya II there are three priests, two African and one European, and in the parish-school complex in Kologho Naba there is one African priest assisted by one French and one German priest. There are only two or three Black Sisters continually in attendance at Dapoya II, but about one dozen Black and White Sisters at Kologho Naba, a number of the latter engaged in teaching in the school. Of the 90 or so missionaries and clerics at the main mission complex in Ouagadougou, the majority are still Europeans. These and the African clerics are engaged in preaching, teaching, and medical work.

The number of Catholics in Ouagadougou has also grown from the small number domiciled only in the "Saint" wards (St. Julien, St. Léon, St. Jean-Baptiste, and St. Joseph) to 32,000 adherents (claimed by the Church in 1964–65) scattered throughout Ouagadougou. According to the census of 1962, the greatest number of Catholics, 3,069 persons, live in Dapoya II, with 1,232 in Koulouba, 1,205 in Larhalle, 1,133 in Bilbalgo, and 1,116 in Ouidi. Nevertheless, the highest percentages of Catholics in specific wards are still found in "Saint" wards, Kologho Naba, and the Zone Résidentielle. Out of a population of 807 in St. Léon, 633 or 78.4 per cent are Catholic; and out of 680 persons in St. Jean-Baptiste, 512, or 75.4 per cent are Catholics. Kologho Naba has 128 Catholics out of a population of 147 persons and the Zone Résidentielle has 151 Catholics out of an African population of 218. The only ward having no Catholics is Hamdalaye, a predominantly Moslem ward.[26]

The presence of a large percentage of Catholics in the "Saint" wards is due to historical factors. The large number of Catholics in Dapoya II and Koulouba reflects the heavy clerk and civil servant settlement in those wards. The presence of a Catholic church and a number of schools in Kologho Naba is the reason for the large percentage of Catholics there, whereas the high percentage of Catholics in the Zone Résidentielle is due to the presence of high-status Africans. In addition, most of the Europeans living in the Zone Résidentielle are members of the Catholic church.

The Catholic church has been responsible for many changes

[26]"Recensement Démographique . . . ," p. 35.

in Ouagadougou, but almost everything it did was, consciously or unconsciously, designed to spread the Gospel of Christ. Thus, the Catholic church in Ouagadougou, like Islam in other times and places in Africa, often used nonreligious techniques to attract converts. Girls were recruited to work in the carpet factory, but they were also viewed as potential wives for alienated youths and the future mothers of Catholic children. Aid to the lepers, the old, the lame, the sick, diseased, and blind was viewed as an act of charity by the missionaries, but their hope always was and still is that these acts would throw light on the beneficial intentions of the Catholic church. The Nurses Training School, still attached to the mission, undoubtedly serves as a recruiting station for many non-Christian students who attend it.

At one period the Catholic church in Ouagadougou held out the hope—sometimes the only hope—for young people interested in getting an education and thereby leading a better life. And for many people in Ouagadougou becoming a Catholic meant, and still means, becoming "civilized." The missionaries were sometimes the only "civilized" persons with whom many of the townspeople came into contact, and, in contrast to the European administrators and businessmen, these churchmen actively tried to pass their knowledge on to their students. True, the Fathers were often more paternalistic than the other Frenchmen in Ouagadougou, but this paternalism did result in the transmission of French culture traits— an important asset to youngsters eager to interact with Europeans. Of course, not all the students recruited for school wished either to be educated or to be acculturated to European ways, but enough of them did to enable the Church to expand.

The Church also made a substantial appeal to women. It was able to offer women new opportunities for self-expression and grant them religious autonomy. Of course, it was the development of new social and economic relations between men and women in the town that facilitated the Church's contact with these women. Indeed, those Mossi women who could or would not tolerate difficult or unhappy marriages, especially polygynous ones, and left their husbands, found ready allies among the missionaries. Young girls who had been promised as wives or had been assigned as *pughsiudsé* to men they did not like sought and received help from the Fathers in choosing their own spouses. They also won the active support of a rather militant feminist nun, Soeur Marie-Andre du Sacré-Coeur, who, with Monsignor Thévenoud of the Catholic mission, besieged the French administration with demands to pass laws "ameliorating" the status of Mossi women.[27]

Interestingly enough, many Catholics in the town believe that conversion of the women to Catholicism gave urban and even rural households the integrity and stability they had traditionally lacked. Wives who were Catholic and monogamous allegedly took their marital vows quite seriously and presented fewer problems for their husbands than their traditionalist sisters. And reportedly, traditionalist men, seeing the virtue of Catholic wives, made little objection to the conversion of their wives, despite their own devotion to ancestral beliefs and ritual. This type of conversion was, moreover, facilitated by the Church which held that women could become good Catholics despite the polygyny of their husbands. The Church's view in this matter was that the women were not to blame for belonging to polygynous households and that it was unjust to punish them for the errors of their husbands.

The Church also made a determined effort to attract young girls and young women. A number of women who had joined the Catholic church as children declared they were attracted by the gentleness of the Catholic missionaries (both men and women); by the willingness of these clerics to permit the girls a large amount of personal freedom; and by the opportunity to go to school and to play. Little traditionalist girls also appreciated the fact that their Christian peers usually received clothes for going to church while they and the little Moslem girls had no religious opportunities for obtaining special wearing apparel. Going to 9:00 Mass on Sunday mornings has become as much a social as a religious event for the school girls, and this has attracted the attention of non-Christian girls. Catholic young women could also look forward to a religious marriage ceremony in church as an integral part of the entire modern wedding ceremony, whereas traditionalist and Moslem girls could not. It is almost a contradiction in terms to talk about traditionalist girls having modern marriage ceremonies since few, if any, girls have modern marriage ceremonies if

[27]Cf. Marie-Andre du Sacre-Coeur, *La Femme noire en Afrique occidentale* (Paris, 1939).

they remain traditionalist. Educated Moslem girls still feel a void in their lives; for, until quite recently, to be modern was to be Catholic.

Except for school boys who saw in the Church a means for socio-cultural mobility as well as spiritual salvation, the men in Ouagadougou, especially the Mossi, have felt ambiguous about conversion to Catholicism. There were periods in the history of the Catholic church in Ouagadougou when the Fathers behaved no differently toward the Mossi than did the other Europeans. True, their goal was to build cathedrals for the Lord and to create industry for "idle hands" in the hope that the minds behind these hands would embrace Christ; but to the Mossi men, building bricks for God or Mammon was the same. It made little difference to them whether they were forced to take bales of cotton to the warehouses of the great commercial enterprises or to the mission yards.

What really interested many Mossi men in the Church was the opportunity to find work, to learn trades, to learn to cultivate new crops, to gain wives, and to obtain the benefits of modern medicine which the Fathers knew how to dispense. The desire to adopt a new religion might also have been a factor in the conversion of many men to Catholicism. Nevertheless, given the fact that attempts at proselytism were so closely associated with more practical types of aid, it is difficult indeed to claim that religious factors were dominant. For example, Father Goarnisson, a medical doctor, stated that at the end of a healing session he would try to convert the patients by showing them that Catholicism was very old and venerable. He has a chart on which he shows his audience that the first Mogho Naba dated to about A.D. 1200. Next, he shows them a longer chart on which Mohammed's Hegira is dated A.D. 632, earlier than the Mossi kingdom. Then he shows them an even longer chart on which Christianity appeared at the year A.D. 1, and, below, stretching backward in time, to "Adama," was Jesus' *korongo* (genealogy). Father Goarnisson explained that the Mossi elders marveled at the length of Jesus' genealogy and often concluded that a religion as old as Christianity must be a good one.

An important factor in the conversion of young Mossi men to Catholocism is that it is a *visible* religion and, despite its antiquity, a *modern* religion. Young Mossi men had no role in their traditional religion except for bringing their chickens to be sacrificed by the elders to their ancestors or as *yagensé* (sisters' sons) being required to be present at their mothers' brothers *(yasenaba)* houses so that sacrifices could be made to those ancestors. Thus, when young men came to town without their elders, they ceased all activities in the traditional religious rituals and ceremonies. Some men returned home for the annual rituals, especially if they were of noble origin, but few could afford this luxury. For some of these young people, traditional beliefs and practices meant no more than taking precautions against illness induced by magical practitioners through the purchase of amulets or in seeking help from these and other practitioners for help in overcoming the normal obstacles of life. For others, Islam and the Catholic church represented active religions with which they could identify and in which they could participate.

Catholicism has had more success among urban men than Islam primarily because it is new in Ouagadougou and, as is obvious to all, most of the important and modern people in the town are Catholics.[28] The desire to be modern and even Western, implicit in conversion to Christianity, is observed during Catholic baptismal rituals. More than 90 per cent of the male converts wear Western-style suits to this ceremony even though they are permitted to wear white, traditional garb. Apparently they view this sacrament not only as a "spiritual regeneration" of man, but as a "cultural" one as well. Catholic priests lament that now when it is possible, and even viewed as desirable, for converts to retain their African names, the converts do not wish to do so. The latter consider their traditional names to be "primitive" and insist upon adopting such "modern" names as Jean, Joseph, and Pierre.

It is difficult to determine whether there is a negative relationship between polygyny and conversion to Catholicism among the men of Ouagadougou. For example, one can never tell for sure whether polygynous men refused to convert to Catholicism because they were polygynous or simply because they preferred to remain traditionalist or convert to Islam. The Catholic clergy in Ouagadougou believe polygyny prevents men from becoming Catholic, and it is usually difficult to

[28]Cf. Skinner, 1960b, p. 397.

disprove beliefs. Nevertheless, the Catholic church has shown itself quite tolerant of polygynous men who wish to have some relationship with the Church. Those members of the Catholic elite who take plural wives are visited by the clergy who "try to show them the errors of their ways" but do little else. The polygynists are forbidden to receive Holy Communion, but normally they are free to attend church services. Polygynous postulants are encouraged to remain as faithful to the Church as possible so that on the point of death they could symbolically repudiate all but one wife and thus be eligible for baptism and the chance for eternal life.

The Catholic church in Ouagadougou has always insisted that its converts be properly instructed before they are admitted to membership. A prospective convert first inscribes his (or her) name in the Church. Then follows four years of instruction during which the candidates receive lessons in Catholicism three times a week: Mondays, Thursdays, and Sundays. The Catholic clergy believe that candidates must receive four years of instruction because the doctrine of the Church cannot be imparted to them in a shorter period of time. Baptism itself is a rather elaborate ritual during which candidates, standing in front of their godparents or sponsors, undergo the elaborate rituals prescribed for the baptism of adults in the Catholic church. During the December 1964 baptismal ceremony (called *Sobo* by the Mossi) at the parish church of Kologho Naba, 328 adults were baptized, 200 men and 128 women. The parish priest could not explain the apparent reversal in the usual ratio of women to men since—both in the Cathedral and Dapoya II this ratio was about the same. That same month, the Abbé of Kologho Naba baptized 48 infants, which according to him was the normal monthly number.

All the Catholics in Ouagadougou, presumably like Catholics all over the world, are expected to attend Mass every Sunday. The churches in the town have at least one Mass every morning; and in those wards where there are mosques as well as churches, if the Catholics had not already been awakened by the muezzin's call to prayer, they are soon awakened by the pealing of their own church bells. These early morning services are normally attended only by devout females, although occasionally male church members may be present. Sundays are the days when most Catholics in the town try to attend at least one of the three Masses held in their churches.

Except for Europeans[29] and some young educated persons, men and women still segregate themselves during Mass in the Catholic churches in Ouagadougou. Men usually sit on the left side and women on the right. The priests state that the reason for this seating plan is that women bring their babies to church, and, since crying babies often have to be taken outside, it is better for the men and women to sit apart. It is true that crying babies make it difficult for the worshippers to hear the songs and prayers. Nonetheless, Catholic priests have learned to accept this since many of the women in town, even educated ones, take their nursing babies everywhere, even, and especially, to the church. Perhaps for ideological reasons, the priests could not accept the suggestion that this seating arrangement might really be a concession to the sensibilities of the Mossi men. However, only the very young married couples normally violate the traditional norm that men and women never sit together, especially in public places.

The Catholic church in Ouagadougou has always encouraged its clergy to use Moré during church services. Thus, most sermons are preached in Moré and announcements are also made in that language. There are several Moré hymnals in use, and a number of Catholic priests, including Abbé Guierma of Kologho Naba and Abbé Robert Ouedraogo of Dapoya II, have written Masses for church use based on traditional Voltaic songs. Despite these innovations, many of the older converts and ex-seminarians take delight in singing Gregorian chants. To these people, steeped in the tradition of the former missionaries and seminaries, the only Catholic music is the Gregorian chant, and, while they take an interest in the attempts to Africanize church music, they feel that a tradition is being lost.

Ouagadougou Catholics, in contrast to the Moslems, have had no difficulty celebrating the major holy days of their church, since even anticlerical administrators celebrated these feasts as holidays if not as holy days. Christmas is by far the most important of the feasts for the Ouagadougou Catholic population, and they make extensive preparations for its cele-

[29]François Djoby Bassolet, *Evolution de la Haute Volta* (L'Imprimerie Nationale de la Haute Volta, 1968), p. 51. He declares "Inside the Churches, the Cathedral of Ouagadougou, the Churches of Bobo-Dioulasso, and Koudougou, the Whites and the Blacks were separated. A strict segregation was thus applied from the steps to the altar."

bration. Almost all Catholics build little mud-brick huts in front of their yards, painting and decorating them with candles and small figurines. A few of these are even decorated with stars, tinsel, and pieces of cotton to represent snow. In their crèches, wealthier people are beginning to place small animals manufactured through the use of the *cire-perdue* process by the smiths of Ouagadougou. Parents buy new clothing for themselves and their children, and on Christmas Eve, every church holds a Midnight Mass. After Mass, friends visit each other to eat, drink, and, sometimes, to sing carols around the "mamosa" tree which serves as a Christmas tree. In a few homes, men, dressed up as Père Noël (Father Christmas or Santa Claus) awaken the sleeping children to give them presents. Christmas Day itself is devoted to visiting relatives and persons of authority in the wards, especially if these persons are Christians.

It is especially at Christmas that one gets the feeling that Ouagadougou, despite its non-Christian majority, is a Christian town, since this holiday is celebrated not only by Christians but also by most of its non-Christian population, especially educated persons. For example, the Mogho Naba of Ouagadougou, though a convert to Islam, customarily builds one of the most imposing creches in town and invites many persons to see it. Again, urban Catholics often invite many of their rural relatives, traditionalist and Moslem alike, to come to Ouagadougou to attend the Midnight Mass. Here the emphasis is not on belief but rather on kinship and sentiment. An interesting side effect of the growing universality of Christmas is a corresponding secularization of this holy day. For example, in 1964, worshippers at the Christmas Midnight Masses in the churches of the town, including the Cathedral, had difficulty hearing the prayers said by the priests because nearby loudspeakers were blaring out cha-cha. This prompted the Mayor to vow that in future years he would enforce the ban against loudspeakers disturbing the residents of the town.

The Feast of the Assumption, in contrast to Christmas, is really a holy day and not a holiday, even though no one works on this day. It is especially holy to the women of Ouagadougou who are the major participants in the processions held in each parish. In Dapoya II, the procession is led by a man carrying the banner of the Legion of Mary, followed by a large crowd of women and a few men who carry a statue of the

Blessed Virgin. Two African priests lead the participants in joyous songs, while a European missionary, in silent prayer, trails at the end of the procession. After completing a tour of the quarter, the procession returns to a plaza in front of the church where, again led by the priests, the women sing and dance to their ritual tunes. The objective here is twofold: to honor the Virgin and to permit the women to participate extensively in a religious ceremony whose central figure is a woman. The clerics hope that the Catholic women will feel a closer link with the Church and that non-Catholic women will witness the joy and participation of women in Church affairs.

Catholics are buried in a number of burial grounds around Ouagadougou, including the main cemetery near the mission and the cemetery behind the Dapoya II parish church. The Church does not interfere in the family rituals (such as the role of the *dakiba* [joking relatives], the preparation of the body, and matters of this kind) which take place within the confines of the homes of the deceased. The clergy hold burial services for the deceased in the church and then preside at the final religious rites at the grave. However, they leave rather quickly after this rite is over so that even good Catholics can perform such traditional rituals as placing wearing apparel and food utensils on the graves of the deceased. The Church does encourage Catholics to light candles for the deceased, and to have Masses said for the soul of the departed in lieu of spending money for the more expensive traditional funerals *(kouré)*. Nevertheless, Mossi Catholics in Ouagadougou do have modified versions of traditional funerals at which friends gather, the dead are spoken about, joking relatives appear and make people laugh by their antics, and where people drink *dolo* and dance in the name of the deceased. But sacrifices are never made to the ancestors, at least not publicly, since it would be considered un-Catholic to do so.

Protestants

The first Protestant American Assemblies of God missionaries arrived in Ouagadougou around 1922 or 1923 from their base in Senegal. By the end of 1923, six missionaries were listed as resident in the town, but by 1929, two had left to establish mission stations in other parts of Mossi country. The Protestants had difficulty gaining their first converts among the Ouagadougou population. In one of their early reports they complained that, in addition to being the headquarters of the French administration and the capital of the Mogho Naba, Ouagadougou was "also the headquarters of the Catholic Mission which has been here for about thirty-five years. These all have considerable influence on the natives, making the work of evangelization more difficult here than in other centers, and the visible fruit for the labor bestowed less."[30] After much effort, the Protestants finally did gain some converts. Here, too, the desire among Africans for education appears to have helped. The report added that,

> For several years now, a number of young men who were attending school in Ouagadougou came to the French Bible class, but just recently some of the natives in the government employ have also become interested and joined the class. At this station, we are having Bible classes most every day, three of these classes being in French. Some of our more advanced Christians have taken over the teaching of reading and writing, and every night when they are free, they go to villages and preach the Word.[31]

The Protestants encountered many of the same difficulties as did the Catholics in trying to convert the Mossi to Christianity. In contrast to Father Thévenoud who had grandiose plans for developing Mossi country (an ambition linked, no doubt, to his being a colonial Frenchman as well as a missionary), the Americans were primarily concerned with preaching the gospel. Second, and in contrast to the Catholics, the administration resented efforts of the Americans to educate the children of Ouagadougou. It insisted that the Americans use French or Moré for instruction, and, since few of them knew French they were at a greater disadvantage. Third, the American Protestants, like the Catholics, incurred the hostility of Mossi fathers and husbands whose children and wives had elected to join their church to escape family control. But they had less success than did the Catholics in freeing young people from kinship and marriage ties in favor of religious ones. Fourth, and here again in great contrast to the Catholics, the Americans

---

[30]"The Assemblies of God in Foreign Lands, The Gospel among the Mossi People." Foreign Missions Department, General Council of the Assemblies of God (Springfield, Missouri, 1934), p. 13.
[31]*Ibid.*

did not dare complain officially to Paris, far less to America, when they felt that the local people were suffering. Geoffrey Gorer, who visited the Upper Volta about 1934, reported that the Protestant missionaries he met there "spoke with a dispassionate 'none of our business' disapproval of the ill treatment of the negroes, who they said were ruled entirely by fear."[32] This decision of the American missionaries to leave unto Ceasar those things that were his is understandable, given their preoccupation with formal conversion. However, within the context of Ouagadougou society and that of the Upper Volta, this approach was detrimental to the rapid spread of Protestantism.

In contrast to the Catholic missionaries, they did not live in the center of town but in Gounghin, an area then fairly remote from the activities of the townspeople. Their decision to do so was as much a function of their concern for sanitation as it was a symbolic retreat from worldly affairs. Their comparative isolation was also conditioned by the fact that the American missionaries often were married couples, as much engaged in domestic activities as in religious work. Thus, unlike the Catholic missionaries, they could not have continuous face-to-face relations with their converts. Whereas the Catholic priests made a total commitment to their charges (mind, body, and soul), the American Portestants were interested only in their souls. The result was that few American Protestants developed that easy comradery or "joking" relationship with their African converts that one witnesses so often between the Catholic missionaries and their former students.

Ouagadougou was the headquarters for the Assemblies of God in all parts of Mossi country, or, more exactly, all parts of the eastern Upper Volta. Actually, the mission there was more an administrative center than anything else. People did go there for conferences and reunions of converts, but the missionaries were fairly decentralized. The mission Bible school was located in Koubri, some 18 kilometers south of the capital, just as the Catholic seminary was located at Pabré, out in the country, but Koubri never gained the reputation for educational excellence as did Pabré. A number of young Protestant students left Koubri when they discovered that they were not getting the same education as were the Catholic boys

[32]Geoffrey Gorer, *Africa Dances* (New York: A. A. Knopf, 1935), p. 149.

at Pabré. Later the Protestants decided to build a regular school for Protestants at Sabin in the northern part of the town. This school received aid from the French Protestants and from the government and has started to graduate students with the B.E.P.C. It is also serving to attract children who would otherwise not have the opportunity to receive an education in the overcrowded Catholic and private schools. As is to be expected, the Protestants are recruiting converts from this school.

The Assemblies of God missionaries in Ouagadougou are sensitive about the number of their conversions and complain that their activities are underreported. But faced with the great success of Islam and Catholicism, they claim that they are not concerned with numbers but in producing "faithful" Christians. According to the 1962 census, there were 717 Protestants in the town. In 1964 the Assemblies of God claimed 1,800 church members in Ouagadougou. This increase in conversion is due to the desire of persons to get an education or to adopt a universal religion. A certain percentage of the latter were converted to Christianity while in the rural areas and have retained their church membership. Some recent immigrants to Ouagadougou reported that they were converted by the Assemblies of God mission in Adjame ward in Abidjan, Ivory Coast and have continued to attend church in Ouagadougou. Friends and relatives of these converts have also joined the church. But the Protestant church does not appear to be expanding as rapidly as the Catholic church because it offers less than the Catholic or even the Moslem church. The Assemblies of God has even lost some of its members to a separatist church in the town and may thereby have lost the opportunity to recruit those persons who, while seeking another religion, may be dissatisfied with both Catholicism and Islam.

Most African members of the Assemblies of God mission are laborers and cultivators. This church does boast five students studying in France, three commanders of *cercles,* a number of police and army men, but has few clerks or civil servants. This is to be expected since, until quite recently, educated persons were produced by the Catholic schools and remained loyal to Catholicism.

The census of 1962 shows the largest number of Protestants, 292 persons, living in Sabin, the quarter in which the Protestant school is located.[33] This number presumably includes a large number of children. There are 159 Protestants listed in Gounghin ward, a fact no doubt linked to the location there of the headquarters of the Assemblies of God mission and also the main church of the Eglise Apostolique. Most of the 37 Protestants reported for Zanguettin and the 26 for Kamsaoghin are Yoruba and do not belong to either of the Protestant groups already mentioned.

The Assemblies of God have four buildings in the town. The Protestant Temple, located near the Auto Gare in the commercial area of the town, is now the main church in which the converts congregate on the major Christian holy days. Another church is located at the school in Sabin; a third church is being constructed near the original mission in Gounghin; and a small chapel is located near the Sankre ra-le between Dapoya II and Bilibambili. These four churches are pastored by the following ministers: one African and one French pastor serve the Protestant Temple, one African pastor is at the church in Sabin, one African at Sankre ra-le, and one itinerant African pastor at the church in Gounghin. Most of the white missionaries in Ouagadougou are engaged in such technical services as printing and selling books.

The Protestants of the Assemblies of God were the first missionaries in town to Africanize the liturgy and ceremonies of their church. As early as February 1934, their general council voted the adoption of "Indigenous Church Principles." These stipulated among other things, that each Assembly should choose its own African pastor and take care of its own affairs, and that the Africans could use tambourines, drums, and other instruments in the church. Nevertheless, until 1955 there were no African pastors in Ouagadougou, because as the missionaries insist, there were no qualified Africans at that time. When political changes began to take place in Africa, the Protestants modified their policy. They appointed African pastors and gave them partial control of the church. By 1964, there were some 30 African pastors in the Assemblies of God in Upper Volta.

The African President of the Assemblies of God is assisted by white missionaries serving as assistant president, secretary, and treasurer. Theoretically, the Africans control their

---

[33]"Recensement Démographique . . . ," p. 35.

churches, even those in Ouagadougou, and the missionaries can do nothing in the churches without the consent of the African pastors. Actually, there is little change in the basic relationships between the African president and the missionaries. In contrast to the leaders of the Catholic church (and the administration where Africans have taken over both the trappings of power and the perquisites of it), the missionaries still live in the main mission complex and are still fairly well separated from their, now African, colleagues. Nor do many of the African Protestants believe that they now control the church. One of the reasons given by the defectors from the Assemblies of God was that, contrary to the rules of the church, they did not have the right to elect their own pastor.

The missionaries of the Assemblies of God in Ouagadougou are "fundamentalist" Protestant Christians, and they have introduced this creed to their converts. Normally prayers are in Moré and are often said individually. A fundamental part of the service is Bible reading and exposition with the accompanying exhortations to God. The Africans have learned this style from the missionaries and use it to full advantage. Hymns are sung to the accompaniment of drums, tambourines, a base viol, and an accordian. Like the Catholics, the Protestants segregate men from women but, in contrast to them, even young educated couples seldom sit together. Like the Catholics also, the Protestants have a Sunday morning service for the French-speaking community which Europeans are especially encouraged to attend. However, owing to the relative absence of Africans at these services, a number of European Protestant families in Ouagadougou have avoided attending what they consider to be mono-racial church services.

The Protestant church is now firmly established in Ouagadougou. But the church has already had one important schism, and, as this has happened once, there is no reason why it might not happen again. The government asked one missionary to leave because he threatened damnation to merchants who would not support the church; and during one crisis, some of the oldest African church members requested the resignation and departure of a missionary family which had spent close to thirty years among them. The missionaries are understandably somewhat disturbed by these events. Many of the younger ones appear to be paying more attention to running a printing and book shop for religious works than in proselytizing. It is only a matter of time before Africans take over the missionary duties and continue the spiritual work of the church.

Eglise Apostolique

The *Eglise Apostolique de la République Voltaique* has many of the characteristics of the classic "separatist" church.[34] As is common with such churches, its origin or separation from the Assemblies of God was accompanied by charges and countercharges of evil, righteousness, adultery, polygyny, theft, ambition, cowardice, political chicanery, and threats of violence. It is perhaps irrelevant to speculate whether the charges are correct or false; the important thing is to see these charges against the background of a conflict which could not be resolved within the structure of the Assemblies of God mission.

According to the mission, the trouble began about 1955 when, in direct violation of church rules, several of the converts in the church took plural wives. Their African brethren initially hid this breach of faith from the missionaries, but when the missionaries found out, they decided that the "sinners" should be punished. The second conflict arose when one catechist, whose delinquency resulted in frequent transfers, came to Ouagadougou and borrowed money both from missionaries and converts. This man allegedly took the money to a "charlatan" in Nobéré who had promised to quadruple it, but who swindled him by giving false money in return. In an attempt to retrieve the money, the dupe sought help from both the police and the mission; when unsuccessful, he joined the polygynists in their hostility to the missionaries. Later he, too, took several wives, was barred from receiving the Lord's Supper, and was dismissed as a catechist.

The situation finally reached a climax in 1958 when the "rebels" took advantage of a new policy granting them the power to decide the relationship between the missionaries and the local church, and decided to expel a veteran missionary of the church. This American was allegedly even "roughed up" by the "sinners" when he attempted to enter the church. The

---

[34]Cf. B. G. M. Sundkler, *Bantu Prophets in South Africa* (London: Oxford University Press, 1961).

missionaries called the police and the rebels were taken to the Commissariat where they were jailed. When they were released, they attempted to reenter the church but were barred and threatened with jail. They accused the president of the Assemblies of God of not being a *Moaga* (pl. *Mossi*) but a *Boussanga* (pl. *Boussansé*) and suggested that he should go back to Tengkodogo and leave the Ouagadougou church in Mossi hands. The president convoked all the pastors and missionaries who vetoed the expulsion of the missionary and voted to suspend the rebels from the church.

Many of the rebels admit that some of the oldest converts had taken plural wives; but all of them insist that polygyny was not the cause for the split. The rebels charged the pastors with many cases of misconduct. They claimed that an African pastor had impregnated three young girls who had been placed under his care in his home and had then sent them out of town. Second, they charged that this same African pastor had taken money from the collection basket on several occasions and when queried about it had declared that he had visitors at home and needed money to take care of them. The rebels further asserted that when they notified the American missionaries of these events, the latter took no action against the pilferer. Finally, the rebels charged that when the Ouagadougou congregation elected a pastor for the Temple in 1959, the American missionaries vetoed its candidate in favor of their own. Some of the church members refused to accept the "imposed" pastor and were asked to leave the church, but they refused to do so. It was this decision, they said, that led the missionaries and their "stooges" to call the police and attempt to jail the dissidents. The police allegedly found the rebels innocent of any crime and released them. The rebels returned to the church the next Sunday and were questioned about their desires and intentions and then told to leave. Thereupon they tried their best to effect a reconciliation with the church, including requesting the good offices of Mogho Naba Kougri. However, the missionaries and their followers refused to readmit them and told them to go and seek a separate church.

When comparing the testimony of both groups of Protestants, it becomes quite obvious that a number of basic conflicts existed within the Assemblies of God mission. It is clear that during the political changes that were taking place in

Ouagadougou in 1956, the Protestants like other Voltaic Christians were anxious to take over their church. They were, however, not aware of the subtleties of "decolonization" and became frustrated when they were not permitted to control the affairs of the church. The "Mossi" element in the Ouagadougou church also wanted the presidency for themselves and were resentful when the position went to a "Boussanga." The missionaries appeared to have been caught in a dilemma. The "Boussanga" was not only well qualified for the job, but he had good political as well as social relations with many politicians in the town. The missionaries were quite anxious about the changing political climate and felt that the interest of the church could be best served by supporting the "Boussanga." This act alienated the oldest Mossi converts.

Having been dismissed from the Assemblies of God, the dissident Protestants were faced with the problem of finding another religious affiliation. "We could not go back to killing chickens," one man declared. By this he meant that the rebels had no intention of returning to the traditional religion, but how they arrived at the decision to affiliate with the Eglise Apostolique is not completely clear. One spokesman declared that the group had discussed affiliating with the Presbyterians, Methodists, and other Protestant bodies, but finally decided to return to the "primeval Church of Christ, the Church of the Apostles which had come down directly from Christ when he left." They had apparently learned about the Eglise Apostolique in 1957, when a white American pastor, who claimed to be associated with that church in Ghana, visited the Assemblies of God in Ouagadougou. This visitor reportedly "prayed and worked miracles, something that the missionaries who had spent 30 to 40 years in the country had been unable to do." The missionaries purportedly discouraged him from remaining in Ouagadougou, but he so impressed the Africans that when the dissident element had to find a new affiliation, they remembered the visitor and his church. Once the decision had been made to seek out the Eglise Apostolique, a mission went to Ghana to seek affiliation with that body, with the proviso that the Ghanaians "should not interfere in the internal affairs of the Upper Volta Church." The Ghanaians agreed to this and the Ouagadougou group joined the Apostolic Church.

The headquarters church of the Eglise Apostolique is in Gounghin, about 1 kilometer from the original mission of

341

the Assemblies of God. The members had wanted to build a church in the center of town, but owing to the cost of land and lack of financial aid, they used a piece of land donated by a member in Goughin. The building, constructed of *banco* and covered with sheets of galvanized iron, is the center for the 350 members of the church in Ouagadougou. They have another chapel in Ouidi ward, and about twelve churches and chapels throughout the country.

The Eglise Apostolique has a written constitution which spells out in detail, "Ce que nous croyons et ce que nous pratiquons" (what we believe in and what we practice). The dogma of the church include: belief in the Bible and in the existence of a single God; belief in the depraved nature of man who can only be saved by grace; and belief in the Saviour, baptism, holy communion, faith healing, and so on. The table of organization of the church includes such statuses and roles as ministers, apostles, prophets, evangelists, pastors, and doctors; and it gives the qualifications which persons must have to be "admitted" to these offices. The constitution also provides rules for marriage, inheritance, discipline, meetings and assemblies, control of property, finances, and councils, and describes the essential characteristics of the "Christian life."[35]

Despite the existence of a formal doctrine and constitution, the religious behavior of the members of the Eglise Apostolique does not differ greatly from that of the members of the Assemblies of God. The women are segregated from the men, the music and songs are the same, and, most interesting of all, the African preachers affect the mannerisms, tone, and accents of American missionaries when delivering sermons in Moré. The church also does not have the categories of ministers previewed in the constitution. The explanation given for this is that the church is young and has not yet produced these ministerial types. The members hope that these offices will be filled in the future, and that the church will be able to put its constitution into practice. The members of the church have no desire to return to "African" social and religious practices. The hope is that the church will enable its members to "go forward" and not "backward."

It is difficult to determine what the future holds for this

[35]"La Constitution," *Eglise Apostolique du Togo, du Dahomey et de la République Voltaique* (Ouagadougou, Haute-Volta [archives of the author]).

separatist church. The government has officially recognized it, but its leaders, unlike those of the Assemblies of God, are seldom invited to official functions. These Protestants have no desire to return to the Assemblies of God since they maintain that they are the devout Protestants in town. Yet, they feel no antagonism toward the American missionaries. The Africans believe that the missionaries were duped and that they refrained from criticizing the frailties of local Christians for fear of harming the mission and its church.

Traditional Religion

It is difficult to obtain much specific data either about the beliefs or the practices of those people in Ouagadougou who follow the traditional African religions. The reason, of course, is that in contrast to the Moslems and Christians, the traditionalists who come to the town do not build any structures, imposing or otherwise; nor do they have complex religious institutions.[36] Moreover, those elders who are normally responsible for the traditional religious rituals and ceremonies among the Mossi and other Voltaic groups are relatively few in number. The young people who migrate to town are neither knowledgeable about, nor responsible for, the traditional religious observances. The chances are that they will never become responsible for them, since they will either convert to Islam or to Christianity and be forbidden by their Imams, pastors, or priests to maintain their ancient religions.

The most formal of the traditional religious rituals still found among the people of Ouagadougou are the *Basgha* ceremonies of the Mogho Naba and the ward chiefs. These rituals[37] do not attract much attention and are performed in private by the Mogho Naba and chiefs, who are now nominally Moslem or Christian. Some civil servants from royal lineages do return to their districts for the *Basgha* of their ancestors, but it is difficult to determine whether these visits indicate family solidarity or lingering belief in the traditional religion.

The Ouagadougou Naba and the Ouagadougou Tengsoba

[36]Pierre Ilboudou, *Contribution a L'Histoire Réligieuse du Peuple Mossi de Haute Volta.* Thèse de Doctorat de 3ème Cycle (Paris, 1970).
[37]Skinner, 1964b, pp. 126ff.

still make sacrifices at the various earth shrines about the capital, such as the presowing rituals at the earth shrine, *Kadyogo,* a pond on the northern edge of town. When a new Mogho Naba is installed, the *tengsobadamba* in the various quarters perform rituals at their *tengkouga* in the name of the new ruler. For example, sacrifices were made at the large *baobab* tree (a *tengkougrê*) in Paspanga quarter in supplication for the health and "force" of both Mogho Naba Sagha II and the present Mogho Naba Kougri. This latter ruler also still observes the daily rituals (the *Wend'pous yan* at daybreak and the *Kwaga Basgha* at sunset) traditionally considered necessary to preserve the *nam* of the ruler and the integrity of the country. His conversion to Islam has not stopped the performance of the traditional religious ceremonies associated with royal power.

There is a good deal of inferential evidence that a considerable number of persons in Ouagadougou, besides those listed as *Animistes* (*Wend'pous neba*) in the census, have retained belief in the traditional systems. Note was made that many infants visiting the health center wear some form of amulet around their necks, arms, wrists, waists, or ankles. These amulets are composed of all sorts of organic and inorganic matter: the teeth and claws of animals; sachets made of leather possibly containing written verses or special powders of stones; pieces of metal shaped in the form of a cross or medal; rings composed of several different metals; and glass beads of various sorts. Some male infants carry pieces of iron (a custom frequently encountered in rural Mossi areas) because the mothers are told by a *barga* (diviner) that the child needs this proof of manhood if he is to live. But the most important characteristic of the childrens' amulets is that they are often mixed up indiscriminately. It is not uncommon to encounter a combination of a Christian cross and an iron ring; or a Moslem sachet and an animal tooth; or a St. Christopher's medal and an iron bracelet. Both the mothers of the children and the social aides affirm that these amulets are given to the children to protect them from normal physical illnesses as well as those supernaturally induced. The social aides feel that since these amulets do no harm to the children, it is folly to insist that the mothers remove them.

Charms of various kinds are found in many Ouagadougou houses. Small bundles of organic matter are often placed above the door of the entrance hall. The presence of these charms does not indicate whether the occupants are Christians, Moslems, or *Wend'pous neba*. Perhaps this is because these entrance halls are frequented by people of all religious beliefs and can be contaminated by anyone. A moot point is whether the pictures of Saints and of the Virgin at the entrances of Catholic houses are charms in the traditional sense or the adoption of a new European trait. It is, however, considered good for Catholics to have these religious objects in their homes, and it is believed that their existence places the houses under supernatural protection.

A constant reminder of the persistence of traditional beliefs among the Ouagadougou population is the presence of oblatory objects at crossroads and at ant hills around the town. Traditionally, the Mossi and other Voltaic groups have made oblations and sacrifices at crossroads to misdirect evil away from villages, and at ant hills in the hope that the ants would take messages to the ancestors. At one crossroad in Ouagadougou, a traditional offering was seen on an ant hill at the foot of a "stop" sign. The offering consisted of bundles of red sorghum, sorghum cakes, cowries, and pieces of local cloth. Undoubtedly they had been placed there by a person who wanted help from the ancestors or from spirits of the area.

The use of Moslem holy men to provide supernatural aid for traditionalists as well as Moslems is well known by the people of Ouagadougou. There is little any official in town can do to prevent *Wend'pous neba* from buying charms from Moslems, getting remedies from them, or paying them to read passages of the Koran believed to bring surcease from illnesses of the body and of the mind. These practices are made more difficult to modify because while many intellectuals and officials bemoan the existence of "charlatans" exploiting the "credulous," they believe that some of the traditional medicines and magico-medical practices are efficacious. For example, in 1964, the alleged ability of a *marabout* from Dori to cure cases of partial blindness created so much excitement in town that doctors at the hospital sought to have him effect cures in the hospital. They were quite aware that he would refuse to reveal the secrets of his remedies for fear that these might lose their efficacy, but they were resigned to permitting him to try to cure persons found to be incurable with Western medicines. The unstated belief here was that some traditional

religico-magical-medicinal practices and lore might cure
psychosomatic diseases and even purely somatic illnesses of
Africans.

A growing number of persons in Ouagadougou now feel secure enough to reject all religions, foreign and indigenous.
Some 1.5 per cent of those questioned about religious beliefs in 1962 denied religious affiliations or considered themselves "free-thinkers." Many educated persons cannot accept
either the traditional religion or the newer universalistic
ones. One characteristic of the educated youth in Ouagadougou is their relative lack of interest in Christianity or Islam.
When questioned about this, students are wont to respond that
either they have no time for the "clergy" or for the *marabout*
or that in time all religions, including traditional ones, will
disappear. Further discussion often reveals that the respondents believe that neither Christianity nor Islam is superior to
their ancestral religion as far as man's relationship to the supernatural is concerned.

Despite a growing disenchantment with nontraditional religions among some people in Ouagadougou, there is no move
on either the part of free-thinkers or "others" to develop a
neo-African religion. One reason is that educated people
still consider the most important ritual of Voltaic religions,
the annual sacrifice of animals, to be extremely barbaric or
"uncivilized." It will be recalled that the group of Protestants
who separated from the Assemblies of God searched about for
another modern religion because as their spokesman said, they
could not "go back to killing chickens." Unless this young
man's father was dead, he could not have sacrificed chickens to
his ancestors in any case. These sacrifices were communal
acts made in the name of the family, whereas the more modern
religions involve the individual with the supernatural. The
free-thinkers in Ouagadougou, by their rejection of all religions, can and do avoid the conflict of choosing foreign religions above ancestral ones. To accept foreign religions would
be to challenge one's Africaness, and to accept the traditional
religion would be to challenge one's modernity.

An important characteristic of the Ouagadougou people is
their religious tolerance. For many of them, membership in
one religion as contrasted with another is an accident of history or situation or a pragmatic act. Catholic household heads
do excuse or rationalize the religious differences of relatives

in the interest of family solidarity at Christmas time. Non-Christians do give their children Catholic names with the hope that they will be given one of the limited number of places in the parochial schools. In most instances where townspeople cited religious differences as the basis for conflict, the issue turned out to be really one of social distinctions. The devout Moslem who founded a "secular" society to break the hold of Catholics on public education did so to provide access of more people to superior social and economic positions.

In conclusion, then, we find that both Islam and Christianity helped the people of Ouagadougou enlarge their intellectual and economic horizons. Moslem traders not only brought Islam, but served as councilors of the Mogho Nanamsé, especially in dealing with outsiders, and of course furnished revenue for the Ouagadougou population. Nevertheless, the Mossi rulers prevented Islam from spreading among the town's population. Because Catholicism appeared in the wake of the French conquerors, it had a greater impact on the people of Ouagadougou. It provided one of the avenues by which the town's inhabitants could get the education so necessary to gain a footing in the administrative and commercial institutions of the colonial power. Modern education laid the basis for the economic and social mobility of the local people and gave them the capability to displace the foreigners. Religion in contemporary Ouagadougou is severing many of its connections with colonial-related institutions and is in the process of developing a new character of its own. It is forced to do so if it would preserve its function as mediator between man and the supernatural in the interest of the relationship between man and man. Christianity, and to a lesser extent Islam, has had to come to grips with the cultural assertiveness of the people of Ouagadougou who in the hope of regaining spiritual independence are beginning to reevaluate their traditional beliefs.

CHAPTER X

Law Enforcement

Law enforcement in Ouagadougou is affected by a complex of factors such as the incompatibility between traditional law and European codes; the immigrant population's lack of familiarity with urban statutes; and the growth of new attitudes among the townspeople toward property, kinsmen, affines, and both traditional and modern political authorities. From all reports, the people of precolonial Ouagadougou were relatively law-abiding.[1] The *kamboinsé* (guards) protected the royal persons and the palace-complex, while officials such as the Samandin Naba and Kamsaogho Naba maintained order within Na'Tenga. The provincial ministers, courtiers, and stranger chiefs and headmen who lived in the quarters of Ouagadougou settled litigations among their people, subject only to judicial review by the Baloum Naba,[2] palace chamberlain, who, when circumstances warranted, took the cases to the Mogho Naba.

These traditional police and judicial practices were modified during the colonial period when the French took ultimate responsibility for security within the town. But the traditional system, though truncated, was not suppressed. It continues to function even now that Ouagadougou has several types of police and an elaborate court system. In fact, it is only when the traditional judicial techniques break down or are not utilized that the police are notified that civil and criminal problems exist, and the municipal or state courts take charge of the problems. Of course, the municipality and the state do intervene to maintain law and order in the town when these governmental systems feel that their ordinances and laws have

[1] Delobson, *The Empire of the Mogho-Naba,* p. 14.
[2] There is controversy as to whether the Samandin Naba or the Baloum Naba should properly be regarded as the traditional "Mayor" of Ouagadougou. The Samandin Naba was charged with protecting Na'Tenga, but the Baloum Naba was in charge of strangers. In time, the role of the Baloum Naba evolved, especially as a large number of strangers arrived in the town. Because of this, the French began to consider the Baloum Naba the "traditional" Mayor, but the Mossi declare that this is a distortion of their traditional political system.

been violated. Nevertheless, any analysis of the maintenance of law and order in the town must take into consideration the presence and function of several types of order-maintaining mechanisms, their interrelationships, their elements of co-operation, and their occasional conflicts.

The official agencies of law enforcement in Ouagadougou are a heritage of the French colonial system. The national army, while an instrument of the Republic and organized for the protection of the state against outsiders, still occupies the same quarters it has occupied since the conquest and has continued to reflect the colonial tradition that the army should also protect the "state" from its own subjects. Thus when, in 1958, the Mogho Naba and his cohorts tried to seize power and surrounded the National Assembly, the army forced them to retire.[3] And again, in January 1966, when rioting inhabitants of Ouagadougou, attempting to overthrow the national government, shouted, "The army to power!" that army heeded the call and seized power in the "name of the people."

Other law enforcement agencies of the national government within Ouagadougou are La Garde Républicaine, Le Gendarmerie Nationale, and La Compagnie Nationale Républicaine de Sécurité (C.N.R.S.). These three groups have the task of guarding the internal security of the state, and, like the national army, are under the control of the state. However, since the state, through its Minister of the Interior, is the "tutor" or "guardian" of the municipality, the state can and does use these bodies to maintain law and order within the town. The Municipality of Ouagadougou has its own police agencies: La Police Municipale (including its secret branches) and the Garde Champêtre. The former is a regular police force charged with policing the town, while the latter is a group charged with aiding the police, supervising market places, serving summonses, and distributing ordinances around town.

The activities of the municipal police of Ouagadougou are similar to those of police in any modern town. They protect the populace from illegal acts and ensure obedience to municipal laws and ordinances. However, the problems of the police of Ouagadougou are different from those of police in many other countries since, in many cases, pleas of ignorance of the

[3]Skinner, 1964b, pp. 199–201.

law are not rationalizations for disobeying the law but reflect a true *ignorance* of the *law*. The reason is that many of the people who run afoul of the municipal laws of Ouagadougou are recent immigrants into the town and do not know the laws. Unfortunately, ignorance of the laws even extends to many persons born in Ouagadougou because the laws often stem from socio-cultural considerations which are foreign to many of them. For example, the inhabitants of the town as well as rural visitors know that fighting is against the law and that they could be apprehended and jailed for so doing. People also know that stealing is a crime and that they can be punished for it. Most people, even those from rural areas, know that bicycles must be licensed or the user could be fined, since this ordinance also holds in the rural areas. However, people must live in the town for a long time before they become aware of the meaning of "Stop," *Sens-unique,* and of those red and green traffic lights (see Table XXXV). Rural

TABLE XXXV. **Traffic Violations in Ouagadougou**
(August 10–September 3, 1964)

Type of Vehicle	Type of Violation	Number
Automobile	No driver's permit	38
	Speeding	17
	Excessive horn-blowing	15
	Faulty driver's permit	6
	Illegal parking	4
	Defective red lights	3
	Lack of vehicle registration	2
	Violation of "One-Way" regulations	2
	Failure to Signal	2
	Overloaded vehicle	4
	Defective lights	1
	Failure to yield right of way	1
Bicycle	Riding without lights	186
	Violation of "One-Way" regulations or riding on left	154
	No vehicle license	88
	Transporting persons	50
	Faulty or no brakes	7
	Dangerous riding	3
	Miscellaneous violations	41
	TOTAL	624

SOURCE: Les Services du Commissariat de Police de la Ville de Ouagadougou.

people arrested for riding bicycles without lights react with incredulity to the "stupidity" of urbanites who would insist that lights be used when the streets are lighted.

"Moving" traffic violations are so common in Ouagadougou that whenever the police enforce the laws, they have to bring large trucks to haul away the hundreds of bicycles seized from violators. True, some persons are aware of the signs and deliberately break the law. But the plight of those violators who truly did not "perceive" the signs and who did not know that such things existed can be seen by anyone who takes the time to stand near the police making arrests. The police, for their part, readily admit, and often with some wry condescension, that *le pauvre type* (the poor fellow) did not understand what the sign was all about. They also point out that they, too, are caught in a dilemma. They must fill the summons book they are given or face censure from the Commissioner of Police.

Another problem with which the police of Ouagadougou have to deal, and one, which though commonly encountered in all countries, takes on a slightly different aspect here, is juvenile delinquency or, more correctly, the "problem of wayward youth." Hundreds of youngsters, ranging in age from seven to sixteen, throng the streets and market places seeking some way of earning money by performing such tasks as carrying baskets and bundles for housewives out shopping; transporting merchandise and beer pots to and from the markets or other establishments; washing dishes in the small foodshops around town; shining shoes; and running errands. Inevitably many of these youngsters steal from their employers, some because they are dishonest and others out of revenge for being exploited by employers who do not pay the promised wages. When this occurs, the police are summoned and the youngsters are arrested. The police arrest other youngsters for loitering around the markets or other places; for visiting places of entertainment after the children's curfew hour; for gambling in vacant lots or empty buildings; and for fighting.

There are approximately 20 to 25 juvenile gangs (or "bands" as they are called by social workers) in Ouagadougou[4] which present a problem for the police and the municipality. These gangs first appeared about twelve years ago,

[4]Hochet, *passim.*

351

having been introduced by youngsters who had been labor migrants to the Ivory Coast. The gangs have a structure, a hierarchy, and are well disciplined.

The typical gang has about 4 to 6 members varying in age from ten to sixteen years. The boys do not necessarily live together—except when they sleep together in the markets or in a park at night—but have regular meeting places before and after their operations. New members for the gang are mostly recruited from among boys who migrate to town and who are observed by gang members for several days wandering around the streets or markets looking for work, shelter, and food. The members of the gang establish contact with the new migrants, help them get something to eat, a place to stay, and gradually incorporate them into the gang.

Each juvenile gang in Ouagadougou has its chief or leader, popularly called, *Docteur en droit* by his fellows because of his long experience and exceptional qualities. A boy becomes leader because of his proven intelligence and his skill in organizing the activities of the group. Most of the gang leaders known to the police are also boys who had been former students, and almost all of them speak some French. The leaders are responsible for assigning the various roles to gang members, for arranging the program of activities, for organizing large operations, and for directing the more difficult ones. This means that each leader continues to work with the members of his gang and has no right to the spoils unless he takes part in the operations. Leaders are, however, seldom caught by the police because they take care to be much better dressed than the ordinary gang members. They are aware that the police are disinclined to apprehend well-dressed persons who are usually thought to have high status. The leaders also remain relatively unknown to the police because they do not normally participate in such ordinary activities of the gang members as playing soccer with tennis balls or simply sitting around talking.

Although the leader is primarily responsible for maintaining discipline within the gang, he expects the members to cooperate by reporting any lapse in discipline. Indeed, one of the primary rules for gang members is that they should never, under any circumstances, even when clouted by the police, divulge the names of their comrades. Second, gang members should never divulge the methods by which things are stolen, nor should they reveal the secret names given to conventional objects or goods. Third, gang members are enjoined never to disclose where they meet, the nature of their projects and operations, the hiding places of stolen goods, and the names of the "fences." Any lapse of discipline—characterized by such acts as attempting to jeopardize an operation because of anger about assigned tasks, quarreling about the distribution of the loot, being unsociable by fighting members of the gang or creating disturbances with them, and revealing gang secrets— is severely punished. Punishments include beatings, suspension from the group, and even denouncement to the police which may result in the troublemaker being jailed and thereby eliminated from the group. So strict is the discipline in the gangs, and so fearful are expelled members that successful police raids on the gangs might be attributed to them, that only former gang leaders, now grown and immune from the sanctions of youngsters, furnish information about the gangs.

The success of many delinquent gangs in Ouagadougou is due to the proper training and socialization of youngsters by older gang members. Each gang has its own slang or argot which is a mixture of, or transformation of, either French or Moré to which are added certain foreign words, signs, and gestures. The names of articles most frequently stolen are also disguised. For example, a bicycle pump (an object which can never be left on a bicycle without it being stolen) is called, *dayoko* (literally, *da,* to sell and *yoko,* hollow). However, a bicycle dynamo is called a *phare,* and a razor blade is called *merchandise.* A wallet, one of the principal objects stolen, is often called *bidon* (tin container), *dynamite,* or *diligence* (an obvious pun on the word, "diligence"). A brief case or saddle bag (usually for carrying money) is called *dynamite bernard* (a large, St. Bernard dog wallet), and the money contained in a wallet is called *net.*

New gang members are taught, by means of practice and imitation, the methods and procedures for stealing specific objects. They are also taught how to pass the stolen object rapidly from one person to another and how to slip behind an innocent individual, a tree, a hut, or a shop. The art of pickpocketing is carefully taught, and neophytes are shown how to use their fingers to take out wallets and how to use a razor blade to cut out a pocket. This latter technique is usually the specialty of the *Docteurs en droit.* Apprentices also learn how to steer a victim by walking in front of him or at his side to slow him down, and how, when a victim, realizing that his pocket has been picked, attempts to run down the thief, to shout the word *caler* so that other gang members can either trip the victim or prevent him from finding the thief by blocking his way. Of course, during such an emergency, the rule is to pass the money or wallet very quickly from member to member so that if the thief is apprehended, the stolen goods are never found upon him. Neophytes are often taught signs by which to set up victims for the pickpocket operation. For example, the sign made by putting the index finger at the left or right side of the collar indicates that the future victim is advancing toward the pickpocket either from the left or the right. This gesture also means that the pickpocket may operate without fear. On the other hand, raising the collar means that there is danger and the thief must be careful; and reversing the shirt means that gang members should leave the area because it is dangerous. Finally, new gang members are taught how, in the case of arrest, to talk rapidly and with conviction so as to convince the police and the public of their innocence.

Members of robber gangs find Ouagadougou a fairly fertile field of operations. True, the police are there, but so are vast numbers of people new to the town and unsophisticated in urban behavior. Thus the women and, sometimes men who journey to the Ouagadougou markets to sell their products and carelessly expose their receipts are robbed. People who are traveling through the town and take the opportunity to shop at the markets or at the European stores are easy marks for the skilled pickpocket. Other travelers at the Auto Gare or train station who fall asleep while waiting for transport wake up to find their wallets and money bags stolen. But even the educated Africans and resident Europeans are not immune. These people have their pockets picked while shopping in the Monoprix, in the markets, or while waiting in line to buy cinema tickets. African and European women who hire young boys to carry their merchandise often discover, too late, that their porters have decamped with their bags. In other words, the members of the gangs are prepared to take risks and advantage of persons whose naïveté or ignorance of town life make them easy victims.

The Ouagadougou police affirm—and this was confirmed

independently—that there is a great amount of cooperation and solidarity between the gangs in the town. There is little or no intergang fighting for such things as prestige, reputation, or control over territories. Nor are the gangs interested, as gangs, in girls or in having female auxiliaries. There is the understanding that the places where certain gangs usually work should be left to them. (Again, shoeshine boys and charioteers have territories which are respected, but there is little actual fighting to maintain territorial integrity.) So far, Ouagadougou has not experienced serious gang wars. The attitude among the boys appears to be that a gang is for work and that their job is a difficult one because they risk their health and their lives. Therefore, gangs believe that it is important to cooperate with other gangs when they can and in areas where their members can be most successful.

There are several so-called "services" or "areas of operation" divided among the gangs of Ouagadougou: a) Market Service, where 7 to 10 gangs operate; b) Cinema Service, where about 30 boys from different gangs operate as individuals; c) Dance Halls Service, also individuals; d) Automobile Service, given to inexperienced gang members who are still timid but who wreak havoc among those chauffeurs who leave their brief cases, flashlights, extra gasoline cans, or any other valuables in open or closed automobiles around town; e) Shop and Store Service, usually individuals and reserved to the older and more expert boys, called *balayeurs* (sweepers); f) Relay Service, consigned to younger members who rent bicycles and ride from market to market to steal goods; and g) Railroad Service, consisting of several experienced gangs who ride different trains between Abidjan, Bobo-Dioulasso, and Ouagadougou. This operation, which involves capital outlay for tickets, is the most lucrative but not the most dangerous. There are no specific "services" covering receptions, parades, or other public gatherings, but wherever many people are gathered in Ouagadougou, gangs are sure to operate. However, the gangs rarely engage in breaking and entering homes or businesses during the night.

There is some evidence that the gangs have an organization for selling their stolen goods. Gang leaders establish verbal accords with merchants and market sellers, usually said to be Yoruba and Lebanese, who sell products brought to them. These goods are taken to the merchants every morning before

355

the opening of business. Normally there is no bargaining since the prices of the articles have been fixed beforehand, and the merchant only ascertains the amount of goods delivered. In fact, the merchant is almost obligated to accept the stolen merchandise if he wants to continue doing business in the market. In the event that the merchant refuses to pay the price agreed upon, the gangs may destroy his stall during the night, if he works in the market, or steal his merchandise from the stands. A gang may even subject a merchant to bodily attack. This, however, brings police action which reveals all aspects of the affair. Moreover, a merchant who tries to cheat a gang finds himself boycotted by other gangs and is so harassed by them that he is unable to do business in the market unless, of course, he is reconciled with the injured gang.

Besides dealing with gangs, the police of Ouagadougou have their share of petty thievery, shoplifting, fraud, personal injuries, and a host of other torts and crimes.

Courts and Litigation

There are several judicial systems in Ouagadougou and they, like the systems of maintaining law and order, are a heritage of the town's past. The Mossi traditional courts still exist, as do the Customary Courts introduced during the colonial period to preside over domestic and some civil cases among Africans. The French colonial court system survives, but it is now modified and supplemented by many French-type legal institutions introduced since independence.

One result of juridical profuseness in Ouagadougou is that people have many tribunals from which to choose when seeking redress for wrongs: the traditional ones, the municipal ones, and those established by the state. Nevertheless, in the absence of a clear knowledge of which system to choose, and also because the court systems themselves are not well articulated, people do have difficulties settling their lawsuits and resolving their problems.[5] Thus, many a man whose wife runs away or whose son or daughter is disrespectful or refuses to support him goes to the Commissariat de Police for redress.

[5]Cf. A. L. Epstein, "Some Aspects of the Conflict of Law and Urban Courts in Northern Rhodesia," *Human Problems in British Central Africa* (*Rhodes-Livingstone Journal*), XII, Manchester University Press, 1951, pp. 28–40.

The chances are, however, that he may be ridiculed by the police and chased away or, at best, told to go to the Customary Court at the Mayor's office. Similarly, if a man wounds his wife during a quarrel and believes that this case should be taken to the Town Hall, he is told to go to the Commissariat de Police where he may be locked up until the case is heard by a state court. Even the state courts may not be helpful to citizens with specific types of litigation since, as of 1964, numerous judicial institutions intended for use in the courts had not yet been introduced.

The traditional courts at the compounds of chiefs and headmen still play an important role in helping the people of Ouagadougou resolve some of their problems. Many people, especially those cultivators who live in Gounghin, Ouidi, Larhalle, Tiedpalogho, Zoghona, and Tampouy, take their marital and other domestic problems to the chiefs and headmen for reconciliation. Even quarrels and fights (during which people are stabbed) are often "illegally" taken to these men for adjudication. Appeals from the "judgments" (now most often euphemistically called "suggestions") of the chiefs and headmen are taken to other chiefs, to the Mogho Naba, and even to his wife for settlement. It is normally only when criminal acts or civil disputes are not settled by the traditional authorities that the police intervene and formal courts are seized with the responsibility of judging them.

The lowest official court in Ouagadougou is the Tribunal de Premier Degré du Droit Local or, more popularly, the Tribunal Coutumier (Customary Court). This court has competence to judge most cases of domestic disputes and simple litigation between townspeople, provided that the amount of property and damages involved is no greater than 15,000 C.F.A., or $60.00. Cases dealing with sums in excess of this amount should normally go up to the next judicial level.

The Customary Court meets twice weekly in the Town Hall: on Tuesdays it hears litigations and on Thursdays it passes judgments on applications for supplementary certificates for civil statuses. For purposes of litigation, the court has a president (at present a retired Mossi civil servant, but formerly the Ouidi Naba, a provincial governor) and twelve assessors drawn from among the major ethnic groups in the town. In 1964, these included eight Mossi, one Hausa, one Dioula, and one Boussanga. All of these men were appointed by the Mu-

357

nicipal Council and confirmed in office by the Minister of the Interior. In addition to these officials, there is a secretary whose job it is to record the testimony offered and to furnish the necessary documents concerning the civil status of the litigants.

The atmosphere of this lower court is fairly informal. The litigants to disputes arrive between 7:30 and 8:00 in the morning on the day their cases are to be tried; the president and his assessors arrive at 8:00 A.M. Due to the lack of room in the court, the disputants and their witnesses have to wait outside until their cases are called. Then they are summoned to the courtroom by a *garde champêtre* who seats them according to the number of places available. The main parties to the dispute are always seated. When husbands and wives are parties to the dispute, they are always seated together. This often disturbs the couples, especially when they do not wish reconciliation.

Normally the trial begins with the president asking the secretary of the court to read a summary of the litigation. He then asks the complainant to state his case. During this recital, either the secretary, the president, or one of his assessors may ask for clarification of the testimony. They may also ask for corroboration from witnesses and may even challenge the veracity of the litigant, especially if contradictory evidence is given. Under no circumstances does the president permit the interruption of testimony from the litigants or witnesses, and, in the event that those persons listening to the case interrupt the proceedings either by laughter or any other noise, they are chased away from the windows and doors by a guard who might even thrash them in the process. Similarly, if anyone in the room shows disrespect to the court, by boisterousness, sloppy posture, or by speaking out of turn, he is reprimanded by the officials there and may be slapped or expelled by either the guard or the police.

After the complainant and his witnesses have been heard, the defendant and his witnesses are called to testify and he, or they, may be subjected to cross-examination from the court officials. Confrontations between litigants frequently take place when the court officials ask for the clarification of some point of fact or testimony. However, if the litigants get too boisterous, they may be manhandled by the police and guards and either expelled or forced to keep quiet. Finally, the president and the assessors confer secretly. They may ask further questions relevant to points at issue, or they simply declare their verdict, informing the litigants of their right to appeal.

An important characteristic of the Customary Court of the First Degree is that the judges make every attempt to use assessors from the ethnic group of the litigants. Thus, on several occasions, when there were no assessors on the board who belonged to the ethnic group of the litigants, or when the particular ethnic assessors for the litigants were absent, the cases were postponed. When there are no authorized assessors from the litigants' ethnic group, the president is authorized to call upon the elders of the groups in question for aid in judging the case. Of greater interest is that once, when non-Mossi but Moré-speaking litigants wished to have their cases heard by Mossi assessors, the president refused to permit them to do so. He declared that while the litigants may have lived among Mossi all their lives and may have been acculturated to Mossi ways, they were socially members of their ethnic group and their ethnic assessors should hear their cases. Although this appears quite logical, there was some indication of "feather-bedding." One suspected that the assessors were striving to maintain jobs which might become supernumerary if all litigants spoke Moré. This suspicion is supported by the fact that, except for non-Voltaics whose language is not known by any assessors or headmen in the town, all litigants must use their vernacular language. This comes as a surprise and an annoyance to civil servant litigants who seek to impress the court with their erudition and the "cartesian" presentation of their case. However, the president and the assessors, probably either because they are not well versed in French (there are some assessors who neither speak nor understand French) or because they refuse to permit themselves to be "up-staged" by educated juniors, compel all litigants to use their native tongues.

It is difficult to determine how the president and the assessors arrive at their judgments since they discuss the points of law raised by the cases in private and do not explain the reasoning behind their decisions. One suspects that the judges have worked together so long or are so familiar with both the Mossi and the other traditional legal systems that they have synthesized a body of law applicable to most groups in town. This consensus may have emerged because most of the major

359

groups in town are from the Voltaic culture area, are patrilineal, or face common legal problems. There is a law book
present in court, *La Justice Locale et la Justice Musulmane en
A.O.F.,* but the judges never refer to it. Nor do they ever raise
any questions of Koranic law, even though there is frequent
evidence in court that the litigants had previously consulted a
cadi (Moslem judge). Nevertheless, a surprisingly large number of litigants accept the judges' decisions in cases which,
while not novel in themselves, reflect the many new problems
facing the Ouagadougou population.

Most of the cases brought before the Customary Court at
Ouagadougou involve domestic problems between husbands
and wives (see Table XXXVI). One reason for this is that most

TABLE XXXVI.   Cases in the Tribunal de Premier degré du Droit Local
(Ouagadougou, 1963–64)

Major Category of Cases	Sources of Conflict	Number
Domestic relations	Wives abandoning husbands	21
	Adultery of wives	12
	Trouble with in-laws	11
	Wives objecting to polygyny	8
	Husbands mistreating wives	7
	Sterility and barrenness	2
	Problems over wives working	4
	Lack of support	2
	Inadequate support	2
	Intention to poison	2
	Husbands abandoning wives	2
	Accusation of witchcraft	1
	Disease of spouse (leprosy)	1
	Wife steals	1
	SUBTOTAL	(68)*
Others		
	Broken engagements and demands for refund of "bride wealth" or "gifts"	5
	Refusal to marry pregnant girls	5
	Disputes over animals	3
	Inheritance disputes	2
	Adoption disputes	2
	TOTAL	85

*Although there are 76 charges, 8 of these are subsumed in cases involving multiple
sources of conflict.

of the people in the town are Mossi, and the Mossi, even in the rural areas, have always had difficulties resolving domestic conflicts between husbands and wives. As we saw in Chapter V above, where a number of court cases were cited, conflicts between spouses have been exacerbated by the urban environment where many of the traditional sanctions imposed on spouses to maintain their marriages are either absent or seriously weakened. Moreover, the Mossi women now take advantage not only of the actual laws giving them the right to choose their husbands, but of the new social climate in the town and the now ambiguous attitudes toward traditional marriage and are prone to rupture any domestic condition they find intolerable.

A growing number of cases coming before the Customary Court in Ouagadougou involve young women who had either been jilted or had been impregnated by young men who subsequently often refused either to marry them or accept paternity of the child and support it. The following case illustrates the complexity of this growing problem and the way in which the judges are attempting to deal with it.

Case Number 15

Complainant: L. B., a young man of Samogho origin, Christian, teacher, residing in Tougan, northwestern Upper Volta.

Defendant: K. O., a young woman of Samogho origin, Christian, nurse, working and living in Ouagadougou.

Testimony

L. B. to Tribunal: "K. O. and I lived in a state of concubinage and we had a child. Unfortunately, I could not marry her at that time because I was a student. However, I made certain that she was taken care of and that she received food and clothing. Now, two years later I have finished my education, but she has renounced any intention of marrying me. She has demonstrated her attitude by returning the money I recently sent her, something she had never done before. I have had further confirmation of her intention when I learned from her relatives that she had married another man. I do not wish to create trouble over the marriage. I will be content to get my child whom she declares she would return to me only with the con-

straint of administrative authorities. I am ready to reimburse her for the three years that I sent nothing for the
child in order that I might be able to get him."

K. O. to Tribunal: "When he heard that I had been dismissed from the *Cours Normal* (Teachers' College), for
having been impregnated by him, L. B. wrote me a letter,
which I still have, telling me how ashamed he was and especially how, if he failed his *brevet* examination, he would
be the butt of his friends' jokes, attributing his failure to
things other than his work. His letter filled me with indignation and I replied to him as follows; 'Since you are
ashamed, I am led to suspect that you are renouncing the
paternity of your unborn child. All right! But I warn
you, from this moment on, the child will belong to me
alone. I shall be its father and its mother. And it will be
my *brevet* because it is the reason for my inability to con-
clude my studies.' Nevertheless, I obtained a supplementary birth certificate in which I declared that L. B.
was the father, since I still believed he would marry me.
Since then, L. B. hurried to get the dossier of the child
in order to collect the family allotment of my issue. For
taking full care of the child, I received only six cans of
millet and these I did not use alone since his elder sister
boarded with me. He did give me three thousand francs,
but his sister alone used the money for trading purposes.
Furthermore, I was taking care of her. Finally, one day
he wrote me a letter in which he declared that it would be
useless for me to depend upon him any longer because he
no longer loved me. Afterwards, he came to reclaim the
child and I refused to give the child to him, and still refuse
to do so."

Tribunal: "Whereas L. B. and K. O. could not realize their
marriage plans;

Whereas out of their concubinage has issued a child
who has been under the exclusive charge of his mother;

Noting the supplementary birth certificate, number ... ,
delivered to L. B. in the name of the child, I. B.;

Noting also that L. B. has regularly received, since October 1957, the family allotment from which he alone
benefitted;

Taking these factors into consideration, the Tribunal
declares on the one hand, that the child, I. B., should be

remitted to his father, L. B., and on the other, orders him to give to K. O. the sum of 52,700 francs, representing the total of the family allotment, as reimbursement for the care of said child."

The problem faced by the judges in this case was the attempt of a modern woman to keep her child, a child which was recognized by its father only for administrative purposes. Nevertheless, the judges would not permit her to do this for fear of introducing the novel idea that women can "own" children. As it was, they gave the child to its genitor, but they penalized him by forcing him to surrender all the money he had received on behalf of the child.

The following case is only one of five in which broken engagements and demands for the return of the bride wealth were the issues before the court. Young persons in town who become engaged are not quite clear as to what their behavior should be, with the resulting conflict, or accident.

Case Number 41

Complainant: Mossi man, twenty-one years old, Catholic, assistant teacher living in St. Léon quarter, Ouagadougou.

Defendant: Mossi woman, twenty-one years old, Catholic, dressmaker, resident of St. Léon quarter, Ouagadougou.

Testimony

Complainant: "I asked for the hand of this woman in marriage, and she consented. From April 1962 onward, I gave her money to prepare for the marriage until she had received a total of 35,000 francs. One day when I went to arrange the date of the marriage, she received me badly and insulted me, calling me a 'bastard.' She said that she knew young men who were better than I was and that she was willing to return my money. I thought that she was joking and returned the next day only to receive the same treatment. Despite the intervention of her family, she refused to change her mind. It was at that moment that I decided to ask for my 35,000 francs."

Defendant: "The essential cause of the breakup of our marriage plans was that he insulted my decency. I told him that we were affianced and asked him to have patience because we should not have sexual relations before our marriage. Since that date, he has demanded that I return his 35,000 francs. I will give him the money when I have it."

Father of Defendant: "I have assumed the debt of my daughter."

The Tribunal ordered the father to pay the complainant 3,000 francs per month until the debt had been repaid.

This case raised a number of conflicting problems but left the judges little room for making any other decision. First of all, there was understanding of the young woman's attempt to preserve her virgin state until marriage, but her insistence upon it created the suspicion that she was not telling the truth. Traditionally, the Mossi did not have what one might call an "engagement," even though men were often given little girls as wives and these girls were reared in their husbands' homes. Of course, the consummation of these marriages did not take place until the girls had passed puberty, but this depended upon the decision of their husbands rather than upon their whims. Even modern Mossi youth, though Christian, tend to place little emphasis on virginity at marriage and try to avoid complications by marrying shortly after the engagement. Thus, the expectation of this young woman that a young man should adhere strictly to Christian teachings was viewed with cynicism, especially since she had allegedly told her fiancé that she knew better men. The judges also did not like the evidence that the young woman had already "eaten" (used) the money that her fiancé had given her to prepare for the wedding and did not have it to reimburse him when the engagement was broken.

Cases dealing with land disputes seldom are brought before the Customary Court of the First Degree because they usually involve amounts in excess of 15,000 francs. But, occasionally, and for reasons which are not always clear, such cases are heard before this court. Among the most important of the four cases in the sample is the following:

Case Number 14

Complainants: H. B. and S. Z., Mossi, orphans of the army veteran, R., of Ouagadougou.
Defendants: M. C. and S. D., Mossi, also of Ouagadougou.

Testimony

H. B. to Tribunal: "My deceased father, R., obtained a place to live from the Kamboin' Naba [Chief of Kamboinse] before the allotment of the Kamboinse quarter. Sometime later he retired to Nagbangré and invited me to occupy his lot, but the Kamboin' Naba opposed this saying that my father wished to sell it. Then, having had recourse to the Manga Naba and to His Majesty, the Mogho Naba, the latter ordered that the lot be given back to me in return for the payment of 80,000 francs to M. M., M. C., and S. D., the new occupants of said lot. This was a sum, indicated by the Mogho Naba's secretary and the Kamsaogho Naba, as representing improvements to the land. Three times His Majesty summoned the latter two [M. C. and S. D.] to give them the money, after having given them a stay of eight months to move away. But it was in vain. On the advice of the Manga Naba, I obtained a permit of Urban Occupancy for the lot."

S. D. (cousin of H. B.) to Tribunal: "When I returned from military service, I found three round huts on the lot. I then constructed a three-room house with its veranda, a small pantry-kitchen for the use of my wife, and five round huts. And as my uncle had the intention of selling this parcel of ground and insisted upon doing so, the Kamboin' Naba ordered me to vacate the lot. Thereupon I had to carry away the iron sheeting which had served to cover the larger building, and I left all the rest intact."

M. C. to Tribunal: "S. D. and I had received from the Kamboin' Naba the lot of land in question practically vacant, since we found nothing there but ruins. Each of us installed himself on a half-lot, and I have constructed a five-room house, of which four are covered, and three small shacks [*maisonnettes*]. I have planted two *neems* and a *gmelina* [species of trees]. Then, during the last rainy season, we were summoned to the house of the Mogho [Naba] who enjoined us to move away. But we have refused to do so. However, even before this, the Land Surveyor [from the Town Hall] had caused our names to be erased from the land allotment register. I cite M. M., D. M., I. F., and D. N. as witnesses."

I. F. (a witness for M. C.) to Tribunal: "About one year ago I

365

was present at the distribution of the Kamboinse lots, and
the lot in question was assigned, in my presence, to M. C.
and S. D. And, when the former wished to obtain a permit of Urban Occupancy, he found out that his name did
not appear on the register. Having taken part in the affair, I hastened to verify this, and it was with astonish-
ment that I discovered that the names M. C. and S. D.
had been erased and replaced by that of M. B., but some
traces still remained. I asked for explanations from the
land surveyor, who told me that the land had belonged to
the army veteran, R., and that it should rightfully be
passed on to his heirs. And he added that he would see
the Mogho Naba who would be able to arrange the affair."

The Kamboin' Naba to Tribunal: "In effect, it was I who
gave the lot to the ex-soldier, R., prior to allotment. And
a little while afterwards, he informed me of his desire to
go to Nagbangré to improve his harvests. When allotment finally took place, a certain man, L., a native of
Koubri [a district about 16 miles south of Ouagadougou],
who then occupied the lot, was given this lot [in the name
of the ex-soldier]. When the ex-soldier learned that L.,
who was a relative of his, had left this land, he ordered
that the lot be sold. I opposed the sale and took back the
land in question by having the ex-soldier's son, H. B.,
move away. After that, I assigned the lot to M. C. and
S. D. One day the land surveyor came to see me and told
me to take the lot back and give it to the son of the ex-
soldier. I told him that I could no longer do this. A few
days later, I was summoned to the Mogho Naba who ordered me to give the lot back to H. B. in return for the
sum of 80,000 francs that were to be given me as reimbursement for the improvements made on said lot by
M. C. and S. D. They promised to give the latter two
men a lot elsewhere and ordered them to move away in
eight months time. But they refused."

The Land Surveyor to Tribunal: "M. M., G. J., H. Y., D. N.,
and I were members of the commission designated for the
apportionment of the lots in Kamboinse quarter. The
Manga Naba had charged me to obtain information from
the Kamboin' Naba about said plot in litigation. The
latter told me that, at the time of the allotment, the ex-
soldier, being in Nagbangré, had sent L., his brother, to

occupy the lot so as to be able to have a lot. When he received this information, the Manga Naba asked Monsieur G. J. to return the lot to the heirs of the ex-soldier. With regard to the aforementioned reimbursement, the testimony is correct.

The Assessors, S. D. and A. O., after making inquiries, have confirmed the declarations, to wit, that the unallotted land had been given to the ex-soldier, R., that the plot had been assigned to his brother, L., and that his sons had built thereupon."

The Tribunal examined all the evidence, and, having studied it carefully, rendered the following verdict:

Tribunal: "Whereas His Majesty the Mogho Naba and Ministers F. B. and M. O. have tried in vain to effect a reconciliation between the two parties;

Noting the official report of August 1, 1961, of the Commission designated by His Majesty and on the proposition of the self-same Ministers, to evaluate the improvements of the plot of litigation;

Noting the permit of Urban Occupancy no. 21/CO of February 1961 of lot no. 0 of terrain no. 1099 of the quarter, Peuloghin-Zanguettin;

Declare the heirs of the ex-soldier, R., to be the proprietors of said lot and order them to reimburse M. C. 52,000 francs and S. D. 21,000 francs. [The defendants] must vacate said lot in the shortest possible time in order to install themselves upon other lots which the land surveyor is charged to find them."

This rather long case is of interest in that it shows the direct involvement of chiefs, administrators from the Mayor's office, and politicians (namely, the two ministers, one of whom is also a chief), in a lawsuit. It was clear to all and sundry that the Kamboin' Naba had wished to assign the plot of land to the defendants because he suspected that the ex-soldier had no intention of living in Ouagadougou and wanted the plot only for his heirs. The question of whether the Kamboin' Naba meant to profit from this assignment of land was not raised in court. The heirs of the ex-soldier, R., had powerful supporters in the persons of the Manga Naba and the ministers. The fact that another chief, the Kamboin' Naba, was involved in the case did not matter because the complainants were also related to an important official who used not only his traditional status but his new political status as well to put pressure on the Mayor's office to have the land returned to both H. B. and S. Z. It should be noted, however, that the judges were not content to return the lot to the heirs of the ex-soldier, but made sure that the defendants would be given access to other plots which were being allotted in the town.

Cases involving inheritance illustrate some of the conflicts between relatives and the problem posed for the judges.

Case Number 35

Complainant: M. S., a Samogho cultivator of Tougan.
Defendant: P. S., a young educated Fulani and her two children.

Testimony

M. S. to Tribunal: "My son died and I have come to see about his estate. I have been told that since my son was married according to the laws of the Europeans, his wife and his children are to receive all of the money which is to come from the government [the deceased in question was a civil servant] and also all his property. What we would like is guardianship of the children."

P. S. to Tribunal: "I am over twenty-one, am literate, and furthermore, I am a teacher. I should be the guardian of my children. I really do not mind my husband's relatives also being guardians over my children, but, since I fear that there would be conflicts, I believe that it would be better if the President [of the court] named me as their official guardian."

A. S. (brother of the deceased) to Tribunal: "We do not wish to take the children away from their mother, but we would like to be able to watch over them when we are in Ouagadougou. And that is why we would like to be their guardians."

S. D. (brother of the widow) to Tribunal: "We do not mind any one of the dead man's brothers living in the household when they come to town, but we feel that to name them guardians would lead to grave conflict."

President of the Tribunal: "If this is indeed the case, then arrangements could be made for the relatives of the deceased to stay at his house while in town, and we can give the mother the guardianship of the children."

The dead man's relatives were aware that they could claim neither the deceased's property nor his wife, but tried to claim guardianship over his children. They had hoped to use the traditional bias against giving children to women, and, once having secured the children, they hoped to receive the family allowances which would come to them. However, since they did not believe that they could reveal this in court, they simply stated that they wanted "to watch over the children" when they came to Ouagadougou. The widow's brother, apparently a discerning individual, countered by offering them a place to stay whenever they came to Ouagadougou. Once this point had been seized, the president quickly closed the case. He was able to take the complainants at their word and give the children over to the custody of their mother. Of interest is that the relatives, who were cultivators, did not express a desire to take the children back to the rural area. They could not hope to train these boys as cultivators since it is generally believed that children born in town are quite different from those born in the rural areas and adapt with difficulty to rural life. Besides, it would not have profitted these rural people to use their scarce resources for sending their relative's children to school. Thus, in this case, the important factor was that the mother of the children was an educated woman, and she won.

Tribunal of the Second Degree

This tribunal, like the Tribunal of the First Degree, also meets in the Town Hall but, in contrast to the twice-weekly meeting of the lower court, it normally meets only once a week, on Fridays. Like the lower court, the Tribunal of the Second Degree has a president, but he is an officer of the Ministry of the Interior and not of the municipality. The incumbent is an administrative secretary to the Director of the Ministry of the Interior. This man is also assisted by twelve assessors chosen by the Mayor, but confirmed in office by the Minister of the Interior. This tribunal hears cases dealing with problems falling under customary law, but involving property valued at more than 50,000 francs. It also hears appeals from the lower courts on all problems treated there. Like the lower court, its rulings are not binding upon litigants who can appeal to the Superior Court of Customary Law. However, just as few appeals are sent from the lower court to this court, so almost no cases go from this court to the highest court of customary law.

So few cases were placed on the docket of the Tribunal of the Second Degree in Ouagadougou during 1964 that the court seldom met more often than twice a month. On most days the president of the court telephoned the secretary of the court to determine whether any cases were on the docket. If there were none, he did not come to court. Sometimes he simply telephoned to say that he was busy at the ministry and that the cases should be postponed.

Table XXXVII gives a breakdown of the cases heard by the Tribunal of the Second Degree on which data were collected.

The reason why the largest number of cases which come before the Tribunal of the Second Degree involve land disputes is that not many people understand the procedure by which urban land is made available; consequently, heirs quarrel over the rights to plots. Until the municipality assumes full control of a ward, the land there remains under the supervision and control of the traditional chief and is subject to customary laws. He may distribute the land as he sees fit, and when a quarter is scheduled for allotment, the municipality tries to satisfy the claims of all persons to whom the chief has given lots. Most difficulties arise for the following reasons: different persons claim rights to the same plot of land; people without full title to land sell it through the ruse of "selling improvements on the land"; chiefs try to take back land and give it to others; and, again, heirs squabble over land. The following case illustrates the problem of disputes between relatives over urban land:

TABLE XXXVII. Types of Cases
Heard at Second Degree Court

Category of Cases	Number
Urban land disputes	13
Appeals from lower court	5
Domestic relations	2
Bride wealth disputes	1
TOTAL	21

Case Number 201

Complainant: B. D., forty years old, barber, residing in Zanguettin quarter, Ouagadougou, of Gourmantche origin, appearing in person and speaking Moré.

Defendant: A. D., forty-five years old, barber, also residing in Zanguettin, of Gourmantche origin, appearing in person and speaking Moré.

Testimony

B. D. to Tribunal: "I have the honor to address to you this complaint against one A. D. by name, who wanted to take my lot by pure force. I have spent the sum of 500,000 francs for building on this lot. A. D. would like to sell this lot. Not being able to obtain justice myself, I beg of you to summon A. D. so that I may have justice and so that he will leave me in peace on my land."

A. D., given the opportunity to address the Tribunal: "The lot belongs to me; I have the permit of Urban Occupancy. When the distribution of lots took place, it was the maize field of my father. The Town Hall gave it to me and I have constructed a four-room house upon it. My father's brother's son lived there at first; then, he asked for authorization to build a house. I refused him permission, but he built the house anyway. I wished to avoid all trouble in the first place, but I have not succeeded—now, here we are. I would like the Tribunal to order him to move away."

The Tribunal then asked the witnesses to come forward.

M. K. (a retired office clerk) to Tribunal: "I am their neighbor. At the death of their father, A. D. took the permit of Urban Occupancy of a lot which included their manioc field. As B. D. is a relative of A. D., the latter allowed him to live on his lot, and now he claims the lot as his own. B. D. would like to sell the lot and leave town. Having worked in the Office of Lands, it was I who made out the permit, therefore the lot belongs to A. D."

B. O. (a neighbor) to Tribunal: "At the time of the distribution of the lots in Zanguettin quarter, I saw that the lot in litigation was assigned to A. D. We have lived side by side for more than twenty-two years. In all that time A. D. has never ceded or sold that lot."

371

M. D. (a municipal councilor of Zanguettin) to Tribunal: "I know that the occupant of the lot in litigation is A. D. The permit of Urban Occupancy has been established in A. D.'s name since 1961. Therefore the lot belongs to him."

Tribunal: "The case having been thus examined, the Tribunal, after due deliberation, has rendered the following judgment:

Whereas customary law does not indicate any special disposition;

On these grounds, the Tribunal firstly decrees that the parcel no. A of lot no. 1073 in the quarter, Zanguettin, is the property of A. D.

The importance of this case, so clear-cut on the surface, is that it dramatizes the impact of modern property considerations on the traditional norms of corporate access of relatives to land and other resources. It is quite clear that B. D. felt that because the lot in question was owned by his father's brother, he had the right to live there on the same terms as A. D. However, agnation aside, it is quite clear that the issue in the case was decided on the basis of possession of the permit of Urban Occupancy rather than on any other grounds. The fact that the judges did not raise the question of kinship is as significant as their decision that customary law did not contain any guidelines for judging the case.

The following case also deals with the issue of urban land, but here, as in the previous case, the judges also had to deal with the problem of kinship as it relates to property.

Case Number 215

Complainant: Y. O., sixty-two years of age, cattle merchant of Mwemne, of Mossi origin, appearing in person and speaking Moré.

Defendant: M. D., forty-seven years of age, Assistant Director of the Ministry of Finance, of Mossi origin, appearing in person and speaking Moré.

Testimony

(At the request of Y. O. on July 22, 1964, this case was transferred from the Tribunal of the First Instance to that of the Customary Court of the Second Degree.)

Y. O. to Tribunal: "I have the honor to submit to your very high approbation the facts which put me in opposition to His Honor, M. D., the First Adjutant of the Mayor of the town of Ouagadougou. In effect, my younger brother, B. O., died in Ouagadougou on June 27, 1963, leaving two concessions situated at lots 155-portion K and 146-portion L in the center of the allotted area of Nyoghsin. In order to meet the property and income taxes on the revenue of the deceased, we [members of the family] have decided to sell one of the concessions. But in the course of inquiries made to the communal authorities, Mr. M. D., the First Adjutant of the Mayor of the town of Ouagadougou, refused our request. Mr. M. D. told us that he was going to confiscate all properties of the deceased because the latter owed him a considerable sum of money.

From an investigation of the facts in the Land Records of the Commune of Ouagadougou, we found out that Mr. M. D. has had himself inscribed as proprietor of lot number 146-portion L of Nyoghsin quarter. Not one bill of sale, of gift, or of recognition of debt had been established between the late B. O. and M. D.; nor between the heirs of the deceased and M. D. Not having known of any judicial action between the former and B. O. while living, we, the family, consider the actions of Mr. M. D. to be an ABUSE OF POWER, and we beseech you to consider the present circumstances as grounds for complaint against M. D.

There are two other matters: 1) In August of 1960 (the 4th or 7th) M. D. and I. T. put pressure on B. O. and extorted a considerable sum of money. This occurred at the home of El Hadji I. T. B. O., who was by profession a money changer, ought to have had sums of money belonging to several merchants of the market with him that day. The victims brought a complaint against him [B. O.] for abuse of confidence, and he was condemned to two years in prison. M. D. and I. T., satisfied, remained in the shadows and did not bring any action against him. 2) On Monday June 17, 1963, while B. O. was en route to the market, he was hailed by M. D. He responded to his call, but as soon as he entered the home of M. D. the latter closed his door and had him whipped until he lost consciousness and confiscated all the papers he had on him. B. O. died eleven days later, on the 27th [sic] of June 1963, from pains in the back and chest. He had made these facts known to the police and to the Sûreté, but did not know enough to obtain a medical certificate. M. D. should still have the papers of B. O.

Personally, I could not reimburse the debt contracted since I am ignorant of the amount. Not one member of the family is capable of doing it. Thus, I equally refuse to give the portions of land to M. D. In the event the Tribunal decides to give the lands to him, I will not be opposed."

M. D. was asked to tell his story to the Tribunal: "I have the honor to submit for your high approbation the affair which separates myself and Y. O. living in Mahomet [Hamdalaye] quarter, Ouagadougou. The man in question, whose cousin, B. O., was the man who owed me money and who is dead, brought action against me before the Tribunal of the First Instance. That jurisdiction did not recognize the penal character of the accusation made to the Commissioner of Police, who then asked that Y. O. be notified of the change of venue.

Besides, I considered that I had been the object of defamation of character and brought action myself. However, since the Tribunal of First Instance, having declared that the affair should be brought before the Customary Tribunal, I ask you, Mr. President, to regulate this affair as soon as possible.

Upon the recommendation of the Larhalle Naba, he [Y. O.] presented himself to me in my office so that I could authorize the sale of the two portions of land. Being municipal councilor of the quarter, it was necessary to obtain my preliminary agreement before any sale of land could take place. Thus I profitted from this opportunity and told him that I was looking for a relative of B. O. I also told him that I was withdrawing the two concessions of the late B. O. while awaiting settlement of the debt he had contracted. The reason for this was that the debt was greater than the price of the two lots in question.

I present to you the witnesses who know that the late B. O. had taken the money."

At this point, the Tribunal, according to custom, tried to reconcile the parties and, failing to do so, called the witnesses:

M. T., fifty-six years of age, cultivator living in Dapoya II, speaking Moré: "I know that the late B. O. owed money to M. D. M. D. often came to see him under our shed [in the market], then B. O. ran away from Ouagadougou, taking my money and that of M. D. However, I do not know the amount of money owed to M. D. Since his flight, M. D. has declared to me that B. O. owed him a large amount of money, more than any of us."

M. S., thirty-nine years of age, a jeweler of Nyoghsin, speaking Moré: "I do know that B. O. owes a certain sum to M. D., but I am ignorant of the amount."

El Hadj I. T.: "I can affirm that the late B. O. had borrowed money from M. D. As to the amount, this I do not know exactly."

A. S., fifty-three years of age, a jeweler of Nyoghsin: "I know that the late B. O. owes money to M. D. But I do not know the amount. When B. O. died, he left two concessions. That is all I know."

Tribunal: "The case having been examined, and the Tribunal having deliberated, renders the following judgment:

Whereas it has been determined that the late B. O. had borrowed money from M. D.;

Whereas Mossi custom does not indicate any special disposition of such a case;

Because of these factors ... [the members of the Tribunal] declare that the two portions K and L of lots numbered 155 and 146 of the allotted area of Nyoghsin will be the property of M. D. ...

The parties have been told of their right to appeal in one month's time."

This is a very unusual case since it is clear that not all the factors involved were brought to the attention of the court. The reputation of B. O. was not good since he had been convicted for fraud by the Court of First Instance and sentenced to prison. This being the case, the judges took no notice of the charge that M. D. had had B. O. beaten and that this beating was responsible for his death. Y. O.'s claim, that B. O. did not have a medical certificate which showed the results of the beating because he was too ignorant to do so, was not acceptable either to the Court of First Instance or to the Customary Court since most people in Ouagadougou who get into trouble try to get a medical certificate to present in court cases. The further fact that the Commissioner of Police had had the case sent back to the Customary Court of the Second Degree was not in B. O.'s favor, nor, subsequently, in his heirs' favor. What requires some explanation is why the actual sum of money allegedly borrowed by B. O. from M. D. was never stated, and why, even in the absence of any written proof, the court accepted M. D.'s word that the debt had been contracted. The obvious reason is that M. D. not only was a respected municipal councilor and the First Adjutant of the Mayor of Ouagadougou, but also an educated man whose word could not be doubted. It is important to note in this context that the complainant did not accuse M. D. of fraud but of "abuse of power." Moreover, the complainant implied that, although he considered M. D.'s action highhanded, he was willing to abide by the judgment of the court rather than indicate that he might appeal. The additional fact that M. D. was supported by witnesses, who included an *El Hadji,* doubtless convinced the president of the court and his assessors that B. O. did indeed owe money to the defendant. The only question which remains unanswered is why the amount of money involved was not revealed in court.

The following case is an example of the types of domestic relations cases which are returned from the higher courts, in this case from the Chambre d'Annulation de la Cour d'Appel de Ouagadougou to the Customary Court of the Second Degree for adjudication. The rejection here was based primarily upon the judge's contention that his court was not competent to hear a case involving persons of specific ethnic affiliations and in which the disposition of the children could be influenced by conflicting traditional customary laws.

Case Number 202

This case was heard on two consecutive dates, September 25, 1964, and September 30, 1964, before the president and two Dahomean assessors, one of Fon origin and one of Mina origin.

Complainant: T. P., thirty-one years of age, nurse, living in Dapoya II, of Pla and Mina origin, represented by Sankara Bolikary, business agent.

Defendant: A. G., thirty years of age, agent of the Postal-Telephone-Telegraph Service, living in Ouagadougou, of Fon origin, representing himself and expressing himself in French.

Testimony

Mr. Bolikary for his client, T. P., to Tribunal: "I am suing for divorce on several grounds: my husband is almost never at home at night; I very often eat alone with my children; once it was nearly dawn when he came back from town; there are insults; he has even threatened to kill me. I have notified Michel Campaore, Chief of the Sûreté, who warned him, but this effort was in vain. On the night of October 8, 1963, he announced to me that this was his last notice, that he was afraid of nothing, neither prison nor the police. Having been threatened, I was obliged to quit the conjugal domicile.

How could one live under these conditions? I have tried to guard my life because no one knows what could happen. When I left the conjugal domicile, my mother took the trouble to call on him, on the 20th of October, and she asked him several questions: 'Why so many threats during the nights? Have you suspected that your wife is going around with someone else? Or have you surprised her somewhere?' 'No,' he replied, 'I do not suspect her, nor have I surprised her.'

The President of the National Assembly [Mr. Begnon Koné] and the Minister of Foreign Affairs [Mr. Lompolo Koné] together tried to effect a reconciliation, but one week later my husband came to the home of my parents and whipped me. He shoved my parents around so much that my mother fell and displaced her kneecap.

In what country in the world has one ever seen such disregard for parents-in-law, especially when they have attained such advanced age? I was obliged to seek the intervention of two policemen who guarded us until morning.

My husband, not having any more respect for, nor any consideration for my parents, I asked myself whether he could have any for me?

I have lost twelve kilograms during the last year. All of the children are dependent upon me. He has promised

377

to drive me crazy and to have me suspended from my work. How can you expect me to return to him under such conditions? How am I going to feed my children if I can not work, since he no longer takes care of them?

On the 2nd of November, he told my mother, 'Thanks to my *gris-gris* from Dahomey, I will be able to drive your daughter to insanity; I will force her to be imprisoned and fired from her job.'

My old mother, frightened, had heart palpitations. I have to watch over her all night. And here are the last unhappy days of my old parents, abused, menaced, insulted by a barbarous son-in-law, drunk, without respect, with a rare type of rudeness, and with a heart of stone.

During the past eight months, I have spent 132,800 francs for the maintenance of the children. I claim payment of this sum before he takes the children. I especially insist that a divorce be granted so that I will be able to live in peace."

A. G. to Tribunal: "The demand for a divorce formulated by my wife cannot be granted, in principle, because she is in an awkward position. She abandoned the conjugal domicile on the 10th of October, 1963 without notifying the Tribunal of the First Degree. Since that time she has lived with her parents. Because she did not go to the Tribunal before going to her parents, she has no right to ask the Tribunal for a divorce.

Herewith are the fundamental reasons which separate my wife and me. She has taken up the practice of frequenting the *marabout* and the *féticheurs* [magical practitioners]. When she leaves the house, she returns late under the pretext that she had gone to see her mother.

On the 8th of October, my wife left the conjugal domicile about three o'clock in the afternoon to go to visit her mother. I went to her mother and I did not find my wife. I then went for a walk. Upon my return, I found her at my mother-in-law's house. 'Where did you go?' I asked her. 'To the market,' she replied. Not satisfied with this reply, I waited for her to return to the house to ask her the same question again. She replied, vehemently, that I had no right even to know where she went, nor to follow her on her excursions. That aroused my ire, and I said to

378

her, 'The day I catch you in adultery will be your death. I do not forgive!'

Five days later, upon returning from work at midday, I found my door wide open and my house empty. I hastened to my mother-in-law's house and saw my wife there with her baggage and my children. I told my mother-in-law that she ought to have come to me to ask what the matter was because it is not proper for her to keep my wife at her house. My mother-in-law replied, 'T. told me that you wanted to kill her, that is the reason why I have kept her.'

When my mother learned that my wife had abandoned her conjugal domicile, she went to my mother-in-law's family to seek forgiveness. My wife refused to return to her conjugal family. She [my mother] returned again with a delegation of old Dahomean women [to seek forgiveness] but without happy results. My wife rejected their pleas, and, discouraged, they never returned again. This attitude of my wife has upset me considerably. The third [sic] time the delegation contacted my wife, she imposed several conditions and said that if these conditions were not fulfilled she would not rejoin the family home.

I let her know that every one of those women who had come to intervene was capable of being her mother and that she owes them respect. It was from that moment that I began to whip my wife.

She went to see Mr. Joseph Conombo [the Mayor of Ouagadougou] and asked him to resolve our problem. During this period, my wife's father sent a letter from Cotonou [Dahomey] pleading with Mr. Conombo to reunite us because, for all the goods in this world, he would not wish to see our separation. Mr. Conombo tried to effect a reconciliation, but in vain. The second intervention was that of Messrs. Lompolo Koné, Begnon Koné, and Joseph Conombo. They requested my wife to rejoin the conjugal family. She categorically refused. In principle, I should have made a complaint against my wife for conjugal abandonment a long time ago, but I was thinking about the juridical consequences that this would produce. For my part, I did not wish to bring her before the

Tribunal. She, seemingly stronger than I am, has been the first to lodge a complaint against me. She asks for a divorce; I refuse. As far as my children are concerned, I ask the Tribunal to place them in my custody."

The Tribunal asked to hear from the witnesses.

M. S., sixty-three years of age, merchant, residing in Dapoya II, to Tribunal: I have been a neighbor of Madame P., the defendant's mother-in-law, ever since the time her daughter, T., returned with her children. Mr. A. G. came often to provoke them, even during the night.

M. C., former Chief of the Sûreté, to Tribunal: "While I was Chief of the Sûreté, I had agents intervene several times in the affairs of this household to restore calm there and to avoid all incidents."

Tribunal: "The testimony and witnesses having been heard, the Tribunal, after due deliberation, renders the following judgment:

Noting Judgment No. 3 of March 17, 1964, rendered by the Tribunal of the First Degree of Ouagadougou;

Noting the appeal made on March 19, 1964, by Madame G., Née T. P., to that same Tribunal;

Whereas that appeal, according to form, has been made in the time legally allotted for it;

Whereas the appellant has been able to prove, with witnesses, maltreatment, calamitously serious abuses, threats of death, insults to in-laws, and nonsupport of children by the father;

Whereas, as the customs of the Fon, Pla, and Mina peoples which, conforming to the disposition of article no. 6 of the decree of December 3, 1931, should apply, the fact which led to the nullification of the judgment given, but which belongs to the Tribunal to evoke and to rule upon;

On these grounds, the Tribunal, sitting in the last resort, and on appeal ...

Declares the appeal made by T. P. to be admissible and annuls the previous judgment;

Therefore, declare that a divorce is granted to T. P.

Order that the custody of all the aforementioned children be given to Mr. A. G., conforming to the customs of the Fon, Pla, and Mina;

Order Mr. A. G. to pay 132,800 francs to T. P.;

Place the visits to the children at the initiative of Mr. A. G.

Upon demand of Mr. A. G., order the provisionary execution in the matter which concerns the immediate return of the children, taking into consideration the imminent date of the beginning of classes. . . .

This case shows quite clearly some of the tensions which do arise in households of the elite or educated civil servant group in Ouagadougou and of the sociological relations between the elite, whether local or of stranger origin. It is quite clear, though not immediately recognizable in the testimony of T. P.'s lawyer, that the latter feared that her husband was involved in serious extra-marital relations which threatened the sanctity of her household. She objected to his behavior, only to be subjected to verbal and physical abuse for presuming to question the sexual or other prerogatives of her husband. Apparently, she then took two kinds of action: she appealed to the religico-magical practitioners for help; and she appealed to important political figures who were also personal friends. Not getting any results, she left her husband's house.

The position of the husband in this case was legalistic but not apologetic. His legalism can be seen in his insistence that his mother-in-law had no right to grant his wife shelter and in stating that he should have brought action against his wife for desertion. However, the fact that he sent his mother, or permitted his mother and delegations of Dahomean women, to seek a reconciliation with his wife shows quite clearly that he felt guilty of mistreating her. Moreover, he was not above appealing to his wife's probably latent respect for old age when he accused her of not heeding the pleas of the older women for the reconciliation.

Two aspects of the relationships between Dahomeans and the local people can be seen in this case. The belief of the local people that the Dahomeans practice witchcraft was supported, ironically enough, both in the testimony of husband and wife when each accused the other of practicing it. Secondly, the ability of the wife to appeal to important local municipal and government officials to help resolve a case of poor domestic relations demonstrates the existence of social networks among the elite which cut across ethnic boundaries. Another important aspect of this case is that it revealed that at least this elite family sought help from members of its own group before resorting to the courts. Had their friends and relatives been able to help, there would have been no evidence of problems.

There was no record in the Town Hall or from any other source to indicate that cases are appealed from the Customary Court of the Second Degree to the Superior Customary Court. The one case which had been taken to the Chambre D'Annulation du Droit Local was sent back to the Customary Court of the Second Degree. Perhaps litigants feel that there is little chance that appeals to higher courts of cases involving traditional customs would result in a reversal of judgment. A more important reason why cases are not taken beyond the Customary Court of the Second Degree may be that any case more complex than the ones judged on this level would certainly have some characteristics which would bring it before the civil or criminal courts of the Republic.

Tribunal of First Instance

The Tribunal de Première Instance of the Republic of Upper Volta, sitting in Ouagadougou, is the court which handles most of the civil, commercial, and criminal problems of the people of the town. It is here that cases of fraud, abuse of confidence, assault, theft, accident, fighting, and various kinds of delinquency are judged. The structure of this court is quite similar to that of the French courts on this level and comprises the *parquet,* which includes the offices and staff of the Procureur de la République or the public prosecutor; the *greffe,* the office of the head law clerk and his assistants; the *cabinets d'instruction,* which include the *juges d'instruction* or examining magistrates and their office personnel; and finally, the *présidence,* which includes the judges and their staffs. Until about 1962 all of the judges and magistrates of the court were either European or French West Indian, but by 1964 Voltaic judges and magistrates had been trained and assigned to the court.

Cases brought before this lower court are usually heard on Thursday mornings at the Palais de Justice, a building in modern Sudanese style located near the business district. On court day, litigants, persons released on bail, and prisoners with their jailers arrive in court at 7:30 A.M. The prisoners sit on the first benches on the right side of the court, leaving the comparable benches on the left side for such court-related personnel as lawyers or persons from the social service agency. Behind both sets of reserved seats are the benches on which litigants and the audience sit. At about 7:55, a junior law clerk, an interpreter, and the lawyers arrive, followed a few minutes later by the public prosecutor and the senior law clerk. These sit on the left and the right of the judge's chair respectively. About 8:00 the judge enters, everyone rises, and the court is called to order.

Normally the first cases called are civil suits involving Europeans or Lebano-Syrians and their African debtors. Almost invariably the Europeans' cases are presented by their lawyers, and, also invariably, the Africans have no lawyers   These cases are usually routine affairs involving either expatriate merchants who have not been paid for goods given on credit to local merchants, or merchants whose creditors claim that they never received the goods or loan, or had already paid their bills. In none of the cases witnessed was the African defendant sent to jail. Usually he arranged to repay the loan or pay for the goods received. The judge usually recesses the court as soon as these civil cases are concluded. The Europeans and their lawyers leave, and the chief law clerk often retires from court for the day.

When, a little later, the court reconvenes, cases dealing with juvenile delinquency are heard. In such cases, the judge summons the boy to approach the bench and also beckons the social worker to come forward. A conference takes place between all of the interested parties and disposition is made of the case. The other cases are treated quite differently. The law clerk calls the name of the litigants and these names are repeated by the interpreters present. If the litigants and their witnesses are all present, they approach the bar of justice and the clerk directs them all to leave the court by a side door. Subsequently they are individually summoned by the clerk to appear and give testimony or bear witness to testimony being given.

The language of this court is French, and an interpreter is employed if the litigants do not speak that language. The two interpreters customarily employed in the court appear to know almost all the important languages of the Upper Volta. When, as happened a few times, they do not know the language of a defendant who can not express himself in French, an attempt is made to find someone from the office of the law clerk to act as interpreter.

The judge usually consults the dossier of a case before summoning the litigants or accused to appear before him. When, as sometimes happens, the judge needs clarification about the case or, in the case of a recidivist criminal, he needs to know the opinion of the public prosecutor, that official is asked to give his opinion.

Both the judge and the public prosecutor question the litigants or the prisoners in an effort to ascertain their guilt or innocence, and the litigants or prisoners have the right to be defended by their lawyers. But during repeated visits to court, only one African lawyer or "pleader" was ever observed defending clients. This man was a consummate actor who never addressed himself to the legal aspects of the case nor challenged the ruling of the judge. Instead, he apparently always accepted the judgment of the court and pleaded for mercy, invoking the Greeks, history, poor relatives, the human condition, and the quality of man.

It is difficult to discover precisely the crime rate among the urban population of Ouagadougou since many of the cases

TABLE XXXVIII. Types of Cases Heard at First Degree Court

Category of Cases	Number	Category of Cases	Number
Willfully inflicted cuts and wounds	114	Illegal hunting	12
Theft	89	Embezzlement	8
Accidentally inflicted cuts and wounds	80	Lack of immigration permits	8
Breach of trust	70	Sorcery	7
Vagrancy	62	Abandonment of the home	6
Receiving stolen goods	60	Contrabanding	5
Robbery	41	Accidents incurred at work resulting from violation of labor ordinances	4
Attempted theft	36	Running an illegal bar	4
Fraud	26	Resisting arrest	3
Accidental homicide (manslaughter)	26	Tampering with meters	2
Insulting an officer of the law	23	Contributing to the delinquency of minors	2
Traffic violations	22	Trafficking in poisonous substances	2
Illegal possession of arms	18	Illegal practice of medicine	1
Civil cases	16	Miscellaneous	8
Evading officers of the law	15		
TOTAL			770

384

judged in the Tribunal de Première Instance are sent there
from the rural areas of the country and even from Dori, Kaya,
and Fada N'Gourma where there are local seats of this court.
Again, so many cases involve persons either traveling through
Ouagadougou or new to the town that one has real difficulty
determining whether their criminality can really be assigned to
the Ouagadougou population. According to the statistics of
the court, 1,242 cases were judged during 1963. Table
XXXVIII gives a breakdown of the first 769 of these. Before
making any analysis of the relative importance and number of
cases in each category, a breakdown will be presented of the
42 cases actually witnessed, including the ethnic affiliations
and provenience of the litigants or prisoners (see Tables
XXXIX–XLI).

The highest number of crimes judged by the Tribunal of the
First Instance were crimes against persons, including both
willful assault and battery and the involuntary infliction of
wounds. A closer look at these cases shows that the majority
of the altercations resulting in injuries were over the affection
of women. The reason why so many persons were wounded is
that many of the Voltaics, especially the Mossi, still carry
staves or, in the case of cultivators, hoes of some kind, and
use these implements in fights.

Theft, receiving stolen goods, robbery, and attempted theft

**TABLE XXXIX. Cases Actually Witnessed at
First Degree Court**

Category of Cases	Number
Assault and battery	11
Vagrancy and juvenile delinquency	5
Theft	5
Traffic accidents	2
Civil suits	2
Dealing in contraband	1
Statutory rape	1
Suspicion of theft and violation of banishment from Ouagadougou	1
Shooting a cow and illegal possession of a gun	1
Accidental homicide (manslaughter)	1
Abandonment of the home	1
Fraud	1
Postponed cases	10
TOTAL	42

**TABLE XL.   Provenience of
Cases Witnessed at
First Degree Court**

Provenience of Cases	Number
Town of Ouagadougou	23
Kombissiri	3
Boulsa	2
Djibo	2
Manga	1
Pô	1
Unknown	10
TOTAL	42

**TABLE XLI.   Ethnicity of
Litigants in Cases Witnessed at
First Degree Court**

Ethnicity of Litigants	Number
Mossi	24
Fulani	4
Gourmantche	2
Senegalese	1
Setba	1
Unknown	10
TOTAL	42

rank second in the crime statistics of Ouagadougou. According to the police, bicycles are the objects most often stolen, and persons visiting the markets, stores, and other establishments in the town are warned to lock their vehicles or risk having them stolen. Motorcycles, rapidly becoming more common in town, are also being stolen in larger numbers. Pilfering from the markets and stores also contributes to the large percentage of reported thefts. The persons responsible for these petty thefts most often are the young boys who loiter about the market in the hope of finding small chores to do and who steal any object not carefully guarded. The *garibous* from the Koranic schools around Ouagadougou are also accused of pilfering any object they see lying around in the yards of those houses to which they go in order to beg for alms. The result is that many householders in Ouagadougou now chase away all Koranic students who approach their houses, especially if the youngsters do not announce their arrival by chanting songs.

Breach of trust, fraud, and embezzlement rank fairly high among the cases brought to court. Most of these cases involve merchants or petty traders who take goods on consignment, sell them, and refuse to pay their debts or decamp with the proceeds, claiming that the goods had been stolen. Many a rural peasant is swindled by urban traders who entice him to permit goods and animals to be taken to town in the hope of a richer return, only to have the trader disappear. Also swindled are persons who give objects they wish to sell to strangers they encounter in the market, only to discover that the intermediaries in the sale have disappeared. The police despair of people who are swindled in this manner and insist that people never learn.

The cases of accidental homicide judged in this court are caused by automobile accidents, usually involving both cyclists and pedestrians. Ouagadougou does have adequate traffic control devices, including signs and stop lights, but many drivers, cyclists, and pedestrians either ignore them or, in the case of recent migrants or visitors to the town, are ignorant of their meanings. Again, many persons, especially the old, panic when being approached by any vehicle and, as a result, are frequently knocked down. Ouagadougou also has its share of reckless drivers and taxi chauffeurs who, because of exhilaration over the possession of a vehicle or contempt for pedestrians and cyclists, either drive too fast or ignore traffic rules and thus cause accidents. Among the more notorious violators of the traffic laws, and thus frequently involved in accidents, are children of high-status persons or their chauffeurs. To make matters worse, most of them are relatively immune from censure or arrest. Not only do the police hesitate to stop and arrest high-status persons, but they recognize the make and license number of these persons' cars and are more interested in greeting them than in noting any possible violations of traffic laws. Status recognition takes priority over the recognition of illegal acts.

Ironically, many cases involving insulting an officer of the law and resisting arrest are the result of altercations between police and vehicularists accused of violating traffic laws. Tempers usually flare and the persons accused hurl insults at the police who then arrest and charge them with abuse. Another source of "abuse to police" is, of course, merchants in the market places who refuse to pay taxes and abuse the police summoned by the tax collectors. A further source of abuse is the drunks around town. However, the police seldom arrest and bring these malefactors to court. They normally ignore the drunks and allow them to sleep off their intoxication.

Most of the cases involving illegal possession of arms and illegal hunting are sent to the Ouagadougou court from the rural areas. Only one case of illegal possession of arms involving Ouagadougou residents was encountered, and this was more a case of theft than possession of arms. This case concerned a young man who stole a revolver from a car belonging to a European which was parked outside a cinema, tried to sell it, and was reported to the police.

Cases of evading justice and failure to answer summonses reflect, in most instances, a disbelief on the part of the persons concerned that the police authorities possess the techniques and procedures for discovering their whereabouts. Such persons believe that if they move from one area of the town to another, or even from one town to another, they will be able to evade the authorities. They are, therefore, quite surprised to discover that they are picked up routinely when they try to pay taxes or when they apply for any state services. There is little doubt that the growth of a French-type bureaucracy in Upper Volta, even though modified by local conditions, will, in time, make evasion increasingly difficult.

The civil suits listed in Table XXXIX primarily involve lawsuits brought by European and Lebano-Syrian merchants against their African debtors, most of whom are also merchants. From the cases actually heard in court, the main problems are complaints by Africans that they had been overcharged or otherwise swindled by the expatriates; charges by the Africans that the expatriates manipulated the credit accounts so that they showed larger sums being owed than the Africans believed they owed; and charges by the expatriates that the Africans had defaulted on their payments, and appeals to the judge to compel compliance with the repayment schedule or devise a new one with rules for enforcing it. Interestingly enough, cases quite similar in nature between Africans, normally involving smaller sums, are simply treated as attempts at "breach of trust" and "fraud." Apparently, the conviction of the judges here is that if Africans cannot reconcile their differences without coming to court, there must be something more involved than a mere misunderstanding.

The crimes of sorcery, trafficking in poisonous substances, and illegal practice of medicine all deal with the attempts of persons to use the supernatural for private purposes and are viewed by the court as attempts to defraud. According to judges interviewed, the court takes cognizance of these acts primarily because they usually involve the eventuality of some specific criminal action such as poisoning, embezzlement, and so on. However, whether or not the persons brought into court on such charges are convicted, their paraphernalia is confiscated.

Surprisingly enough, a number of cases which belong in the category of "domestic relations," usually judged at the Customary Court in the Town Hall, are brought to the Court of the First Instance. On the docket one finds cases dealing with women abandoning their husbands and, when such cases are actually heard, it becomes quite clear that similar cases are indeed judged in the Customary Courts. The only apparent reason why these cases are brought to the Court of the First Instance is that the Customary Court's power is limited to attempts at reconciling a man and his wife. It normally cannot punish the person responsible for the separation. In the Court of the First Instance, however, the judge does try to ascertain whether the man living with a runaway wife knew her before she left her husband. If this turns out to be the case, he can be charged with and fined for alienation of affections. In this way the Court of the First Instance also attempts to support the marriage system by showing that persons cannot destroy marriage and family life with impunity.

Such crimes as contrabanding, running illegal bars, violating labor ordinances, and contributing to the delinquency of minors are not too numerous in Ouagadougou, but they represent a growing field of litigation in areas formerly marginal to judicial control. The cases dealing with tampering with meters placed on water and electric outlets show not only the spread of new services among the townspeople but also the spread of crimes associated with these services.

In 1963 the Court of the First Instance heard no cases dealing with prostitution. As far as the police and judges are concerned, prostitution does not constitute a crime. The prostitutes who appeared in court were summoned there for such offenses as drunkeness, fighting, and, in the case of foreigners, not having the proper visas or visitor's permits. The one case

389

of statutory rape which was brought to the court during 1964 did not result in a conviction.

The following examples of cases recorded from the Court of the First Instance are presented with the aim of providing some data on the nature of cases brought to the court and their judgments.

Case Number 300

This case concerned a young Mossi man, about twenty-three years of age, who had been picked up by the police for violating the court's order to stay away from Ouagadougou since, every time he came to the town, he was jailed for theft. His record showed that during the last four years he had been imprisoned for theft four times.

When asked to state why he was in Ouagadougou, the defendant replied that he had not intended to violate the ban, but had come to Ouagadougou to obtain transportation to the Ivory Coast. He admitted that he had been in town for two months, a fact which amazed the court who said that it did not take more than twelve hours to get transportation out of town. The court then scolded the young man, telling him that he could be jailed for fifteen or even twenty years. The judge then asked the public prosecutor whether he had any comments, and the prosecutor replied that the prisoner was a recidivist thief and should be severely punished.

The judge asked the prisoner's lawyer whether he had anything to say. The lawyer, who had sat throughout the previous testimony busily taking notes, started to speak. He first appealed to the judge to have mercy on this "weak" individual. He said that the prisoner had left home as a small boy and since had followed evil ways. But to send the prisoner away for fifteen years or more was, in his opinion, too severe. "How," he asked, "would the prisoner support his family?" The lawyer said that it was quite understandable why the prisoner was in Ouagadougou. He said that he did not believe that the prisoner could get a good job either in the rural areas or in the town since he could not get the necessary identification cards. "Who would hire this man?" asked the lawyer. He said that people would say, "Hire him? He has a prison record and he is a thief, a robber." The lawyer pleaded for mercy for his client and rested his case.

390

The judge listened quite carefully to the lawyer's plea, then sentenced the defendant to one year in prison.

The judges in Ouagadougou try to keep recidivist thieves out of the town, but, as the lawyer pointed out, this is an impossible task. The culprits return again and again, especially now that they find it increasingly difficult to obtain the necessary papers to cross the frontiers into neighboring countries. The judge could have sentenced the prisoner to life imprisonment as he had been jailed on several other occasions, but, although recidivism is quite high among prisoners in Ouagadougou, there was no instance of recidivists being sentenced to life.

Case Number 327

This case concerned a young man accused of fraud. According to the evidence, the defendant, a newcomer to Ougagdougou, bragged to his neighbors that he could buy cattle inexpensively in his native district, Béré, and sell them at a profit in Ghana. The complainant stated that he had given the defendant 50,000 francs in order to purchase the cattle. After not having heard from the defendant for several months, he dispatched a messenger to Béré to find out what the matter was. The messenger saw the defendant and was told to inform the complainant that everything was being arranged and that he would come to Ouagadougou in a matter of weeks. When the allotted time had passed and the defendant had not appeared, the complainant sent another messenger to Béré. The defendant allegedly sent the same message back to the complainant, but he still did not appear for several weeks. Finally, the complainant heard that the defendant was in Ouagadougou and, after waiting for several days to see whether or not he would come to him, he notified the police of an attempted fraud and had the defendant arrested.

When asked to testify, the defendant confirmed the statement of the complainant. The judge then asked him why he thought he could buy the cattle and make a profit for all concerned. The defendant replied that the cattle at the place where he customarily bought them were suffering from dissease. Asked by the judge why he had not returned to Ouagadougou with the money, the defendant replied that the money was just spent. He said that the reason why he

391

had not returned to Ouagadougou sooner was that he was afraid of the consequences but eventually decided to return and face any problem he would encounter. The judge then asked the complainant what he wanted done to the defendant. The latter replied that he simply wanted his money back. The judge ordered the defendant to make arrangements through the court to refund the money and placed him on probation for one year.

Noteworthy was that the judge did not ask what the defendant had done with the money. Questioned about this later, the judge said that he had assumed that the defendant had simply taken the money back to his district, bragged about his good fortune in town, and spent it. Many of the cases of fraud and embezzlement are of this kind and reflect a willingness of people to take the word of others rather than inquire too carefully into the business qualifications of their neighbors.

Case Number 328

This case was one of the few civil cases involving Africans which came to the court during 1964. It concerned a merchant of Mossi origin and a Fulani civil servant. It appears that these two men had known each other for more than twelve years while they both lived and worked in the town of Kaya. The merchant moved to Ouagadougou where he built a house, and when, a few years later, the Fulani civil servant was transferred to the town, he sought and obtained the merchant's house at a monthly rental of 10,000 francs. Since the two men were friends, the merchant permitted the Fulani civil servant to fall in arrears, and, even when he paid his rent, no receipts were given or received. The civil servant was in arrears for some months when he was transferred to Dori in the northern part of Upper Volta. The merchant asked the civil servant to pay him the money owed, a sum of 54,000 francs (he had said 56,500 when he had made a statement to the police) or give him a document accepting this debt for, according to the merchant, "In this life one never knows what will happen." This the defendant refused to do stating that true friendship never needs any papers and that he would pay his debt. He told the court that he had made this statement before witnesses, but failed to produce witnesses in court. Nevertheless, the complainant declared that he wanted documentary proof of debt or the money. The judge postponed the case until witnesses could be produced.

This case showed that either the merchant did not trust the civil servant whose tardiness in paying the rent might have been interpreted as an indication of bad faith, or he felt that friendship alone was no guarantee of good intentions and a written contract was necessary for protection. It is not known why the judge called for witnesses, nor is the final judgment in this case known.[6]

Case Number 320

This case concerned a young civil servant employed by the postal service who was arrested for stealing a motorcycle and selling it for 15,000 francs. The prisoner pleaded guilty to the crime. When pressed by the judge as to the reason for the theft, he replied that he had been asked for money by a brother who was getting married. Having none to spare, he stole the vehicle in order to provide the gift of money. He added that he had a wife and children and that was the reason why he had no extra money with which to help his relatives.

At this point the public prosecutor intervened and declared that the prisoner was lying. He said that no person being pressed for money would steal a vehicle and keep it hidden for several days before disposing of it. Nor did he believe that members of a family would insist that one of their kinsmen help with a marriage when the kinsman in question did not have money with which to take care of his own family. The prosecutor said that he believed that the defendant had a weak character, so weak that even during the time he had possession of the stolen vehicle he could not reflect upon the inherent dishonesty and danger of the theft.

The judge said to the young man that he did not believe his story about indigent kinsmen or of his wish to obtain money to give a wedding present to his brother. He added

---

[6]I encountered this civil servant in the town of Léo on the Ghanaian border in 1968 and questioned him about the case. He said that the court made him pay the money because the judge did not understand "friendship."

that no family would like to know that one of its members had to steal in order to help them. He wished to know from the defendant how his family would feel if the members had heard that he was being accused of theft. He then placed the young man on probation for three months and warned him never again to come to court under such circumstances.

The lawyer who had been retained by the young man had apparently not heard the nature of the sentence; he approached the bar of justice and wanted to plead. The judge, obviously amazed at this request, declared that there was indeed nothing to be said since the young man had pleaded guilty and had been given a rather light sentence. This remark brought forth laughter from the people in court and the judge had to rap for order.

Later on in his chambers, the judge used this case to explain to me some of the problems he faced in court. He said that in many lawsuits he faced what he called a "Lambrosian" problem, that is, the problem of impartiality when judging cases in which one or more of the litigants involved were personally known to him. He said that he personally knew the family of the defendant and knew that the man had been lying when he asserted that he had stolen because he wanted to help his brother. The judge said that the young man's father was a deputy in the National Assembly and the brother mentioned by him did not need his money because he had an important job. The judge added that the defendant was known to have a bad character and that the older brother had told him to put the defendant in prison for a while in the hope of teaching him a lesson. The judge stated, however, that it was both against his principles and sound penal practice to imprison an individual on his first offense because this often started the individual on a criminal career.

The judges in the Court of the First Instance in Ouagadougou are not in the habit of dealing with points of law in judging cases. They cross-examine litigants and witnesses, listen patiently to the pleas of the lawyers who, as far as could be ascertained, also never raise points of law, and then lecture the litigants before passing judgments. From the cited statement of the judge, it is obvious that many of the judges take the problems of culture change, urbanization, sociological factors, and frequent incongruity into consideration when

TABLE XLII. Penalties Levied for Crimes Judged by First Degree Court

Category of Crime	Penalty
Accidental homicide	3 months' imprisonment
Assault and battery	2 months' imprisonment, 10,000 francs fine, and 26,200 francs damages
Wilfully inflicted cuts and wounds	Probation for one year and 10,000 francs damages
Attempted theft, infliction of wounds	6 months' imprisonment
Attempted theft by juvenile	Probation in custody of parents
Theft	1 month imprisonment
Theft by two persons	7 months' probation for each
Theft by juvenile (fifteen years old)	Probation in custody of father
Theft by juvenile (fifteen years old)	6 months' imprisonment because he acted with malice aforethought
Theft	13 months' imprisonment
Theft	1 year imprisonment and 5 years on probation
Accidental homicide	3 months' probation, made to surrender his gun
Attempted fraud and trickery	3 months' probation
Theft	18 months' imprisonment; permitted to post bail on appeal
Sale of meat unfit for human consumption	15 days' imprisonment and 5,000 francs fine
Contraband importation of one tin (20 liters) of alcohol	15 days' imprisonment, 20,000 francs fine, and confiscation of alcohol and bicycle on which it was imported
Illegal hunting	10,000 francs fine and confiscation of gun
Illegal possession of arms	5,000 francs fine and confiscation of gun
Attempted theft	Recidivist; 1 year imprisonment and 5 years' probation
Theft and vagrancy	8 months' imprisonment and 5 years' probation
Theft	Recidivist; 6 months' imprisonment
Theft of 2,400 francs by a juvenile	Sent to reform school at Orodara; money returned to victim
Wilfully inflicted cuts and wounds	3 months' imprisonment and 4,000 francs in damages
Theft	10 months' imprisonment
Theft and attempted theft	2 years' imprisonment and 5 years' probation
Theft	2 months' imprisonment in addition to 1 year suspended sentence in early 1963
Wilfully inflicted cuts and wounds	400,000 francs damages to victim
Refusal to pay taxes	1,000 francs fine and payment of taxes

Category of Crime	Penalty
Theft by seventeen-year-old male	Declared to have acted with malice aforethought; 1 year imprisonment plus restitution of stolen articles
Theft by seventeen-year-old	Declared to have acted without discernment; 6 months' imprisonment
Theft by fifteen-year-old	Declared to have acted with malice aforethought; 3 months' imprisonment
Theft by thirteen-year-old	Declared to have acted without discernment; released in the custody of relatives
Theft by fourteen-year-old	Declared to have acted with malice aforethought; 6 months' imprisonment
Theft by sixteen-year-old	Declared to have acted without discernment; sent to reform school at Boulbi
Attempted theft	6 months' imprisonment
Theft by a minor	1 year imprisonment; sentence suspended
Theft	2 years' imprisonment; sentence suspended
Illegal entry into Upper Volta by a Yoruba of Nigeria	1 month imprisonment
Theft	4 months' imprisonment
Theft	3 months' imprisonment plus restitution of stolen articles
Theft and receiving stolen goods	6 months' imprisonment
Theft	1 month imprisonment; sentence suspended
Illegally wearing police uniform	15 days' imprisonment
Abuse of confidence	4 months' imprisonment
Theft	6 months' imprisonment
Theft	15 days on bond
Theft	3 months on bond plus 5 years' probation
Accidental homicide (vehicular) involving two persons	Person #1: 3 years' imprisonment, 650,000 francs damages, and 675,000 francs fine (Appealed)
	Person #2: 2 years' imprisonment, and 18,000 francs fine
Attempted theft and vagrancy	8 months' imprisonment and 5 years' probation
Accidental wounding (vehicular)	20,000 francs damages plus repair of automobile

applying French law to Africans of different ethnic and educational backgrounds. There are, however, other factors, such as shortage of space in the prisons or the absence of proper reform school facilities in the country, which determine whether judges incarcerate adult prisoners and juvenile delinquents or simply suspend their sentences and place them on probation. The sentences meted out in the first fifty cases on the docket of 1963 give some indication of penalties assigned to crimes by the Court of the First Instance (see Table XLII).

Litigants and accused persons who appeared before the Court of the First Instance in Ouagadougou during 1963 seldom appealed the verdicts rendered and the sentences meted out by the judges. A careful perusal of the docket, where the appeals are marked in red, revealed only five such cases. Another characteristic of justice in this court is that persons accused of crimes requiring imprisonment remained in prison so long awaiting trial that they literally served their sentences before being sentenced. When their cases finally came to trial, the judge usually took the time spent in jail into consideration before passing sentence. The sentence frequently was the time already spent in jail. The result was that jail terms meted out for the same crimes differ greatly, the differences often reflecting the length of time the accused was held in prison before being brought to trial.

There were no opportunities to visit or gather data on the higher courts, such as the Superior Court of Appeals, the Assizes Court, the Supreme Court, and the High Court of Justice which serve not only the people of Ouagadougou but all the people of Upper Volta. In general these courts do not meet very often, and when they meet their dockets are devoted to special types of litigation. Data gathered from one meeting of the Assizes Court in Ouagadougou during 1963 show that this court deals primarily with homicide and other serious crimes. The president of this court was a Frenchman assisted by six citizens of Ouagadougou, among whom were a school teacher, a male nurse, and the chief of Ouidi ward of the town of Ouagadougou. Following are ten cases which came before the Assizes Court and the sentences meted out:

1. A. P., accused of "correcting his wife so energetically that she died," was sentenced to 2 years' imprisonment.

397

2. G. S., accused of murdering his rival for the affection of a woman, was sentenced to 10 years' forced labor.

3. P. S., accused of "ignorantly murdering the man who he believed had attracted illnesses to his village" (witchcraft), was sentenced to 10 years' forced labor.

4. D. S., a relative of P. S., was implicated in the above affair but his role was "only supportive." He was sentenced to 5 years' forced labor.

5. D. B., accused of "committing murder after having lost his head over an insult which he felt was particularly offensive," was sentenced to 10 years' forced labor.

6. O. O., accused of "suspicion of having violated the daughter of his employer," was acquitted.

7. P. D., accused of "murdering his aunt for various motives, among which sorcery was not absent," was sentenced to 20 years' forced labor.

8. S. Z., accused of "murdering a young man while drunk," was sentenced to 5 years' solitary confinement.

9. N. K., accused of "murder," was sentenced to 5 years' solitary confinement.

10. S. C., accused of "suspicion of embezzling funds from the Post Office administration," was acquitted.

Prisons

There is one prison in Ouagadougou for incarcerating sentenced criminals. Until the end of September 1964, the prisoners were housed in a city-block-long building constructed in 1920 by Lieutenant-Governor Hesling to house all short-term prisoners of the Upper Volta colony. Prisoners sentenced for more serious crimes were either imprisoned in Bamako (Mali) or Dakar (Senegal). When Upper Volta was granted independence in 1960, the prison in Ouagadougou became the main prison for criminals of the country. Smaller prisons in towns such as Bobo-Dioulasso and Koudougou were used to incarcerate persons found guilty of lesser offenses.

There were approximately 600 prisoners in the Ouagadougou jail on July 30, 1964, including 6 women and approximately 40 juveniles. The women were kept separately in one part of the prison, but the men and juveniles were housed together. There were no special provisions for keeping those persons awaiting trial separated from those who had already been sentenced, so there was a great deal of fraternization between the two groups. The only distinction was that most of the male prisoners wore a blue uniform while persons awaiting trial wore their own clothing—except that their belts were taken away to prevent them from committing suicide by hanging.

The prisoners in the Ouagadougou jail, even those sentenced to hard labor, had little physical work to do. On some mornings, truckloads of prisoners left the prison compounds to work in the municipal gardens, to clean the municipal abbattoir, or to cut down trees, but these men often returned to their compounds by 3:00 P.M. There were no workshops in the prison except those which permitted the prisoners to take care of their own domestic chores, and prison labor was not used in any capacity to construct the new prison which the prisoners occupied in September 1964. Many persons in the Town Hall believed that the prisoners were not even made to clean their own quarters. The Mayor of Ouagadougou constantly received complaints from the housewives in Bilbalgo quarter, where the old prison was located, about the foul odors which wafted over the prison walls. The municipality did try to mollify the housewives by telling them that attempts were being made to deodorize the waste disposal facilities there, and that in any event their woes would soon cease since the whole prison would be moved.

The shortage of facilities at the old prison in Ouagadougou not only influenced the judges to mete out prison sentences which had already been "served" by prisoners awaiting trial, but also hampered the jailers' ability to punish prisoners. Prisoners condemned to "hard labor" could not serve these sentences, nor could prisoners be safely kept in solitary confinement for any extended period of time. The jailers were able to maintain discipline by means of the customary technique of reducing a prisoner's diet to bread and water and were not above using harsher measures, such as whipping, when they proved necessary. Nevertheless, discipline was fairly lax, and after learning prison routine, the so-called *zazzous,* or rebellious youths, were able to obtain stylish haircuts and effect the air of the "hipster." Those long-term prisoners who, by their good behavior, had become trustees, abandoned prison garb for street dress and spent most of the day sitting on benches outside the prison. They served the function of allaying the fears of relatives of newly incarcerated prisoners; bought and distributed cigarettes, kola nuts, and other luxuries to prisoners; and passed on the food brought daily by relatives to some beloved prisoners.

The women prisoners also had a great deal of liberty, a fact which in time created some embarrassment for the prison officials. Two female trustees not only sold food and vegetables outside the prison to those guards, visitors, and trustees who wished to buy, but these two women also took sewing lessons at the social service center of Bilbalgo. That one of the women had been jailed for the homicide of a French soldier who allegedly had tried to cheat a group of prostitutes in Tiedpalogho, did not prevent her from going outside the prison. The relative freedom of the other women prisoners resulted in the allegation, by townspeople, of prostitution in the prison and of the birth of two babies to the women inmates.

The decision to move the prison to a site just a few kilometers north of the town's boundaries did produce a crisis for the inmates. For one thing, many of them felt that they were being taken out of town and placed "in the bush," and many also resented the fact that female relatives, who daily brought meals to them, would now have to walk almost 2 kilometers out of town to do so. The result of this disquietude was that, when word was received that the move to the new prison was imminent, the prisoners attempted a jailbreak on the night of September 24, 1964. About four prisoners escaped, but by early October the move was carried out.

The new prison, in contrast to the old, is a three-story concrete structure. The building itself is about 300 feet long by 40 feet wide and about 40 feet high. It has two rows of 30 cells (60 in all) on each floor, and space allotted for offices, dispensary, kitchen, and so forth. Each cell is designed to hold six prisoners and has an interior toilet and shower. This arrangement permits the prison officials to segregate young inmates and boys awaiting trial as juvenile delinquents from the hardened prisoners, a practice which the social service had long requested. Also, the women now have one wing on the ground floor of the building so that they can be supervised easily by the senior officials. Thus, from the point of view of space, living conditions, sanitation, and security, the new prison is superior to the old.

400

The only problem with the new prison is that, although it was built according to modern prison specifications, it anticipated by a few years the requirements of the prisoners for whom it was built. The prisoners keenly feel that they are "in the bush" and cut off from life. As of December 1964 the people in the area had not yet discovered that they had in the prisoners a good market for cigarettes and kola nuts, and this displeased the prisoners.[7] Again in contrast to the old prison which had walls and thus permitted the prisoners to get air and sunlight when they came out of their cells each morning, the new prison was initially not surrounded by walls and the prisoners were kept inside their cells and inside the building. Many prisoners complained that it was only when they were moved to the new prison that they really felt that they were imprisoned. The people in town even began to make jokes about the prison stating that, true, the prisoners were in a *gratte-ciel* (sky scraper), but that once a man went in there he never saw the sun again until he got to paradise.

A rather serious problem for the prison administration was the inadequacy of the kitchen facilities. Provisions had been made for a kitchen within the building and a chimney had been built to carry away the smoke. However, the chimney was not intended for fires in which the fuel would be wood. Any attempt to use wood would have resulted in the whole beautiful white kitchen space turning a dismal black in a short time. The fact is that the architects had planned for the use of butane gas, a luxury found only in the homes of the top African elite and of the Europeans in Ouagadougou. After a few days of short rations cooked over makeshift fires in the prison yard, the administration built an outdoor kitchen for the prisoners.

If the adult prisoners in Ouagadougou are now being adequately housed, the problem of providing facilities for the juvenile delinquents now living in the prison still remains. These youngsters range from six to seventeen years of age, and from youths who had been imprisoned for committing crimes with malice aforethought to boys awaiting trial. The prison authorities did segregate the youngsters on the top floor— much to the annoyance of the older prisoners who now have to

[7] By 1968, a village with small shops and bars had sprung up near the prison.

do without the services of their "boys" (domestics)—but the social service would like to remove the youngsters from the prison environment altogether.

The provision of adequate care and training for the juvenile delinquents of Ouagadougou became a political problem and has suffered as a result. The first institution to which juvenile delinquents were sent, La Maison de l'Enfance d'Orodara, was established by the White Fathers' Catholic mission at Oro-dara. But this establishment had no one qualified to reeducate the delinquents and was closed in December 1958 after suffer-ing financial difficulties. It was subsequently taken over by the government and reopened in April 1959 under the direc-tion and control of a Frenchman. It is still functioning and the courts, both in Ouagadougou and Bobo-Dioulasso, send young juvenile delinquents there. One problem is that young-sters must volunteer to go to Orodara since it is a minimum security institution and youngsters sent there against their will might just run off. A more serious problem is that the Maison can only accommodate 70 boys at a time, and the rate of juvenile delinquency in both Ouagadougou and Bobo-Dioulasso is much higher than that.

The other institution for reeducating juvenile delinquents was established in 1958, about 8 kilometers from Ouaga-dougou, by the initiative of a Brother of the White Fathers missionaries. By 1960 he had about 50 youngsters ranging in age from about six to fifteen who, besides being taught disci-pline, were put to work making bricks, cultivating crops, cooking preserves, and so on. However, since the Brothers wished to focus most of the attention of these boys on agri-culture and the available land there was insufficient to do so, a piece of land for the school was obtained at a place called Boulbi, 15 kilometers south of Ouagadougou. Trouble started almost immediately because many boys who had accepted the discipline of the school when it was close to town, absolutely refused to live "in the bush" and fled. Only the very young boys were left until the government recognized the reeducative possibilities of Boulbi and sent older juvenile delinquents there. A private group, the Association Voltaique pour la Sauvegarde de l'Enfance et de l'Adolescence (A.V.S.E.A.), organized in 1959 at the height of the association-building period in the Upper Volta, came to the aid of Boulbi by giving

402

it a modest subvention. Nevertheless, two problems arose to plague the school. One occurred in 1963 when the Brother who ran the school left for vacation. Discipline became so lax that the villagers in the Boulbi area complained about the depredations of the boys and the decision was made to remove the camp further into the bush and away from the villagers. Second, some of the leaders of A.V.S.E.A., realizing the concern of many Voltaic parents with the growing problem of juvenile delinquency, tried to use their connection with Boulbi to enhance their political prestige and ran afoul of the politicians. The result was that A.V.S.E.A. was disbanded. Since then, the school at Boulbi has become a strictly private institution supported by the Archdiocese of Ouagadougou with the aid of some prestigious persons in Ouagadougou, local as well as foreign.

As of 1968, the problem of reeducating the juvenile delinquents of Ouagadougou was still not being satisfactorily approached. The division of L'Enfance Inadaptée, created in 1961 as a subdivision of the Service of Social Affairs under the control of the Ministère de la Santé Publique et de la Population, has been vainly trying to obtain more personnel for its work and more facilities for reeducating delinquents. Today it comes into contact with delinquents only after they have been arrested by the police and are awaiting trial. Staff members then interview the delinquents, their employers (if they had been working in the town), and their guardians or people with whom they were living in Ouagadougou; and they even make trips to the rural areas to interview relatives of those boys who had migrated to the town. With this information, they counsel the judge at the Court of the First Instance as to the possible disposition of the young delinquents. The social workers may recommend that the youngsters be released in the custody of rural relatives or even urban relatives or, with the consent of the boys, be sent either to Boulbi or to Orodara. If the boys do not agree to go to either of these institutions, the only recourse the judge has is to send them to the regular prison. Everyone concerned believes that doing so exposes the boys to confirmed lawbreakers and may start them on a criminal career. But in the absence of any other facilities, this is the only solution. The fear is that this absence of proper facilities for reeducating the growing number of juvenile delinquents coming through the courts of the town will contribute toward future and greater problems of law and order for the people of Ouagadougou.

The data in this chapter show the predicament of migrant youths, cultivators, and literate clerks and civil servants as they attempt to cope with the new economic, moral, social and legal imperatives of modern urban life. Some people break urban codes through ignorance; others attempt to manipulate the law by claiming ignorance of it. The municipality in its quest for funds is not above penalizing individuals who unconsciously break the law. Young men faced with unemployment or unwilling to look for work have organized gangs which use techniques learned from the most recent movies. These youngsters attack property, and the highest proportion of crimes committed in Ouagadougou involve property. But the large number of offenses involving injuries suggests that strained social relations are an important element of conflict in the town.

The urban milieu of Ouagadougou has exacerbated many of the problems, such as marital discord, that have historically plagued Voltaic societies. Some men, but especially women, manipulate the new alternatives generated by economic change, nucleation of extended family, social mobility, changing cultural values, and French-derived laws to break irksome conjugal ties and other social relations. Both the traditional and modern judges are aware that litigants use traditional mediators and high-status persons, and also manipulate customary law and the new legal codes, to affect reconciliation, obtain justice, or subvert it. But faced with a mass of incongruities, the judges in Ouagadougou often make *ad hoc* decisions in order that justice be served. There is, however, evidence that a consensus about law and order is emerging in Ouagadougou. Both the people and the judges are learning to blend novelty with tradition, even as they recognize that the "Lambrosian" problem of "impartiality" must be viewed with a full awareness of the nature of the changing African urban environment.

404

CHAPTER XI

Politics and Government

Ouagadougou has always been a center of government, and politics the principal task of its most prestigious inhabitants. The Mogho Naba ruled his kingdom from Ouagadougou, and his resident ministers maintained law and order in the town. When the French conquered Upper Volta in 1896, they used Ouagadougou as their capital and instituted colonial-type municipal administrators. Then as Upper Volta progressed toward independence, the French upgraded the town's municipal system. The result was that when Ouagadougou became the capital of an independent Upper Volta Republic it possessed three distinct political and administrative systems: the persisting traditional system, a modern municipal system, and the political apparatus of the Upper Volta nation-state. And while these three systems have facilitated the adaptation to modern urban life of a largely rural-born population, competition between them has frequently led to conflict within the town.[1]

Despite their penchant for "direct-rule," the French permitted the traditional government of the Mogho Naba and his chiefs to survive and help run the town.[2] Even when, in April 1920, the administration created the Conseil de Notables (Council of Native Notables)[3] as a consultative institution within the town, no attempt was made to bypass the chiefs. The French intended to use the members of the council as

[1] Elliott P. Skinner, "Chiefs, Politicians and Municipal Councillors: The Problem of Government in a West African Municipality," *Proceedings of Conference on the Government of African Cities,* Institute of African Government, Department of Political Science, Lincoln University, Lincoln University, Penna., pp. 96–104; cf. A. L. Epstein, *Politics in an Urban African Community* (Manchester, England: Manchester University Press, 1958), pp. 224–40.

[2] Skinner, 1964b, p. 155; Gomkoudougou V. Kabore, *Organisation Politique Traditionnelle et Evolution Politique des Mossi de Ouagadougou,* Recherches Voltaique 5 (Paris—CRRS/Ouagadougou-CVRS/1966), p. 174.

[3] *Journal Officiel de la République Française* (Circular of June 16, 1919); see also Skinner, 1964b, p. 165.

intermediaries with the local population in an attempt to introduce the ideals and standards of French policy. The administration also wished to establish closer contact with the townspeople, who "had been almost totally ignorant of the functioning of [the French] administration." It also foresaw the members of the council as "an elite who [would] later be able to contribute in a closer and more personal way to the economic and financial life of the colony."[4]

The Conseil de Notables of Ouagadougou had 10 to 16 members, among whom were a number of traditional provincial ministers of the Mogho Naba (with life membership). In addition, there were representatives of the Moslem community of the town; representatives of the stranger populations living in the town; representatives of the French community; and representatives of the large number of African veterans of World War I who had settled in the town after their return from service. The Commander of the *Cercle* of Ouagadougou served as the president of this council, and the body discussed such matters as personal taxes, the allocation and execution of prestations for the administration, the use of Voltaic laborers in foreign areas, the licensing and taxation of local traders and merchants, and the status of women. But since the council's work was mainly advisory, it had little effect on the administrative procedures which had been evolving between the administrators and chiefs in the emerging wards of the town.

As we have already seen, the first major step in the evolution of modern administration in Ouagadougou was the designation of the town as a *commune-mixte* in 1927. Its Administrateur-Maire was responsible for distributing colonial ordinances within the town and could promulgate simple ordinances to deal with minor local problems. More serious ordinances for the town had to be approved by the colonial administration. Moreover, the Administrateur-Maire of Ouagadougou did not have a municipal council but was given a "Municipal Commission of the First Degree," composed of important French citizens appointed by the Governor of Upper Volta. As far as the local population was concerned, the inception of the Administrateur-Maire in the town, while representing a stage in the evolution of the Municipality of

[4] *Ibid.*, pp. 165–66.

Ouagadougou, had little or no effect on their relations with the local chiefs.

By 1927, the administrative roles of the local chiefs in Ouagadougou had been fairly well adapted to and institution-alized by the colonial system. The provincial chiefs and chiefs in the emerging wards of the town were now confirmed in their task of collecting taxes for the administration. For example, the Dapoya Naba (formerly the head of a group of serfs serv-ing the Mogho Naba) was given the task of collecting taxes from his people in Dapoya II and from those who subse-quently settled there. The provincial chiefs, such as the Ouidi Naba, the Larhalle Naba, the Samandin Naba, the Baloum Naba, and the Gounghin Naba, also collected taxes from the inhabitants of their wards. Local Christians, who had emerged as "chiefs" or "headmen" in the "Saint" wards around the mission, also collected taxes for the administration. When, as often happened, the chiefs or headmen did not sub-mit the taxes on time, they were reprimanded by the adminis-tration. In 1930 the chief of St. Joseph ward was sent the following memorandum from the Administrateur-Maire:

> I regret to note that your quarter is one of the last to pay its taxes. You still owe the office 3,255 francs. You would do well to collect these taxes before the end of September. Otherwise, I will have the painful task of suppressing your commission on the taxes for the year because of negligence in the performance of your duty. Please inform me when these present instructions have been executed and your tax collection has been completed.[5]

The colonial governments' use of chiefs in the town's admin-istration resulted in interesting political compromises. For example, when the administration wished to use provincial ministers as tax collectors and give them the usual commis-sion, it discovered that the decree concerning tax collection authorized commissions only to "village chiefs." The only way the government could compensate the ministers was to con-sider them the "village chiefs" of the wards in which they lived. The results were memoranda such as the following:

Concerning Sana Rouamba of Ouidi.

In view of the situation created by Honorable Sana

---

[5] *Archives du Cercle de Ouagadougou* [unedited], 31 August 1950.

Rouamba exercising the functions of chief of the Village of Ouidi concurrently with the function of chief of the Province of Ouidi;

On the recommendation of the commandant of the North Subdivision of Ouagadougou that these functions are necessary for his service;

It is decided:

Article one: to ratify the traditional designation of the Honorable Sana Rouamba as chief of the village of Ouidi (Province of Baloum).[6]

The French thus officially subordinated the provincial chiefs in Ouagadougou to the Baloum Naba, traditional chamberlain of the royal court, an act which was contrary to Mossi political organization.

In most cases, the French administrators of Ouagadougou accepted the Mogho Naba's nominations for the chiefship of the Mossi wards of the town. An early circular in the files of the *cercle* shows that the administration accepted the Mogho Naba's designation of Finsi Ilboudou as chief of the "village" (actually ward) of Kamsaoghin, replacing Amadou Compaore who had died. It is noteworthy that the Mogho Naba was careful to state in his letter that "the nomination of M. Finsi Ilboudou, actually chief of Nomgana village, Loumbila Canton, Subdivision of Zinaré, was responsive to the desires of the inhabitants of Kamsaoghin, whose notables had been consulted."[7] The administration exercised more control over the choice of the representatives of the non-Mossi groups within the town. Once, when a chief of the Fulani subsection of Bilibambili died, the French officials in the town summoned some 56 household heads and the representative of the Mogho Naba, the Baloum Naba, to ascertain whether they wished the deceased's brother's son to be the new chief.

The French practice of indirect rule in Ouagadougou was advantageous for all concerned. Those local people who preferred to avoid the French administration could be admin-

---

[6] *Ibid.*, 20 April 1950; Kassoum Congo, *Conséquences de la colonisation sur la vie coutumière en pays mossi.* Essai sur l'intégration du pays mossi dans le système francais avec *les conséquences sur la vie archaique* (Montpellier, Université de Montpellier, Faculté de Droit, 1955), multigr. (Thèse pour le doctorat de droit), p. 23.

[7] *Ibid.*, 8 October 1957.

istered by their own chiefs and elders. If these persons could not solve the problems of their people, appeals could be made through the Baloum Naba to the Mogho Naba. Sometimes when the French found out that serious criminal cases had been tried by the traditional authorities, they summoned the litigants to appear before the colonial courts. In most cases, however, the French permitted the townspeople to solve their own problems with the help of their chiefs. The chiefs, for their part, welcomed the opportunity to retain some of their traditional power.

The dismemberment of the Upper Volta colony in 1932 arrested the development of Ouagadougou and stymied the evolution of administrative structures within the town. The departure of many European and African civil servants for the Lower Ivory Coast and the loss of such amenities as the printing press deprived the town of those persons and processes which were conducive to further growth and development.[8] The erstwhile capital of the colony of Upper Volta was now reduced to its former status—headquarters (*chef-lieu*) of the *Cercle* of Ouagadougou. Nevertheless, the chiefs continued to play their traditional roles as well as the newer roles that had been given them by the administration. Mogho Naba Kom gained so much respect among the town's inhabitants that when he died in 1942 his death was seen as a portent of changes that would take place in the political status of Upper Volta after World War II. The French Resident in Ouagadougou took note of the rumors, but he reassured his superiors in Abidjan that he would watch the situation very closely. Except for some abortive acts of the ritual license which customarily marked the interregnum among the Mossi, the situation in the town remained calm. Naba Kom's eldest son was inaugurated as Mogho Naba Sagha II and the country remained peaceful to the end of the war.

The end of World War II set in motion forces which were to shape the future administration of Ouagadougou. The Brazzaville Conference of high French officials, convened in 1944 at the instigation of General Charles de Gaulle, sought to establish a new relationship between France and her overseas territories. In 1945 the people of the "Ivory Coast Colony," including those in the town of Ouagadougou, were asked to

[8] Tiendrébéogo, 1964b, p. 181.

vote for political representatives to the Constitutional Convention of the Fourth French Republic. Mogho Naba Sagha II initially refused to take the new political situation seriously. When visited by a delegation of elders who had been approached by representatives of political groups forming in the Lower Ivory Coast, he allegedly told them that he did not think very much of the politicians and that he would send his *tansoba* (war minister) to talk to them. A number of young educated Mossi were alarmed by the king's attitude and convinced him that the political campaign was important both for the Mossi people as well as for their chiefs. He authorized his Baloum Naba to run for office against Félix Houphouet-Boigny of the Lower Ivory Coast[9] on a platform that included, above all else, the restoration of the Upper Volta territory with Ouagadougou as its capital. The Baloum Naba carried the town of Ouagadougou and much of the Upper Ivory Coast during the election, but lost to· Houphouet-Boigny by 1,030 votes.[10] Nevertheless, the French became aware of the desire of the Mossi to secede from the Ivory Coast. They struck a bargain with the Voltaic chiefs in which they attempted to curb the power of Houphouet-Boigny's R.D.A., and obtain laborers to extend the railroad to Ouagadougou, by promulgating a law on September 4, 1947, reconstituting the Upper Volta with Ouagadougou as its capital.

The selection of Ouagadougou as the capital of the territory of Upper Volta greatly changed its physical appearance but had no immediate effect on its municipal status nor its local government structure. Ouagadougou had not been chosen for elevation to the status of *commune de moyen exercice* (a status transitional to full *commune* status) when the decree of November 26, 1947 modified the structure of several African towns. Ouagadougou's lack of financial resources "capable of supporting the charges of full communal development"[11] was probably the reason for this omission. The people of Ouagadougou really could not afford to build a capital, and it fell to François Bouda and Joseph Conombo, two newly elected Mossi parliamentarians, to obtain funds from France. The success of the politicians demonstrated to the people of Ouagadougou that henceforth the fate of their town was closely

[9] Skinner, 1964b, p. 181.
[10] *Ibid.*, p. 183.
[11] Thompson and Adloff, p. 183.

410

linked with the activities of elected representatives. It was the politicians who obtained ordinances controlling the use of land, tracing streets, and providing a more adequate water supply for a growing urban population. They thus proved that they were able to persuade the French to undertake major projects.

The next two stages in the political evolution of Ouagadougou followed so quickly upon each other that many people did not realize they had taken place. On January 1, 1953, Ouagadougou became a *commune de moyen exercice* with the right to elect a municipal council. But before M. Chabron, the Administrateur-Maire, could start the process for electing this council, the African politicians in France were already demanding full *commune* status for the capital towns in French-speaking Africa. They also wanted to eliminate the double-college electoral system which had been foisted upon most of French-speaking Africa in 1946 and place the towns under the control of local African populations. A new law of November 18, 1955 made Ouagadougou a *commune de plein exercice,* and gave it the right to elect a municipal government. But once again political events outside the town, and even outside the territory and federation, delayed elections. It was not until one year later that the Ouagadougou people prepared to hold elections for their municipal council. The 28 wards or neighborhoods recognized by the administration (traditional ones such as Gounghin, Ouidi, and Bilbalgo, and modern ones such as St. Léon, Camp Fonctionnaire, and Zone Résidentielle) were divided into 7 election districts. There was to be one municipal councilor for each 1,000 persons. Thus, the most populous Fourth District (Gounghin, Larhalle, Ouidi and Tampouy) with a population of 6,579, was allotted 6 councilors, and the least populous Sixth (St. Léon, St. Joseph, and Mission) with 1,949 inhabitants, could elect 2 councilors. Adults of both sexes had the right to vote. Excluded from the franchise were criminals and foreign (non-French) nationals.

Most of the political parties in Upper Volta and a few independent candidates contested the municipal council election on November 18, 1956. The Parti Démocratique Unifié—a fusion of the Union Voltaique Parti Social d'Education des Masses Africaines (P.S.E.M.A.) and the Parti Démocratique Voltaique (R.D.A.)—contested every seat in Ouagadougou. The Mouvement Démocratique Voltaique, representing the

411

northern and western parts of Upper Volta, contested seats in all the districts except the First, Sixth, and Seventh. The latter were strongholds of the Baloum Naba, the Catholics, and a combination of the military, Europeans, and African civil servants respectively. The Indépendants (independent candidates) contested seats only in the First and Seventh Districts. Out of 60 candidates, 36 were Mossi, 22 were non-Mossi Voltaics, 1 a European, and 1 a Haitian-Syrian mulatto. As to be expected, the European and the mulatto contested seats in the Seventh District inhabited by Europeans and businessmen.[12]

The P.D.U. won a clear majority in Ouagadougou, taking 25 out of the 31 seats on the council. The M.D.V. received 5 seats, and an Indépendant, 1 seat. An analysis of the voting shows that 21 of the elected councilors were Mossi, thus giving the Mossi twice as many seats as the other councilors combined. Mossi candidates carried all seats in the wards of three traditional provincial chiefs (the Larhalle, Ouidi, and Goun-ghin Nanamsé) and the Catholic mission ward. The relative ethnic complexity of the Second and Fifth Districts facilitated the election of a Hausa, a Fulani, and two Mossi (one from Koudougou and the other from Ouahigouya, both known for their opposition to the followers of the Mogho Naba of Ouagadougou). Non-Mossi were elected to all three seats in the Seventh District: one was Gurunga, the second a mulatto, and the third a Frenchman. The *Bulletin Quotidien,* commenting upon the election, stated:

> Present among the new councilors elected at Ouagadougou were: the Deputy, Mr. Gerard Ouedraogo, elected at the head of the list in the Second District; the Territorial Councilors, Messrs. Joseph Ouedraogo, Oscar Nikiema, and André Kaboré; as well as several traditional notables among whom were the four ministers of the Mogho Naba.[13]

Thus the council represented a good cross section of the important political factions within the town itself.

The Municipal Council, exercising its constitutional rights, elected as Mayor, Mr. Joseph Ouedraogo, a territorial councilor and an important member of the P.D.U. Besides appointing the Mayor and providing adjutants for him, the council was to form itself into committees for the special services

[12] *Bulletin Quotidien,* 23 November 1956, p. 4.
[13] *Ibid.*

412

needed by the town, to meet twice annually in ordinary sessions to deal with the problems of the town, and to meet in extra-ordinary sessions whenever the situation so warranted. The municipal councilors fully expected to deliberate on all the affairs of the commune and to ascertain the wishes and desires of their constituents. If these matters fell within the competence of the council, they were to be brought up for approval and, if they were accepted, passed on to the Mayor, other bodies, or individuals for execution.

The Mayor named a general secretary to coordinate the various services of the municipality: the secretariat, bookkeeping, military, civil status, Customary Court, census, municipal property, water works and markets, streets and highways, and public health. His main functions included the administration of the town's property; the preparation, submission, and administration of the budget; the direction of public works; and the execution of the decisions of the Municipal Council. As the chief executive of the town, the mayor had a great deal of power. He could pay off his political debts and mobilize support among the townspeople by giving them jobs, house lots, and contracts for many essential services. As the chief agent of the Civil Status Bureau in the town, he was able to help those many immigrants to Ouagadougou who needed official papers. Moreover, as an officer of the judiciary police, he could intervene on behalf of those persons who, out of ignorance or intent, had violated the statutes of the municipality.

The Mayor was relatively free from censure by the Municipal Council for actions taken as a function of his office. Nevertheless, he was subject to the state whose agent he became upon being elected Mayor. In this latter capacity, he was responsible for announcing and executing the laws, ordinances, and security measures of the state. He supervised elections, tax collection, and military recruitment; kept statistics on population and municipal affairs; and utilized his police powers to maintain public peace and order. He was also responsible to the Minister of the Interior for the affairs of the municipality and could be censured by the state for malfeasance in office.

The first elected Mayor of Ouagadougou found himself in a difficult position because the status of the territory of Upper Volta was still ambiguous. The *loi-cadre* of June 23, 1956,

413

envisaged devolving executive power to the local Territorial Assembly and its parliamentarians, but in November 1956 this process was incomplete. People were, therefore, unsure about the nature of the authority to which the Mayor was subjected. The situation was further complicated by the Mayor's active candidacy for the highest office in the state available to Africans. The result was that the mayoralty in Ouagadougou became highly politicized and the Mayor used his power to gain support on a territorial level. Many of the municipal councilors in Ouagadougou were also active politicians and, during the first period of uncertainty, used their status to further their territorial ambitions.

During the period 1956 to 1960 the Municipal Council and the Mayor of Ouagadougou, paid more attention to their political careers and to improving the physical appearance of the town, than to developing its governmental apparatus. The council voted money for paving several streets in the town, improving the town's water supply, providing electric services, and constructing a covered market and a Town Hall. Speaking at the inauguration of the new Town Hall on June 7, 1958, Mayor Joseph Ouedraogo declared:

> It had been necessary that the mayoralty, which had already made a great effort for the construction of a spacious and organized market, rid itself of its tired, old, mud-brick building with its decayed walls and lizards. It had been necessary to rid itself of offices, glorious in times past, but today unworthy to serve the population. The Municipal Council and I have to uphold the pride of our city and that is why we, your elected members, thought that the Capital of the Territory, though economically poor, should possess a vast and attractive Community House, a Town Hall bearing witness to the vitality and the force of our city.[14]

The Mayor, a former seminarian, evoked the image of the Town Hall as a "Civil Cathedral, a secular basilica, where one works for the people, where the people come to be counseled and helped, and where the peoples' representatives try their best to secure for them, well-being, justice and social peace."[15]

The social peace that the Mayor promised the town did not

---

[14] *Ibid.*, 8 June 1958, p. 11.
[15] *Ibid.*

414

materialize. During the years 1958–59 he lost a series of skirmishes in the political arena. On August 29, 1959, the president of the Council of Ministers of the Upper Volta Government accused him of malfeasance in office and dismissed him and his municipal council. Now, once more, the government of the town of Ouagadougou was directly influenced by territorial political problems. The president of the council, Mr. Maurice Yaméogo, himself an elected municipal councilor from the Second District of the town, appointed a delegation consisting of Messrs. Joseph Conombo (a former Secretary of State in the Mendès-France Government of the Fourth French Republic), Nader Attié (a municipal councilor from the Seventh District), Laurent Ghilat, and Daga Hama to run the town. This delegation chose Dr. Joseph Conombo as its president, and he conducted the affairs of the town until the independence of the Upper Volta Republic on August 5, 1960.

By this time, the political climate in Upper Volta had changed: the U.D.V.–R.D.A. had emerged as the victorious party in Upper Volta and Maurice Yaméogo, its leader, became President of the Republic. The other political parties in the country either disbanded or were proscribed. The former Mayor, Joseph Ouedraogo, had been interned by the President, and the Mogho Naba had been deserted by many of his prominent chiefs after he attempted a *coup d'état* in 1958.

The elections for the post-independence Municipal Council of Ouagadougou were fairly calm. Candidates of the U.D.V.–R.D.A. contested every seat in the town and had little opposition. Some 28,380 persons registered to vote and, on December 18, 1960, the 20,845 who voted gave the U.D.V.–R.D.A. party 73.4 per cent of the vote and all 48 seats on the council. On Friday, December 23, 1960, the new Municipal Council met and, by a vote of 46 to 1, with 1 abstention, named Dr. Joseph Conombo, Mayor.

Despite the U.D.V.–R.D.A.'s total control of the Municipal Council, the composition of the council itself reflected the social and economic structure of the town. For example, 25 or 52.1 per cent of the municipal councilors were "civil servants," 9 were traditional notables, 7 were merchants (including the 1 mulatto), and 5 were war veterans. Among the 25 "civil servants" were such men as Alexandre Tiendrébéogo, a brother of the Larhalle Naba of Ouagadougou. Among the 9 notables on the Municipal Council were such provincial ministers as the Larhalle Naba, the Baloum Naba, the Ouidi Naba, and some village (now ward) chiefs of the Hausa community. The traditional notables were also well represented in the various bodies established by the municipality. The Larhalle Naba was appointed one of the five adjutants of the Mayor; the Baloum Naba headed one of the five commissions—the one dealing with municipal property; and the Ouidi Naba presided over the Customary Tribunal of the First Degree. Thus, although Mr. Nader Attié expressed the hope that within the U.D.V.-R.D.A. dominated council "we ought to be able to find again the fraternal road to unity and concord," many of the councilors' political, professional, occupational, and traditional allegiances did not coincide with those of the national political party.

The presence of three political organizations in Ouagadougou after 1960 was as much an asset to the people of the town as it was a danger to successful municipal government. Although the chiefs were eclipsed by the politicians, they still played an important political role in the various wards. The municipality, whose responsibility it was to govern the town, took over control of various services; and the national government, which was a guest in the town, sought to provide the same services to the townspeople as it did to all the citizens of the Republic, urban as well as rural. This afforded each member of the various groups in the population—from the newly arrived migrant to the Ouagadougou-born civil servant—the opportunity to select from among the various institutions of the several political organizations the services which he needed at a specific time and for a specific purpose.

The overall problem of government in the town lies in the severe structural if not functional differences between the traditional, municipal, and national organizations since, by definition, the three are organized for different purposes. The traditional political representatives still see themselves as mediators between their people on the face-to-face community level where most of the daily problems develop; the Municipal Council defines its task as taking care of all the people of the town regardless of specific quarter; and the national government regards the people of Ouagadougou as only one group, albeit an important one, of the citizens of the Republic. This situation would not have created difficulties for the governing officials had there been mediating structures between the three political systems of the town. But, even though many of the officials in the three systems were related to each other and often held positions simultaneously in each of the structures (i.e., until 1965 the traditional minister of the Larhalle Naba was a municipal councilor, an adjutant mayor, as well as a technical councilor to the President of the Republic), there was a lack of coordination between the three systems and a paucity of mediating structures between them. The result was not only competition among the three systems but also opposition among them, often to the detriment of the town's population.

Except in the Zone Résidentielle, the Zone Commerciale, and to a lesser extent, the quarters around the mission, the traditional chiefs and headmen still play important roles in governing the people. The chiefs have lost control of land in the allotted wards of town but still control it in those areas not yet allotted. They, therefore, derive a great deal of power from their right to distribute land to persons who need it, be they civil servants, politicians, or migrant cultivators. If and when the municipality subsequently takes over an area, the chief there is consulted about the disposition of the land and about the need for people to retain plots or be given new ones as compensation for areas appropriated for public roadways. But even in areas already taken over by the town, the chiefs keep an interest in the transfer of land so that they can give evidence in the event of litigation and inheritance, if and when that becomes necessary.

Second, the chiefs also provide invaluable service to the municipal commissions charged with census taking, military conscription, and tax collection because of their intimate knowledge of the movements of persons, especially in the areas peripheral to the center of town. Practically no one from the municipality goes into an area of the town for these purposes without notifying the chiefs or headmen there and seeking their aid.

Third, the chiefs continue their traditional role as judges and conciliators between disputants because many people still do not trust municipal and national officials. Interestingly enough, this service is now technically illegal, but both municipal and national officials ignore its occurrence when, during the course of trials on these levels, the disputants reveal that their cases had previously been heard in the chiefs' courts.

417

Fourth, the chiefs act as communicators of municipal and national ordinances, statutes, and regulations to the people in their wards; and they are used by the local branches of the political party, the U.D.V.-R.D.A., as instruments for propagandizing party matters and for providing places for party meetings and rallies.

Despite the chiefs' functions in all the above capacities, their activities are not officially recognized either by the municipality or by the national government. Nevertheless, everyone in the town takes it for granted that the chiefs perform important services for their people. The result is that even though the chiefs may not be recognized officially, they have succeeded in preserving much of their prestige among the people and receive gifts from them. For example, those chiefs who give land to immigrant laborers receive gifts of money and often labor from them. In January 1965, both the Paspanga and Ouidi Nanamsé were able to obtain volunteer labor from their people tó thresh millet which had been transported to the town from peri-urban farms. The chiefs also receive presents of money from civil servants and politicians to whom they give land. More important, perhaps, to the chiefs are the personal contacts established with officials through the gift of land which could help them provide such important items for their people as birth certificates, identity cards, family cards, and the many other documents needed by citizens of modern towns and states.

The municipal councilors in Ouagadougou, as those members of the municipality in direct contact with the population, interpret their role in the light of their traditional or modern statuses, education, and occupation. As far as the traditional chiefs who are also councilors are concerned, there is no indication that they conceive their new functions as separate from the old. Conversely, it is also problematical whether those municipal councilors who are also members of noble families perceive their status and role as councilors to be different from that of the traditional ones as nobility or chiefs. On the other hand, the younger civil servants who serve as councilors are aware of the theoretical role and function of municipal councilor. One councilor quoted de Tocqueville to the effect that, "The *commune* is the only association so basic to nature that wherever men are gathered, they form themselves into *communes.*" He also took as his guide the statement in the French law of April 5, 1884, that, "the aim of the commune is to organize elementary social life, and the Mayor and Municipal Councilors are expected to look after the common interests, protect the public weal, regulate the communal life, and defend rights and liberty." But whether chief-councilor, councilor-chief, or plain councilor, all these men face numerous problems in their appointed tasks.

The major problems faced by the municipal councilor in governing the town are due to the presence of a socio-culturally complex population ranging from poor rural immigrant cultivators to foreign embassy populations from modern affluent societies. The immigrants need such services as housing, schools, medical care, official papers and, most of all, employment. The higher ranking people in Ouagadougou need many of the same services, but, in addition, desire such modern conveniences as electric lights, fuel, running water, paved roads, sewers, recreational parks, and hygienic markets.

What makes the tasks of the councilors difficult is that many of the townspeople have different opinions as to what is important or necessary, or even what constitutes a problem. Consequently the people often resent efforts of the council to deal with certain matters or to resolve certain problems. Thus, when the municipality banned the cultivation of cereals in backyard plots in an attempt at mosquito control (since mosquitoes breed in water retained in the leaves), the poorer people expressed indignation. And when the council did not similarly prohibit civil servants from growing leafy vegetables or ornamental shrubs, the cultivators and some intellectuals complained of class and cultural discrimination. The critics of the council were partly correct in decrying this as a class-based ordinance, but the cultivation of cereal in the town does create a health problem. Again, when the municipality sought to prohibit the construction of mud-brick houses, a measure designed not only to live down Ouagadougou's former sobriquet of Bancoville but also to impose higher taxes on the more expensive concrete structures, the poor cultivators and laborers who could not afford to build in concrete complained that the municipality was chasing them out in order to make room for wealthier people. Even when the municipality tried to take action to aid the citizens there were complaints. Thus, when drains were dug in order to prevent the flooding of house plots during the rainy season, many people complained that the excavations undermined their mud-brick walls to such an extent that they collapsed.

On the other hand, some of the ordinances proposed by the municipal councilors not only came into conflict with the local customary social system, but could easily have come into conflict even with Western social systems. One councilor proposed that a tax be levied on each household head in order to provide for more efficient garbage collection. The conflict started when another councilor requested that the term "household head" be defined. "Did it mean," he asked, "the head of each nuclear family? Or the head of an extended family in one household? Or in several households? Or the owner of the house plot in front of which the garbage is deposited? Or the head of each family living in the tiny rooms in multiple-room compounds?" Even the sponsor of the bill was asked whether he meant that his married son, who lived under his roof, should pay the tax, and did he consider his son to be the head of a household? The bill was pigeonholed.

Many of the councilors' difficulties stem from their lack of communication with the people and from the absence of mediating structures through which new ideas can be communicated. The councilors themselves are the first to concede that they have not yet created the necessary structures through which the people can voice their complaints or make their needs manifest. The Municipal Council meets officially and publicly only twice a year except for extra-ordinary sessions. These few meetings are meaningless for the majority of the townspeople who were accustomed to soliciting the chiefs whenever they had pressing problems. Yet, only if it were to meet more frequently would the townspeople become used to visiting the council to press their complaints and demands.

The municipality has no local offices in the wards. People with problems have to chance meeting the councilors on the streets, visit them on their jobs, or wait for them at their homes—a not too satisfactory arrangement for some councilors who dislike having their midday siestas interrupted by people who, as one stated, "do not understand that there is a time for everything." When a councilor wishes to communicate with his constituents he has less difficulty because, working with comparative ease through the traditional chief, he can summon the people to the chief's compound. Asked whether such use of the chiefs compromised the position of the councilors in the eyes of the people, one young councilor replied, "not at all." He added, "there is a 'mixed' governmental system in Ouagadougou," and using the chiefs' compounds for meetings is especially helpful if the councilors want to communicate with the elders who often visit the chiefs but would only come to see the municipal councilors if they had a pressing modern problem. However, it is quite clear that using the chiefs' compounds for municipal business does not especially help the municipal councilors' prestige; on the contrary, it only reinforces the position of the chiefs.

Like the chiefs, the members of the Municipal Council of Ouagadougou receive no salary for their services. Moreover, they are expected to attend the regular sessions of the council each year and the many extra-ordinary sessions to which they are summoned. Those councilors missing three sessions of the council without valid excuses may be dismissed by the Minister of the Interior for dereliction of duty.

On the other hand, men do gain a certain amount of prestige for being councilors, and the traditional chiefs and members of noble lineages consider it an act of *noblesse oblige* to continue to serve their people even within a new governmental institution. Then there are the perquisites which come from being a municipal councilor. Since the municipality is one of the largest employers in the town, employing some 619 persons, municipal councilors are able to secure jobs for their relatives and friends. Again, the municipal councilors are necessarily involved in any discussion concerning the allotment of land being developed by the municipality and often secure plots for themselves, for their relatives, and for their friends. Finally, as municipal councilors, men can use their prestige and influence to help their relatives, friends, and constituents resolve financial, civil, and legal problems with which they may be confronted as residents of the town or as citizens of the state. Thus, despite the occasional problems which men do encounter because of their membership on the Municipal Council, the perquisites and the prestige are substantial enough to make many men seek that office. Even those men who show little concern for the material gains to be obtained from serving as municipal councilors seek the prestige they receive from helping to govern the town in which they live.

The greatest problem faced by the Municipal Council in governing Ouagadougou is the lack of adequate revenue; for, in the

421

TABLE XLIII.   Budget of the Municipality
of Ouagadougou

Year		Amount (in C.F.A.)
1954		52,000,000
1957		72,042,650
1959		100,977,250
1961		267,769,630
1962		237,273,435
1963		315,393,709
1964	Preliminary Budget	244,826,000
	Supplementary Budget	69,541,006
	Total	314,367,006

absence of an adequate budget, the council cannot create the instruments necessary to run the town. The budget of the municipality increased astronomically from 1954 to 1963, but decreased in 1964 because of growing economic austerity (see Table XLIII). The sources of revenue are as follows: a) 85 per cent of the taxes collected by the municipality for the Republic levied on moveable and stationary property, and land and house rates; b) 60 per cent of the fines collected by municipal officials; and c) diverse taxes on such things as market permits, vehicular licenses, civil certificates, water and light rates, theater tickets, land transfers, and use of the abattoir.

The budget of the town for the fiscal year (January 1 to December 31) is prepared by the secretary-general of the municipality under the supervision of the Mayor. This official first prepares a preliminary budget which is discussed and voted upon by the municipal councilors during their budget meeting in November. After the budget has been voted upon, it is submitted to the Minister of the Interior who, as "tutor," examines it to see whether or not it meets the requirements of a municipal budget. Once his approval is given, the Mayor may execute the budget according to the prepared plans, but whenever he wishes to spend any sum in excess of 500,000 francs (C.F.A.), he must consult the Minister of the Interior. In most years the preliminary budget voted by the Municipal Council proves to be insufficient and a supplementary budget is prepared. This, too, must be voted upon by the Municipal Council and approved by the Minister of the Interior.

Most of the money spent by the municipality in years gone by, and most of the money voted in the 1964 budget, was for public works directly involved with improving the appearance of the town. Thus, 40 per cent of the 145 million francs "ordinary" expenses section of the budget was allocated for road construction, the largest single expense. Some 20.7 per cent of the budget was for administration; 6.2 per cent for markets; approximately the same for industrial development; and about 4.1 per cent for ceremonies, beautification, etc. About 48 per cent of the 99 million C.F.A. allotted for "extra-ordinary" expenses was spent for new construction, which included building an addition to the Town Hall, paving the market, constructing urban lighting, building maternity centers and schools, piping water, etc. About 24 per cent of these expenses was for the purchase of vehicles, and about 20 percent was allocated to the allotment of Koulouba and Gounghin wards. Other expenses included money for the Customary Courts, education, public assistance, support for organizations, and so forth. The reduction of the preliminary and supplementary budgets of the municipality for 1964 by 1 million C.F.A. below that of 1963 did create a problem for an administration bent on improving the town and its services.

One complaint heard from the Mayor and the councilors is that the tax-gathering machinery of the municipality is still inadequate to collect even the ordinary funds due it. Collecting taxes in the market places and from itinerant traders is still a battle of wits between inexperienced young civil servants and lynx-eyed men and women traders who quickly disappear when the tax collectors show up. Collecting taxes from the more formal French businesses in town is even more difficult— it is a well-known national trait of Frenchmen to keep faulty tax records. Moreover, since the French Government supplies a significant part of the deficit in the budget of the Upper Volta, the municipality can do little or nothing to gain more revenue from these people.

The municipality did try to increase its revenue from taxes on vehicles of all kinds by making periodic checks of all vehicles entering or moving about town. This was not too successful because persons without licenses and permits heard about the spot checks and left their vehicles at home until the checking had stopped. More remunerative than the vehicular checks, from the point of view of income for the municipality, are drives enforcing traffic regulations. During this period each member of the municipal police force is given a book of traffic summonses which he is expected to utilize by a certain date. Motorists must pay fines on the spot or their vehicles are impounded. Bicycles are usually impounded and taken to the Commissariat de Police where their owners may retrieve them upon paying a fine. Doubtless, these fines help the municipality meet some of its budgetary needs, but the techniques for obtaining these funds work hardships on many persons who are either ignorant of the traffic signs or have not lived in Ouagadougou long enough to learn to obey them. Moreover, it is quite clear that fines alone could never meet the financial needs of the municipality, especially since the cost of modernization is so high.

Ouagadougou's status and function as capital of the Upper Volta Republic is certainly one of the reasons why the municipality spends large sums of money on urban construction. René Dumont, in his very critical book *L'Afrique Noire est mal partie*,[16] has described how towns such as Ouagadougou have to use most of their resources for what he considers to be display purposes. It is true that many of the roads in Ouagadougou were paved in honor of those presidents who attended the Conférence des Chefs d'Etat et de Gouvernement de L'Union Africaine et Malagache in March 1963. And the municipality annually spends hundreds of thousands of francs in order to display a profusion of flags whenever the President of the Republic makes an official trip or when foreign dignitaries visit the town. As a matter of record, under the category of "ordinary" expenses, the budget of 1964 allotted 6,782,000 C.F.A. for *cérémonies et beaux arts* and only 3,988,000 C.F.A. for all types of education in the town, including money for the communal schools, and physical education, and funds for the upkeep of the different recreational parks and services in town. Some 6,500,000 C.F.A. was earmarked for new schools, but this was listed under "extra-ordinary" expenses, meaning that this was not expected to be a usual form of expenditure.

It is also partly because of a desire for municipal and national prestige that there are traffic lights in Ouagadougou. However, René Dumont was probably wrong when he alleged that it was civic pride that caused "the Mayor of Ouagadougou to pass an ordinance forbidding the use of Citroën *deux-chevaux* as taxis."[17] The Mayor's explanation for this

[16] René Dumont, *L'Afrique Noire est mal partie* (Paris, 1962), p. 67.
[17] *Ibid.*

424

ordinance was that these small cars, while perhaps adequate for family use, presented too many inconveniences for the taxi-riding public.

The Mayor of Ouagadougou was exceptionally aware of the danger of fiscal irresponsibility for the development of the town. He also knew that "fiscal incompetence" had been one of the reasons given by the Minister of the Interior when, in 1959, he dismissed the first elected Mayor of Ouagadougou and suspended tne Municipal Council. When he took office in 1960, Dr. Conombo declared, in an article in *Carrefour Africain* (December 25, 1960):

> It was not only bad management, but also lack of decision in the face of the financial problems of the town that caused its bankruptcy. The *commune* employs more people than any other enterprise in town but the taxpayers show a lack of civic spirit, especially with respect to paying income taxes, thus leaving budget deficits and unpaid bills. This fact called into question the morality of the town's officials and the ability of the town to meet its obligations.

He concluded by expressing the wish for a strong fiscal policy not only to "expedite civic improvements," but also to "rid the capital of the nation of mosquitoes, dust, darkness, and old mud-brick houses."

Being host to the government of the Republic also creates political problems for the Municipality of Ouagadougou. The municipality, in terms of number and quality of employees, its rather substantial budget, and the leadership capabilities of the mayors (both of whom have been seasoned politicians), has always been a formidable political rival of the national government. Thus, it is not surprising that one of the first acts of the political leaders of the U.D.V.–R.D.A., in their drive for political supremacy during the immediate preindependence period, was to curb the power of Mr. Joseph Ouedraogo, the first elected Mayor of Ouagadougou. This was not too difficult a task since the Mayor, being under the supervision of the Minister of the Interior, could easily have been dismissed for alleged fiscal irresponsibility or some other malfeasance in office. The U.D.V.–R.D.A. made sure that both the Mayor and the members of the Municipal Council who took office after the election of 1960 were party members, but the structural conflict between the municipal government and the Re-

425

public's government was not completely solved by this allegiance.

One basic source of conflict between the municipal government and the Republic's government was that the political party controlling the national government had to use certain of the basic structures of the municipality to gain the support of the urban population. Thus, the political party found itself utilizing the municipal councilors, and through them the traditional political system, for such purposes as political recruitment, mobilization, and socialization. It used the municipal councilors to summon branches of the political party in their respective wards to perform certain tasks, to meet at specific times, and to parade at other times.

Sometimes, the conflict in statuses and roles of party functionaries, municipal councilors, and chiefs created difficulties for all the groups concerned. For example, in preparing for Independence Day celebrations in December 1964, a radio broadcast announced that the youth section of the political party in the Larhalle ward was to meet at the home of the Larhalle Naba. In the middle of the session, a man stepped forward, interrupted the proceedings, identified himself as a municipal councilor, and complained that he had not been notified that this event was taking place in his ward. The young members of the party reacted strongly. One young man from the President's office suggested that the councilor should leave as he was elderly and this meeting was for the youth of the party. The councilor replied that, as municipal councilor, he was, so to speak, the father of the people in the ward and was responsible to the Mayor for their activities. This brought hoots of laughter and protests from the party workers. The councilor stalked off mumbling to himself. This incident is significant because it shows that both the municipal and national governments see themselves in actual competition for leadership. Apparently this councilor did not know where his powers and functions began and where they ended. His being the brother of the traditional chief in whose compound the meeting was held also did not help matters. Indeed, the question could be raised as to whether this municipal councilor perceived himself as being "municipal councilor," "national party member," or *na-biga* (son of a chief).

Another source of conflict between the Municipal Council and its Mayor on the one hand, and the national government

426

and its president on the other, was the municipality's activities on behalf of the most significant group of people in Upper Volta, the elite of Ouagadougou. The municipality was responsible for schools, streets, electricity, and the like, and when people had either complaints or praises about these services they went to the Mayor. The national government resented the attention paid to the municipality by visitors and resident Frenchmen and acted somewhat like a hostess slighted by guests in favor of her domestics. Indeed, it was suggested that some national government officials feared that the municipal government officials would use their prestige to seek power on the national level. Thus when the municipality decided to try to obtain some outside aid by becoming the "twin" of the city of Bordeaux, France, the national government was agreeable. But when it appeared that by so doing the Mayor of Ouagadougou would be establishing too close a relationship with the head of a powerful city, anxiety was expressed, and the relationship between the towns did not materialize. No doubt the fear here was that the Mayor of Ouagadougou would use his influence with the Mayor of Bordeaux to gain national power in Upper Volta.

In August 1964, the relations between the municipal government and the local European population did create a rather serious conflict between the Republic's government and that of the town. A ravine passing through the middle of Ouagadougou had posed such a health hazard and was such an eyesore that, with the encouragement of both the local Voltaics and resident Europeans, the municipality proposed to have a regular canal built. Arrangements were made to have the cost of the project included in a request for funds which the national government was making to F.E.D.O.M. (Fonds d'entr'-aide et de développement pour L'outre-mer) and with the understanding that the local European community, working through France, would support the request. When the municipality was not given its share of the funds received from F.E.D.O.M., and when flooding occurred during the rainy season of 1964, many persons in town raised questions as to the disposition of funds earmarked for the canal. On Tuesday morning, October 20, 1964, the following announcement appeared in the *Bulletin Quotidien:*

> The Municipal Council of Ouagadougou, meeting in plenary session yesterday, October 19, after having heard

427

the explanations of his honor the Mayor on the execution of the F.E.D.O.M. program, concerning the drainage, purification of water, and the construction of a water tower, moved to express its distress over the delay in the realization of said public works. It fervently wished, in the interest of the population, that all obstacles to carrying out these public works would be removed as rapidly as possible.[18]

It was quite clear that this message, also released the evening before to the audience of Radio Haute-Volta, was an attempt to absolve the municipality of tardiness and fix the blame on the national government. The President of the Republic was away in France on one of his customary visits, and no one replied to the announcements. When the President returned and summoned the leaders of the national party to the capital to report upon his visit to Europe, he took the opportunity to castigate the Mayor for what he considered to have been a political trick. Moreover, he declared that, from 1965 on, the budget of the Municipality of Ouagadougou would be subsumed under the budget of the national government. By so doing, the President sought to deprive the municipality of one of its most important means of autonomous actions and thereby cripple it.

By the end of 1964 it was quite clear that the national government not only distrusted the Mayor and the Municipal Council, but that the President of the Republic was determined to eliminate these sources of conflict and competition. The opportunity to do so was to come in 1965, the year when elections were to be held for all elective offices in the country. The Mayor and municipal councilors of Ouagadougou knew that their days in office were numbered, but, in the absence of a multi-party system where they could stand for election as members of other parties or even as independents, they could do little. Their chances of influencing the U.D.V.-R.D.A. to renominate them for office were further reduced when the rules for the nomination of officers and the nature of the elections were made known. First of all, the members of the party were not to have a convention at which candidates for all offices in the country could be presented and their qualifications discussed. Instead, it was decided that there would be three nominating sessions and three elections. Candidates for the presi-

[18] *Bulletin Quotidien,* 20 October 1964, p. ix.

dency of the country would be nominated first and elections held for that office; the candidates for the Chamber of Deputies would be nominated and that election held; and finally, candidates for municipal offices nominated and those elections held.

The politicians in Ouagadougou and throughout the country suspected that these nomination and election procedures were designed to eliminate all opposition to the leaders of the party. They surmised that since many of the politicians in office as well as out of office hoped to be nominated as a deputy by the man who was named President, these men would close ranks behind the incumbent who, after all, still controlled the party during the nomination period. Furthermore, they believed that once the President was elected, he would then be free to disregard or double-cross all those who had supported him in the hope of becoming a deputy, and he would influence the choice of candidates for the Chamber. The belief also was that the President could then easily choose his candidates for the municipal councils, since by this time he would not only be in office but would have the support of his hand-picked members of the Chamber of Deputies.

As the Mayor, the municipal councilors, and other politicians suspected, the election procedures permitted the leaders of the U.D.V.-R.D.A. to control the party quite effectively and to obtain the support of the rank and file for their chosen candidates. On August 17, 1965, President Maurice Yaméogo was nominated for the presidency by his party, and he accepted its invitation to run for a second term in that office. But, before the presidential election, an event occurred which was to have grave implications for the President of the Republic, for the people of Ouagadougou, as well as for the country at large. Madame Yaméogo, who had been in France on a visit, was accused by the President of gross misconduct while there. She was publicly humiliated and mistreated by a relative of the President and imprisoned in Koudougou. Mathias Konaté was later to declare that, "This ... event was not only prejudicial to an individual and though strictly national in character, had implications for the whole African continent; 'Love in the Tropics' was the title that the 'Canard Enchaîné' [a well-known French humor magazine] gave to this affair."[19]

Despite this personal setback, on October 3, 1965, Maurice

---

[19] *Afrique Nouvelle,* No. 967 (17–23 February 1966), p. 2.

Yaméogo was reelected President of the Republic by more than 99 per cent of the vote. No sooner had he been elected, than, on October 17, Mr. Yaméogo decided to marry Miss Nathalie Monoco Adama, the twenty-two-year-old "Miss Ivory Coast." This act displeased many of the citizens of Ouagadougou. Again, according to Mathias Konaté:

> Yes, even though people had kept silent about the repudiation of the legitimate wife, this did not prepare them for the shameful and mournful events that followed. The pomp of the new union surprised and shocked international opinion. Yet, the fact of the remarriage was not upsetting nationally—although from a Catholic who constantly has the name of God on his lips—ordinary mortals would have expected something different. What was unacceptable were the conditions and the circumstances of the marriage. More discretion would have been wished; Yaméogo did not wish it. The people were not able to impose that upon him. It is nonetheless true that they have been shocked and humiliated by it.[20]

To make matters worse, the President reportedly spent some 40 million francs ($160,000.) on a marriage and honeymoon which took him to Brazil by way of New York. In the course of this trip he met some of the same important international political leaders who just over a year ago had entertained him and his ex-wife in the United States.

The presidential party returned to Ouagadougou for the national election for the Chamber of Deputies which was scheduled for November 7, 1965. The U.D.V.–R.D.A.'s list was the only one registered for the election. Such well-known deputies as Dr. Joseph Conombo, the incumbent Mayor, and Mr. Joseph Ouedraogo, the former Mayor, were only two of the former deputies who were not nominated by the party. The people of the town had no ready means of redress, but they showed their disaffection by staying away when the President gave his preelection speech at the party headquarters. In fact, so poor was the turnout, that party members had to chase people out of the market to go and hear the President's speech. But the party workers could not persuade people to vote the next day. A substantial percentage of voters stayed home, and 404 blank ballots were cast by the Ouagadougou electorate.

[20] Ibid.

Despite this poor showing in Ouagadougou, the party candidates reportedly received 98.6 per cent of the vote.

As was expected, Mr. Joseph Conombo and many of the municipal councilors who served with him were not renominated as candidates by the party for the Ouagadougou municipal election to be held on December 5, 1965. The party had decided to eliminate men who had embarrassed the national government. The people again showed their concern over their lack of choice of candidates by remaining away from the polls. It is estimated that between 20 and 42 per cent of the Ouagadougou voters abstained, but this did not prevent the party from claiming a victory of 98.97 per cent of the votes cast.[21] When, in the subsequent vote among the elected municipal councilors for Mayor, three councilors voted against Mr. Mathieu Ouedraogo, the party's candidate, and four others abstained, an R.D.A. stalwart seized upon this fact as evidence of "Voltaic Democracy."[22]

Less than one month after their municipal election, the people of Ouagadougou revolted against the national government and brought it down. True, they were distressed about the plight of Madame Yaméogo and about the manipulation of candidates for the Municipal Council, but the event that led to the revolt was the adoption by the National Assembly of a proposal to reduce the salaries and perquisites of the civil servants, most of whom lived in Ouagadougou. The decision to introduce austerity measures was due to a diminution of external aid, especially from France, and the heavy strain of paying the salaries of civil servants and temporary technical personnel. Faced with these two problems, the National Assembly, on December 30, 1965, under the chairmanship of Mr. Begnon Koné, adopted an austerity budget of 9,038,700,000 francs. It also decided to approve a slash in the salaries of all civil servants by 20 per cent, reduce family allowances for all sectors of the population from 1,500 to 700 francs per child per month, to raise the fixed tax by 100 francs in the three large towns, including Ouagadougou, and to prohibit all civil servant promotions for two years. The only relief for the civil servants was the suspension of a 10 per cent tax on all incomes over 10,000 francs.

Unfortunately for the government, the adoption of these

[21] *Ibid.*, No. 961 (12 January 1966), p. 5.
[22] *Ibid.*

431

measures coincided with the meeting in Ouagadougou of the Second Congress of the Union Syndicale des Travailleurs Voltaïque (U.S.T.V.), attended by representatives of some of the most powerful unions in the country, including those of the civil servants. Already on December 27, 1965, the labor syndicates, under the leadership of the secretary-general, Mr. Zoumana Traore, an Inspector of Primary Education, had taken exception to the national government, opting for "capitalism" as the economic system for Upper Volta. Covering the walls of the Bourse de Travail (Labor Exchange), where the unionists were meeting, were banners bearing the following inscriptions: "Raise the minimum wage," "Down with high prices," "Long live the Organization of African Unity," "Down with the racist domination of [Ian] Smith," "Work for our Young People," "No more vagabond children," "Yes to austerity! No to austerity on the backs of the Workers!" "Schools for our children," "Medicine for our Sick," "Planning without the assistance of Workers is planning against them," "Liberty for Labor Unions."

These signs were not only critical of the economic policies of the government and of the relative lack of fraternal spirit which many of the elite felt the President had shown to Africans and their problems, but they also represented the real concern felt by many people about the problems created by urbanization and culture change. It was true that there were too few schools in the country, especially in such heavily populated areas as Ouagadougou; it was true that crime and delinquency were problems in the growing urban centers; and it was also true that there was a shortage of employment for the youth. The union leaders also felt that the politicians of the national government had not shown themselves capable of fiscal moderation in the past and feared that any planned austerity would be at the expense of the people.

The national government apparently did not fear any hostile reactions to its austerity program for the labor leaders, and the President of the Republic was not even in Ouagadougou when the program was adopted. He had journeyed to the Ivory Coast where he and President Houphouet-Boigny had signed protocols establishing "double-nationality" for the citizens of their two countries. The labor unions' concern about the possible harmful effect of double-nationality on the ability of Voltaic labor migrants to redress grievances against

432

the Ivory Coast planters had caused the President to insist upon economic guarantees in the agreement. Thus, when, on returning to Ouagadougou, he was confronted with the news that the labor unions were preparing to protest against the austerity measures taken by the National Assembly, President Yaméogo was not only surprised but angry. And when, on December 31, 1965, the morning after the National Assembly's action, ten labor leaders signed a petition requesting an audience with the authorities in the hope of obtaining an explanation of the austerity measures, the Minister of the Interior, Mr. Denis Yaméogo, summoned them to the ministry, insulted them, rejected their request for a meeting, and sent them away.

Faced with what they considered to be a rather serious problem for the laboring population of the capital and for the country, the labor leaders decided to hold a meeting, scheduling it for 5:30 P.M. that same Saturday afternoon, New Year's Day. Meanwhile, the labor leaders were being castigated by the President who, in response to the New Year's greetings proffered by politicians, stated that he would deal severely with those who pretended to speak in the name of the nation. About 6:00 P.M., the Minister of the Interior and Security went to the Labor Exchange where he found the meeting in progress and again insulted the unionists. He was shouted down and withdrew. A few minutes later, a number of policemen invaded the hall, but they were expelled by order of an action committee set up by the unions and headed by Mr. Joseph Ouedraogo. The committee declared that there would be a general strike on Monday, January 3, 1966, and that it would remain at the Labor Exchange until the political leaders spoke to the unionists. At about 10:30 P.M., that night, police and gendarmes arrived, threw tear gas grenades into the hall, and scattered the unionists. The police then instituted a search for the signers of the motion who were hiding among the town's population.

A number of minor syndicalists were arrested on New Year's Day, 1966, but no labor leaders were found. About 6:30 P.M. on January 2, the President addressed the nation declaring that:

Subversion, inspired by Communists, has entered the country, having as its leader a national of the country, Mr. Joseph Ouedraogo, now in hiding. Under the pretense of

433

unionist activities, he has indoctrinated some workers who tried to disturb the established order in the capital. Joseph Ouedraogo wishes to deliver our country into the hands of Ghana, and thereby to Peking, China. The proof is in our possession. I ask every one of you to have confidence in our national army whose officers, noncommissioned officers, and enlisted men are not ready to submit themselves to any foreign country, whatever. That is why I have declared a state of emergency. I invite the entire population of Ouagadougou to remain calm and to have complete confidence in me. All provisions have been made against the effectuation of the general strike called for tomorrow, January 3. The unionist dramatics which animated the evening of December 31 are now over and will not have their normal epilogue: I myself will see to that![23]

This statement was rebroadcast that night about 8:00 P.M., and throughout the evening, the Minister of the Interior, accompanied by two gendarmes, made the rounds of most of the bars in town, much to the annoyance of the population. The union leaders remained hidden from the dragnet set out for them.

A state of emergency was proclaimed for January 3, 1966, as the President had threatened. All public buildings and the presidential palace were surrounded by law enforcement officers. The President had hoped that he could prevent the strike. He was counting on his threats to force the civil servants to report to work. He was also counting on his appeal to the religious authorities in town to request their employed followers to report for work at the normal time of 7:00 A.M. on Monday. This, however, was not to be, since the civil servants had decided to strike. All of Sunday, January 2, the civil servants used their great influence with those of their relatives employed in the private sector to do likewise.

By 8:00 A.M., on Monday, January 3, it was quite clear that the unionists had prevailed upon the working population of Ouagadougou to obey the call for a general strike. The civil servants did not report for work at 7:00 A.M. as ordered, nor did the workers in the private sector report for work at 7:30 A.M. as usual. However, the students at the Lycée-Philippe Zinda Kabore, the Cours Normal des Jeunes Filles, and the Ecole Normale, who had grievances against the government

[23] *Ibid.,* p. 4.

434

and who had seen some of their teachers arrested, were up and about at 8:00 A.M., bearing placards with the words, *Du Pain, De l'Eau,* and *De la Démocratie* (Bread, Water, Democracy). They paraded to the Place d'Armes, followed by a growing crowd of people, especially the young unemployed youths from the market area. The procession then turned around and headed back up Binger Avenue to Independence Avenue which terminates at the presidential complex. Here they encountered police barricades which they pushed aside. As they encountered the forces of law and order someone shouted, *Vive l' Armée! L'Armée au Pouvoir!* (Long Live the Army! The Army to Power). These slogans were taken up by the whole crowd. The throng made no attempt to attack the soldiers, gendarmes, and policemen. Reports allege that the army had been given orders "twenty times" to fire on the crowd; it did launch some tear gas grenades into the shouting multitude. The crowd then broke into three groups, one of which reached the palace and shouted insults at the President; another reached and attacked the house of the Minister of the Interior; and the third group attacked the house of the President of the National Assembly. This group also invaded the National Assembly itself—destroying the bottles of whiskey, beer, and champagne in its bar—and burned several of the Mercedes automobiles of the deputies. The armed forces tried to set up other barricades, and again under the order of the President, launched tear gas grenades into the crowd which continued shouting, *Penez le Pouvoir! Où est le Colonel Lamizana? Pourquoi Protégez-vous Un Seul Homme Contre le Peuple? A bas la Dictature! L'Armée au Pouvoir! Vive l'Armée* (Take Power! Where is Colonel Lamizana? Why Protect a Single Man Against the People? Down with Dictatorship! The Army to Power! Long Live the Army!).

Meanwhile, inside the palace and military camp a number of anxious discussions began to take place between the politicians, union leaders, and the army. Mr. Joseph Ouedraogo, who had come out from hiding, declared that he had nothing to do with Ghana much less Peking and demanded the release of the imprisoned union leaders. About 1:15 P.M. a sound truck moved through the town asking the people to go to the Place d'Armes to continue to petition the army to take power. The union leaders told the people that the President had cried "wolf" so many times that it was useless to believe him. The

President, himself, had been consulting with the army regarding what he should do in the face of a popular revolt. He expressed a desire to talk with the union leaders, but these men and women rejected his request and continued to ask the army to take power. At 6:30 P.M. the army announced that the President had agreed to suppress the 20 per cent reduction in salaries and that the family allotments would remain the same. The crowd, now numbering some 25,000 persons, rejected this proposal, shouting, "Resign!" "No!" "The reduction does not interest us any more!" "We do not want Maurice any longer!" "Maurice to the gallows!" "Return and demand his resignation!" "We will sleep here if that becomes necessary, but we will not leave as long as Maurice has not resigned!" "The Army to power!"

Colonel Lamizana, the army chief of staff, held talks with the unionists and with the President and, at 9:45 P.M., announced to the crowd that the army "has assumed its responsibilities." The people of Ouagadougou had brought down the Government of the Republic. Colonel Lamizana assumed the responsibilities of the government "until the new order" could be effected and declared a state of emergency.[24] About 10:45 P.M., the ousted President publicly declared that he resigned to avoid bloodshed within the town and to prove to the world that "we are truly a people attached to our unity, that we are a people dedicated to realizing our economic and social advancement, and, therefore, I am persuaded that those who replace us are also as patriotic as we are, for the simple reason that they are Voltaics."[25]

The people of Ouagadougou had accomplished what they had set out to do—to replace a national government whose overall policies appeared to them as detrimental to their own municipality. They now have the dubious distinction of being the first group of urban African civilians to have overthrown a national government. Ironically, the fall of the national government also resulted in the dissolution of the Municipal Council that had been elected on December 5, 1965. By presidential order, a special delegation was provisionally constituted to supervise communal affairs. Thus, here again, the very close relationship between the Municipality of Ouaga-

[24] *Ibid.,* p. 5.
[25] *Fraternité Matin,* 7 January 1966, p. 5.

436

dougou and the nation-state of Upper Volta was emphasized. It is not known what provisions have been made in the Constitution of the Second Upper Volta Republic for municipal institutions, but unless there are drastic structural changes in the municipal system, future municipal governments in Ouagadougou face comparable difficulties.[26]

The data of this chapter demonstrate that the problems of government in Ouagadougou, as in many African towns, are exacerbated by the multiplicity of political systems within the town which, while facilitating the adaptation of rural migrants to urban life, often come into violent conflict with each other. Not only are the political institutions and structures in conflict, but the processes governing decision-making, compliance, and implementation are still inchoate. The resulting lack of legitimacy makes government in most African towns highly vulnerable to attack from dissatisfied interest groups. Unless and until politicians can create methods for mediating between individuals and groups that manipulate persons, symbols, and institutions as they compete for power, the emerging African towns may well be the crucible for revolutionary movements which ultimately create new types of relationships between African municipalities and their nation-states.

[26]Elliott P. Skinner, "Political Conflict and Revolution in an African Town," *American Anthropologist,* Vol. 74, No. 5 (October 1972), pp. 1208–17.

Meeting of Municipal Council

The transformation of Ouagadougou was begun by a colonial regime intent on tapping all the human and natural resources of Upper Volta. Therefore, the processes of urbanization that took place in the town cannot be separated from the colonial situation of which they were an integral part. Nor can the town be viewed as a sociological isolate in which social relationships could be examined without consideration of the external imperatives of colonial policy. Ouagadougou's physical and demographic growth was largely determined by French administrative policies which set parameters to the type of adaptation which both indigenous inhabitants and immigrants could make to the urbanization process.

First of all, the Europeans' demand for land for administrative and commercial purposes—and their decision to make Ouagadougou a territorial headquarters and, subsequently, a colonial capital—changed the physical, social, economic, and political characteristics of this traditional royal seat. With the demotion of the Mogho Naba and his removal from the physical and political center of the agglomeration, his chiefs, courtiers, and other groups of residents sought new quarters. A number of them followed the ruler, but a significant number of them separated along religious and economic lines. The traditionalistic retainers of the Mogho Naba moved north, founding new wards, while the Moslem merchant strangers moved south doing likewise. The provincial chiefs, bowing to European demands for laborers, quartered labor recruits within their hamlets, thereby laying the basis for future wards. When the military and the mission recruited soldiers and pupils from the outlying areas, many of these persons sought food, shelter, and companionship in the emerging wards of the provincial governors of their home districts.

That Ouagadougou developed as an administrative center also affected its demographic characteristics. Many men who were quartered in town, or who settled in town after discharging their military or labor conscription, sent for their wives. Therefore, almost from the beginning, there was a balance between the sexes in town and family groups. Later generations

438

of voluntary migrants brought their wives and families with them since they considered Ouagadougou to be in their own country. Thus, although the town was developing as an urban center controlled by, and in the interest of, the Europeans, the incoming migrants found there many traditional institutions which could serve as a means of adapting to life in the town.

The lack of mines, industries, and important commercial activities in Ouagadougou conditioned the occupational choices of its inhabitants. Most of the town's indigenous and immigrant population, needing to earn a living in the absence of salaried employment or commercial enterprises, were forced to practice subsistence agriculture in the town's peri-urban areas. Later on, when a substantial class of persons with European food habits appeared, a number of "urban" cultivators switched to the production of garden vegetables. Nevertheless, both types of cultivators still consider agriculture as only a poor substitute for salaried employment. They, and most people, deem civil service employment and clerking to be most congruent with urban life. The observable fact is that office workers earn much more money than cultivators, merchants, or tradesmen, and that their life styles more closely approximate those of the Europeans who formerly controlled the town. To be a highly paid *fonctionnaire* is the ideal, and it is only in the absence of achieving this goal that the people of Ouagadougou seek and practice other professions.

The inability of people in Ouagadougou to find those jobs or earn the income commensurate with their needs, social obligations, or aspirations often leads to conflict. Some youngsters selling merchandise in the markets or renting chariots to transport goods in the market find that they have to resort to prostitution (in the case of the girls) or to petty theft (in the case of the boys) in order to meet their needs. The female *dolotière* who was able to sell beer in the rural villages without conflict with her husband finds that similar activities in town lead to conflict and divorce. The unlettered wife of a high-status urban civil servant also finds it difficult to earn money, whereas her equally unlettered sisters married to nonelite men can do so, even if only by selling water in the market. In such cases, the lack of congruence between the necessary skills, the social dimensions of work, the new status, and the need for money dramatize the problems of earning a living in Ouagadougou. These factors also indicate the boundaries beyond which

439

people cannot manipulate the existing institutions and other components of urban life.

The changing patterns of kinship, courtship, and marriage in Ouagadougou reflect the different life chances of the different occupational and status groups within the town. People find that traditional kin relations are difficult to maintain in the town. The result is that both rural and urban dwellers exploit and manipulate their kin ties. Often the lack of correspondence between kin terms and expected behavior leads to changes in forms of address and reference. Most of these changes are conditioned and sustained by residential dispersion, differential occupations and incomes, and differences in education, interests, and associations among relatives. These differences also affect the control by parents over the lives of their children, resulting in individualization of marriage choices and living arrangements. New patterns of household arrangements and individualization of incomes are now more common, especially among craftsmen, merchants, and civil servants. Moreover, the greater the desire to conform to the legal prescriptions of the municipality and the state, the more the norms of courtship and marriage deviate from the traditional ones. The distinction between civil and religious ceremonies does create problems for some people, but often young Moslems use the civil ceremony to satisfy most of the social and psychological requirements of modern marriages.

Family life in Ouagadougou has been affected as much by official policy and economic changes as by the urban environment. Women and wives are no longer the economic and legal wards of their husbands and male relatives. Moreover, with the concurrence of the government, women are able to terminate unsatisfactory marriages. The ability of women to benefit from these new laws and norms is conditioned by age, education, and income. As is to be expected, the older wives of cultivators deviate less from the traditional norms, whereas the younger and literate wives are more conscious of their modern prerogatives for social recognition and the like. The wives of cultivators in town still react to an unsatisfactory marriage by running away. "Abandonment of the conjugal domicile" is the most frequent reason for divorce in Ouagadougou. Elite women are more apt to seek divorce because of polygyny, but they fear the stigma of divorce more than do

440

their traditional sisters. Men and not women are the ones to seek divorce on grounds of adultery. The double standard here is still maintained. What is not maintained, however, is a husband's ability to dispose of his educated wife's income. Economic cooperation between most couples seldom survives attacks by relatives, the desire of husbands for additional wives, or the desire of wives to spend money on the children. The desire for children is still strong among all social groups in Ouagadougou, with divorce demanded by either husband or wife on the suspicion of sterility in the other. Mothers still exhibit anxiety about rearing their children to adulthood, and most are now eager to take advantages of modern maternities and child care clinics.

European-derived patterns of education are becoming dominant in Ouagadougou. Some Moslem children still attend Koranic schools, but even Moslem parents demand that their children receive the modern education considered by all to be the passport to modern life and affluence. The lack of employment in Ouagadougou for school dropouts has led a few intellectuals to question the efficacy of attempts at universal education of both boys and girls. But most people try to have their own children educated. People in Ouagadougou still emphasize the humanities in the schools and pay lip service to those sciences and specializations deemed necessary for the development of Upper Volta. Moreover, the desire of students to be "educated" in the European way of life rather than to be "instructed" accounts for their preference for French universities rather than for comparable African ones.

Similarly, European-derived recreational forms, since they were originally linked to education and thus offered greater economic rewards, have eclipsed traditional recreational activities. Thus the *nam,* a recreational association based on the traditional political organization, serves only a limited group of Mossi immigrants. The *gumbé,* an import from neighboring countries, provides entertainment and mutual aid for a more modern and heterogenous group of urban youths. All of these activities are, however, subordinate to modern sports with their chances of economic gain and national and international recognition. Perhaps in reaction to this emphasis on these aspects of European culture, there is an effort of the town's elite to assert the importance of African culture. Local artists are

441

encouraged, Voltaic and African dance, folklore, and traditions are honored, and people strive to conquer their admitted complexes derived from European conquest and domination.

The religious paradox of Ouagadougou, a "Christian" town in which most of the inhabitants are Moslem, is a direct result of the colonial situation. Islam existed in precolonial Ouagadougou only at the sufferance of the Mogho Naba, but its followers took advantage of his loss of temporal power to spread their beliefs at the expense of the traditional religion. Nevertheless, it was not Islam but Christianity that gave many people the opportunity for education and elite status; and it is the European and African Christian elites who now dominate Ouagadougou. The conversion of migrants to Catholicism in contemporary Ouagadougou is as opportunistic a move as it was for earlier generations of urban dwellers. African women can play a more active role in Christianity than in either Islam or the traditional religions. Moreover, Catholic parents have the first choice in mission-run schools for their children. Partly because of this, and despite the right of African converts to retain their traditional names on baptism, they still choose such names as Jean and Paul. They see in this name change the possibility, if only symbolically, of becoming *civilisé*. A number of younger African priests have started to Africanize the liturgy, but for many former seminarians who are now mature civil servants, only the Gregorian chants evoke the "true" sentiment of their religion.

The Protestants in Ouagadougou failed to secure the same adherence to their sect because initially they were uninterested in providing their converts with the tools of Western education. This has now changed, but the Protestant church Africanized more slowly than did the Catholic and is now rent with schisms. The dissenters, for their part, have not changed their doctrinal approach and have evinced no desire to return to the religion of their fathers. The traditional gods are in full retreat in Ouagadougou; their surviving worshippers now make sacrifices to them at the base of modern "stop" signs.

The problem of law-breaking in Ouagadougou is more a result of a general ignorance of the law by rural migrants to Ouagadougou than deliberate attempts to break the law. This phenomenon throws into relief the often ignored truism that laws are culture bound and usually reflect the biases of the law-givers rather than the existence of evil. Must the police insist

442

upon bicycle lamps on lighted streets when rural people customarily ride at night without lights on unlighted roads or paths? But if some law-breakers are ignorant of urban laws, there are others who seek to profit from wrongdoing. The delinquent youth gangs in Ouagadougou are organized to steal from the townspeople. They have many characteristics in common with gangs found in many urban areas in Africa as well as outside of Africa, but their main activity is stealing rather than fighting over territory or women. In contrast, most of the adults brought before the municipal and national courts in Ouagadougou are accused of misdeeds stemming from conflict over women—a situation exacerbated by the urban setting, not caused by it. The judges in both the customary tribunals and national courts make *ad hoc* decisions reflecting the ambiguity of changing norms and the attempts of litigants and lawyers to benefit from the uncertainty. The judges experience no such difficulty in judging the large number of crimes involving property, even though this condition is doubtlessly linked to urban life where differences in wealth are more marked than in the rural areas.

The French colonial authorities permitted the traditional authorities in Ouagadougou to perform certain political functions within the town. Even when colonial municipal government was introduced to Ouagadougou, the French found it administratively and economically necessary to permit the Mogho Naba and his provincial ministers to hold court and to mediate between Africans and the Europeans. When, finally, African officials assumed control of the municipality, and even when Ouagadougou became the capital of an independent Upper Volta, the traditional authorities were used as political agents of both the municipality and the national government. Throughout these different periods, the urban people manipulated the various systems in an effort to deal with the exigencies of modern life. Nevertheless, the latent conflict between the various political and administrative systems within the town could not always be controlled or contained. The conflict became acute when politicians in all the political systems within the town tried to use the urban people as pawns in competition for power. The national government, overestimating its strength, attempted to destroy both the traditional and municipal authorities of the town. In revenge, the urban masses— led by the traditional and modern political leaders and labor

443

organizers—overthrew the national government. The military government which assumed power over the Upper Volta state formally abolished all political authorities in the town.

Ouagadougou can be considered a prototype of post-colonial administrative towns in Africa. The town does have some superficial characteristics of what Southall characterized as "towns of type A."[1] It was the traditional royal seat of a king, the Mogho Naba; it did have an "indigenous population core of considerable homogeneity";[2] and many contemporary "town dwellers also have farms even at considerable distances to which they go and work and from which they obtain supplies."[3] Nevertheless, in contrast to Southall's type A towns, Ouagadougou is *not* characterized by "occupational diversity." It is predominantly clerical and commercial rather than industrial, and there are few, rather than numerous, groups of small and independent entrepreneurs within Ouagadougou. Moreover, the town does not possess "a continuous and very wide range of variations from wealthy proprietors of business, land, or property, and professional men down to poor dependents, casual workers, and beggars."[4]

In contrast, Ouagadougou does have a number of features characteristic of what Southall[5] called "towns of type B"—those relatively new and rapidly growing urban centers created by the Europeans for mining, industrial, or plantation purposes. For example, Ouagadougou's population is largely immigrant and of recent origin; second, its "occupational structure is based on clear distinctions between clerical, skilled, and unskilled workers and dominated by relatively few but large corporate organizations which are foreign to their African employees. African managerial, entrepreneurial, landlord, and professional roles are little developed and independent African economic activity is slight. Emergent class structure tends to follow the occupational structure closely."[6] Nevertheless, and again in contrast to Southall's town of type B, Ouagadougou is *not* characterized by a "continuous gradation between short-

---

[1]Southall, *Social Change,* pp. 6–9.
[2]*Ibid.,* p. 7.
[3]*Ibid.*
[4]*Ibid.,* p. 8.
[5]*Ibid.,* pp. 6–9.
[6]*Ibid.,* p. 8.

444

and-long-term migrants in relation to their economic status and distance from home," and the migrants *did* find a social reality with which they were able to deal and "traditional institutions to provide a focus."[7]

The missionary groups in Ouagadougou functioned as postulated by Southall for both type A and type B towns. The missions did use Ouagadougou as headquarters for rural and ethnic operations, but they were also engaged in educational, welfare, and medical activities within the town. Moreover, they played an important role as a "positive factor in social change and the emergence of new groups and leaders."[8]

Ouagadougou's significant differences from the polar types of Southall can be explained by the specific historical processes that transformed the town. Thus, while Ouagadougou was a traditional royal seat with a fairly homogeneous population, its transformation into a modern colonial administrative center transcended its previous functions.

Second, the French authorities induced or facilitated the influx of so many rural Mossi and non-Voltaic strangers to staff or service their colonial administrative structures that over a period of time Ouagadougou lost its homogeneity and became a cosmopolitan town. It was only after independence and the exodus of "strangers" and the continuing influx of Mossi migrants that Ouagadougou reverted to its relative ethnic homogeneity of precolonial days.

Third, the continuing dependence of large numbers of Ouagadougou inhabitants on peri-urban subsistence cultivation is related to the lack of industrial development in Ouagadougou and in Upper Volta as a whole. The French administration and a few commercial companies did provide jobs for a clerical elite, but the absence of industries prevented "occupational diversity" and the development of a wide range of professional men or businessmen. Therefore, many persons who had been drawn to Ouagadougou in the hope of finding salaried jobs had to rely upon traditional means of earning a living when these jobs failed to materialize.

Fourth, the presence of an indigenous Mossi core culture, which had made provisions for precolonial stranger groups, facilitated the adaptation to town life of various migrant groups during the colonial period.

[7]*Ibid.*, p. 7.
[8]*Ibid.*, p. 9.

Last, the missions profited from the town's political status to use it as a headquarters, but equally took advantage of both the administration's need for clerks and the people's need for education and social welfare to extend their activities in these areas. By so doing they laid the basis for an urban elite which later was to replace the white colonial elite.

Ouagadougou's dissimilarities from the towns described by Southall raise once again the perennial question as to the representativeness of the samples used for typologies in Africa. Nevertheless, it appears to be true that most of the interior towns of Africa do have characteristics similar to Ouagadougou. Moreover, the transformation of many of these interior towns to the status of national capitals, or, in the case of the larger countries, such as Nigeria, into regional or state capitals, will undoubtedly increase these similarities. The reasons for these similarities are partly historical. The colonial towns were developed to serve specific needs, but the needs of the urbanizing populations changed even before the colonial period ended. Whereas the Europeans used the towns as administrative centers for the maintenance of law and order throughout the territory, or as commercial entrepôts, the African migrants were permanently attracted to the towns by the new economic and social opportunities that they provided. Whereas the lack of industrialization in the African towns redounded to the interests of the metropoles, the lack of industrial jobs frustrated the growing African urban populations. The rise of nationalism ended European rule, but it only quickened the urbanization process in Africa. The resulting towns in Africa will be different from the colonial ones, but the chances are that they will be quite similar to each other.

One of the major behavioral characteristics of the people in contemporary Ouagadougou has been their attempt and ability to use or to create procedures or institutions in the effort to adapt to the exigencies of urban life. The relatively complex urban environment does provide a wider range of alternative institutions, strategies, and behavior patterns for people than did the rural areas from which they came. Nevertheless, what is characteristic of the people of Ouagadougou is the ingenuity with which they use the available choices open to them.

The ability of individuals in Ouagadougou to create or to take advantage of a given number of options was shown not to be unlimited, but was conditioned by their personal characteristics, kin ties, and associations. Moreover, people used traditional as well as modern institutions or syntheses of both in such a way as to invalidate many existing models developed to account for African urban behavior. Gluckman's model of "townsmen" or "tribesmen" is just too rigid and Janus-faced to characterize the adaptations of the Ouagadougou population to urban life. Cohen's notion that Africans did become "retribalized" when they attempted to deal with new elements or events in towns is equally atavistic or reactionary, because his model fails to take into consideration the manipulative, opportunistic, and creative qualities in the behavior of urban Africans. It is not really whether a man's ethnic or rural ties or institutions are of primary or secondary interest in the "urban system of relations" but whether or not he can use them in adapting to town life. If they are not useful, he discards them or suffers the consequences; if they are useful, he keeps them. However, in keeping and using his traditional institutions and ties, the African changes them because the context in which they are used is different. This means that there can never be any such process as "retribalization" in Africa (or in any other country for that matter) except in the thinking of social scientists convinced that African behavior is basically "tribal" whatever its manifestation. Cohen and Gluckman are victims of the idea that "primordial" social bonds between people persist despite everything and are ready to reassert themselves when given the opportunity. They would "tribalize" all kinds of conditions of men so as to retain their belief in "tribalism."

The people of Ouagadougou have accommodated and adapted to change by manipulating their traditional values and institutions; by utilizing a mixture or syncretization of traditional and modern traits when they could do so; by adopting and adapting modern European traits or institutions when possible; and by attempting to de-Westernize these traits in an attempt at psychological accommodation. This process has not been easy. Social conflict did take place, and is perhaps inevitable in urban Africa given the socially heterogeneous populations, multiplicity of behavior patterns, and often incompatible social, economic, and political institutions. Caught in kaleidoscopic social fields, immigrants in town, and even urban-born individuals, often misjudge the situations in which they find themselves. The resulting behavior is far from normative, but neither is it normless. Life in a changing African

447

town demands a certain transiliency that is rarely found in most societies except during crises, such as war, when rapid changes must be accommodated if the society is to survive. The issue in African towns is to determine and to be aware of the point beyond which this transiliency breaks down.

A major problem confronting Ouagadougou and similar post-colonial administrative or capital cities in Black Africa without major industries, commerce, or economically viable hinterlands is how to provide a livelihood for most of their populations. As the focal towns of the nation-states and centers of modernization and urbanization, they will continue to attract the rural population also intent on modernizing. These rural immigrants and nonelite urban populations also expect to benefit from the development that is occurring in the capitals. The dilemma is that the new countries cannot afford the "service industries" needed in a modern capital. They do not have the funds to finance "industries" to provide employment for urban populations whose main source of salaried income is the government itself. In order to survive, the nonemployed or underemployed urban masses find that they must practice, when possible, peri-urban agriculture. A growing problem is that, whereas the early rural immigrants in town could and did cultivate, their town-bred children eschew agricultural activities as being unworthy of urban dwellers. Like the urban elite, they, too, insist upon salaried employment as the preferred source of income. The result is that the politically powerful urban populations drain revenue from the rural peasants, the major productive group in the country. The rural masses, in turn, follow their resources to the capital in order to profit from the relatively better opportunities found there.

The urban elites of such towns as Ouagadougou may appear to have the option of attempting to slow down urbanization and modernization by using their scarce resources for rural development. This could also presumably maximize and guarantee their future incomes. In reality, these urban elites, locked as they are into the cultural complex of the modern world, are seldom willing or able to make the necessary sacrifices, and to do so in time. Try as they would, they are unable to escape the influences of the outside world on their behavior. True, they live in an African town, but their style of life, their public behavior, and even their private behavior reflect adherence to norms of a wider community. Thus, Mitchell is in

448

error when he would study the behavior of Africans in towns as though the imperatives of the outside world did not affect their patterns of social relationships.

The effect of the outside world on the behavior of urban Africans is not all pervasive, however, and does not equally influence the behavior of all of them. Differences in education, income, aspirations, and the like condition the behavior of the urban people. These factors also affect how they participate in or relate to the major institutions within the town. There is an increasing gap or differentiation in the social and cultural institutions of the elites and nonelites within the towns, and the result of this gap could well spell disaster. Ouagadougou has already experienced political difficulties created by struggles for power within the elite group. Future struggles for power within the town may well take place between the elite and nonelite as both groups seek to manipulate the institutions within the town for their own benefit. If this happens, not only could the municipal institutions of the town be attacked again, but the very structure of the nation-state might well be modified.

APPENDIX I

                                    Work Site MTCA
                                    Abidjan
                                    23 September 1963

To: The Director of Works in the Ministry of Labor,
    The Director of the Office of Manpower, Ouagadougou

Mr. Director:

Born in Koupéla, subdivision of the Republic of Upper Volta, the
son of Bila Kaboré and of his wife Pogo Zougou, and being of
Upper Volta nationality, I have lived in the Ivory Coast since 1953,
where I am employed as the chief iron worker, category 6, and chief
metalic carpenter, category 6C.

I have the honor of soliciting from your high person, a position in
the occupation cited above so that I can return to Upper Volta, my
native land.

In the hope of receiving a favorable response.

Please accept, Mr. Director, the expression of my distinguished
sentiments.

                                    Yamba Kaboré

                                    Treichville, Abidjan
                                    Ivory Coast
                                    23 October 1964

To: The President of the Republic of Upper Volta, Ouagadougou

Mr. Minister (*sic*)

We beg you to honor us with a special audience. In effect, we
would like to tell you confidentially of certain difficulties which we
do not believe could be resolved without the help of your high
authority. We have been in Abidjan for several years, but because
of the severe criticisms of us as strangers, we have not been able to
find work. Thus we have sent you a short note to acquaint you with

450

our situation as precisely as possible. We will be brief, since we know how precious is your time. Please believe us, we would never have attempted to bother you personally if it were not indispensable that we communicate with you personally about this very delicate situation, and one which touches the interest of all of us. We have attached our birth certificates in the hope that you will summon us soon.

We wish to thank you in advance. Please accept, Mr. President, the assurance of our most respectful consideration.

Your devoted servants,

Lamine Danogo Paul
and
Gningnande Ouedraogo

22 November 1962

To: The Director of the Office of Manpower

Sir:

I have the honor to write you very respectfully to ask you for a position as a cook-butler in Ouagadougou. I am attaching to this letter my recommendations and a money order for 300 francs so that you may return them to me. I am leaving my present employment the 15th of November, 1962, because my boss is leaving for France. I judge myself capable of filling, with zeal, any function that should be given to me.

Hoping that my request would be accepted by you, please agree to accept, Sir, the expression of my most respectful sentiment.

Eugene Some
Cook-Butler,
now employed by
Mr. Ceauplace
in Abidjan

451

Abidjan
4 November 1962

To: The Director of the Office of Manpower, Upper Volta

Mr. Director:

I am writing a short note that will permit me to acquaint you with my problem as precisely as I can in a few words. I know how precious is your time. Please believe me that I would not have disturbed you if it were not indispensable to bring this delicate problem to your attention. It is in the interest of all of us.

I am a young Voltaic, born in Banfora, Upper Volta. I have a C.E.P.E. Diploma, and would like to obtain a position as an assistant clerk, preferably in the capital, Ouagadougou, or in Bobo-Dioulasso. I am 18 years old and hope that you will satisfy my request if there is a vacancy.

In the hope of receiving a favorable reply, please accept, Mr. Director, my most anticipated sentiments.

Gabriel Soma

Man, Ivory Coast
28 September 1964

To: The President of the Republic of Upper Volta, Ouagadougou

Sir:

I have the honor of beseeching your highness most urgently to employ me as a butler-washerman or a general servant. I would be very happy, Mr. President, if you would respond to my desire as rapidly as possible. Mr. President, I am counting entirely on you and I believe that my desire would be satisfied.

In the hope of receiving from you a favorable and rapid response please accept, Mr. President, my profoundest respect.

Maurice Momboulou

B. P. 317, Abidjan
4 October 1962

To: The Minister of Public Works
of the Upper Volta at Ouagadougou

Mr. Minister:

I have the honor to solicit from your august personality a job as an automobile chauffeur in Ouagadougou, or in any place within Upper Volta. I promise you that if I am hired, to be a model employee, devoted, honest, hard-working, and willing to fulfill all that you expect of me. I will send you my driver's license if you wish to see it.

Hoping to receive a favorable response from you.

Please accept, Mr. Minister, my most distinguished sentiments.

Mr. Maiga Youssuf
Chauffeur in the Compensation
Service of the Ivory Coast

453

The labor unions in Ouagadougou, like the associations, have been as interested in politics as in unionism per se, that is, in seeking a "better economic deal" for their members. It might even be said that the unions in Ouagadougou are more interested in politics than in anything else, and in fact, they formed the political opposition to the government of the Republic. Perhaps this was unavoidable given the colonial context in which the unions developed and the fact that the early syndicalists were in actuality proto-politicians. The proscription of opposition political activities in the post-independence period had a comparable effect of transforming the proto-politician-syndicalists into pseudo-politician-syndicalists. And just as the early syndicalists played an important role in ending colonialism, the post-independence syndicalists in Ouagadougou were to use their associations to bring down the political party in power.

The present unions in Ouagadougou are the end products of an intensive period of union-building which started with the passage of the Overseas Labor Code by the French National Assembly in December 1952. At that time three important French metropolitan unions (the radical and Communistic Confédération Générale du Travail (C.G.T.), the reformist French Socialist (S.F.I.O.) Force Ouvrière (F. O.), and the Catholic Confédération Française des Travailleurs Chrétiens (C.F.T.C.) tried to organize the numerous guild-like unions that were developing in all industries and among all occupational groups, public as well as private, in French Africa. Initially, only the F. O. and the C.F.T.C. gained any meaningful number of adherents among the Ouagadougou population. According to Balima,[1] by 1956 the F. O. had some 3,400 members in the entire country, the C.F.T.C. approximately 780, and the autonomous unions some 11,000. The apparent reason for the strength of the F. O. among the workers was that it

[1] Albert S. Balima, "Notes sur la situation sociale et les problèmes de travail en Haute-Volta," *Revue internationale du Travail,* LXXXII, No. 4 (October 1960), 404–408.

was supported by many Europeans in the country and had the approval of the administration. This was in contrast to the C.G.T. which the administration distrusted and of which the Catholic church disapproved. The C.F.T.C. gained adherents primarily among Mossi Catholics led by Joseph Ouedraogo, an ex-seminarian of the Catholic church, who not only distrusted the C.G.T. because of its ideology, but disliked the F. O. because of its control by Europeans and its tendency to seek the interest of this group above that of the local people. The autonomous guild-like unions felt that they had more to gain by remaining independent of the metropolitan syndicates since many of their problems lay in seeking better wages for their own members, often against the disapproval of resident European workers.[2]

Despite the fact that the workers in Ouagadougou distrusted the C.G.T., it was the branches of this union in French Africa that best articulated the grievances of the local people against the colonial economic and political policies. Thus when, in April 1956, Sekou Touré of the Guinean branch of the C.G.T. broke with the metropolitan union and created the Confédération Général des Travailleurs Africains (C.G.T.A.) in the name of decolonization, the other French African unions were quick to follow. In June 1956, the members of the C.F.T.C. met in Ouagadougou under the sponsorship of the local branch and under the chairmanship of David Soumah, and declared their independence from their parent union. They created the Confédération Africaine des Travailleurs Croyants, thus emphasizing not only the African nature of their association, but also the fact of religious diversity by enabling Christians, Moslems, and traditionalists to gather under the umbrella of "believers."

The F. O. members in Ouagadougou, like their confreres in the other parts of French Africa, remained attached to the S.F.I.O.; and many of the autonomous unions in the town again elected to remain independent. Nevertheless, the political pace which had been quickened by the Africanization of the branches of the metropolitan unions in Africa was soon to affect them all. In January 1957, all the unions of French West Africa were invited to Cotonou in Dahomey ostensibly to

---

[2]Thompson and Adloff, pp. 491–510.

form an African union, but in reality to hasten the decolonization process. The C.A.T.C. and some of the autonomous unions attended, but only those unions affiliated with the C.G.T.A. and sympathetic to Skeou Touré united. Despite this setback, the Union Générale des Travailleurs de l'Afrique Noire (U.G.T.A.N.) emerged and, together with the Rassemblement Démocratique African (R.D.A.), a political grouping, set in motion the last stage of the process toward independence for all of French Africa.

The period between 1957 and 1960 witnessed as much fusion and fission among the unions in Ouagadougou and the rest of French West Africa as it did among the political parties and groupings. This was the period, also, when the C.A.T.C. affiliated with the International Confederation of Free Trade Unions and the U.G.T.A.N. established loose ties with the World Federation of Trade Unions, two world labor organizations representing both East and West.

When independence for the Upper Volta, as well as for most of French Africa, finally arrived in 1960, many of the unions became highly localized. As a matter of fact, the ruling party in the Upper Volta, the Union Démocratique Voltaique (U.D.V.-R.D.A.), attempted to force all the unions and union groups in the nation into one large party-run organization, the Union National des Syndicats des Travailleurs de la Haute Volta (U.N.S.T.H.V.). This attempt failed primarily because of the political opposition of members of the C.A.T.C. and the local members of U.G.T.A.N. Nevertheless, out of the U.N.S.T.H.V. came the Organisation Voltaique des Syndicats Libres affiliated, like the C.A.T.C., with the I.C.F.T.U. Meanwhile, the local grouping of the U.G.T.A.N., the Union Syndicale des Travailleurs Voltaique, followed its parent body and affiliated with the All-African Trade Union Federation, a Pan-Africanist group. However, the external ties of the unions in Ouagadougou to international and inter-African labor unions were not important, being more sentimental than anything else. Furthermore, the local government discouraged such ties.

By 1964, the general picture of unionism in Ouagadougou was as follows.[3]

[3]Main source: "Direction du Travail, de la Main-d'Oeuvre et de la Formation Professionnelle," Ministère du Travail et de la Fonction Publique, République de Haute-Volta, 1964.

CENTRALES

Union Syndicale des Travailleurs Voltaique (U.S.T.V.)
(Federation of Voltaic Workers' Trade Unions)

Estimated Membership: 4,500

Affiliates

Syndicat National des Enseignants Africain de Haute-Volta (S.N.E.A.H.V.)
  (National African Teachers Union of Upper Volta)
Syndicat des Agents du Trésor
  (Treasury Workers Union)
Syndicat des Agents des Services Sociaux de Haute Volta
  (Social Services Employees Union of Upper Volta)
Syndicat des Infirmier-Infirmières et Sages-Femmes d'Etat
  (Union of Government Male Nurses, Female Nurse, and Midwives)
Syndicat des Infirmiers des Grandes Endémies
  (Union of Male Nurses of the Endemic Disease Service)
Syndicat des Agents de la Météorologie
  (Weather Bureau Employees Union)
Syndicat EMCIBAN Ouagadougou
  (Commerce, Industry, and Bank Employees Union of Ouagadougou)
Syndicat des Agents de la SAFELEC
  (SAFELEC [Electric Power] Employees Union)
Syndicat des Travailleurs Scolaires de Ouahigouya*
  (Union of Ouahigouya School Workers)
Syndicat des Assistants d'Elevage
  (Union of Animal Husbandry Assistants)
Syndicat des Travailleurs de la Mine de Pourra*
  (Union of Pourra Mine Employees)
Syndicat des Travailleurs de la Mairie de Bobo*
  (Bobo-Dioulasso City Hall Workers Union)
Syndicat EMCIBAN Bobo-Dioulasso*
  (Commerce, Industry, and Bank Employees Union of Bobo-Dioulasso)
Syndicat des Travailleurs de la Métallurgie
  (Metal Workers Union)
Syndicat des Travailleurs du Bâtiment
  (Construction Workers Union)

*These are local unions and have no branches in Ouagadougou

Syndicat SYMEVETOPHARSAF
(SYMEVETOPHARSAF Union)
Syndicat des Gens de Maison
(Domestic Servants Union)

Organisation Voltaique des Syndicats Libres (O.V.S.L.)
(Voltaic Organization of Free Trade Unions)
Estimated membership: 2,470

Affiliates

Syndicat des Conducteurs de Taxis
(Taxi Drivers Union)
Syndicat des Employés du Commerce, de l'Industrie et des Banques
(Commerce, Industry, and Bank Employees Union)
Syndicat des Travailleurs de Boulangeries
(Bakery Workers Union)
Syndicat des Infirmiers Vétérinaires
(Union of Male Veterinary Nurses)
Syndicat des Travailleurs des Hotels
(Hotel Workers Union)
Syndicat des Travailleurs de la "King" Haute-Volta
(Employees Union of "King" Upper Volta)
Syndicat du Personnel de la Radiodiffusion de Haute-Volta
(Employees Union of the Upper Volta Broadcasting System)
Syndicat des Gens de Maison de Ouagadougou
(Domestic Servants Union of Ouagadougou)

Confédération Africaine des Travailleurs Croyants (C.A.T.C.)
(African Confederation of Believing Workers)
Estimated Membership: 2,000

Affiliates

Syndicat Unique des Agents de l'Agriculture
(Single Union of Agricultural Agents)
Syndicat des Agents des Grandes Endémies
(Endemic Disease Service Employees Union)
Syndicat des Agents des Travaux-Publics
(Public Works Employees Union)
Syndicat des Enseignants Privés
(Union of Private School Teachers)
Syndicat des Employes des Dragages

(Dredging Workers Union)
Syndicat des Employes de la Société Hersent
  (Union of Employes of Hersent Company)
Syndicat des Employés de l'Enterprise Travaux-Afrique
  (Employees Union of the Company Travaux-Afrique)
Syndicat des Employés et Membres de la Société Cooperative Ouvière de Meubles et Bâtiments
  (Trade Union of Employees and Members of the Workers Furniture and Buildings Cooperative Association)
Syndicat des Employés des Missions Catholiques
  (Catholic Mission Employees Trade Union)
Syndicat des Employés des Ambassades
  (Embassy Employees Union)
Syndicat EMCIBAN
  (Commerce, Industry, and Bank Employees Union)

AUTONOMES

(Nonaffiliated, Autonomous Trade-Unions)

Estimated Total Membership: 1,150

Syndicat des Travailleurs de l'Aviation Civile
  (Civil Aviation Workers Union)
Syndicat Unique des Travaux Publics
  (Single Union of Public Works)
Syndicat des Cheminots de l'Abidjan-Niger (S.C.A.N.)
  (Abidjan-Niger Railway Workers Union)
Syndicat des Travailleurs de la Santé
  (Health Service Workers Union)
Syndicat des Douanes Voltaiques (S.D.V.)
  (Voltaic Customs Workers Union)
Syndicat des Travailleurs des Postes et Télécommunications
  (Postal and Telecommunications Workers Union)
Syndicat des Travailleurs de la Commune de Ouagadougou
  (Ouagadougou City Employees Union)
Syndicat Unique des Services de l'Administration Générale
  (Single Union of the General Administrative Services)

The biggest problem facing the unions in Ouagadougou during 1964, as before, was the political competition between their leaders that prevented effective cooperation in the interest of trade-union goals: formulating policies for their members;

459

protecting the unions themselves from political control; and gaining more adherents. In 1964 there was a great deal of sentiment among union leaders for the weaker *centrales,* such as the C.A.T.C. and the O.V.S.L., to merge with the more powerful U.S.T.V.-U.G.T.A.N. and for the autonomous unions to cease their *corporatif* (corporate) particularities and activities and merge with the *centrales.* But since union leadership gave certain individuals "political" power, this was difficult to accomplish. On the other hand, the lack of unity made it difficult for the unions to take much action when the national government, apparently in an effort to prevent the unions from increasing their power by being able to affiliate with interterritorial and international agencies, passed law No. I/AN of 24 April 1964 making such affiliations illegal. The unionists complained that this law violated Articles 86 and 97 of the Conventions of the International Labor Office promulgated in 1948 and 1949, to which the Upper Volta, in 1960, had promised to adhere. However, they could do nothing about this; nor could they do anything about the refusal of the government to permit local unions to accept invitations to attend labor conferences in the Soviet Union, among other places. Finally, lack of unity prevented the unions from controlling either the adhesion or lack of adhesion of workers to the syndicates.

There is little precise information on the actual number of union members in Ouagadougou. One important leader of the C.A.T.C. declared that there were some 5,000 unionists in the capital alone. Data from the Ministry of Labor for 1963 showed some 2,063 union members among a non-civil servant salaried work force of 11,561, thus indicating that only some 17.8 per cent of these workers had joined the union. The only way that the C.A.T.C. leader's estimate of 5,000 unionists could be correct would be to assume that close to 100 per cent of the 3,242 civil servants in the town belong to the *centrales* or the corporate occupational unions. Since this is unlikely, the actual number of unionists in the town may not be more than 4,000.

During 1964 the people of the town were aware of the presence and activities of the unions. On May Day 1964 the unionists in town held a parade despite the disapproval of the national government. Persons passing the Bourse de Travail in Ouagadougou at 5:30 in the afternoons often saw unionists gathered there, discussing problems of an economic as well as a political nature. The greatest union activities in the capital took place when the powerful S.N.E.A.H.V. (Syndicat des Travailleurs de la Santé Humaine et Animale de Haute-Volta) invited most of the unions in town to send delegates to attend its Tenth Congress in the town of Koudougou from July 8 to July 11, 1964.

The work of this Congress of the National African Teachers Union of Upper Volta demonstrated many of the concerns of the unions in Upper Volta.[4] The opening speech by its secretary-general, a professor in the Government Lycée of Ouagadougou, dealt with the generalities of African education, the role of the teachers, and the need to "safeguard the traditional values which constitute the measure of the permanence of Africa and its modest contribution to universal civilization."[5] He said nothing either about the economic problems facing the teachers or their hopes for a better life. The representative of the Minister of National Education, who had traveled from Ouagadougou to attend the conference, said in response that the profession of teaching was "different from others, *it not being simply a matter of earning a living. It demands from us a total involvement of the self* in order not to deceive those who have confided to us their offspring" (emphasis his).

A number of speakers underscored the remarks of the government representative that the teachers should be interested in other than economic matters, and gave frankly political speeches. The Secretary-General of the U.S.T.V.-U.G.T.A.N. from Ouagadougou complained that the lack of economic development had resulted in the expatriation of 300,000 Voltaics in Mali, 500,000 in the Ivory Coast, and 500,000 in Ghana, a fact which, according to him, posed social, political, and economic problems of overwhelming proportions, unless they could be "resolved by the unity of Africa, winning the fight against racial discrimination, a rise in the standard of living of the peasant, and the education of all the people." He complained that the peasants won only idleness and misery from independence; that workers in the public sector had

[4]"Motion contre la loi No. I/AN du 24 Avril 1964." Travaux du Xe Congrès du Syndicat Nationale des Enseignants Africains de Haute-Volta (Koudougou, 8–11 July 1964).
[5]"Travaux du Xe Congrès du Syndicat Nationale des Enseignants Africains de Haute-Volta," unpublished M. S., 1964.

461

seen a 25 per cent increase in unemployment; and that in the private sector, "capital has fled and the system functions only on bank credit." Another speaker from the C.A.T.C., this time the head of S.C.O.M.B. from Ouagadougou, suggested that the situation in Upper Volta resembled that described for neo-colonialist Africa by Frantz Fanon in his book, *The Wretched of the Earth.*

The "Committee on Grievances" sounded the only note concerning the material problems of the teachers. Here were demands for better lodgings, better provisions of foodstuffs, better furnishings for teachers' housing, better provisions for traveling costs, a demand for better examinations both for teachers and students, the desire for the Africanization of school inspections, demands for an end to the lack of access of the teachers to radio time and publication opportunities. The congress finally passed resolutions in favor of rural education; for the preparation of examinations by Voltaics; condemning oppressive labor in Angola, Mozambique, and the so-called Portuguese Guinea; in favor of union unity and the right of unions to support the Union Générale des Etudiants Voltaique under proscription by the government; the right of unions to affiliate with extra-territorial unions, especially the U.S.P.A. (Pan-African Syndical Union); and condemning the law which prevented such affiliations.

The overall tone of the congress was more political than syndicalist, and members of the S.N.E.A.H.V., like those of the other unions in Ouagadougou, became increasingly hostile to the politics of the Yaméogo Government during the rest of 1964 and 1965. By December 1965 the unions had become completely disenchanted with the government, and when the President announced an austerity program at the same time that the U.S.T.V.-U.N.S.T.V. was meeting at its Second Congress in Ouagadougou, the unionists all came together, formed a joint action committee, and precipitated the revolt that led to the downfall of the government.

Abderahman, As-Sadi. *Tarikh As-Soudan.* Trans. O. Houdas. Paris, 1900.

Afrique Nouvelle. No. 961 (12 January 1966); No. 967 (17–23 February 1966); No. 94 (25–31 August 1966); No. 1, 156 (2–8 October 1969).

Archives du Cercle de Ouagadougou. 20 April 1950; 8 October 1957; 31 August 1960.

Archives of the Centre Voltaique de la Recherche Scientifique (formerly I.F.A.N.). Ouagadougou, Haute-Volta.

Arensberg, Conrad M. "The Community Study Method," *American Journal of Sociology,* LX (1954).

———. "The Urban in Crosscultural Perspective," in Elizabeth M. Eddy (ed.), *Urban Anthropology: Research Perspectives and Strategies,* Southern Anthropological Society Proceedings, No. 2. Athens: University of Georgia Press, 1968.

Balandier, Georges. "The Colonial Situation," in Pierre L. Van den Berghe (ed.), *Africa: Social Problems of Change and Conflict.* San Francisco: Chandler Publishing Co., 1965.

———. *Ambiguous Africa.* New York: Random House, 1966.

Balima, Albert S. "Note sur la situation sociale et les problémes de travail en Haute Volta," *Revue internationale du Travail,* LXXXII, No. 4 (October 1960).

Banton, Michael. "Social Alignment and Identity in a West African Town," in Hilda Kuper (ed.), *Urbanization and Migration in West Africa.* Berkeley and Los Angeles: University of California Press, 1965.

Barlet, Paul. "La Haute Volta (Essai de présentation géographique)," *Études Voltaiques* (N.s. 1962), Mémoire No. 3, Ouagadougou.

Barth, Henry. *Travels and Discoveries in North and Central Africa.* New York: Harper and Brothers, 1859.

Bascom, William. "Urbanization among the Yoruba," *The American Journal of Sociology,* LX, No. 5 (March 1955).

Bassolet, François Djoby. *Evolution de la Haute Volta.* L'Imprimerie Nationale de la Haute-Volta, 1968.

Baudu, Paul. *Vieil Empire, Jeune Eglise.* Paris: Editions La Savane, 1956.

Bellot, F. (P). "Etude sur la toponymie des quartiers de Ouagadougou," *Notes Africaines,* XLII (April 1949).

Binger, Louis. *Du Niger au golfe de Guinée par le pays de Kong et le Mossi, 1887–1889.* Paris: Hachette, 1892.

Boahen, A. Adu. "The Caravan Trade in the Nineteenth Century," *Journal of African History,* III, No. 2 (1962).

Bohannan, Laura. "Dahomean Marriage: A Revaluation," *Africa,* XIX, No. 4 (1949).

Bouche, Denise. "Les écoles françaises au Soudan à l'époque de la conquête, 1884–1900," *Cahiers d'Etudes Africaines,* VI, No. 22 (1966).

Bouniol, Joseph. *The White Fathers and Their Missions.* London: Sands and Company, 1929.

Breese, Gerald. *Urbanization in Newly Developing Countries.* Englewood Cliffs, N.J.: Prentice-Hall, 1966.

Buell, Raymond. *The Native Problem in Africa.* 2 vols. New York: Macmillan, 1928.

Bulletin Quotidien d'Information. Distribué par le Service de l'Information de la République de Haute-Volta, 22 January 1956; 8 June 1958; 15 April 1959; 20 October 1964; 2 November 1964; 18 September 1966.

Carrefour Africain. Troisième Année, No. 12 (8 July 1962); No. 111 (31 May 1964); Sixième Année, Nos. 170–71 (25 July–1 August 1965); Sixième Année, No. 174 (22 August 1965); Septième Année, No. 255 (11 March 1967), No. 257 (25 March 1967); Huitième Année, 27 July 1968; 10 August 1968; 26 October 1968; Neuvième Année, No. 349 (28 December 1968); Dixième Année, Nos. 363–64 (5–12 April 1969).

Challenor, Herschelle S. "Expatriation, Discord and Repatriation: A study of Dahomeyan Strangers in French West Africa as a Problem in the Colonization and Decolonization Process." Unpublished Ph.D. dissertation, Faculty of Political Science, Columbia University, New York, 1970.

Clapperton, Hugh. *Second Voyage dans L'intérieur de L'Afrique.* Trans. M. M. Eyries and de la Renaudière. Paris, Arthus Bertrand Libraire, 1829. Vol. II.

Cohen, Abner. *Custom and Politics in Urban Africa.* Berkeley and Los Angeles: University of California Press, 1969.

Cohen, Ronald and John Middleton (eds.). *From Tribe to Nation in Africa.* Scranton, Penna.: Chandler Publishing Co., 1970.

Congo, Kassoum. *Conséquences de la colonisation sur la vie coutumière en pays mossi.* Essai sur l'intégration du pays mossi dans le système francais avec *les conséquences sur la vie archaique,* Montpellier: Université de Montpellier, Faculté de Droit, 1955, multigr. (Thèse pour le doctorat de droit).

Crozat, Dr. "Rapport sur une mission au Mossi, 1890," *Journal Officiel de la République Française* (5–9 October 1891).

Delafosse, Maurice. *Haut-Sénégal-Niger.* Paris: Larose, 1912. Vol. III.

Delavignette, Robert. *Les Vrais Chefs de L'Empire.* Paris: Larose, 1934.

Delobson, A. A. (Dim). "Le Mogho Naba et Sa Cour," *Bulletin du Comité d'Etudes Historiques et Scientifiques de L'Afrique Occidentale Française,* XI, No. 3 (July–September 1928).

————. *The Empire of the Mogho-Naba.* Trans. Kathryn A. Looney. Human Relations Area Files, New Haven, Conn., 1959.

Deshler, W. W. "Urbanization in Africa: Some Spatial and Functional Aspects," *Items* (Social Science Research Council), XXV, No. 3 (September 1971).

Direction de la Statistique et des Etudes Economiques. Ouagadougou, Haute-Volta.

Direction du Travail, de la Main-d'Oeuvre et de la Formation Professionnelle. Ministère du Travail et de la Fonction Publique. République de Haute-Volta, 1963, 1964, 1966.

Dobkin, Marlene. "Colonialism and the Legal Status of Women in Francophonic Africa," *Cahiers d'Etudes Africaines,* VIII, No. 31 (1968).

Dumont, René. *L'Afrique Noire est mal partie.* Paris: Editions du Seuil, 1962.

Dupuis, Joseph. *Journal of a Residence in Ashantee.* London: Henry Colburn, 1824.

École Nationale d'Administration. Ministère du Travail et de la Fonction Publique. République de Haute-Volta, 1961.

"Education catholique en Haute-Volta." Anonymous manuscript in archives of the author.

Epstein, A. L. "Some Aspects of the Conflict of Law and Urban Courts in Northern Rhodesia," *Human Problems in British Central Africa* (*Rhodes-Livingstone Journal*), XII (1951).

————. *Politics in an Urban African Community.* Manchester: University of Manchester Press, 1958.

Fallers, Lloyd A. *Bantu Bureaucracy.* London and Chicago: The University of Chicago Press, 1965.

Fanon, Frantz. *The Damned.* Paris: Présence Africaine, 1963.

Foreign Missions Department. "The Assemblies of God in Foreign

Lands: The Gospel among the Mossi People." Springfield, Missouri: General Council of the Assemblies of God, 1934.

Fraternité Matin. 7 January 1966.

French Union Assembly Debates. June 24, 1949.

Gans, Herbert J. "Urbanism and Suburbanism as Ways of Life: A Reevaluation of Definitions," in Sylvia F. Fava (ed.), *Urbanism in World Perspective.* New York: Thomas Y. Crowell, Co., 1968.

Geertz, Clifford. "The Integration Revolution: Primordial Sentiments and Civil Politics in the New States," in Clifford Geertz, *Old Societies and New States.* New York: The Free Press, 1963.

Gluckman, Max. "Anthropological Problems arising from Industrial Revolution," in Aidan Southall (ed.), *Social Change in Modern Africa.* London: Oxford University Press, 1961.

Gorer, Geoffrey. *Africa Dances.* New York: A. A. Knopf, 1935.

Gutkind, Peter C. W. "The African Urban Milieu: A Force in Rapid Change," *Civilisations,* XII, No. 2 (1962).

Hammond, Peter B. "Economic Change and Mossi Acculturation," in William R. Bascom and Melville J. Herskovits (eds.), *Continuity and Change in African Cultures.* Chicago: The University of Chicago Press, 1959.

———. "Mossi Joking," *Ethnology,* III, No. 3 (July 1964).

Hance, William A. "The Economic Location and Functions of Tropical African Cities," *Human Organization,* XIX (1960).

———. *Population, Migration, and Urbanization in Africa.* New York and London: Columbia University Press, 1970.

Houchet, Jean. *Inadaptation Sociale et Delinquance Juvenile en Haute Volta.* Recherches Voltaiques, No. 9, Paris-Ouagadougou, CNRS-CVRS, 1967–68.

Hunton, W. Alphaeus. *Decision in Africa.* New York: The International Publishers, 1957.

Ilboudou, Pierre. *Contribution a L'Histoire Réligieuse du Peuple Mossi de Haute Volta.* Thèse de Doctorat de 3ème Cycle. Paris 1970.

Jeune Afrique. No. 431 (7–13 April 1969).

Jeune Volta. December 1965; February 1967; April 1968.

Journal Officiel de la République Française. Circular of June 16, 1919.

Kabore, Gomkoudougou V. *Organisation Politique Traditionnelle et Évolution Politique des Mossi de Ouagadougou,* Recherches Voltaique 5, Paris-CNRS, Ouagadougou-CVRS, 1966.

Kahl, Joseph A. "Some Social Concomitants of Industrialization and Urbanization," *Human Organization,* XVIII (1959).

466

Kamarck, Andrew M. *The Economics of African Development.* New York: Frederick Praeger, 1967.

Kargougou, Emile. "Le Cinéma en Haute Volta: Comportement et goût d'un public africain," *Voix Voltaiques,* I, No. 4 (January–March 1969).

Kennedy, Raymond. "The Colonial Crisis and the Future," in Ralph Linton (ed.), *The Science of Man in the World Crisis.* New York: Columbia University Press, 1945.

Khuri, Fuad I. "Kinship, Emigration, and Trade Partnership among the Lebanese of West Africa," *Africa,* XXXV, No. 4 (October 1965).

Kilson, Martin. "African Political Change and the Modernization Process," *Journal of Modern African Studies,* I, No. 4 (1963).

Krause, Dr. "Krause's Reise," *Peterman's Mittheilungen* (Berlin, 1887–88).

Kuper, Hilda (ed.). *Urbanization and Migration in West Africa.* Los Angeles and Berkeley: University of California Press, 1965.

"La Constitution," *Eglise Apostolique du Togo, du Dahomey et de la République Voltaique.* Ouagadougou, Haute-Volta. [Archives of the author.]

L'Afrique Française: Bulletin du Comité de l'Afrique Française et du Comité du Maroc. Paris, X (1900); XLII (1932).

Lambert, G. E. "Le Pays Mossi et sa Population," *Etude historique, économique et géographique suivie d'un essai d'ethnographie comparée.* Ouagadougou, 1967. [Archives de CVRS, Ouagadougou.]

La Voix des Enseignants. No. 22, 1968. Ouagadougou, République de Haute-Volta.

Lerner, Daniel. "Comparative Analysis of Processes of Modernisation," in Horace Miner (ed.), *The City in Modern Africa.* London: Pall Mall Press, 1967.

Les Services du Commissariat de Police de la Ville de Ouagadougou.

Little, Kenneth. *Some Contemporary Trends in African Urbanization.* Melville J. Herskovits Memorial Lecture (II), Northwestern University (20 April 1965). Evanston: Northwestern University Press, 1966.

Lloyd, P. C. *Africa in Social Change.* Baltimore: Penguin Books, 1967.

Lugard, Frederick D. *The Dual Mandate in British Tropical Africa.* London: W. Blackwood, 1929.

Mabogunje, Akin L. *Urbanization in Nigeria.* London: The University of London Press, 1968.

Mair, Lucy. *Primitive Government.* Baltimore: Pelican Books, 1962.

467

Mangin, Eugène. *Les Mossi: Essai sur les us et coutumes du peuple Mossi du Soudan occidental.* Paris, 1921 (reprinted from *Anthropos,* 1916). Trans. Ariane Brunel and Elliott Skinner and reissued by Human Relations Area Files, New Haven, Conn., 1959.

Maquet, Jacques. *Power and Society in Africa.* London: Weidenfeld and Nicolson, 1971.

Marie-Andre du Sacre-Coeur, Soeur. *La Femme noire en Afrique occidentale.* Paris: Payot, 1939.

Mathieu, M. *Notes sur L'Islam et le Christianisme dans la subdivision centrale d'Ouagadougou.* Cercle d'Ouagadougou (Haute-Volta), Paris, 1956. (Mémoire 2,619 du Centre de hautes Etudes d'Administration Musulmane), Paris.

Meillassoux, Claude. *Urbanization of an African Community.* Seattle: University of Washington Press, 1968.

Miner, Horace (ed). *The City in Modern Africa.* London: Pall Mall Press, 1967.

Ministère du Travail et de la Fonction Publique. Ouagadougou, 1967.

Mitchell, J. Clyde. "Structural Plurality, Urbanization and Labour Circulation in Southern Rhodesia," in J. A. Jackson (ed.), *Migration.* Cambridge, England: Cambridge University Press, 1969.

Nikiema, Roger. "Le Folklore: Une Force," *Visages d'Afrique.* Deuxième Année, Numéro Speciale, 1968.

N'Krumah, Kwame. *Neo-Colonialism: The Last Stage of Imperialism.* London: Nelson Co., 1965.

Northrup, Bowen. "The Lure of Lagos: City Is Beset By Woes, but People Flock There." New York: *The Wall Street Journal,* January 25, 1972.

Ouagadougou: Chef-Lieu de la Haute-Volta. *Renseignements Coloniaux et Documents.* Supplément à *L'Afrique Française,* XXXI (January 1921).

Owusu, Maxwell. *Uses and Abuses of Political Power: A Case Study of Continuity and Change in the Politics of Ghana.* Chicago and London: The University of Chicago Press, 1970.

Pageard, Robert. "Théâtre Africain à Ouagadougou," *Présence Africaine,* No. 39. (Paris, 1961).

Perham, Margery. *Colonial Sequence: 1930–1949; 1949–1969.* London: Methuen and Co., Ltd., 1967, 1970.

Plan de la Ville de Ouagadougou. *Annuaire de L'Afrique Occidentale Française,* Plan IX, 1921.

Plotnicov, Leonard. *Strangers to the City: Urban Man in Jos. Nigeria.* Pittsburgh: University of Pittsburgh Press, 1967.

Pons, Valdo. *Stanleyville: An African Urban Community under Belgian Administration.* London: Oxford University Press, 1969.

Présence Voltaique. No. 18 (April–May 1969).

Projet de Classement Indiciaire et Echelle des Traitements. Tableau No. 1, Ministère du Travail et de la Fonction Publique. République de Haute-Volta, 1967.

"Recensement Démographique de la Ville de Ouagadougou [Resultats Provisoires]." République de Haute-Volta, Ministère de l'Economie Nationale, Direction de la Statistique et des Etudes Economiques. Ouagadougou, Haute-Volta (June 1962).

Schwab, W. B. "Social Stratification in Gwelo," in Aidan Southall (ed.), *Social Change in Modern Africa.* London: Oxford University Press, 1961.

Sirjamaki, John. *The Sociology of Cities.* New York: Random House, 1964.

Sjoberg, Gideon. "The Preindustrial City," *The American Journal of Sociology,* LX, No. 5 (March 1955).

Skinner, Elliott P. "Christianity and Islam among the Mossi," *American Anthropologist,* LX, No. 6 (December 1958).

————. "The Mossi Pogsioure," *Man,* XXVIII (February 1960a).

————. "Labour Migration and its Relationship to Socio-Cultural Change in Mossi Society," *Africa,* XXX, No. 4 (October 1960b).

————. "Intergenerational Conflict among the Mossi: Father and Son," *Journal of Conflict Resolution,* V, No. 1 (March 1961).

————. "Trade and Markets among the Mossi People," in Paul Bohannan and George Dalton (eds.), *Markets in Africa.* Evanston: Northwestern University Press, 1962.

————. "Strangers in West African Societies," *Africa,* XXXIII, No. 4 (October 1963).

————. "The Effect of Co-residence of Sisters' Sons on African Corporate Patrilineal Descent Groups," *Cahiers d'Études Africaines,* IV, No. 16 (1964a).

————. *The Mossi of Upper Volta.* Stanford, Calif.: Stanford University Press, 1964b.

————. "Islam in Mossi Society," in I. M. Lewis (ed.), *Islam in Tropical Africa.* Published for the International African Institute by the Oxford University Press, 1966.

————. "Chiefs, Politicians and Municipal Councillors: The Problem of Government in a West African Municipality," *Proceedings of Conference on the Government of African Cities.* Institute of African Government, Department of Political Science, Lincoln University, Lincoln University, Pennsylvania (April 18–19, 1968).

469

────── . "Processes of Political Incorporation in Mossi Society," in Ronald Cohen and John Middleton (eds.), *From Tribe to Nation in Africa.* Scranton, Penna.: Chandler Publishing Co., 1970.

────── , "Political Conflict and Revolution in an African Town," *American Anthropologist,* Vol. 74, No. 5 (October 1972).

Snyder, Louis L. "The Conquest and Exploitation of Africa," in Snyder (ed.), *The Imperialism Reader.* New York: D. Van Nostrand Co., Inc. 1962.

Southall, Aidan (ed.). *Social Change in Modern Africa.* London: Oxford University Press, 1961.

────── . "The Impact of Imperialism upon Urban Development in Africa," in Victor Turner (ed.), *Colonialism in Africa.* Cambridge, England: Cambridge University Press, 1971.

Statistiques Scolaires. Bureau des Statistiques Scolaires, Direction Générale des Services. Ministère de l'Education Nationale, République de Haute-Volta.

Sundkler, B. G. M. *Bantu Prophets in South Africa.* London: Oxford University Press, 1961.

Tauxier, Louis. *Le Noir du Soudan: Pays Mossi et Gourounsi.* Paris: Larose, 1912.

Thiemko, Bely. *La Prostitution: Vue sur le drame social en Haute Volta.* Ouagadougou, Ecole Nationale d'Administration, 23 June 1961.

Thompson, Virginia and Richard Adloff. *French West Africa.* Stanford, Calif.: Stanford University Press, 1958.

Tiendrébéogo, Yamba. *Histoire et coutumes royales des Mossi de Ouagadougou.* Ouagadougou, 1964a.

────── . *Contes du Larhalle.* Chez Le Larhalle Naba, Ouagadougou, 1964b.

Toumani, Triande. "Message du Président de la Ligue Voltaique des Oeuvres Laiques," Travaux de Xe Congrès du Syndicat Nationale des Enseignants Africains de Haute-Volta (Koudougou, 8–11 July 1964).

Traore, Bakary. "Le Théâtre Negro Africain et ses fonctions socialiques," *Présence Africaine.* Nos. 14–15 (Paris, 1957).

────── . "Le Théâtre Moderne au Mali," *Présence Africaine.* No. 3 (Paris, 1965).

Travaux de Xe Congrès du Syndicat Nationale des Enseignants Africains de Haute-Volta (Koudougou, 8–11 July 1964).

Trimingham, J. Spencer. *Islam in West Africa.* Oxford: Clarendon Press, 1959.

470

Turner, Victor (ed.). *Colonialism in Africa.* Cambridge: Cambridge University Press, 1971.

Van den Berghe, Pierre L. *Africa: Social Problems of Change and Conflict.* San Francisco: Chandler Publishing Co., 1965.

Van Velsen, J. "Labour Migration as a Positive Factor in the Continuity of Tonga Tribal Society," in Aidan Southall (ed.), *Social Change in Modern Africa.* London: Oxford University Press, 1961.

Vincent, Joan E. "The Dar es Salaam Townsman: Social and Political Aspects of City Life," *Tanzania Notes and Records,* No. 71 (May 1970).

Visages d'Afrique. Revue bimestrielle, Première Année, No. 1 (1967). Ouagadougou, Haute-Volta.

Voix Voltaiques, I, No. 1 (April–June 1968).

Wallerstein, Immanuel. "Ethnicity and National Integration in West Africa," *Cahiers d'Etudes Africaines,* Vol. I, No. 3 (1960).

Welch, Claude E., Jr. (ed.). *Soldier and State in Africa.* Evanston: Northwestern University Press, 1970.

Wilks, Ivor. "The Northern Factor in Ashanti History: Begho and Mande," *Journal of African History,* XI, No. 1 (1961).

Zolberg, Aristede. *Creating Political Order.* Chicago: Rand McNally & Co., 1966.

INDEX

Samogho (people), 17, 121, 195
Sanum, Mogho Naba, 23, 304
Sanwide, Ignace, 297n
Saponé, 316
Sarraut, Albert, 31
Sawadogo, Mogho Naba, 218, 303
Sawadogo, Moussa, 293, 294, 300
schools, see education
Senegal: missionaries from, 333; students in, 237, 259
Senegalese, 197, 213, 280
servants, domestic, 52–54; boys and girls, 78, 80; employment, 82, 85; salaries and job descriptions, table, 53; women, 52, 54
shoeshine boys, 79
Service de la Jeunesse et des Sports, 292
Sibire, El Hadj Ousmana, 308
S.I.C.O.V.O., 63
Sighiri, Mogho Naba, 23
soccer, 265–72
social categories, 12, 16
Socialists, French (S.F.I.O.), 454, 455
Société Africaine de Culture (S.A.C.), 297, 298
Société Auxiliaire d'Entreprise de Constructions en Afrique (S.A.D.E.C.), 60
Société Commerciale de l'Ouest Africain (S.C.O.A.), 64
Société Commerciale du Soudan Français, 64
Société Coopérative pour les Oeuvres Meubles et Bâtiments (S.C.O.M.B.), 60, 66, 462
Société Française d'Entreprise de Dragages et de Travaux Publics (S.F.E.D.T.P.), 60, 63
Société Lorraine de Travaux Publics Africains (S.L.T.P.A.), 60
Société Monoprix, 64, 67
Société Voltaïque d'Equipement, 274
Songhay (people), 197, 303, 312; marriage, 122; prostitutes, 75, 197
songs, popular, 262, 280–83
Soudan, French, 29
Soumah, David, 455

Southall, Aidan, 8n, 9n, 444–46
SOVIMAS, 274
sports, see recreation
standard of living: of cultivators, 144–45, 148–51; of high-status families, 157–67; of middle-status families, 151–57; occupations and, table, 146–47; status differences summarized, 192–94
stores, table, 65
strangers, see ethnic interaction
strike, general, 434–35
Superior Court of Customary Law, 370, 382
Syndicat des Petits et Moyennes Entreprises de Haute-Volta, 213
Syndicat des Travailleurs de la Santé Humaine et Animale de Haute-Volta (S.N.E.A.H.V.), 461
Syndicat Nationale des Enseignements Africains de Haute-Volta, 461n
Syrians, see Lebano-Syrians

Tall, Sekou, 296n
Tampouy (quarter), 44, 74, 144, 322, 324, 357, 411
Tanga (deity), 17
Tanghin (quarter), 144, 157
Tanghin-Dassouri, 70, 324
Tapsoba, Prosper, 280
Tassembedo, Tiga, 274, 275
Tauxier, Louis, 304, 312
taxes, 423, 431; and residence in Ouagadougou, 103–104; on urban land, 144
television, 290–92
Tema Naba, 205
Templier, Father Guillaume, 25, 318
Tengkodogo, 264
Tengkodogo Naba, 205
theater, 292–96
Thévenoud, Joanny, Monsignor, 221, 318–22, 327, 334
Tiedpalogho (quarter), 30, 76, 77, 151, 153, 158, 159, 206, 304–306, 314, 324, 357
Tiendrébéogo, Alexandre, 415
Tiendrébéogo, Yamba, see Larhalle Naba
Tijaniyya sect, 305, 310, 314, 315

485

Library of Congress Cataloging in Publication Data

Skinner, Elliott Percival, 1924–
    African urban life.

    Bibliography: p. 463
    1. Ouagadougou—Social conditions.   I. Title.
HN810.U63097   301.29'66'25   72-14032
ISBN 0-691-03095-2